D0152180

Developments in the

VOLUME III

Aspects of Personality Structure

Rorschach Technique

EDITED BY

BRUNO KLOPFER
formerly, University of California, Los Angeles

MORTIMER M. MEYER
Reiss-Davis Child Study Center, Los Angeles, California

FLORENCE B. BRAWER
University of California, Los Angeles

ASSOCIATE EDITOR

WALTER G. KLOPFER
Portland State University, Portland, Oregon

HARCOURT BRACE JOVANOVICH, INC.
New York / Chicago / San Francisco / Atlanta

Other publications relating to the Rorschach Technique

BRUNO KLOPFER AND HELEN H. DAVIDSON
The Rorschach Technique: An Introductory Manual (1962).

BRUNO KLOPFER AND HELEN H. DAVIDSON
Rorschach Method of Personality Diagnosis: Individual Record Blank, Revised Edition (1960).

BRUNO KLOPFER AND OTHERS
Developments in the Rorschach Technique, Volume II: *Fields of Application* (1956).

BRUNO KLOPFER, MARY D. AINSWORTH, WALTER G. KLOPFER, AND ROBERT R. HOLT
Developments in the Rorschach Technique, Volume I: *Technique and Theory* (1954).

Developments in the Rorschach Technique, Volume III

ISBN 0-15-517628-5

Library of Congress Catalog Card Number: 54-8471

Printed in the United States of America

Editors of Volume III

Florence B. Brawer

ERIC Clearinghouse for Junior Colleges, Graduate School of Education, University of California, Los Angeles

Mortimer M. Meyer

Director of Psychological Services, Reiss-Davis Child Study Center, Los Angeles, California

Bruno Klopfer

formerly Clinical Professor of Psychology, University of California, Los Angeles

Walter G. Klopfer

Professor of Psychology, Portland State University, Portland, Oregon, and Executive Editor, *Journal of Projective Techniques & Personality Assessment*

Contributors to Volume III

Gertrude Baker

Staff Psychologist, Veterans Administration Center, Los Angeles; Associate Clinical Professor of Psychology, University of California, Los Angeles; Chief Psychologist, Westwood Community Mental Health Clinic, Los Angeles, California

Elaine Caruth

Senior Clinical Research Psychologist, Reiss-Davis Child Study Center, Los Angeles, California

Fred Cutter

Research Psychologist, Central Research Unit, Veterans Administration Center, Los Angeles, California

Norman L. Farberow

Principal Investigator, Central Research Unit, Veterans Administration Center, Los Angeles; Co-Director, Suicide Prevention Center, Los Angeles, California; Professor of Psychiatry (Psychology), University of Southern California School of Medicine, Los Angeles, California

Robert R. Holt

Professor of Psychology, New York University, New York, New York. (Formerly, Director, Research Center for Mental Health, New York University)

Martin Mayman

Professor of Psychology, University of Michigan, Ann Arbor

Harvey Mindess

Beverly Hills, California

Helmut Würsten

Associate Clinical Professor of Psychiatry (Child Psychology), School of Medicine, University of Southern California, Los Angeles, California

Seymour L. Zelen

Department of Psychology, Fernald School, University of California, Los Angeles

Foreword

Originally, *Developments in the Rorschach Technique* was envisioned as a two-volume work. However, in the fourteen years that have passed since the publication of Volume II, additional developments have occurred that merit a third volume. The contents of Volume I were essentially "Technique and Theory." Volume II was "Fields of Application." Volume III adheres more strictly to the concept of "developments," specifically in the assessment of personality structure. The literature that has appeared since the publication of Volume II is extensive, and no pretense is made here of having represented all the new developments. However, we hope that the material included does provide a fair sample of the new directions taken and will be a source of stimulation to practitioners and innovators.

We wish to thank the many organizations and people who, visibly and invisibly, assisted in the creation of this book. The *Journal of Projective Techniques and Personality Assessment* unhesitatingly gave permission for the reprinting of an article which appears as Chapter 2 of this volume. We also appreciate the ready cooperation of the clinicians whose material illustrates the various chapters. Finally, deep appreciation is expressed to Mrs. Faye Pocrass, who handled so competently the many details an editor delegates to his secretary.

Bruno Klopfer
Mortimer M. Meyer
Florence B. Brawer

(photo by Sidney Brawer)

BRUNO KLOPFER

It is a special pleasure to the participants in this venture that its publication coincides with the seventieth birthday of Dr. Bruno Klopfer. At the request of the junior editors, Dr. Marguerite Hertz has graciously provided the appreciation that follows and that represents, surely, not only the feelings of those whose writings appear herein, but of hundreds of other workers who have known Dr. Klopfer throughout the years.

M. M. M.
F. B. B.
W. G. K.

Bruno Klopfer: An Appreciation

It is a moving privilege for me to speak for the co-editors and authors of this volume in dedicating their efforts to the senior editor, Bruno Klopfer, on the occasion of his 70th birthday, October 1, 1970. I do so with a special sense of affection and gratitude since for me Bruno Klopfer has been not only a colleague and adviser but also a warm and loyal personal friend. In honoring him we speak not only for ourselves but for those throughout the world who have had the privilege of working with him and who have shared the inspiration of that experience.

For almost four decades, Bruno Klopfer has served clinical psychology as both teacher and scholar. In each role he has made contributions of lasting significance to the science and profession of psychology.

Best known of his achievements is the development of the Rorschach method. His technical innovations, his differentiations and elaborations of Rorschach's original scoring system, his contributions to the interpretative power of the original instrument, and his imaginative applications of the method to a variety of problems are well known to us all. His classic work on the Rorschach method, of which this is the third volume, is a standard text throughout the world. He is preeminent among those who have made the Rorschach technique of prime importance for clinical practice and research.

Bruno Klopfer came upon the American scene in 1934 and kindled a flame which since has illuminated the paths of thousands of students and colleagues. Very early at Teachers College, Columbia University, and later at the College of the City of New York, he established centers of Rorschach studies and projective methodologies.

Bruno Klopfer has had a unique talent for attracting others to share his interests, labors, and enthusiasms. In the early days, with marked generosity, he contributed his time, his classroom, and his home to students of various disciplines in his eagerness to introduce the projective methods to the world of psychology and to place them on firm theoretical foundations. Many workers in the field of projective methods traveled to New York to visit his classes, to attend meetings organized under his leadership, and to exchange ideas, experiences, and insights at impromptu sessions generated by his presence. Those of us who had the privilege of knowing Bruno Klopfer in the early days will always be indebted to him for the opportunities which he alone offered for presentation, discussion, and exchange of information and for the dissemination of the results of our early research efforts. And we will remember him as a man who was always open to approach for those who needed guidance and as one who gave unsparingly of time and strength. In turn, he won the respect of all and the love of those who were fortunate enough to be his friends.

With his superb talent for organization, he became the leading spirit in the emergence of the *Rorschach Research Exchange,* which is now the *Journal of Projective Techniques and Personality Assessment.* He was the first editor and today continues as Senior Editor. The early *Exchange,* mimeographed in form, was devoted to the technical aspects of the Rorschach method, research studies, case studies, and discussions dealing with theoretical problems. It was the first organ of communication in this field of study and the first to give us an opportunity to collate and integrate early findings in a single publication.

Through the years, the *Journal* has extended its range of interests and gained ever wider recognition. It has been a prime source of knowledge concerning projective methodologies and assessment in general and has served as a catalyst for discussions on controversial issues and crucial problems in personality theory and psychopathology. Those of us who were present at the birth of the *Journal* will always remember that its character, vitality, and success are due in no small measure to the initial efforts, foresight, energy, and dedication of Bruno Klopfer and the people he inspired.

In 1939, Bruno Klopfer participated in the founding of the Rorschach Institute, which later developed into the Society for Projective Techniques and Personality Assessment. Under his guidance, membership in the Institute increased rapidly. Regional divisions were established not only in the United States but also in Canada, Australia, England, and South America, as the Institute grew from a small group to an organization of world-wide prominence.

At about the same time, Klopfer started his summer workshops at Crafts, New York, and these too soon spread to various parts of the United States. Later, when he made his home in California, he continued to conduct workshops with the same enthusiasm and limitless energy. He also conducted classes at the University of California at Los Angeles and at Claremont, and engaged in both government consultation and private practice. Again he attracted students and colleagues from various disciplines, always sharing his knowledge, his creative thoughts, and his diagnostic skills with the generosity that was uniquely his.

For many of us, Bruno Klopfer's chief contributions were in the area of theory and teaching. His approach to psychology was from a Jungian psychoanalytic and phenomenological orientation, reflecting his personal background. An expert on Jungian personality theory, he made it understandable to many of us. It was, however, his phenomenological approach which had the greatest impact.

At first his approach on the subjective aspects of the projective methods and his phenomenological emphasis ran counter to the behavioristic attitudes so deeply entrenched in American psychology in the early 1930's. For Klopfer, behavior was determined not by external, objective, and physically described reality but by the phenomena of experience. He insisted that to understand the individual, we must go beyond observable overt behavior and penetrate the inner world of the individual. This he thought could be done through the medium of the projective methods. Projective data could reveal inner processes and experiential events involved in behavior better than any other diagnostic instrument. He therefore espoused and taught the phenomenological approach in personality assessment, and it was not long before his thinking found a favorable climate of opinion among many other clinicians in the field.

Klopfer was, of course, aware of the limitations and uncertainties of subjective judgments. He appreciated the difficulties in conceptualizing, specifying, and measuring the more nebulous dimensions of man's inner world through the medium of projective methods. After all, the human interpreter was involved. Despite the fallibilities of human interpretation, Klopfer was willing to rely on the skills, experience, and knowledge of the interpreter, confident that with training and experience he could develop the necessary skills for penetrating the inner world of an individual. Further, Klopfer believed that the research clinician well trained in the use of projective methods had the necessary creativity and ingenuity to produce good research with projective methods.

Thus Klopfer's goal as a teacher was to develop clinical and intuitive ability among his students. He was eminently successful. He had a rare talent for teaching a subtle kind of clinical judgment. With infinite skill, he would guide his students in the evaluation of the qualitative aspects of a Rorschach protocol not caught by the usual scores. He taught them how to be sensitive to experiential data, and how to make intuitive inferences about the symbolic and dynamic meanings of both the verbal behavior and nonverbal communication of a subject. He taught them how to integrate all the rich qualitative and quantitative data gleaned from a protocol and to weigh them with contextual and environmental factors for purposes of prediction. More than any other teacher in the field, Klopfer demonstrated how clinical judgments and "intuitive feel" can be developed and communicated and how subjective evaluations can be made public with proper teaching, training, and experience.

Klopfer's phenomenological orientation was likewise reflected in his research interests and efforts. He devoted little attention to the possibility of analyzing scores statistically. He minimized traditional psychometric procedures in the compilation of frequency data. He refused to be enthralled by objective quantitative measures which deny the existence of experiential data merely because they cannot be counted. Throughout the years, Klopfer steadfastly refused to bow to sterile quantification.

This does not mean that with time and the accumulation of research data he did not agree that some aspects of the Rorschach are amenable to quantification and objectification. In his research and his case studies, he tempered his subjective and intuitive results in terms of more normative findings, but his emphasis was always toward the qualitative and the subjective. Today, even those of us more behavioristically inclined have come to appreciate more and more the importance of subjective data and to agree that such data can be used productively in Rorschach analysis and research.

A true scholar, Klopfer was always tolerant of the viewpoints of others. Through the years, there were many of us who persistently challenged what we thought was an overemphasis on subjectivity. We questioned his disdain for standardization and his delay in subjecting his intuitive hypotheses to empirical test. Klopfer heard us and respected our views.

He was never afraid to discuss the broad implications of his phenomenological approach. He always took a critical stance with respect to his own work. He welcomed research to test his hypotheses. Indeed, he gave steady encouragement to our research efforts, despite differences in theoretical or procedural orientations. He was primarily interested in research to refine the projective methods in order to establish their validity and improve their effectiveness.

Our differences stimulated friendly controversy and led to exciting activity in the attempt to attack the problems and the uncertainties in the field. The ferment certainly stimulated those of us who had the privilege of working with Klopfer. For us, his workshops, his seminars, his informal gatherings, and even his correspondence will be long remembered and valued intellectual adventures. We were stimulated by his enthusiasm, inspired by his creative ideas, challenged by his standards of scholarship, and, not the least, strengthened by his magnificent friendship. He stimulated us to venture into new areas of research, to explore new horizons, to subject all kinds of hypotheses to empirical test, and to attack knotty theoretical and methodological problems in the larger field of personality.

The entire field of projective psychology profited from this activity. The ferment contributed in large measure to the development of the Rorschach, perhaps even ensuring its survival. The wide use of projective methods in hospitals and clinics today and the extent of the research they have stimulated are due largely to the inspiration of Bruno Klopfer and his students.

It is not unusual in the history of any discipline that when theories, methods, or therapies are subjected to the scrutiny of time, there is need to redefine and perhaps modify them. The clinical field is no exception. Projective psychology is no exception. Bruno Klopfer early led the way in modifying viewpoints and in broadening perspectives to include new conditions, new requirements, new developments, and new knowledge.

Whatever the future direction of clinical psychology, many of us believe that the clinician will continue to be concerned with the phenomenological field and with psychodiagnostic tools to study that field. We shall then be indebted always to Bruno Klopfer for his pioneering contributions to the development of projective methods and to their diagnostic usefulness and for providing sound training and leadership in professional development. We shall be indebted to him for inducting so many students into clinical practice and psychological research, many of whom are today gifted psychologists who have contributed to clinical theory, research, and practice.

Since his retirement to Carmel in 1963, he has won international recognition. In 1965, he received the award from the Division of Clinical Psychology of the American Psychological Association for his distinguished contributions to the science and profession of clinical psychology. In 1966, he received the "Great Man" award from the Society of Projective Techniques and Personality Assessment for his contributions to the Society and to the field of clinical psychology.

With this volume, we again honor Bruno Klopfer. We proudly dedicate this book to him, in admiration for his long record of achievement and his distinguished career as a teacher, and in gratitude for his generous guidance, encouragement, and friendship throughout the years.

Marguerite R. Hertz
Case Western Reserve University

Contents

Introduction 1
WALTER G. KLOPFER

Part One: Scoring and Interpretation

1. **Reality Contact, Defense Effectiveness, and Psychopathology in Rorschach Form-Level Scores** 11

MARTIN MAYMAN

Introduction 11
Form Perception and Reality Testing 13
The Scores and Their Meanings 15
Test Administration 20
Test Scoring 21
Case Examples 22
Validity Studies 32
Reliability 41
Summary 44

2. **Rorschach Indices of Ego Processes** 47

MORTIMER M. MEYER, ELAINE CARUTH

3. The Symbolic Dimension 83

HARVEY MINDESS

Recognizing Symbols 84
Conducive Conditions 86
Interpretation Procedure 88
Utilizing Symbols Diagnostically and Therapeutically 95
Conclusion 97

4. The Relationship between Piaget's Developmental Theory and the Rorschach Method 99

HELMUT WÜRSTEN

Introduction 99
Our Conclusions 106
Piaget's Developmental Theory 110
Practical Application of Some of Piaget's Specific Concepts 132

5. Rorschach Patterns in Three Generations of a Family 143

SEYMOUR L. ZELEN

General Family Background 145
First Generation 146
Second Generation 157
Third Generation 186
Summary 203

Part Two: New Approaches

6. The Consensus Rorschach 209

FRED CUTTER, NORMAN L. FARBEROW

Review of the Literature 211
Theory of Content Polarities and Consensus 216

Choice of Reference Group for Consensus Rorschach 249
Implications for Further Research 254
Conclusion 260

7. **Artistic Creativity and Rorschach Measures of Adaptive Regression** 263

ROBERT R. HOLT

The Psychoanalytic Theory of Creative Thinking 264
The Development of a System for Scoring Primary Process Manifestations 268
Empirical Studies of Creativity and Primary Process in the Rorschach 279
Discussion 298
Appendix. A Glossary and Index to Special Terms and Symbols in the Primary Process Scoring System 311

8. **Post-Diagnostic Use of the Rorschach** 321

GERTRUDE BAKER

Introduction 321
Kinds of Subjects Suitable for Test Discussion and Goals 326
Sources of Illustrative Materials 328
Choice of Tests 329
Problems in Paranoia 352
Homosexuality 359
Integration of an Interpretation 364
Conclusion 371
Appendix. A Therapeutic Application of Psychodiagnostic Test Results 374

9. **The Rorschach in Academic and Vocational Research: A Review** 385

FLORENCE B. BRAWER

History 387

The Literature Since 1956 395
Overview 429

Author Index 438
Subject Index 442

Walter G. Klopfer

Introduction

Since its inception, the Rorschach technique has survived many changes of style and preference. The current volume presents the latest and most stimulating developments in the administration, scoring, and interpretation of this method. Combining some new approaches with the amplification of older, more established ways of using and viewing Rorschach protocols, Volume III should provide a good basis for judging the current status of this instrument.

The first chaper by Mayman makes explicit a form-level score that has been designed to measure reality contact, effectiveness of defense, and absence of psychopathology. In developing this scoring system, Mayman points out that previous suggestions for the systematic evaluation of form level have not proven very popular. Beck's approach, for example, is based upon an empirical comparison of schizophrenic and controlled subjects and, accordingly, does not necessarily guarantee goodness of fit. Because of its dichotomous nature (*F*+ or *F*—), it tends to be a rather general measure. The other most popular approach to assessing level of performance, developed by Klopfer and his colleagues, is so cumbersome that very few people can afford the time to use it extensively in their work.

Because the question of gauging somebody's reality ties is so important that the quest for doing it well must continue, Mayman feels that the search for a good form-level rating should not be abandoned. In many instances the clinical psychologist is asked to make a very fine distinction between the states within the patient where the reality ties are barely adequate and those where they are barely inadequate. Many of the questions that are asked in an interview could be answered on the basis of experience rather than accurate perception. For instance, if asked to distinguish between a table and a chair, the patient might remember that one object is called a table and the other a chair, even though he may regard them quite differently. When shown an ink blot, however, he cannot rely upon stereotypes of past memory and thus the question of whether his perceptions are actually like those of other people can be judged more effectively.

Mayman describes his own form-level system in great detail and demonstrates various ways of evaluating its validity. This form-level score has been found to distinguish between creative and noncreative students; between mature and immature individuals as judged from other sources; between neurotic and non-neurotic subjects; and between organized and disorganized persons. The reader becomes aware that Mayman's score is an excellent research device which makes the Rorschach useful for studies comparing groups, for roughly screening individuals for psychopathology, and for the prediction of success in any endeavor in which efficiency and good reality contact are vital. Whether Mayman's score will succeed where its predecessors have failed—namely, in becoming part of the standard scoring system of the clinician evaluating a case—is difficult to say.

Another scoring innovation is described in the chapter by Meyer and Caruth and concerns Rorschach indices of ego processes. Deeming the Rorschach blots to represent external reality and considering the manner of dealing with this reality to be a product of the interaction of impinging outer reality, the economy of inner needs, and the structure of the psychic organization, the authors purport to explicate the principles of Rorschach interpretation as applied to ego processes. The indices used in this context relate not only to the accuracy of perceptions but to multiple criteria: form; accuracy; reaction time; effectiveness in responding to a variety of stimuli, such as location and determinant categories; the integration of stimuli and reaction time; the interpretation of reality as measured by content; and the presence or absence of ego boundaries.

Although the Meyer and Caruth scoring system could be used for the comparison of groups, it is quite complex. In contrast to Mayman's form-level score, it seems more designed to aid the individual diagnostician and to be made useful for his purposes. In terms of individual prediction and treatment planning, it appears more analogous to the Rorschach Prognostic Rating Scale. The fact that the authors share their methods of studying ego processes and illustrate them copiously increases this system's usefulness to the clinician. Perhaps this system would have the best chance of all of being adopted for routine clinical practice.

The chapter by Mindess addresses itself to a dimension which he feels has been the subject of some neglect; namely the interpretation of content. Content analysis is described as the stepchild of Rorschach interpretation, and the author's approach to using content is spelled out in an imaginative manner with several examples. Actually, content has been emphasized previously in various ways: attempts at using this dimension have ranged all the way from the purely empirical approach of Lindner (1950), who simply compared the frequency of contents in various diagnostic categories, to the highly symbolic ones illustrated in books by Schafer (1954) and Philips and Smith (1953).

Mindess states that the dimensions of significance are originality, emotional cathexis, imaginativeness, and repetition, and that the most productive focus may be on the dramatic symbol. He describes interpretation of this kind as intuitive and deems it to be self-evident, although it would be possible to study both the reliability and the concurrent validity of the interpretations proposed. One way of documenting interpretations of this kind is by the use of the semantic differential. In a review of research on the Rorschach during the past decade (Klopfer, 1968) it is suggested that hypotheses concerning content can easily be put to the test and verified by this means. Mindess emphasizes the dramatic symbol, which is opportune when the examiner (clinician) comes across it and perhaps it would be possible to extend this system to include some of the more common kinds of content collected in the clinic or hospital.

Würsten addresses himself to the integration of the Rorschach with developmental theory as enunciated by Piaget and with the known literature in the field of child development. Such a frame of reference helps to bind together a lot of work which has been fragmented. This theory offers the best chance of an integrated continuum for the use of Rorschach at all ages, and presents an interesting comparison to the psychoanalytic approach which has been the most prominently described in the literature. Würsten compares Piaget's theory with Gestalt theories and finds interesting differences such as the reversibility of structures according to Piaget in contrast to irreversibility in the other framework. He emphasizes the concept of homeostasis in human activity and the fact that it is a dynamic system which is constantly shifting about and readjusting itself. When such shifting does not occur, a dangerous kind of rigidity appears and this can produce problems with further development. Rigidity and flexibility on Rorschach performance may be related schematically to the fluctuation of effective behavior and the ability to shift when environmental pressures seem to demand it.

The Rorschach, in the view of this author, is used most appropriately in understanding the total personality in terms of its implications for both the past and the present. Rather than being a picayunish approach in which fragments of test behavior are related to segments of non-test behavior, an attempt is made to put the entire behavior of the individual including both Rorschach and non-Rorschach behavior on a solid theoretical footing in which everything can be connected and in which the individual can be perceived structurally, developmentally, dynamically, and conceptually. Certainly this is a very laudable effort and may inspire others to be as comprehensive in their attempts to theorize as Würsten.

In the chapter by Zelen we have essentially a very fascinating case study consisting of a saga of three generations of a family in which Rorschach protocols are used to illustrate both the intra- and interpersonal traits. Interactional hypotheses are made on the basis of individual protocols. It becomes clear that the Rorschach profiles show some similarities and also some differences, and that anyone interested in the use of this technique for in-depth understanding of many related people will find this chapter fascinating reading.

Zelen has a particularly captivating style in presenting his material. It would have been additionally intriguing if some of the interactional methods mentioned in the following chapter by Cutter and Farberow were employed in the study by Zelen. It may be that some of the similarities and differences could have been negotiated by the members of the family.

As a variation of the administrative procedure, the chapter by Cutter and Farberow presents the most exciting innovation since the Rorschach's inception. The consensus or interaction Rorschach comes in almost infinite varieties. Decision making concerning Rorschach responses can occur between couples, families, co-workers, therapist–patient pairs, children in a class, therapy groups, etc. Analyses of this information can occur in terms of process, product, or content polarities. This latter procedure is the one emphasized in the chapter. In this section, the literature is reviewed and the process is illustrated; the discussion and the cases cited will enable the reader to apply the technique or one of its variations. The whole consensus approach is of particular value because most patients who appear in the offices of clinical psychologists today come in for essentially interpersonal reasons. They are there because of their behavior toward significant others rather than primarily because of internal discomfort. By giving the Rorschach simultaneously to several people the possibility is created that the unknown stimulus (Rorschach) will lead into the immediate revelation of transactions without sacrificing the role of the Rorschach in laying bare the *intra*personal dynamics revealed in the responses preferred by each individual. Relationships can be evaluated in terms of such dimensions as dominance–submission, enrichment versus impoverishment, and reinforcement of strengths versus reinforcement of pathology. Use of the Rorschach as a consensus measure can do a good deal to update the intrapsychic orthodoxy of the past and integrate it with the behavioral interpersonal focus of the present.

Another innovative use of the Rorschach is presented by Holt, who discusses a quantification of primary process scoring and its relationships with creativity and "adaptive regression." This chapter contains a thorough review of the theory of primary process and a discussion of how it can be measured by means of the Rorschach.

Holt considers creativity as being "loose" or "regressing constructively." In reviewing the theoretical underpinnings of this assumption, he demonstrates a preference for the emergence of primary process in the Freudian sense. In addressing himself to the question of how this primary process is to be measured by means of the Rorschach, Holt considers content scores, formal scores, and administrative variations. The measures are designed to include thought content, control and defense, and creativity, as demonstrated in the person's ideation and perception.

Holt reviews the construct validity of Rorschach measures of "adaptive regression" by contrasting groups who produce creatively with those who do not and by measuring people on a continuum of creative behavior. The results seem to be encouraging. In discussing the findings the author demonstrates enthusiasm about where the data lead him, but mentions the literature's neglect of the inspirational phase. He considers it regrettable that there is less emphasis on process of creativity than on outcome. The non-Rorschach studies alluded to tend to demonstrate that creative people do have more access to primary process material, although their product does not always gain social acceptability.

It is evident that Holt has existential interests and that he is more concerned about what is going on inside the box in the way of human potential and inner flexibility. The author admits that his measures have a certain irrelevance for social adaption and thus may not show high correlation with behavioral measures of adjustment. However, he feels that the Rorschach is primarily valuable as a means of discovering otherwise hidden resources.

One of the most important points made in the book is in the chapter by Baker on the use of feedback. Feedback is described by her as both a means of gaining additional assessment information and as a lead-in in counseling and psychotherapy. It has many added advantages as well, including the facts that the examiner learns more about the test's meaning through discussing it with the patient and that the patient is greatly loosened up by this sign of trust on the part of the diagnostician. Much of the suspicion with which psychological testing has been regarded can be overcome by techniques such as those described in this chapter. Some of the subjects suitable for discussion include diagnosis, style of behavior, defenses, and thought content. This feedback session can set the trend for future collaboration.

Another chapter dealing with interpretation and prediction is the one by Brawer, which reviews in detail the use of the Rorschach in vocational prediction and related areas. It is evident that the Rorschach has had success in many fields of prediction, such as in certain medical and military decision areas. The use of the Rorschach in colleges and other schools is apparently primarily justified in terms of the in-depth understanding of the students which results on the part of the counselors. According to this review, it has not proven as useful in the detection of artistic ability, which might not be surprising in terms of the results described in Holt's chapter. The discussion of the use of the Rorschach in industry reveals, as noted before, that psychological tests are more useful in detecting the absence of psychopathology than in making specific predictions for vocational success. The author mentions that particular new scoring methods which are not described in this book in detail, such as Piotrowski's perceptanalysis (1957) and Stone's SORT, show utility in the area of industrial selection. As it has been employed in the selection of teachers and scientists, the Rorschach thus far has not been studied sufficiently to demonstrate fairly what role it can play. The research literature described in this chapter indicates both the utility and the limitation of the Rorschach testing in predicting for specific areas.

Even though the Rorschach is one of the most comprehensive means of assessment ever invented, still it does not tap some areas of functioning as concretely and specifically as other tests, such as tests of vocational interests, ability, etc. If we try to make the Rorschach do all things for all men we elevate it to the status of a fetish and guarantee its eventual demise. If, on the other hand, we use it for screening of psychopathology, in-depth understanding of people's motives, and other appropriate goals, we can use this information together with that from other sources to assist people in planning vocational, academic, and personal goals much more effectively. Thus I lead into many interviews with both children and adults with a Rorschach test, not because Rorschach tests will reveal all, but because they will give sufficient cues to enable a much more rapid establishment of empathy and the initiation of effective problem solving. When the Rorschach is asked to carry more weight than it can legitimately bear, the attempt is bound to be destructive.

After reading this book, the reader should be in a good position to judge the current status of the Rorschach. Despite many changes of style and preference in the field of clinical psychology, it continues to be employed widely and innovatively. The authors of these pages have been in the forefront of research and theorizing in the field of clinical psychology and they have found the Rorschach useful in each step along the way. The instrument is sufficiently flexible and the normative data sufficiently profuse that it continues to be a tool of progress rather than part of a discarded past. Every aspect of Rorschach procedure, including administration, scoring, interpretation, and use of test findings, has been studied over the years since the publication of the last volume in the series, and the results are herein made available in one place for all concerned.

References

Klopfer, W. G. 1968. "The Present Status of the Rorschach Test." In *Advances in Personality Assessment,* Paul McReynolds (Ed.). Palo Alto: Science & Behavior Books.

Lindner, R. M. 1950. "The Content Analysis of the Rorschach Protocol." In *Projective Psychology,* L. E. Abt and L. Bellak (Eds.). New York: Alfred A. Knopf, Inc.

Philips, L. and Smith, J. G. 1953. *Rorschach Interpretation: Advanced Techniques.* New York: Grune & Stratton.

Piotrowski, Z. A. 1957. *Perceptanalysis: A Fundamentally Reworked, Expanded and Systematized Rorschach Method.* New York: Macmillan.

Schafer, R. 1954. *Psychoanalytic Interpretation in Rorschach Testing: Theory and Application.* New York: Grune & Stratton.

PART ONE

Scoring and Interpretation

1

Martin Mayman

Reality Contact, Defense Effectiveness, and Psychopathology in Rorschach Form-Level Scores *

Introduction

A scoring system is helpful only if it calls attention to those aspects of a test response from which the clinician or the researcher may draw useful inferences. Form quality was thought by Rorschach to be one such attribute of ink-blot percepts, but until recently form-level scoring has consistently failed to catch and hold the interest of most Rorschach practitioners. Many clinicians seem to feel there is little they can learn from form-level scores that they do not already know from their impressionistic scanning of Rorschach protocols.

Those who do score form quality often settle for a rough-and-ready classification of responses as either "acceptable" or "poor." Rorschach himself apparently believed that there was not much to be gained by more than a rough dichotomy of this kind. Beck (1948) followed Rorschach's lead in this respect, although he did urge that statistical norms be used to decide whether a response is acceptable or not.

---

* A briefer version of this chapter was read at a symposium entitled "Measuring Reality-Adherence in the Rorschach Test," American Psychological Association meeting, New York, September 3, 1966.

Those Rorschach investigators who have advocated a more discriminating approach to form-level scoring have not yet convinced clinicians that their proposed innovations would increase the clinician's diagnostic effectiveness, but a good case could be made for the research value of such innovations. Klopfer (1942) was the first to break with Rorschach's approach to form-level scoring. Instead of a single cutting point he used two, one at each extreme of the form-level continuum, separating out for special attention the unusually good forms and the unusually poor forms. This left about 90 percent of all responses in an undistributed middle category where form quality had no special significance. Rapaport and associates (1945) and Schafer (1948) introduced a further scoring refinement, developed also independently by Bohm (1958). They divided all responses into "good" or "poor," as Rorschach did, but added a further differentiating grade in each of these categories, "±" for substandard but acceptable percepts, and "∓" for poor but defensible percepts. However, the criteria for scoring "±" or "∓" remained ambiguous, and the meaning of these scores remained unclear.

Klopfer, in 1944, proposed a new approach to form-level scoring. He suggested that form level be rated on a 15-point scale according to the care and accuracy with which a response is developed. Starting with a base value of zero for each response, he suggested adding a half-point for each good elaboration and subtracting a half-point for each distorting elaboration. This score provided primarily a measure of effective intelligence brought to bear in the Rorschach response process. While this proposal probably has merit, it has so far failed to appeal to the busy clinician who has other, better established and probably more reliable techniques for assessing intelligence.

The most original innovation in form-level scoring was introduced by Rapaport (Rapaport et al., 1945), but was used by him only for research purposes. Rapaport distinguished six discrete grades of response quality: *F+*, *Fo*, *Fv*, *F—*, *special F+*, and *special F—*. The "+" score designated a well-differentiated, well-perceived response; the *"o"* score a "gross response," i.e., a loose but acceptable generalization from no more than one or two crudely seen elements. The *"v"* (vague) score designated a response in which the shape of the object seen in the blot is *intrinsically* ambiguous or amorphous, e.g., "island," "a piece of coal," "Spring." The "—" score was given for poor, ill-conceived responses. *"Special F+"* referred to unusually well articulated, often original *F+* responses, and *"special F—"* referred to well-differentiated but very arbitrary responses, usually original *F—*'s. The value of this approach was demonstrated, but on a limited scale, and these scores were never adopted by Rapaport for use in clinical practice.

Friedman (1952) picked up where Rapaport left off. The only change made in Rapaport's qualitative form-level scores was to distinguish "amorphous" from "vague" responses, both of which had been scored "vague" by Rapaport. However, Friedman attributed different meanings to all these scores. He saw them as representing points in a scale of "developmental maturity" of the perceptual process. The "arbitrary," "amorphous," and "vague" responses were considered to be relatively primitive, "syncretic" perceptual structures. *F++* and *F+* responses were looked upon as highly differentiated, developmentally advanced perceptual structures. This scoring scheme and its rationale have been applied successfully in a series of subsequent studies (Hemmindinger, 1960).

All these approaches, with the possible exception of Beck's, emphasized the perceptual and cognitive implications of form level. They related form-level scores to the impact of emotional factors on intellectual efficiency. Beck (1948) went a step beyond these formulations when he suggested that form level was also a measure of "ego strength," but he used the term as synonymous with the presence or absence of severely disruptive psychopathology. I would like to suggest a somewhat different approach to form-level scoring based on the assumption that the form quality of Rorschach responses is an index of reality testing, i.e., indicates the range and general level, the fluctuations and flaws, in a person's capacity to test reality.

Form Perception and Reality Testing

A person gains a firm hold on reality only gradually in his development. There is a time in the young child's life when his "Really?"

expresses a profound uncertainty as to what is and what is not what it seems to be. There is a time when the child has no reason yet to disbelieve his impression that people and things do, in fact, change, perhaps into radically new forms. If children can change into adults, why not adults into children, why not boys into girls, why not people into monsters? Before the age of three or three and a half, object-constancy is not yet entrenched as the *sine qua non* of reality. The child playing with a stick of wood is limited neither by shape nor substance as he assigns to it a series of ever-changing identities in the shifting fantasms of his unfettered imagination. Stable, well-delineated form emerges only gradually as a relatively invariant object-property of the things in his world. But form-constancy does eventually gain the ascendancy in the child's view of things. This process of coming to terms with an outer reality made up of structural configurations stable enough to withstand the autistic pull of moods, wishes, or impulses, marks the hard-won triumph of the reality principle over the early primacy of the pleasure principle in human thought (Freud, 1912; Ferenczi, 1913).

The excessive subjectivity of a person's early view of his world is outgrown in time, but never completely. In daydreams, in imaginative play, and in creative productions, a person is free to return to the more relaxed, freely ranging, less scrupulously disciplined perceptions of childhood.

In much the same way, Rorschach blots invite relaxation of stringent standards of reality testing, an invitation which some people accept willingly in the service of enhanced creativity. Others, however, may welcome the opportunity to ease up on reality testing because their egos are weak, hard-pressed and quick to abandon adult imperatives. Still others with more brittle egos may staunchly resist any temptation to relax standards for fear of losing control.

The form quality of Rorschach responses indicates in microcosm the attitude with which a person maintains his hold on his object-world. Some people find it easy to shift from well-defined representations of real objects to more malleable representations of fantasy objects. For other people reality is more intractable and subjective imagery gets short shrift if it does not conform with strictly imposed standards of reality testing. For some, reality is looked upon as open-ended and free to be played with. For others, it seems a stringent, even harsh, taskmaster. For some, reality testing is an ego function, employed in a constructive exploration of their world. For others, the self-checking, self-corrective aspect of this exploration may have hypertrophied into a superego function; self-criticism may have become an end in itself, a form of self-castigation, and self-scrutiny may have become only a form of pained self-consciousness. Reality testing, if it is too rigorous and unrelenting, can be maladaptive and even pathogenic.

The Scores and Their Meanings

A form-level scoring system can be devised to reflect such qualitatively distinct modes of reality testing. Each of the seven form-level scores defined below identifies a distinct balance of subjective and objective considerations achieved in the discovery of a familiar form on the Rorschach test. At one extreme (the *F*+ response) the subject maintains an objective, realistic, appropriately critical attitude toward a given response. He stays close to the determining influence of the blots and maximizes the fit between the associated idea and the blot outline. His associations, however rich, will form themselves around the outlines he finds in the ink blots. At the other extreme (the *F*— response) an idea may be permitted to emerge and become more compelling than the reality represented by a blot outline. An idea may take hold of the person so completely as to weaken his hold on reality, leading him even to ignore indications which contradict that idea. He is so immersed in his associations as to disregard the goodness of fit between the idea and its projected representation in the ink blot. He forgets the tacit social obligation to "test" the appropriateness of his response and to see to it that he reports only what others can see and share with him.

Fo. This score ("ordinary" form) is reserved for those responses which are so obvious, so easily noticed, as to be rather unimpressive achievements. These are the responses which need not be sought out, which make little call on ingenuity or imagination. They require little or no creative effort to produce. *Fo* responses include not only the most popular percepts, most of which are seen by at least half of any normal group, but also the near-popular percepts seen by about one out of three normal subjects and the fairly commonplace percepts which occur in one out of five or six protocols.

The *Fo* response indicates only that the subject was able to see the obvious. Conversely, the absence of any acceptable minimum number of *Fo* responses indicates a significant failure to notice the obvious. Protocols with a disproportionately high percentage of *Fo* responses are obtained most often from superficial or banal subjects who feel most secure with patently obvious, directly palpable realities. But a high *Fo* percent record may also indicate a superficiality which is situational rather than characteristic of that person; for a variety of reasons he may choose to remain uninvolved in the test situation. Occasionally, high *Fo* Rorschachs reflect the extreme caution of someone uncertain of his ability to distinguish the real from the unreal, the valid from the arbitrary, in his thoughts and actions. He may not trust himself to express an idea which others might deem inappropriate, so he limits himself to the safest responses he can find.

A Rorschach protocol which is grossly lacking in *Fo* responses may well indicate a serious deficiency in reality contact. A well-balanced record would be one which includes a sizable proportion of *Fo* and *F+* responses, indicating a person who can appreciate the obvious without being limited to banalities, someone who can break away from the obvious without losing his moorings and without being carried off into projective misrepresentations of reality.[1]

F+. This score is reserved for those responses which represent the successful combination of imagination and reality-congruence. They depart from the commonplace but remain realistic. At their

---

[1] It would require too much space to include here any useful discussion of scoring criteria and statistical norms. For such concrete suggestions concerning form-level score patterns, the reader is referred to the Form Level Manual (Mayman, 1956).

best, they show a measure of creativity within the framework of a socially shared reality; they may express originality in a way which permits others to participate in the idea, benefit from it, and reward it. *F*+ responses bend to the strictures of reality testing without sacrificing spontaneity, thoughtfulness, or even originality.

One *recognizes* an *Fo* response, whereas one *discovers* an *F*+. In the *F*+ response one does not have as ready-made a prod to the associative processes as in the *Fo* response. The perceptual configurations more often must be pulled out of their embedded, sometimes even well-camouflaged, place in the blot mass.

A low *F*+ percent score is usually a valid indication of poor reality testing or limited intelligence. On the other hand, a high *F*+ percent score is not necessarily a measure of good reality testing or high intelligence. It may, as was suggested above, indicate a person hemmed in by harsh, inflexible standards of acceptable behavior. One might say that the egos of such people have been overshadowed by their superegos. Excessively high *F*+ percent scores do, in fact, occur most frequently in patients with hypertrophied superegos, i.e., those who are neurotically depressed, constrictedly paranoid, or characterologically compulsive.

Where the superego is easily circumvented, as in messy obsessional states, we may find quite low *F*+ percent scores. And in patients where the superego is archaic and the ego correspondingly regressed, *F*—'s will appear, A high *F*+ percent with interspersed lapses into *F*— responses may well indicate regressive lacunae in an otherwise compulsive character structure. In such cases, sporadic breaks with reality are indicated by the person's bland acceptance of blatantly arbitrary interpretations.

Fw (*Fw*+ and *Fw*—). The "weak" form responses mark a significant shift away from the reality adherence characteristic of *Fo* and *F*+ percepts. The *Fw* responses are unconvincing but not arbitrary; they fail to "click." For example, a tiny round area with a jutting point may be called a "face." It doesn't look much like a face, but on the other hand it might be a face if one were to fill in more of the details and perhaps correct a contour or two. The subject obviously reads a great deal into the area to be able to see it as a face. He could just as easily have called it a breast, or a hill, or the glass tip of an old-fashioned light bulb, or anything else with a rounded contour which comes to a point.

A response is scored *Fw*+ when the general contours of the area do not clash with the suggested response. It should be scored *Fw*— when some clash does occur. That is, the *Fw*— response may have only one blot detail in which image and blot outline are congruent, while other attributes of that blot area not only lend little support but actually make the idea somewhat incongruous. If in the "face" response, for example, it were not oval in shape and if the only justification for the response "face" were the jutting nose, it would be scored *Fw*—.

Unlike the *F*+ response, which effectively integrates image with reality, the *Fw* responses accept fantasy representations (images) without much concern about their veridicality. A reality-oriented subject can be expected to permit himself an occasional relaxation of this kind in his stringent adherence to the reality principle but will choose the most favorable conditions under which to do so. He may already have given a number of good responses before he slips into an *Fw* response, and even then he may take the precaution of slipping off into a relatively inconsequential area of the blot, an area whose outline is sufficiently ill-defined that any one of many images may be read into that area without contradiction.

Too many *Fw* responses in a record may indicate a too easily corrupted standard of reality testing, too much readiness to slip away from the most reality-attuned level of response in order to play more freely with images or fantasy fragments. A record with too few *Fw*'s, on the other hand, may indicate a very exacting approach to reality testing (in which case the *F*+ percent will be high), or it may indicate a person given to simple, unreflective, matter-of-fact contact with reality, with a relatively shallow "inner life" (in which case the *Fo* percent will be high).

Fv. The *Fv* ("vague") form response is much like the *Fw* in the slackness of the fit between image and blot outline. But here, the freedom from stringent reality testing comes from the choice of image which is fitted to the blot. If someone sees an object with intrinsically variable or nondefinitive shape, any question as to goodness of fit becomes more or less irrelevant. He has made it unnecessary to work with that idea until it does fit the blot outline, or to reject the idea because it does not fit. The *Fv* response provides perhaps one more degree of freedom to the response process than is available in the *Fw+* response but somewhat less freedom than one permits himself when he gives an *Fw—* response. The *Fv* is not an unrealistic response, but simply noncommittal.

Too much reliance upon *Fv* responses, especially if these are not prompted by a direct response to color or shading in the blots, suggests a poverty of available ideas which may, in fact, be ominous in its implications. It may indicate the kind of constriction and estrangement from reality which sometimes occurs in preschizophrenic conditions or severe anxiety states. Occasionally, we get a massing of such responses from persons in blunted schizophrenic states, and sometimes from retarded or brain-damaged persons.

Fs. The *Fs* ("spoiled") response represents a more serious departure from reality than does the lassitude of the *Fw* response or the noncommittalness of the *Fv*. The *Fs* indicates, in fact, a partial break with reality. The *Fs* score is used to designate an incipient *Fo* or *F+* response in which an important oversight or a striking distortion spoils what might otherwise have been a good response. Most of the response may be well seen, but one part is grossly misperceived. Something has gone awry, and the subject arrives at a surprisingly idiosyncratic *mis*perception of a percept commonly seen "correctly" by others. The configurational properties of the blot which for others prove so compelling are not compelling enough for the person who sees an *Fs;* he slips out of touch with reality long enough for some significant "error" to find its way into an otherwise good response which should be relatively impervious to such distortion. The distortion occurs almost as if a fragment of the blot reality had faded out—had dissolved—while the rest of the form remained intact.

F—. The *F—* response is a wholly arbitrary percept where the blot outline exerts little or no influence on the response process. An idea is imposed on an area of the blot with virtually complete disregard for the structural properties of that area. The idea is totally autistic and acquires its subjective validity only from the vivid attachment this person can have to any of his ideas, however arbitrary. With such an approach, reality is easily brushed aside, or delusionally reorganized, to better fit an inner conviction concerning what must be true.

To avoid construct diffusion, it is important to remember that reality testing assessed by this scoring system refers only to the form quality of a percept, not to the fantasy or inner object-world in which that percept may have become embedded. A person may elaborate an *F+* response into a psychotic confabulation without spoiling the *F+* properties of the percept. For example, the popular figures on Card III may be seen as "two men in evening dress, bending over doing something. I can't make out exactly what, maybe dissecting the body of a third person in order to eat it." This is a bizarre fantasy, probably a psychotic fantasy, but the two men if well seen are not scored *F—*. This confabulation represents a different form of disorganization than appears in *Fs* or *F—* percepts. The dereism of confabulatory *fantasies* should not be confused with arbitrary *misperceptions* of reality. The *F—* response is not a crazy thought, or image, or fantasy; it is an arbitrary *percept* in which the person claims to see something which simply is not there.

Even one *Fs* or *F—* response in a record may have severe pathognomonic implications. At best, it indicates too cavalier an attitude toward reality, a blitheness which may serve as a cover for actual inability to deal more appropriately with reality. At worst, *Fs* and *F—* responses in a record indicate an imminent or overt psychotic abandonment of reality.

Test Administration

Changes in a scoring system necessarily change what one must look for in Inquiry. The rationale presented here for form-level scoring is based upon an ego-structural approach to personality assessment. The scoring system is consistent with the Rapaport mode of test administration in which the examinee is primed to test reality rather than indulge in a free play of fantasy. Examiners who follow Klopfer's mode of test administration should make appropriate corrections before they apply the norms suggested in the Form Level Manual.

To use this scoring system properly, the examiner must pay more attention to details of a response which he may previously have found it more convenient to disregard. He must be alert for *Fs* or *Fs tendencies* in otherwise good responses. He must be quick to inquire into a response if there is something nebulous or deviant in the way the response is verbalized. He should pin down in some detail the various elements of a suspect percept. When the subject sees a face, the nose and chin are key reference points. When he sees the body of a person, the nose, waist, and feet may be details the examiner asks him to point out. One need not have a subject tediously trace all the details of every response; this is an unnecessarily heavy-handed approach to Inquiry. The examiner must learn to rely on his empathy with the response process, but he should be careful not to presume too often that he knows what the subject had in mind, or how well the subject saw what he claims to have seen. The examiner should remember that form-level scoring is based on what the subject actually saw, not on what he had in mind.

Test Scoring

A word is in order, too, regarding the advantages of making routine use of a scoring system in clinical practice. The harassed clinician often does not take the trouble to score Rorschach protocols. Without recording and summating form-level scores, he registers his impressions of the form quality of responses and carries these impressions into his conclusions about the person. The general drift of such inferences are, of course, in the same direction as those drawn from a carefully scored protocol. But most impressionistic statements if examined closely prove to be rough approximations—freer, less precise generalizations about the person than one would draw from a more precisely scored record. One might draw a parallel between free-style versus score-disciplined interpretation and the modes of reality testing described in the scoring system itself. A casually impressionistic approach to interpretation not tied to a scoring system exposes one to the danger that he will unwittingly slip into *Fw+* kinds of inferences. On the other hand, an *F+* kind of approach to clinical inference may be overly rigid at times but is not inevitably so nor even generally so. Working with exacting standards in clinical inference can be—often is—optimally productive and not merely compulsive. One can commit himself to an *F+* approach without surrendering the kind of flexibility represented by an optimal number of *Fw+*'s in a record. One need not sacrifice his relaxed, impressionistic, freely ranging subjectivity when he commits himself to the careful checking of his impressions against the strictures of objectivity and consensual validation.

Case Examples

One way to test the usefulness of a scoring system is to compare it with another and see whether it produces richer and more accurate inferences. A convenient set of cases to use for this purpose appears in Schafer's *The Clinical Application of Psychological Tests* (1948). Schafer used Rapaport's approach to form-level scoring. Five of Schafer's cases were selected at random and rescored according to the system proposed in this paper, and the new scores were submitted some months later to a quasi-blind analysis at a Rorschach Institute. In all but one of the cases it was apparent that considerably more information could be gleaned from the more refined form-level scores than was inferred from a more traditional scoring system.

Case 1

The first test case in which revised scores presented a strikingly different picture from the conventional scores was that of a 30-year-old salesman. The original form-level scores were as follows: [2]

$$F\% = 65$$
$$F'\% = 95$$
$$F+\% = 85$$
$$F'+\% = 85$$
$$R = 20$$

A high form level in a rather unproductive record suggests overly constrictive control. The one redeeming feature here is the fact that 35% of the responses do use some secondary determinant as well. Such rigidity and overcontrol could be found in a variety of clinical syndromes: hysteria, mixed neurosis, or, not inconceivably, an anxious, conscientious normal, or a rigid, paranoid character with a good façade.

Schafer said of these scores

> The $F+\%$ is high . . . indicating (along with other supporting evidence) that in the main he is likely to be able to delay the expression of impulses cautiously and that truly impulsive acts are likely to occur only sporadically.

And again,

> Pitting his verbalizations against the actual color and movement distribution and the high $F+\%$, we can conclude that much of his gaiety is feigned, put on for effect and used as cunningly as possible to gain an advantage in social situations.

When the record is rescored according to the scoring system proposed above, the scores take on a very different complexion. The revised scores are as follows:

---

[2] The F' score is Rapaport's "modified F" score, which is based on all form-dominant responses, not just those responses in which no determinants other than form are involved.

$$\left.\begin{array}{r}\left.\begin{array}{r} F'o\% = 65 \\ F'{+}\% = 25 \end{array}\right\} 90 \\ F'w{+}\% = \ \ 5 \end{array}\right\} 95$$

$$F'v\% = \ \ 0$$

$$\left.\begin{array}{r} F'w{-}\% = \ \ 0 \\ F's\% = \ \ 0 \\ F'{-}\% = \ \ 5 \end{array}\right\} 5$$

The $F'+\%$ seems high only if we do not separate the *Fo* from the *F*+ scores. Once we do, we find a massive reliance upon commonplace responses. Even in grossly hysterical patients one does not expect an $Fo\%$ much above 50%. This patient, if he "puts up a good front," does so only by relying heavily on banalities—a degree of shallowness masked by the grosser $Fo,+\%$ score.

One should be careful not to draw inferences from a single response, such as the single *F*— response in this protocol. Yet, in view of the stringent criteria for scoring *F*—, even one such response suggests the possibility that this patient may at times experience serious though transient lapses in reality testing. One begins to wonder whether this man might not be capable of sporadic distortions, or even grossly projective misperceptions of reality.

Clinical Summary [3]

This patient was a 30-year-old salesman referred because of alcoholism which had become especially severe in the last year. He was active, energetic, popular in school, bright, but not very industrious. He worked for his father for several years, was underpaid because he was supposed to be "working his way up." He left at the age of 21, either because, as he claims, he felt his talents were too great for his position or, as his father claims, because he was fired for being insulting and unreliable. In the army, where he served for five years, he was court-martialed frequently for alcoholism, insubordination, and AWOL's. He had been promiscuous, had written bad

[3] For a fuller description see Schafer (1948), pages 159–161.

checks, made an impulsive marriage while drunk, was resentful of being "railroaded" into the hospital. He was rather paranoid, fractious, and flippant. He was demanding and chafed at all restrictions. His frustration tolerance was conspicuously low. The diagnosis was narcissistic character disorder with alcoholism and paranoid features.

Case 2

The Schafer-Rapaport form-level scores in this case are very similar to those in Case 1, but this 37-year-old woman proves to be a very different kind of person.

$$\begin{array}{rl} F\% = & 89 \\ F'\% = & 100 \\ F+\% = & 88 \\ F'+\% = & 89 \\ R = & 19 \end{array}$$

The high $F+\%$ in a low response record suggests highly constrictive control with no apparent disturbance in reality testing. The inferences drawn from scores based on a simple dichotomous form-level scoring system would be much the same as in Case 1. Schafer's only comment about the form-level scores in this case refers to other test information as well and indicates that the clinical picture which would best fit these scores would be that of a neurotic depression.

The revised scores are as follows:

$$\left.\begin{array}{r} \left.\begin{array}{r} F'o\% = 53 \\ F'+\% = 26 \end{array}\right\} 79 \\ F'w+\% = 0 \end{array}\right\} 79$$

$$F'v\% = 0$$

$$\left.\begin{array}{r} F'w-\% = 11 \\ \left.\begin{array}{r} F's\% = 11 \\ F'-\% = 0 \end{array}\right\} 11 \end{array}\right\} 22$$

The rescoring points up a sharp distinction between Case 1 and Case 2. Although the $F'o$ *and* $F'+$ add up to the same high

F′o,+% score in Case 2, there is clear evidence of some disturbance in reality testing in the *Fw—* and *Fs* percentages. The alternation between cautiously constrictive control and intermittent, rather serious misperceptions of reality suggests some kind of borderline state in which the tenuous reality contact is masked by this woman's constriction and guardedness until a more subtle analysis of the quality of her reality testing is done. The *Fo,+%* score indicates only the potential for maintaining some façade. This pattern of scores would be consistent with an incipient paranoid state, an incipient paranoid schizophrenia, or even an openly psychotic paranoid schizophrenia.

Clinical Summary [4]

The patient, a 37-year-old married woman, had apparently led a very seclusive life. In the past six months she had become depressed, even more seclusive, neglected her household, cried frequently, threatened suicide, and had become suspicious of her "hostile" neighbors. She believed that the radio news had a hidden meaning which only she could understand. When agitated, she would laugh and cry at the same time. She believed her fellow patients talked about her and she "heard them" make "smart remarks." She believed that her marriage had disgraced her family and felt no hope for recovery from her illness. The diagnosis was paranoid schizophrenia with symptomatic depression.

Case 3

Again we find the relatively well retained *Fo,+%* score masking a psychotic condition, but this time in a more dilated protocol. The unrevised form-level scores were as follows:

---

[4] For a fuller description see Schafer (1948), page 197.

$$
\begin{aligned}
F\% &= 53 \\
F'\% &= 100 \\
F{+}\% &= 70 \\
F'{+}\% &= 69 \\
R &= 51
\end{aligned}
$$

One is impressed here with the high productivity and with the degree to which other determinants enter into the response process, despite which the patient maintains effective, even excessive, control. In view of the openness to other determinants, the $F'{+}\%$ is excellent and only further underscores the indications of impressively good control. This could easily be the record of a well-functioning normal person, with perhaps some compulsive features in the character structure, compulsiveness which does not necessarily assume neurotic proportions.

Rescored, the form quality is as follows:

$$
\begin{aligned}
&\left.\left.\begin{aligned} F'o\% &= 23 \\ F'{+}\% &= 37 \end{aligned}\right\} 60 \atop F'w{+}\% = 6 \right\} 66 \\
&F'v\% = 2 \\
&\left.\begin{aligned} &F'w{-}\% = 19 \\ &\left.\begin{aligned} F's\% &= (3 \text{ tend} = 15\%) \\ F'{-}\% &= 13 \end{aligned}\right\} 13 \end{aligned}\right\} 32
\end{aligned}
$$

Again, as in Case 2, the relatively good $Fo,{+}\%$ indicates only superficially good reality contact. The severe disturbance of reality testing, masked by the traditional scores, emerges clearly in the rescored psychogram. Schafer drew no inferences from the form-level scores in this case, but his inferences from other features of the test protocol are fully confirmed in the rescored form-level analysis:

> Fantasy with vivid imagery is all-pervasive and colors perception of reality so strongly that very likely she loses distance from her thoughts and is unable to distinguish fantasy from reality. The extensiveness of the withdrawal into fantasy, the absence of adaptive efforts . . . indicate the imminence of a psychotic break.

Clinical Summary[5]

The patient, a 26-year-old married woman, had from a very early age been sensitive to criticism. She ran away from home in her teens, worked as a waitress, drank, had an unhappy marriage which led to her attempted suicide, was divorced, and resumed drinking until she was remarried happily to a man whom she loved and who was gentle and affectionate. Following his death in an automobile accident the day before she gave birth to her second child, she felt "dazed" for several months and tried to keep herself from "going to pieces." She showed little emotion, even over the recent death of her second child. The diagnosis was mixed neurosis in a schizoid personality, but the possibility of a psychotic break was considered. She moved to a different state shortly after her examination, and several months later she suffered an acute schizophrenic break.

Case 4

Unlike the preceding three cases, this patient presents us with a conspicuously low $F+\%$ score:

$$\begin{aligned} F\% &= 88 \\ F'\% &= 100 \\ F+\% &= 50 \\ F'+\% &= 56 \\ R &= 16 \end{aligned}$$

Again the picture is one of constriction—very few responses, a completely form-dominant record, and very little use of other determinants. The low $F+\%$ would suggest first a psychotic record in a flat, constricted personality. Schafer, considering the low $F+\%$ score in the context of the other features of the record, said only

5 For a fuller description see Schafer (1948), pages 266–268.

that the score indicates "noteworthy reduction of intellectual efficiency."

The rescored record removes a large part of the ambiguity of the low $F+\%$:

$$\left.\begin{aligned} F'o\% &= 44 \\ F'+\% &= 12 \end{aligned}\right\} 56$$

$$F'w+\% = 0$$

$$\left.\begin{aligned} F'v\% &= 31 \\ \left.\begin{aligned} F'w-\% &= 12 \\ F's\% &= 0 \\ F'-\% &= 0 \end{aligned}\right\} & \ 12 \end{aligned}\right\} 43$$

This patient's failure to come up with good responses is due to a massive constriction of the associative process, rather than to any drift into autism or dereism. There are no *Fs*'s or *F*—'s to suggest a psychotic disturbance, although of course such a possibility cannot be ruled out. However, the high $Fo\%$ and $Fv\%$ and the low $F+\%$ argue strongly for ideational shallowness due either to a congenital intellectual deficit or to the ideationally and motivationally impoverishing effects of repression.

Clinical Summary [6]

The patient, a 43-year-old barber, married and with two children, had for the past two years complained of much somatic distress, localized mainly in the back and inguinal regions, which he attributed to some type of prostatic disease. He had become increasingly anxious, despondent, and irritable and had had frequent crying spells. Prior to the onset of these symptoms he had been a compulsive worker and a successful businessman. The clinical diagnosis was neurasthenia.

---

[6] For a fuller description see Schafer (1948), page 291.

Case 5

In this instance, the traditional scores reveal rather accurately the patient's character structure, but the more differentiated form-level scores provide a fuller picture of the man.

Schafer's scores on this patient were as follows:

$$
\begin{aligned}
F\% &= 57 \\
F'\% &= 96 \\
F{+}\% &= 77 \\
F'{+}\% &= 84 \\
R &= 45
\end{aligned}
$$

This pattern of scores is much like that of Case 3 and would suggest essentially the same inferences, with perhaps one exception; namely, that the control in this case is, if anything, excessive, suggesting that the compulsive features of the character structure of this person reach neurotic proportions. Schafer looks more leniently on these scores and says, "The $F\%$ and $F{+}\%$ are within normal limits and do not contribute directly to the diagnostic picture." It is from other test data that Schafer infers,

> Intelligence functioning bears the stamp of an obsessive-compulsive character development. Extreme compulsive attention to detail and rigid rationalistic and intellectualistic efforts . . . pervade his thinking.

The rescored record yields the following:

$$
\left.\begin{aligned}
&\left.\begin{aligned} F'o\% &= 27 \\ F'{+}\% &= 39 \end{aligned}\right\} 66 \\
&F'w{+}\% = 22
\end{aligned}\right\} 88
$$

$$
F'v\% = 0
$$

$$
\left.\begin{aligned}
&F'w{-}\% = 12 \\
&\left.\begin{aligned} F's\% &= 0 \\ F'{-}\% &= 0 \end{aligned}\right\} 0
\end{aligned}\right\} 12
$$

The total $Fo,{+}\%$ of 66 is optimal in the new scoring system (somewhat lower than the optimal 70% in the Rapaport system, because we exclude *Fw+* responses, many of which would have been scored *F+* by Rapaport and Schafer). If we look at the scores which fall outside the *Fo* and *F+* categories, our attention is drawn to an unusual feature of this record: there are no *Fv, Fs,* or *F—* responses and only 12% *Fw—*, this in a somewhat dilated record. It would appear that the patient is scrupulous in his unwillingness to allow himself to produce responses that are not readily defensible. He does not let himself make many mistakes and is likely, when he says or does something, to sift it through a self-critical screen and approve it as "correct" in the variety of connotations of this word. Yet, at the same time, the man gives an unusually high number of combined *Fw+*, *Fw—* responses (34%). In fully a third of his responses he finds easy outs. There is a laxness, a willingness to accede to other pressures and sacrifice quality in his responses so long as he remains within certain proscribed limits. Whether this laxness is the product of quantity ambition, or excessive fantasy, or some other form of decompensation of his compulsive defenses cannot be ascertained from these form-level scores alone.

Some comment might also be made of the relative size of the *Fo*% as compared with the *F+*%. We find relatively little banality, although the patient certainly is aware of and responsive to the readily seen responses. Apparently, he gears himself to a high qualitative level of productivity; he reveals in the *F+* responses both his ideational potential and his compulsive needs.

Clinical Summary [7]

The patient, a 32-year-old surgeon, had carried mature personal responsibilities from an early age and appears to have incorporated his father's high and rigid ethical standards. He was obedient as a child, ambitious and hard driving in school years. He developed a duodenal ulcer in medical school and since that time has had several stomach operations and many blood transfusions, several attacks of

[7] For a fuller description see Schafer (1948), pages 118–121.

pneumonia, and frequent and severe headaches. Following an unhappy marriage he became generally fatigued and tense, his headaches grew worse, he began staying away from home, and a year ago he began to rely on increasing doses of Seconal. A few months ago he began using codeine for relief of his headaches and began to feel depressed. He seemed apathetic during the examination, and he felt that he had lost interest in his work and himself. Nevertheless, he struggled to give "perfectly correct" answers. The clinical diagnosis was anxiety state with psychosomatic symptoms and symptomatic addiction in a compulsive personality.

Validity Studies

Anecdotal clinical material may illustrate the diagnostic advantages of a new score but is not in itself sufficient evidence of validity to justify replacing a familiar scoring system with a new one. However, when one adds to the balance the cumulative weight of a variety of validity studies in support of the new score, the conclusion that a substitution of the new for the old is in order becomes quite compelling.

The studies reported below employed the seven-category scoring system described in this chapter and applied the scores to a variety of groups of experimental subjects, ranging from creative art students and empathic psychotherapists to hospitalized schizophrenics and disorganized murderers.

Cohen (1960), studying the creativity of undergraduate art students, found that of 27 Rorschach variables studied, only two successfully differentiated creative from noncreative art students. One was the number of responses, and the other was the individual mean form-level score of those responses which showed some intrusion of "primary process" ideation into the response content (Holt and Havel, 1960). It is important to emphasize that the groups did not differ in their primary process scores, but only in their ability to maintain good reality testing when primary process ideation was activated. The more creative students maintained a significantly higher form level than noncreative students while under pressure from primary process ideas. When form level was scored by another scoring system it failed to separate creative from noncreative subjects.

Using the same set of subjects, Pryor (1962) factor-analyzed a matrix of 23 scores in an attempt to isolate significant determinants of creativity. The form-level score yielded a factor loading of .71 on the factor designated by Pryor as "secondary process thinking."

Holt's more recent papers on his primary process scoring system include findings on a group of 50 members of Actors Equity (see Chapter 7). Table 1 reports some unpublished form-level data from that study, which Holt has graciously permitted me to cite here. In this group, form-level scores are meaningfully related to a variety of personality variables, some measured by other Rorschach scores, but some measured by non-Rorschach indices of character structure, defense organization, and preferred life style.

In still another intensive study of normal subjects, this time a group of junior and senior students at a small liberal arts college, Heath (1965) turned up several other correlates of form-level performance. He gathered data separately from three groups of carefully selected subjects. Members of one group of 20 were those students judged to be the 10 least and the 10 most "mature" of their class. Another group of 24 consisted of the 12 most and 12 least "organized" students in their class. A third group was made up of 36 volunteers from among the remaining 150 students and comprised a "standard" group. Form level was inversely related to various MMPI and Bernreuter measures of neuroticism, especially in the mature–immature group, effectively separated mature from immature students in all three groups, and was demonstrably related to a number of other measures of adaptive capacity and ego strength.

Form level is the largest single factor in Holt's measures of "defense effectiveness" and "adaptive regression." As scored by Rabkin (1967), for example, in a study done in close consultation with

TABLE 1 *Correlations of Mayman's Form-Level Scores with Other Test Scores*

	WEIGHTED FORM LEVEL	$\%F+$ [a]	% BAD FORM [a]
Weighted form level	—	**.79**	**−.79**
$\%F+$	**.79**	x	**−.52**
Selected Holt Primary Process scores:			
Sum DD × DE/*R*	*.32*	.17	*−.32*
Sum DE/*R*	**.72**	**.41**	**−.51**
% "Good *R*"	**.56**	**.52**	*−.33*
Sum Autistic Logic Level 1	**−.52**	**−.38**	**.40**
Sum Contradictions: Inapprop. Impossible 2	*.29*	*.39*	−.23
Sum Contradictions: Inapprop. Unlikely 1	*.28*	**.47**	−.14
Sum Peculiar Verbalizations Level 2	−.27	.03	*.35*
Sum Remoteness, Figures of Speech	*.32*	**.45**	−.17
Sum Negation Plus (adaptive)	.25	*.31*	**−.40**
Sum Aggression Level 1	*−.35*	−.18	*.33*
Sum Level 1 Condensations	−.25	.01	**.40**
Sum Level 1 Verbalizations	*−.33*	−.09	*.31*
Sum Remoteness Plus (adaptive)	**.45**	**.54**	*−.28*
Reported frequency of hypnagogic imagery	*−.38*	−.17	**.63**
Dyn. Pers. Inv.: OI (emotional lability)	−.27	**−.40**	.11
DPI: AH (anal hoarding)	**.38**	**.41**	*−.35*
DPI: WS (liking for seclusion)	*.29*	.11	*−.36*
Paths of Life: Pragmatic adventure, action	*.30*	**.41**	*−.35*
MMPI: Hs (Hypochondriasis)	**.36**	*.30*	**−.37**
MMPI: Hy (Hysteria)	*.31*	*.35*	*−.28*
Wechsler-Bellevue, Total IQ	.06	.24	−.17

NOTE: Subjects are 50 (mostly unemployed) members of Actors Equity studies at the Research Center for Mental Health, NYU, in 1959. Italic type denotes $p \leqq .05$; boldface denotes $p \leqq .01$ or better. (Some tests were not given to all subjects, so degrees of freedom vary slightly).

[a] $\%\text{ Bad form} = \frac{Fs, Fv, F-}{R} \times 100; \quad \%F+ = \frac{Fo, F+}{R} \times 100$

Holt, the procedure for scoring defense effectiveness (DE) was as follows:

> The scorer was first required to enter the DE score appropriate for a given response based solely on its form level. If this rating needed to be adjusted in terms of other factors, the scorer indicated what these factors were in each case, checking the appropriate alternative. The choice for such modification of DE based initially on form level included: (1) correction for affect; (2) correction for the controls and defenses used; and (3) correction based on clinical judgment. The score for Adaptive Regression is based in turn on Defense Effectiveness, and measures a subject's ability to maintain form quality when primary process elements intrude openly into his response content.

In view of the close link between these three measures,[8] any research findings which support the validity of the defense effectiveness and adaptive regression scores provide presumptive evidence as well of the validity of the form-level score. Several studies which directly compared form level with defense effectiveness found form level to be at least as effective a predictor as adaptive regression or defense effectiveness (Cohen; Kahn; Zukinsky). Two others (Rabkin; Heath) found defense effectiveness and adaptive regression to be better than form level in predicting the independent variables employed in their studies.

Through the efforts of Holt, his students, and colleagues, there is a growing body of research on defense effectiveness (and form level). Pine and Holt, for example, found defense effectiveness positively and significantly related to various measures of creativity in 13 college men, but not in their group of 14 college women. Wright and Abbey, also using college students as subjects, found DE to be positively correlated with the ability to complete an isolation experi-

[8] This link exists not only by definition; it has been statistically established as well. Rabkin reports a correlation "in the neighborhood of .80" between form level and defense effectiveness. Holt obtained a correlation of .72 between FL and DE in the unpublished data cited above. Heath (1965) reports somewhat lower correlations between FL and DE (.63; .35; .70) in his study.

ment. Bergan found vividness of visual imagery in dreams to be positively correlated with adaptive regression in both 14 male and 14 female undergraduates. These and other similar findings are cited in Rabkin's review of the experimental literature on adaptive regression (1967, Appendix A), and in Holt's chapter in this volume.

At the other extreme of the health–sickness continuum are three studies by Kahn, Zukowsky, and Saretsky. Kahn (1967) found the mean form-level score of all responses in a protocol to be a useful measure of disorganization in a group of 43 murderers. It was one of the few measures which significantly differentiated "legally sane" from "legally insane" murderers.

Zukowsky's (1961) study of "process" and "reactive" schizophrenics, the mean form-level score of all responses in a protocol failed to differentiate the two groups. But when, as in Cohen's study, the mean form-level score was computed only for those responses which showed some trace of primary process influence, the schizophrenics with good pre-morbid adjustment scored significantly higher than did schizophrenics with poor pre-morbid adjustment after the two groups were equated in other respects.

Saretsky (1963) found significant improvement in mean form-level scores of 20 newly admitted VA schizophrenic patients who were given chlorpromazine for three months, and no change in 20 others who were given a placebo. Increases in form level (and defense effectiveness) correlated with improved clinical behavior as measured by the Lorr scale for the combined clinical and control groups.

If form level does indeed measure a person's spontaneous readiness to test reality, as is suggested in this chapter and attested to by the studies cited above, it should be possible to show that form level improves with age throughout childhood, and especially during those years when children accomplish most of their transition from primary to secondary process modes of thought. Ginsparg (1965) undertook to test this assumption by comparing preschool with latency-age Rorschachs of 21 children in Lois Murphy's study of children's coping styles. As anticipated, Ginsparg found 50% fewer poor responses (*Fs* and *F*—) in the latency-age Rorschachs, even though there were 50% more responses in the older group. Good responses (*Fo*, *F*+) increased 50% in number, but because there were also 50% more responses in the average protocol of the older children the improvement in *Fo*,+% was not statistically significant. Similarly, Lohrenz and Gardner (1966), comparing two groups of older subjects, found that the form-level scores in each of two matched groups of identical twins aged 9 to 19 were significantly lower than the form-level scores of the parents' Rorschachs ($p < .001$ and $p < .025$, respectively).[9] Moreover, there was some evidence that form-level scores were positively correlated with age in the 9- to 19-year-old subjects. The correlations for the two twin groups were .48 and .12, respectively ($p < .01$ and $p =$ n.s.).

However, none of these construct-validating studies would carry much weight if form-level scores did not also differentiate in the extensive range of psychopathology which falls between the extremes of gifted college students and institutionalized psychotics. Such a group was available for study. It comprised the largely neurotic and borderline subjects who made up the subject pool in the Menninger Foundation's Psychotherapy Research Project (Wallerstein and Robbins, 1958). To study the relationship of form level to various measures of ego strength in this group, I selected 15 pretreatment Rorschachs and rescored them according to the Form Level Manual. The protocols were selected randomly except for the stipulation that the sample chosen should span approximately the same gamut of psychopathology as the entire patient population in that study, and that it include a liberal representation of patients who showed marked changes for better or worse following treatment. Participants in two Rorschach seminars were then asked to predict from the form-level scores alone the rating which a team of senior psychiatrists gave each patient on the project's Health–Sickness Rating

---

[9] To ensure the best possible estimates of relationship between mean form level and other Rorschach variables, those subjects with one or more card failures were not used. This procedure reduced Twin Sample 1 to an *N* of 45, Twin Sample 2 to an *N* of 38, and the Parent Sample to an *N* of 62.

TABLE 2 *Intercorrelations of Form-Level Ratings with Health–Sickness Ratings (15 patients)*

COLORADO RATERS

RATER:	#1	#2	#3	#4	#5	GROUP MEAN RATING	H-S PRE-TREAT-MENT	H-S POST-TREAT-MENT
#1	—	.94	.82	.79	.89	.97	.60	
#2		—	.67	.85	.91	.97	.58	
#3			—	.44	.70	.76	.41	
#4				—	.82	.87	.72	
#5					—	.95	.60	
Group mean						—	.64	

Correlations of .76 or higher are significant at the .001 level of confidence; .64 or

Scale (Luborsky, 1962) based on extensive pretreatment clinical evaluations. Raters were given the form-level scores for all the responses in a protocol, as well as the form-level score summary, and were told to base their ratings on the configuration of form-level scores in each protocol, i.e., the general level of form perception and the kinds and degrees of fluctuations around this level which characterized each protocol. Ratings were made independently by each of the students after an initial practice case was rated and discussed in the group. The first set of Rorschach raters were advanced predoctoral clinical trainees at the University of Colorado. Half of the second group of raters were predoctoral interns at Topeka State Hospital and the other half were post-doctoral psychology Fellows at the Menninger Foundation. Rorschach predictions of Health–Sickness ratings were based *only* on form-level scores; all other indications of the nature of the Rorschach responses were withheld, as were all other identifying data including age and sex of the subjects.

The first group's pooled form-level derived ratings correlated .64 with the psychiatrists' ratings of Health–Sickness, significant at the

MENNINGER RATERS

	RATER:	#1	#2	#3	#4	#5	#6	GROUP MEAN	H-S PRE-TREAT-MENT	H-S POST-TREAT-MENT
Predoct.	#1	—	.50	.71	.74	.59	.77	.87	.67	.61
	#2		—	.78	.56	.61	.74	.77	.52	.64
Postdoct.,	#3			—	.74	.84	.89	.94	.46	.53
1st year	#4				—	.69	.64	.85	.49	.41
Postdoct.,	#5					—	.83	.81	.19	.48
2nd year	#6						—	.93	.44	.54
Group mean								—	.56	.62

better, at the .01 level; .51 or better, at the .05 level; .44, at the .10 level.

.01 level of confidence (Table 2). Four of the five students individually predicted as well or virtually as well as the combined group.

The second group's pooled scores correlated .56 with the criterion, significant at the .05 level, with three of the six raters equalling or bettering the collective performance of their group.

Six months later, the Menninger–Topeka State group made similar ratings on an additional 19 patients, selected at random from the remaining psychotherapy research cases. The effectiveness of form-level ratings in this larger group is summarized in Table 3. No significant correlations were obtained with Health–Sickness ratings, probably because two of the new cases had severe ego weaknesses which did not show up clinically until these patients had been in treatment for some time but which did show up clearly in their pretreatment Rorschachs. This would help explain the correlation of .45 ($p < .01$) with the clinical status of these patients following termination of treatment. Eliminating the two patients with deceptively good pretreatment façades brought the correlations of form level with the clinical assessment of psychopathology at the start of treatment up to .40, significant at the .05 level of confidence (Table 2).

TABLE 3 *Intercorrelations of Form-Level Ratings with Health–Sickness Ratings*

MENNINGER RATERS (34 CASES)

RATER	H-S PRETREATMENT	H-S POST-TREATMENT
1	*.38*	*.40*
2	.26	**.49**
3	.14	*.41*
4	.16	.25
5	.08	.33
6	.17	*.42*
Group mean	.25	**.45**

MENNINGER RATERS (32 CASES) *

RATER	H-S PRETREATMENT	H-S POST-TREATMENT
1	**.47**	
2	*.40*	
3	.31	
4	.33	
5	.14	
6	*.35*	
Group mean	**.40**	

* Without the two grossly discrepant cases.
Italic type denotes $p \leq .05$; boldface denotes $p \leq .01$.

Rorschach form-level ratings of these 34 cases were correlated not only with their psychiatric Health–Sickness ratings but also with all other available ratings for patient variables, treatment variables, and situation variables (Table 4). We predicted that there would be no correlation between form-level scores and the 7 situation variables or the 12 treatment variables, but that form level would correlate with 4 of the patient variables: "severity of symptoms," "anxiety tolerance," "ego strength," and "quality of interpersonal relations." This was essentially what we found. None of the situation variables and 13 of the 14 treatment variables yielded nonsignificant correlations as predicted. On the other hand, 5 of the 12 correlations with patient variables were significant, including three of the four for which a significant relationship was predicted ("anxiety tolerance," "ego strength," and "quality of interpersonal relationships"). The significant correlations ranged from .36 to .46 (Table 4).

TABLE 4 *Relationship of Form Level to Patient Variables in the Menninger Foundation Psychotherapy Research Project*

PATIENT VARIABLES	CORRELATION OF FORM-LEVEL WITH RATINGS ($N = 34$)
1. Anxiety Level	.08
2. Severity of Symptoms	–.18
3. Self-Directed Aggression	.19
4. Extent to which Environment is Made to Suffer	–.14
5. Externalization	–.07
6. Level of Psychosexual Development	*.40*
7. Patterning of Defenses	.24
8. Anxiety Tolerance	*.36*
9. Insight	.22
10. Ego Strength	*.36*
11. Motivation	*.37*
12. Quality of Interpersonal Relations	**.46**

Italic type denotes $p \leq .05$; boldface denotes $p \leq 01$.
It should be noted, however, that these ratings are probably highly correlated with each other. For example, in the entire subject group of the PRP study, Level of Psychosexual Development correlated .73 with Anxiety Tolerance, .74 with Ego Strength, .86 with Quality of Interpersonal Relations, and .63 with Motivation.

Reliability

The reliability with which form level can be scored is attested to indirectly by the success of the validity studies cited above. There are some studies, however, which have attempted to measure directly inter-rater reliability in the use of the Form Level Manual.

The most definitive reliability study conducted thus far was completed recently by Lohrenz and Gardner (1966). From a pool of volunteers in a developmental study of twins and their parents, Gardner selected Rorschachs of 20 subjects, 10 children and 10 adults, ranging in age from 9 to 51. Two under-graduate research Fellows scored these Rorschachs independently after a preliminary period of training in form-level scoring. All responses in which form was the sole or the principal determinant were scored, and a mean form-level score was computed for each subject by assigning quantitative values to each form-level score ($F+ = 7$; $Fo = 6$; $Fw+ = 5$; $Fv = 4$; $Fw- = 3$; $Fs = 2$; $F- = 1$). The 20 mean form-level scores yielded an inter-rater reliability coefficient of .90.

There was also generally good reliability in each of the seven form-level categories. The inter-rater agreements distributed as presented in Table 5.

TABLE 5 *Inter-rater Agreements within Each Score Category*

FORM-LEVEL VARIABLE	PERCENT AGREEMENT	
	RATER 1 WITH RATER 2	RATER 2 WITH RATER 1
F+	89	85
Fo	98	94
Fw+	81	89
(*Fo, F+*)	96	92
(*Fo, F+, Fw+*)	90	91
Fv	77	96
Fw−	68	70
Fs	75	75
F−	71	52

The highest proportion of agreements, over 90%, occur on those scores (*Fo, F+, Fw+*) which ordinarily comprise about 80% of all responses in a protocol (72% in this sample). It should also be noted that score disagreements (especially in the *Fw*— and *F*— categories) were mostly trivial, of a sort not likely to change the complexion of a psychogram or create errors in clinical judgment. Serious disagreements, i.e., those in which one scorer rated a response as good or marginally good (*o*, +, or *w*+) and the other scorer rated it poor or bad (*w*—, *s*, or —), were limited to only 6% of the responses.

Another careful study of reliability was carried out by Rabkin and Holt (Rabkin, 1967). The two scorers, who were thoroughly trained in the use of the Form Level Manual, obtained a Pearson correlation coefficient of .90 between their form-level scores of 25 protocols, after first converting the form-level scores of all responses in each protocol into a single weighted form-level score for each subject. They also scored 513 Rorschach responses independently of each other, and were in complete agreement on 367 of the responses (72%) and only one point apart on 58 others (11%).

Several other studies, in which form-level score reliability was of only incidental interest, provide further evidence that the Form Level Manual can be used with good inter-rater agreement. Bachrach (1966) was able to train raters until they could attain an inter-rater reliability coefficient of better than .90 in two consecutive training protocols, and better than .90 agreement with Holt's scores of those same protocols (Bachrach, 1966). Fromm (1967) was able to train scorers to the point of inter-rater reliability of .75 or better on three consecutive Rorschach protocols and .75 or better with Holt on three more protocols. Bergan (1963) obtained good inter-rater reliability (.90) with Holt's adaptive regression score.

In a longitudinal clinical study of ten adolescents which is still underway (Ramsay, 1966), two raters with almost no prior training in the use of the Form Level Manual (i.e., after only one practice case) came up with the distribution of agreements presented in Table 6 in the first five protocols scored. Ramsay found 96% agreement in scoring *Fo* and *F*+ responses, which together usually comprise well over half the responses in a protocol. The two raters gave identical scores on 91% of all responses.

TABLE 6 *Inter-rater Agreements and Disagreements in the Use of Each of the Form-Level Scores*

FORM-LEVEL SCORE	NO. OF TIMES SCORED	NO. OF INTER-RATER AGREEMENTS	NO. OF INTER-RATER DISAGREEMENTS	PERCENT AGREEMENT
F+	48	45	3	94
Fo	52	51	1	98
Fw+	40	35	5	88
Fv	7	6	1	86
Fw−	16	11	5	69
Fs	2	2	0	100
F−	1	1	0	100
	166	151	15	91

Agreements between raters in their intuitive estimates of the degree of psychopathology reflected in form-level scores is almost as high. In the form-level study of Menninger Foundation Psychotherapy Research Project patients cited above (Tables 2 and 3), Pearson product–moment correlations ranged from .44 to .94 in one group of raters and from .50 to .89 in the second group, with median reliability coefficients of .82 and .74, respectively.

Summary

The quality of form perception in the Rorschach test can be scored on a seven-point scale, with each point on the scale representing a qualitatively distinct mode of reality testing. This scoring system can be used both qualitatively and quantitatively to assess a subject's level of reality adherence. Reliability data on the use of the scoring manual and results of the application of this scoring system to a diverse range of clinical research problems have been reviewed.

References

Bachrach, H. 1966. "A Scale for the Measurement of Conjunctive Empathy." Unpublished doctoral dissertation, Univ. of Chicago.

Beck, S. J. 1948. "Rorschach *F*+ and the Ego in Treatment." *Amer. J. Ortho.* 18: 395–401.

Bergan, R. 1963. "A Study of the Relationships between Pitch Perception, Imagery and Regression in the Service of the Ego." Unpublished doctoral dissertation, Univ. of Michigan.

Bohm, E. 1950. *Rorschach Test Diagnosis.* New York: Grune & Stratton.

Cohen, I. H. 1960. "Adaptive Regression, Dogmatism, and Creativity." Unpublished doctoral dissertation, Michigan State University.

Ferenczi, S. 1916. "Stages in the Development of a Sense of Reality." In *Contributions to Psychoanalysis.* Boston: R. C. Badger Co.

Freud, S. 1912. "Formulations on the Two Principles of Mental Functioning." *Standard Edition,* Vol. 12, pp. 213–226.

Friedman, H. 1952. "Perceptual Regression in Schizophrenia: An Hypothesis Suggested by the Use of the Rorschach Test." *J. Gen. Psychol.* 8: 63–98.

Fromm, E. 1967. Unpublished manuscript.

Ginsparg, S. 1965. Personal communication.

Heath, D. H. 1965. *Explorations of Maturity.* New York: Appleton-Century-Crofts.

Hemmendinger, L. 1960. "Developmental Theory and the Rorschach Method." In *Rorschach Psychology,* M. Rickers-Ovsiankina, (Ed.), ch. 3. New York: John Wiley & Sons.

Holt, R. R., and Havel, J. 1960. "A Method for Assessing Primary and Secondary Process in the Rorschach." In *Rorschach Psychology,* M. Rickers-Ovsiankina, (Ed.), ch. 10. New York: John Wiley & Sons.

Kahn, M. W. 1967. "Correlates of Rorschach Reality Adherence in the Assessment of Murderers Who Plead Insanity." *J. Proj. Tech.* 31: 44–47.

Klopfer, B., and Davidson, H. H. 1944. "Form Level Rating: A Preliminary Proposal for Appraising Mode and Level of Thinking as Expressed in Rorschach Records." *Rorsch. Res. Exch.* 8: 164–177.

Klopfer, B., and Kelley, D. M. 1942. *The Rorschach Technique.* New York: World Book Co.

Lohrenz, L. J., and Gardner, R. W. 1967. "The Mayman Form-Level Scoring Method: Scorer Reliability and Correlates of Form-Level." *J. Proj. Tech.* 31: 39–43.

Luborsky, L. 1962. "Clinician's Judgments of Mental Health." *Arch Gen. Psychiat.* 7: 407–417.

Mayman, M. 1956. "Rorschach Form Level Scoring Manual." Unpublished. 63 pp.

Pryor, D. B. 1962. "Regression in the Service of the Ego: Psychosexual Development and Ego Functions." Unpublished doctoral dissertation, Michigan State Univ.

Ramsay, M. 1966. Personal communication.

Rapaport, D., Gill, M., and Schafer, R. 1945. *Diagnostic Psychological Testing*. Cleveland: Year book Publishers.

Rabkin, J. G. 1967. "Psychoanalytic Assessment of Change in Organization of Thought after Psychotherapy." Unpublished doctoral dissertation, New York Univ.

Saretsky, T. 1963. "The Effect of Chlorpromazine on Primary Process Thought Manifestations." Unpublished doctoral dissertation, New York Univ.

Schafer, R. 1948. *The Clinical Application of Psychological Tests*. New York: International University Press.

Walker, R. G. 1953. "An Approach to Standardization of Rorschach Form Level." *J. Proj. Tech.* 17: 426–436.

Wallerstein, R. S., Robbins, L. L., and associates. 1958. "The Psychotherapy Research Project of the Menninger Foundation: Second Report." *Bull. Menninger Clinic,* 22: 115–166.

Wright, N., and Abbey, D. S. 1965. "Perceptual Deprivation Tolerance and Adequacy of Defenses." *Percep. Mot. Skills,* 20: 35–38.

Zukowsky, E. 1961. "Measuring Primary and Secondary Process Thinking in Schizophrenics and Normals by Means of the Rorschach." Unpublished doctoral dissertation, Michigan State Univ.

Mortimer M. Meyer
Elaine Caruth

2

Rorschach Indices of Ego Processes *

At Reiss-Davis, as part of an ongoing research project dealing with childhood psychosis, the authors have been working with the Rorschach, among other instruments, in an attempt to formulate more systematically the cues which are being used in the evaluation of such cases. It has become increasingly necessary to refine the interpretation of psychological instruments so that these differentiate not only the psychotic, nonpsychotic, and borderline psychotic patients, but also so that they describe within these groups the variations of ego functioning which characterize different kinds of patients. The wide range of interest in this problem is represented in the vast amount of literature dealing with schizophrenia and its treatment which has appeared in the last ten to fifteen years. As the above work proceeded it became evident that the task was not one of formulating cues in relation to schizophrenia as such, but rather the formulation of cues to evaluate ego process in general.

All tests provide an opportunity for observing ego processes, particularly around the individual's attempt to cope with the task. Some

---

* Reprinted, with minor modifications, from *Journal of Projective Techniques & Personality Assessment,* Vol. 29, No. 2, 1965, with permission of the copyright owners.

types of tasks more than others permit refined observation of the nature of the specific circumstances under which the individual is able to cope successfully and those in which he is unsuccessful, as well as the manner in which he proceeds. The terms *ego* and *ego processes* are used here in a general way and refer to those ego functions that are involved in the coping processes (Ekstein and Wallerstein, 1954), that is, to the capacity of the individual to fulfill a task. This capacity has many aspects. In this paper only those aspects of ego functioning are being considered which can more readily be inferred from the subject's responses to the Rorschach. For the Rorschach the specific task assigned can be defined as that of responding, integrating, and interpreting a sample of outer reality. We assume that the manner in which the subject deals with this sample is determined by the interaction of the outer reality impinging upon him, the economy of his inner needs, and the structure of his psychic organization. The blots themselves may be considered as representative of external reality and because of the highly unstructured nature of the stimulus provide maximum opportunity for the projection of the inner needs and fantasies. His response is the product of the fusion of his perception of this outer reality with his inner needs and fantasies. The current state of the personality is a result of psychic as well as cultural determinants and will determine the manner of selecting and experiencing particular parts of this reality as represented by the blot. It is the interaction of these outer and inner stimuli which determine the response that the individual gives to the card. These responses then serve as the basis for inferences concerning the nature of the individual's ego processes. Thus, one of the crucial factors is the evaluation of the manner in which the individual copes with the outer stimulus as contrasted to his coping with the inner stimulus. Hartmann (1953) has suggested such a concept when he states,

> Actually, as mental phenomena are no less "real" than the outer world (though we often refer to the latter only in speaking of "reality"), it might prove useful to include testing of the within besides testing of the without . . . we could say that with the neurotic

> testing of inner, with the psychotic testing of outer reality is interfered with. However, a higher complexity is introduced by the fact, among others, that the two aspects of reality testing often interact.

The application of such a differentiation of reality testing to the Rorschach offers the opportunity to refine inferences concerning the operation of ego processes.

This presentation is an attempt to examine, refine, and expand current principles of interpretation of the Rorschach as they relate to ego processes. The suggestions offered are representative of a technique rather than a total or complete method. The familiar and well-used systems of Rorschach scoring and evaluation are the basis of the suggestions. In the customary systems, the effectiveness of the reality-testing function of the ego is inferred from form evaluation. This aspect of evaluation of ego functioning has been well described previously and will not be dealt with by itself but rather as it provides a basis for a more detailed consideration. In addition to reality testing, the degree to which the subject invests his interest in intellectual control over his response is also inferred from form. The degree to which the individual's effort at intellectual control is successful can be determined from examination of the combination of intellectual control with adequacy of form. Many subjects indicate a strong wish or need to exert intellectual control, as evidenced by a high number of responses with form priority, but fail to give sufficient attention to the adequacy of form. In contrast, many individuals manifest less interest in intellectual control but give sufficient attention to the adequacy of form so that the intellectual control achieved is far more efficient. Table 1 suggests a schema for evaluating this interrelationship between the use of form and its appropriateness.

A second indicator of the degree to which the ego can cope effectively can be derived from the interrelationship between form level and reaction time. Reaction time represents the readiness of the ego process to attempt to cope with the stimulus. Form level indicates the ability of the ego process to make appropriate perceptual judg-

TABLE 1 *Emphasis on Intellectual Control*

1. *F* is main determinant	1. (a) Form level is + (b) Form level is 0 (c) Form level is −	1. The use of form as primary suggests that interest in intellectual control and the desire to test reality is high. Form level indicates the degree to which this interest can be effectively implemented. Thus, successful use of *F* in this category indicates either the absence of disturbing anxiety or the presence of successful defense against anxiety. The less adequate the form, the more the conflict impairs the implementation of the wish to achieve appropriate control.
2. *F* is secondary to another determinant	2. (a) Form level is + (b) Form level is 0 (c) Form level is −	2. Where the form is secondary, the wish for control and the desire to test reality is only moderate and on a less mature level. This may represent the capacity for spontaneity or a lowered level of control because of conflict. The successful use of *F* in this category indicates either the absence of disturbing anxiety or the presence of successful defense against anxiety. The less adequate the form, the more the conflict impairs the implementation of the wish to achieve appropriate control.
3. *F* is absent from response		3. Where *F* is absent, there is no evidence of interest in intellectual control or in testing reality.

ment about it. Increased reaction time reflects the diminution of such readiness and implies a cautiousness about the coping process which is indicative of anxiety. This anxiety may be in the service of the coping process and simultaneously may also interfere with it.

This anxiety can be considered a signal to be cautious and thereby create a delay in responding so that the individual can search for a means of coping with the task. This use of anxiety can thus be interpreted as "signal anxiety" (Fenichel, 1945). Where the delay provides time for the individual to mobilize some psychic means for coping effectively with the task, we see the results of successful signal anxiety. Such a result can be interpreted as the adaptive use of anxiety. Where the delay is followed by ineffective coping with the task, such as in a response with a minus form level, there is unsuccessful signal anxiety and a breakdown in the coping process which is indicative of impairment of both adaptive and defensive functions. Thus, the interrelationship of the objective measures of form level and reaction time can be used to infer the interplay of the adaptive and defensive function. Table 2 suggests a schema for use of this concept.

A third aspect of ego functioning which can be evaluated is the effectiveness with which the individual can respond to a variety of stimuli in the environment. This effectiveness can be inferred from the success with which he integrates appropriate perceptual judgments and a variety of stimuli in the Rorschach (specifically, location category, determinants, and content categories) as evidenced in the relationship of form level and stimulus acceptance. The varying levels of form serve as a basis for estimating the consistency of good or poor ego functioning over the range of stimuli and differentiating whether specific stimuli are a greater source of disturbance than others. This type of evaluation provides information which differentiates individuals who have greater or lesser breadth in their response to stimuli in the environment in terms of the success of their response. Such evaluation differentiates not only the individual with a limited range of responsiveness from those with greater responsiveness but also indicates whether the responsiveness is in the service of effective functioning. For a successful adaptation it may well be that in the case of some individuals it would serve them better, for example, to limit their responsiveness to the areas they can master effectively rather than attempting to cope with the greater breadth of stimuli. The ability to use stimuli freely and well is indicative of

TABLE 2 *Form Level and Reaction Time*

1. No time delay	1. Accurate form	1. Indicative of a smooth operation of the ego process which is evidence (a) of the absence of disturbing anxiety or (b) the presence of an effective defense against anxiety.
2. Time delay	2. Accurate form	2. Indicative of the subject experiencing some anxiety which causes a delay in responding and thereby provides time for the individual to mobilize some psychic means by which he can cope effectively with the stimulus.
3. Time delay	3. Rejection	3. Indicative of the subject experiencing anxiety to the degree that he cannot mobilize any psychic means of coping effectively with the task. Thus the signal anxiety serves the function of warding off a breakthrough of impulses or ineffective responses. However, the limitation of the success is seen in the primitive or gross defensive maneuver necessary which actually results in a failure to act.
4. Time delay	4. Inaccurate form	4. Indicative of the subject experiencing anxiety to such a degree that time is not sufficient to prevent an impulsive or ineffective response. The result is the poor form response which thus indicates the failure of the signal anxiety to function successfully.
5. No time delay	5. Inaccurate form	5. Indicative of the subject experiencing either (a) inability to adapt to coping or (b) lack of attempt to adapt to the coping process. Thus, an impulsive, ineffective response occurs, which indicates the absence of signal anxiety.

the readiness with which the individual can adapt to and integrate a wide range of external stimuli and hence utilize the full potential of his inner resources and integrate it with his inner reality. This relationship thus provides an opportunity to observe the individual's mode of coping in terms of the range from the constricted personality where the limitation is necessary to maintain effective functioning, through a personality structure with optimal responsiveness, to a personality structure that reacts to a very wide range of stimuli. Where the latter is the case and the form is not maintained at an adequate level, there is present the pathologically dilated personality unable to limit reactivity even in the service of more effective functioning. The schema suggested for this analysis appears in Table 3.

A fourth way of evaluating ego functioning is to examine the individual's ability to adapt effectively and to integrate a wide range of stimuli in relation to reaction time. This relationship provides qualitatively finer cues to help clarify the functioning of the ego mode of coping with the specific stimuli categories under consideration. For example, when there is an omission of the expected stimuli without an initial time delay it is more likely that a character problem is present than when the omission occurs in conjunction with a significant time delay, which is suggestive of the subject's experiencing anxiety over the task. Table 4 represents the schema for evaluating the relationship.

So far we have been evaluating the manner in which the individual copes with the task rather than examining the content of his responses. A fifth way of evaluating the ego process is to examine the content of the responses for further information about the manner in which the individual copes with the task as noted from the way in which he reflects about and gives meaning to his reality. Severe disturbances in content are considered indicative of a primary thought disorder which may or may not be accompanied by impairment of the perceptual functions. The interrelationship of disturbance in perceptual functioning, as reflected in form level, and disturbances in cognitive functioning, as reflected in a variety of conceptual disturbances, appears related to a number of diagnostic

TABLE 3 *Stimulus Acceptance and Form Level*

1. Optimal use of appropriate variety of stimuli	1. (a) Good form of all determinants	1. (a) The use of good form in relation to the use of stimuli provides information about the capacity for differentiated reaction to a variety of stimuli with good reality testing. Thus the responses can be classified in terms of the variety of stimuli used, ranging from an excessive responsiveness to stimuli, to an appropriate responsiveness, to an inadequate responsiveness. Normally it is expected that appropriate ego functioning will be selective. Thus the excessive use of a variety of stimuli represents a failure of normal selectivity and indicates an ego process which can be flooded from without.
	(b) Poor form of a few determinants	(b) The use of poor form in relation to the use of stimuli provides information about the area in which the ego process can interact effectively and ineffectively with the environment. Comparison of form level with each of the variety of stimuli used provides a basis for differentiating which aspects of the environment the ego can cope with. By contrast, those areas in which form level is poor indicate a failure of ego functioning and thereby provide a clue to the sources of conflict.
	(c) Poor form of all determinants	(c) The use of poor form in relation to the total variety of stimuli responded to is indicative of a more pervasive impairment of functioning and ineffectiveness of the coping processes. However, insofar as the capacity to respond to an opti-

(*continued*)

TABLE 3 (*continued*)

		mal variety of stimuli remains unimpaired, we see evidence of a characterological disturbance to which an adjustment and an adaptation have been made rather than of an active conflict which is expressed in neurotic symptomatology.
2. Excessive variety of stimuli used	2. (a) Good form of all stimuli	2. (a) The excessive use of a variety of stimuli represents a failure of normal selectivity and indicates an ego process which can be flooded from without. Where the form level is good this difficulty is present but without impairment of reality testing.
	(b) Poor form of a few stimuli	(b) The use of poor form in relation to a few of the stimuli used in a record in which there is an excessive variety of stimuli responded to is indicative of ego failure with respect to both the inability to be selective and a beginning impairment in reality testing.
	(c) Poor form of all stimuli	(c) The use of poor form in relation to all stimuli in a record with an excessive variety of stimuli used is indicative of a severe ego impairment manifested by an individual who is bombarded by stimuli from within and without and is under pressure to respond to both.
3. Limited variety of stimuli	3. (a) Good form of all stimuli	3. (a) Where the form level remains intact we have a constricted individual who is able to function without impairment as long as he can limit and select out those aspects of the environment to which he can safely respond.

(*continued*)

TABLE 3 (*continued*)

	(b) Poor form of a few stimuli	(b) Where the form level begins to become impaired we see evidence of increasing intrusion of the conflict and failure of the coping process.
	(c) Poor form of all stimuli	(c) Indicative of the failure of the defensive maneuver of selectivity to screen out the conflict-arousing stimuli with the result that impairment of the reality testing appears.
4. Excessive use of any particular stimuli	4. (a) Good form of all stimuli	4. The excessive use of a particular stimulus reflects an overinvestment in some aspect of the environment arising out of an inner need. This thus creates an imbalance in the distribution of ego investment in different aspects of the environment. Where the form level is maintained this imbalance has not as yet created an impairment of reality testing, although we might predict that the excessive investment of energy in any one aspect of the environment might potentially lead to inadequate attention to other aspects of reality. Inasmuch as the form level is impaired we see evidence of such failure.

problems. For example, there is the problem of the "burnt-out" schizophrenic record. This is the empty, barren Rorschach, in which there is poor reality testing as evidenced by minus form level without overt indications of a breakthrough of primary process functioning, as is found on more florid schizophrenic records which contain a variety of disturbed responses such as confabulations, contamina-

TABLE 4 *Stimulus Acceptance and Time*

1. Optimal use of the appropriate variety of stimuli	1. No initial time delay	1. Indicative of an ego process capable of interacting with appropriate aspects of the environment which is interpreted as (a) absence of disturbing anxiety or (b) absence of an inhibiting defense against anxiety.
2. Optimal use of the appropriate variety of stimuli	2. Initial time delay	2. Indicative of the subject's experiencing some anxiety which causes a delay in responding. By means of this delay the individual is able to master the anxiety sufficiently to cope with the task in terms of responding to the variety of stimuli optimally expected of him.
3. Omission of the appropriate variety of stimuli	3. No initial time delay	3. Indicative of an ego process which avoids the experiencing of anxiety through psychic mechanisms which constrict and limit the ego's responsiveness to an appropriate variety of stimuli.
4. Omission of the appropriate variety of stimuli	4. Initial time delay	4. Indicative of an ego process which experiences anxiety despite the attempt to avoid the anxiety through limiting and constricting the responses to less conflict-arousing stimuli.

tions, etc. In the barren Rorschach we have evidence of a breakdown in reality testing with reference to external reality, which is not, however, accompanied by overt manifestations of regression to more archaic modes of thinking. In contrast, there is the record where the form level may be maintained despite the breakthrough of conceptual disturbances directly related to fluctuations between primary and secondary process thinking. In this instance we are confronted with what may appear to be a normal, meaning a pseudonormal, adjustment to an external reality with, however, a complete breakdown in the area of reality testing of the inner fantasy life. An illustration of such a response is present in the accompanying record where the subject responds to Card I with a flying doll without any suggestion that she recognizes the fantasy nature or unreality of such an object. The central figure is used appropriately for the doll, and the side details are used for the wings. Thus form remains appropriate but there is a failure to test the fantasy for reality.

The area of primary process is one in which extensive work has been done and a variety of systems of classification have been developed. The reader is referred specifically to the detailed work of Holt and Havel (1960), who have further expanded and refined the work of Rapaport (1946) and Schafer (1954) on disturbances in concept formation in order to distinguish more discriminatingly between primary and secondary process functioning.

Holtzman et al. (1961) have attempted to compile some of the more typical categories of content disturbance. These are listed below in order to help illustrate the kind of responses we are including under inappropriate content. They are very roughly ranked according to the degree of pathology that they reflect, but they must not be considered rigidly ordered nor exhaustively described.

Fabulation (FB)
Fabulized Combination
Queer Response
Incoherence
Autistic Logic
Contamination
Self-reference
Deterioration Color
Absurd Response

Table 5 presents a schema for evaluating these disturbances. The presence or absence of a time delay is related to the effectiveness

TABLE 5 *Content and Reaction Time*

1. No time delay	1. Appropriate content	1. Indicative of a smooth operation of the ego process which is evidence of (a) the absence of disturbing anxiety or (b) the presence of an effective defense against anxiety.
2. Time delay	2. Appropriate content	2. Indicative of the subject experiencing some anxiety which causes a delay in responding and thereby provides time for the individual to mobilize some psychic means by which he can cope effectively with the stimulus.
3. Time delay	3. Rejection	3. Indicative of the subject experiencing anxiety to the degree that he cannot mobilize any psychic means of coping effectively with the task. Thus the signal anxiety serves the function of warding off a breakthrough of impulses or ineffective responses. However, the limitation of the success is seen in the primitive or gross defensive maneuver which results in a failure to act.
4. Time delay	4. Inappropriate content	4. Indicative of the subject experiencing anxiety to such a degree that delay is not sufficient to prevent an impulsive or ineffective response. The result is the failure of signal anxiety to function successfully.
5. No time delay	5. Inappropriate content	5. Indicative of an impulsive ineffective response which indicates the lack of signal anxiety and failure of inner reality testing.

of such anxiety in helping the individual to cope with pressures from primary process. Thus, the presence or absence of time delay permits inferences about the degree to which primary process overrules secondary process. For example, the individual who indicates that he was about to give a response which was a contamination but recognized its inappropriateness and therefore did not actually give it has less interference from primary process than the individual who after long delay gives it haltingly, and he in turn has less intrusion from primary process than the individual who gives such a response without delay or recognition of its inappropriateness.

A sixth way of evaluating the functioning of the ego process is to consider the presence or absence of disturbances in ego boundaries. By ego boundaries we refer to the ability to distinguish inner from outer reality and to maintain appropriate distance from fantasies. This ability is reflected in an appropriate affective involvement with the stimulus material from which can be inferred the underlying capacity to maintain the above distinction. (See Table 6.)

Although Rapaport (1946) suggests that loss of distance is found in many of the indicators of pathological concept formation that we described in Table 4, it appears valuable to score separately as a distinct dimension the different kinds of variations possible in distance. Distance devices have been described by Ekstein and Wallerstein (1954) as particularly significant in understanding and treating the fluctuating ego states of the borderline and schizophrenic patient. Loss of distance may be related to loss of object constancy, which has occasionally been described in schizophrenia (Sechehaye, 1951) and is being experimentally investigated by Ittelson and Kutash (1961).

Impairment of the ability to maintain distance can be inferred from the degree to which the individual projects highly personalized attributes onto either the stimulus or his perceptual response to the stimulus. When these attributes are projected primarily onto the stimulus and elaborated as a description of the card, there is evidenced an attempt, although successful, to maintain appropriate distance between self and stimulus and to avoid being overcome by

TABLE 6 *Disturbances in Ego Boundaries*

1. Appropriate involvement in fantasy.	1. Indicative of effective flexible ego boundaries so that the individual is capable of an optimal involvement with both his inner and outer life. There is the freedom to permit fantasy productions and the capacity to recognize the difference between fantasy and reality.
2. Complete denial of fantasy as in a Blot Bound record.	2. Indicative of a rigid, constricted operation of ego functions in an individual who needs to deny and defend against experiencing his inner life. This is reflected in an excessive preoccupation with "objective" reality, which is described rather than interpreted.
3. Excessive fantasy involvement and a diminution of distance from the fantasy.	3. Indicative of a weakness in ego boundaries so that the individual tends to confuse and fuse his inner needs and fantasies with his recognition and understanding of the stimuli impinging from without. His ability to test and discriminate between what comes from within and from without is beginning to weaken, but the testing of outer reality remains relatively unimpaired.
4. Excessive fantasy involvement with complete loss of distance so that either card or percept appears as reality.	4. Indicative of an ego process in which the capacity to test reality, both inner and outer, is totally impaired.

the inner reality. Where the attributes are projected onto the percept to the degree that the percept is experienced as the materialization of the fantasy, the individual is so dominated by the inner need system that separate images become inappropriately fused or inappropriately enlivened.

Finally, it is important to know whether the individual himself can recognize appropriately the quality and adequacy of his func-

TABLE 7 *Adequacy of Response and Adequacy of Documentation*

1. Adequate response	1. Well documented	1. Indicative of an ego process capable of coping successfully with the task and of recognizing and evaluating the adequacy of its own production.
2. Adequate response	2. Minimal documentation	2. Indicative of an ego process which is capable of coping with the task successfully as far as performance but at the same time reflecting some limitation of the ego capacity to evaluate and justify its performance.
3. Adequate response	3. No documentation	3. Indicative of an individual who can act upon the demands of the situation although not necessarily understanding the meaning of his own behavior or being able to justify and explain it.
4. Poor response, improved or rejected in inquiry	4. Critical documentation which (a) improves the initially inappropriate response or (b) explains the rejection	4. Indicative of an impairment in the coping process but in an individual whose critical functions are relatively unimpaired so that he can still evaluate appropriately his own behavior even though he cannot act upon his evaluation too successfully.

(*continued*)

tioning. It is ordinarily anticipated that in effective ego functioning there is present a critical observing aspect of the ego that can recognize and evaluate the adequacy with which a task has been dealt with, or, in some instances, to justify the necessity for dealing with the task on a different kind of level as, for example, when there is a healthy regression in the service of art or of other creative or empathic experiences. Ordinarily this critical process functions automatically and on an unconscious level, resulting in the appropriate

TABLE 7 (*continued*)

5. Poor response	5. Critical documentation but with impotent recognition and helpless acceptance; no ability to make the necessary corrections but may attempt to justify response through rationalizations	5. Indicative of an ego process which appears to be in the process of fragmentation. Critical functions are still operating but individual is unable to synthesize different aspects of his ego functioning.
6. Poor response	6. Recognition of inadequacy of response but without initial documentation and inability to correct or rationalize inappropriate response	6. Indicative of a severe impairment of ego functioning in an individual whose greatest strength is in the critical capacity of the ego but this is accompanied by deficiency in the integrating and synthesizing functions. Thus the individual feels helpless and under the domination of his illness.
7. Poor response	7. Complete acceptance of response with comfort about or indifference to the inappropriateness of response	7. Indicative of a disorganized ego functioning in an individual who appears to have lost all hold on both outer and inner reality, thus reflecting severe impairment of all aspects of the ego process.

response. However, when disturbance is present, resulting in ineffective coping as evidenced by poor form or poor content, a deficiency in the critical aspect of the ego must also be present. The degree of the impairment of the critical process can vary, and such variations provide a basis for inference concerning the capacity or readiness of the individual for insight and self-exploration. The degree to which the individual documents his response indicates the degree to which he is ready to be self-critical. It is possible, furthermore, for there to be weaknesses in this critical process even where the coping process remains relatively undisturbed. For example, the individual may appear to be dealing effectively with the task but does so with limited or no rationale for his behavior. This critical process is related to those aspects of ego functioning referred to in Schafer's (1954) concept of the capacity for reflection and self-exploration.

In addition to the individual readiness to be self-critical, the appropriateness of his self-criticism must be assessed. One objective test manifestation of this process is the adequacy of documentation with which an individual can justify a response, whether it be a good or a poor one. In Table 7 we present the schema for evaluating the interrelationship of the adequacy of functioning with the recognition of the adequacy of functioning as indicated by documentation of the response.

In the following discussion we will analyze the Rorschach protocol of a 15-year-old schizophrenic adolescent girl at the beginning of treatment.

Rorschach Protocol [1]

CARD I

40″

They showed me this already

1. Looks like two dolls and in the middle is a —	1. Two sides. *D*. They're dolls. Their arms are out like this. They're flying. (Why dolls?) Looks cute like dolls.
2. Person with a dress on, doesn't have a head. Can I tell you what I imagine when these are backwards?	2. (Lady?) (*D*) No head and feet—just standing still there. Just a lady with a dress.

[1] Permission to use the protocols was generously granted by the psychological examiner, Dr. Bernice Eiduson.

3. Looks like a person. A man without a head, with his two arms out, and that's all—I can't imagine any more.

3. Holding two dolls like that. Center is a man, like dropping them on the floor, or something.

There is a forty-second delay, which suggests that there is some difficulty in finding a solution, which in turn can be interpreted as suggesting the presence of initial anxiety that interferes with coping with the task. However, at the end of forty seconds a solution is found as if the ego now had organized itself effectively. However, even though there is an initial effective coping with the material (Table 2, item 2), there is, nevertheless, evidence of incomplete ego effectiveness as noted by the intrusion of an inappropriate attribute (flying doll) in the solution (Table 5, item 4). Further, there is failure of insight or attempt at self-evaluation in her failure to explore the basis for this response (Table 7, item 7). Thus it is evident in this response that the signal anxiety provided time for her to mobilize herself and recognize the outer reality appropriately. However, the intrusion of the inappropriate attribute indicated that the inner need dominated the response so that the actuality became somewhat distorted.

The subject continues with a second response which is again appropriate form, which indicates a continuation of the ability to recognize the outer reality appropriately. However, there is evidence of disturbance in the conceptual aspect of the ego process, noted in the peculiar attribute that there is a lady who is "standing still there" but doesn't have "head and feet."

The third response continues in a similar vein, but with increasing difficulty in the coping process. Here there is the peculiar attribute but the form level also becomes questionable. Thus, not only does the inner need dominate in the actuality, but it interferes with the appropriate recognition of the external stimulus. Examination of the inquiry reveals no ability to improve the coping process. In fact, if anything, the inquiry to Card I indicates comfort and failure to recognize the inappropriateness (Table 7, item 7).

Evaluating the responses to this card in terms of the various charts, the following observations are made: lack of stimulus acceptance of expected variety of stimuli can be noted in terms of the absence of the popular response to this card (Table 3, item 3). This omission suggests further the preoccupation with inner needs. There is also omission of any animal response with a limited use of appropriate stimuli plus excessive use of any particular stimuli (Table 3, item 1c). In terms of affective involvement with the card (Table 6), there is an appropriate degree of involvement in the fantasy rather than a loss or increase in the distance.

In summation, Card I indicates that this is an individual whose ego functioning tends to be effective in defending the subject against experiencing anxiety, but that the ego process is ineffective in that this is accomplished by accepting inappropriate intrusion of the inner needs as she acts on the reality to achieve her actuality. The absence of critical documentation indicates the diminution in the effective functioning of the critical observing aspect of the ego.

CARD II
25″

1. These are two boys that are fighting. (frowns) That's all I imagine there.	1. *D.* Hands are together (shows) and banging their feet together. (Banging?) Feet are closed and the red—the red is like banging together. One boy on each side. It doesn't look like anything when I turn it around the other way.

Card II has a twenty-five-second delay, suggesting that the subject again needed time to organize the ego process, but it is less than that needed for the first card. At the end of the twenty-five seconds a response was given, which indicates good coping process (Table 2, item 2). Here the time delay serves the useful function of permitting the individual opportunity to find an organized appropriate means of dealing with the task. However, it is evident that she is not able to integrate all the appropriate stimuli, nor is she able to avoid that which she cannot integrate. Thus, the red, representing affect, is something she experiences as impinging upon her and requiring coping. But she is not able to integrate into the response (as is indicated by use of symbolism) nor is she able to find any effective defense (such as omission of area or of the determinant) against it (Table 3, item 1c). Nevertheless, this difficulty does not result in ego disorganization or failure of reality testing. Rather, the affect is treated in a sense as an isolated part of functioning and has a pseudo quality of coping. This is more an indication of the subject's feeling that the task has been dealt with than an actually successful integrated process of ego functioning. This mode indicates a weakness of the integrative function of the ego process for which the subject has found a defensive method against breakdown. The question which can be raised here is whether the divorcing of the stimulus serves the constructive function of permitting the ego process to avoid disturbance by a partial isolation from the main stream. In this response it can be seen that the uncomfortable aspect of what is stimulated in the subject by this card is separated out and away from the main response. This technique may be what permits effective coping with the major portion of the task. It is interesting to note further that the symbolism here does not reach complete separation from the response; although the red is used symbolically, in this response it remains closer to the action and the objects involved, rather than becoming an abstract representation. This lower level of symbolization of representation suggests a less effective defense against the affect stimulus, and the possibility that the subject is actually closer to the concrete action suggested than somebody who could react to the color with a higher degree of abstraction.

In summation we see that this is an individual who can cope effectively with a major portion of the task by means of isolating from the major portion that aspect of the stimulus which is disturbing to her. This combination gives the surface impression of coping effectively, but actually reveals that there is effective coping in part of the situation and a thin intellectual veneer of coping with another part.

CARD III
10″

1. These are two black men and they're cooking something in their pot there —they're cooking meat in their pots.	1. *P*. Shows head, legs, one arm on each side.
2. They have two meats hanging on their wall on something. That's all I see there.	2. Meats on the wall, like red, looks like a roast or a chicken or something —chicken legs. Meat on the side and it's going into the pot. This part down here could be a red bone with meat on it. The form of a big pot and everything.

The time delay has dropped considerably now to a point where it cannot be considered delay, and the response to the card is appropriate content and use of expected stimuli (Table 2, item 1; Table 5, item 1; Table 4, item 1). The fact that the subject is able to respond with a popular response implies the presence of ego capacity for dealing with social situations in a conforming manner. Initially her attempt at responding to the color appears adequate, but as she continues to explore and justify the response some degree of uncertainty and discomfort enters, indicating that the coping attempt was not quite as secure as initially observed (Table 2, item 1). Nevertheless, the adaptive achievement on this card indicates a large degree of success, in that there is no failure in the reality testing, nor is there any of the concept difficulty previously noted.

Summation

The subject's functioning on this card indicates the capacity to make an adaptive achievement, although it may be accompanied by some ego-process difficulty in integrating affect comfortably. If the sequence of the three cards thus far be summarized, it can be noted that gradually the subject has moved from responding with considerable difficulty in the ego process to a far more successful adaptive functioning. Comparing Card II and Card III particularly, there is the marked difference in level of success in integrating the color. It may be that Card III is dealt with more successfully because the card itself, structurally, is in congruence with the kind of defense she tries to use; that is, the color is separated from the rest of the blot so that part of the ego defensive operation is done for her.

CARD IV
10″

1. This is a big giant and big feet.	1. Shows head, body, large feet.
2. Sitting on top of a little bench.	2. *D.* That's a bench she's sitting on—just something she's sitting on—like a bench.
3. (frowns) An animal coming out of—	3. It's like an animal. I don't know what kind—maybe like snails—like an animal coming out of a shell.
4. Out of a cage—sort of a cave.	4. It's like a cave—big and black and it has the form of a cave.

Again the initial reaction time remains at a level that does not merit special consideration and the subject is able to give a response which is effective in terms of reality testing and adaptive to the blot material (Table 2, item 1). The expected determinants and areas are used (Table 4, item 2). The fantasy involvement is appropriate (Table 6, item 1). Subject is able to complete this card on an adaptive level in terms of the ego process.

In the total record thus far, it is noted that the subject was initially quite disturbed, as assessed by the ego process, but that gradually she has been able to recoup and reach a level of functioning which could readily be part of an average record. Thus far it could be interpreted that under the impact of a new, strange, and unstructured situation, ego weakness is revealed in the form of some helpless responding to the stimulus without insight or attempt at self-evaluation. However, this does not reach major proportions and relatively quickly disappears as the subject proceeds. Therefore, one would infer at this point that only under periods of initial stress would the subject be likely to directly evidence a disturbed thought process, but that these might be sufficiently fleeting that to the non-clinical eye they would not be considered significant. A possible explanation for the improvement noted as the subject reached Card IV could be related to the explanation on Card III. There the chromatic color is separated from the major portion of the blot. On Card IV the chromatic color is eliminated completely. It is as if the removal, then, of the intense color relieves the ego of stress and strain in the integrative process. If this is maintained through the balance of the record, it would mean that the personality is in some state of organization in which the erratic and irrational parts are focused and related to a recognizable stimulus, rather than rising totally from internal confusion.

CARD V
Oh! What do you call those?
5″

1. This is a bat eating people like vultures. What do you call them? I never saw anything like that.	1. Shows horns, legs, wings—he's black. This one's black. (?) He's flying.
2. These are two animals fighting, like some goats or lambs, they're just fighting.	2. *W.* Hat is covering the head which is inside the rock. They're crawling or they're fighting or something. It's the form of like goats or lambs and they're just together there just like they're fighting.

The subject takes only five seconds and gives a popular response, thus indicating no delay and good form (Table 2, item 1). However, within this popular response of good form there is a strange and peculiar concept, that is, "a bat eating people like vultures." (Table 5, item 5, peculiar content.) This response evidences the emergence of some primary process in terms of the inappropriateness of the relationship implied in the response as she speaks of bat eating people. It should be observed that this primary process appears within an appropriate form response. The emergence of this archaic material occurs without any seeming discomfort on her part. Thus there is indication of a breakdown in the effective ego functioning. This is important in terms now of answering the question raised above as to whether it was a focused stimulus that created difficulty for the patient. It is clearly observed here that without any chromatic color present, one of the most seriously disturbed responses emerges. This response is also an illustration of the concept of actuality, wherein the perceptual function seems to remain intact in terms of the individual's recognizing reality for what it is and having to impose the conflict onto the reality framework without directly distorting the perceived reality. The result is an inappropriate response to a correctly perceived reality, as contrasted to the inappropriate response to the distorted perception of a stimulus.

In summation, with the record thus far, it becomes evident that the subject's functioning is highly erratic and includes severe ego disturbances to the point where the presence of a psychotic process must be considered.

CARD VI
15″

I remember what the other teacher said it was like. Sort of looks like— (bites on nails)

1. Sort of a big animal. Something like a squirrel.	1. Shows body, head, a big squirrel. You can tell it's a squirrel from the whiskers. The head looks like a squirrel's head and all the body. (?) Still. It's just standing only.
2. Now I am imagining. There are two	2. Two men sitting on little benches.

men sitting down on their seats, one on each side—they're sort of fighting. One on each side—one on one side and one on the other, and then they're apart. That's all I see.	They're fighting. Their arms are out. Shows head, bodies, and their arms. Yah, it's like a little bench, right this lower part here.

The initial reaction time goes up to fifteen seconds as the subject says, "I remember what the other teacher said it was like." Thus we see the appearance of some anxiety as the subject faces the card and an attempt to use an external ally to the ego and to remove the threat of personal failure. She implied that the response "sort of a big animal, something like a squirrel," can again be considered deficient ego functioning regardless of appropriateness or inappropriateness of the response to the blot. To describe the squirrel as a big animal fails to take into account the reality of what squirrels are in relation to other animals. It may well be that the interpretation by the subject of the big squirrel is related simply to the relationship of the blot to the card. The blot takes up a large portion of the card, and in this sense, therefore, it is conceived of as "big," rather than being tested against the reality of the concept. The response itself, in terms of form, is inappropriate and further evidence of the failure of the reality-testing process. If one examines the inquiry the subject says, "you can tell it's a squirrel from the whiskers." She goes on to say that "the head looks like a squirrel's head and all the body." However, the comment about the whiskers suggests the possibility that this actually is a confabulation in which her conclusion was based more on the whiskers than anything else, and that the vague description of head and body was simply an after-rationalization.

This disturbed response is followed immediately with considerable recovery in her response to the same card. Its fluctuation gives evidence again of the unpredictable ups and downs of the ego process in this subject. Comparison of the first response with the second provides an opportunity to illustrate ego functioning on primary process and secondary process levels. In the first response the content appears conflictual and emerges with primary process thinking. In the second response, although the content may reflect directly conflictual material, the manner in which it emerges is representative of secondary process thinking.

CARD VII
5″

1. Two little Japanese girls that are dancing. They have little pigtails up, and that's all I imagine.	1. A girl dancing. One girl dancing, pigtail up in the air, and the other pigtail up. No, two girls dancing. (Part of them?) These are their legs. The lower part is their legs. (Japanese?) Looks like two faces, their arms out—just like Japanese girls, just Japanese girls dancing.

The response to this card emerges without time delay and with accurate form and appropriate content (Table 2, item 1; Table 5, item 1). It is a well-documented response with appropriate involvement in fantasy (Table 6, item 1; Table 7, item 1). However, in the inquiry there appears to be a momentary lowering of the good level of ego functioning which is related to her apparent inability to maintain the concept of two little girls. In the inquiry it is called one girl, as she describes "pigtail up in the air, and the other pigtail up" as if both of these belonged to one girl. Then she corrects herself and returns to the original well-seen response. Here the functioning of the critical observing aspect of the ego process served to help her recognize the inappropriateness and then to carefully document the well-seen response.

CARD VIII
10″

Oh, this is easy.	
1. Two tigers, no, two bears going up a	1. *P.* Shows head, body, eyes.
2. A mountain, a mountain, or a little hill.	2. Pointed top and it's just like a little hill.

3. Oh, mama, what is this? That's a monster that's scary—the two bears, they're going down because they're so scared. (Gets very frightened, puts card down, hides face in hands.)

3. Oh, what a horrible face. Oh, it's just horrible. The bears are scared, they're running away and they're going downhill after they're going up—that monster has very big eyes, deep big eyes, little holes in his eyes, the nose is long and hanging through the mouth, and his hands are out hanging down. Oh, he's just horrible.

The initial reaction time is slightly higher than the previous card, but is accompanied by the remark, "Oh, this is easy." This remark is followed then by the popular response with minimal but adequate documentation (Table 7, item 2; Table 2, item 1). This is a response in which the actuality clings closely to the reality, and in this sense represents conformity with outer individuality. In this way the inner experience has minimal opportunity to act upon the perception. The succeeding response to the card is an extremely disturbed one, in which she becomes overinvolved in the fantasy and loses her sense of distance from the blot (Table 6, item 4). The marked contrast from the first response to the third deserves special comment because these two responses can be considered opposite ends of a continuum in which the popular response with minimal documentation represents the minimal influence of inner experience, whereas the third response presents a maximum ascendancy of inner experience with minimal attention to the reality and conformity. We see here the extremely idiosyncratic response occurring to the same card in which a completely benign response occurs. This represents a repetition of the extreme fluctuation which has been noted repeatedly in the record.

CARD IX
10″

1. Two persons playing ball, throwing a ball to each other.

1. One person is throwing ball to each other. (Ball?) No, it just looks like

it. (Persons?) Two boys, you see their heads and their bodies.

2. They're sitting on top of big chairs, sofa chairs.
2. The green or sofa chairs (?) The form in the green.
3. Oh, I see another monster. This monster is scary.
3. They're both horrible. Fat and big. Pink, two eyes, holes also. Long nose and hanging down and the bears are just afraid of them, because that monster is scaring them.
4. Two deers and they're running down the hill because the monster is scaring them. And they're afraid of them.
4. The faces look like deer faces—you see only the heads and bodies—this is the bodies in the green.

The first response is well seen without time delay (Table 2, item 1), with appropriate content (Table 5, item 1). The second response has a surface appearance of appropriateness, but as the inquiry verifies, the form actually is poor and the response was only superficially appropriate and accurate. This response is then followed by another highly disturbed response which has the appearance of a perseverative trend, especially when it is considered with the fourth response. This pair of responses is almost a duplication of her dealing with response to Card VIII. Consequently, no further discussion is needed, except to add the observation that perseveration of such disturbance permits the inference of even greater disturbance in the personality than has thus far been estimated. The record ends with a confabulated response, wherein she uses the frequently seen deer heads but overgeneralizes by adding "the bodies in the green," which is completely inappropriate.

CARD X
10″

1. These are two, how do you call these? crabs.
1. *D.*
2. Holding a stick.
2. *D.*

3. And some spiders—one side is one spider and one side the other spider.	3. *P.* Blue spiders (blue?) No, just spiders.
4. And two ladies like ghosts and they're blowing.	4. Two little girls like ghosts playing, they have no legs or anything. They're made out of smoke. They look just like ghosts.
5. Horns.	5. Horns.
6. Two worms getting inside a shell.	6. Two worms inside a shell. (Center *D*)
7. Two deers running—one on each side.	7. Running down a hill.
	8. (Additional response) Two yellow fishes on the side.

The subject begins Card X easily and well. But during the course of the responses it is evident that effective ego process diminishes, as noted in the response where the well-seen people gradually become vague and almost inappropriate in that they are people and playing and yet they now "have no legs or anything. They're made out of smoke." In addition there can be some question about Response 6 in which two worms are getting inside a shell that is smaller than either of them so that a fabulized combination must be considered. On the whole, however, none of the severe disturbances which appeared on previous cards is evident in Card X.

Testing the Limits

(Like?) Cards VII and III best because "two black men cooking meat and two Japanese girls dancing, very easy to see."

(Dislike?) Cards IV, IX, and VIII because "it is an ugly monster, that's very bad picture they have, a very bad picture. I like II and X also."

(Animal rug?) Select VI, looks like a squirrel skin or a rug, furry on top, black and furry, or it could be an animal rug of a bath. IV (could be, no it couldn't be).

(E. asks S. to divide cards.) (S. won't try.) (E. does it.) S. says, "Here's all the pretty ones and here's all the ugly ones, the black."

In summarizing the Rorschach evaluation, we start with the girl's immediately evident capacity to make a seemingly conforming, although somewhat anxious, surface adjustment to her surroundings. However, this adjustment is soon interfered with by the intrusion of an underlying thought disorder. Thus, it becomes apparent that although she may be capable of behaving like others initially, her actual understanding of events and her own motivations in a situation are strange and inappropriate and begin to interfere with her effectiveness in coping with the situation. It is important to note that not only does this ineffectiveness occur, but she herself is not aware of it. For example, in this patient's first hour of treatment, several months after her initial visit with the therapist, she remarks that she understood he had not seen her since "because he was making a machinery or something." The therapist understands this remark to be a reference to the social worker's preparation of the girl and her family for the research aspects of the case which necessitated electrical recording equipment which is actually visible in the room. When she again asks what the machinery is for he explains it to her on this rational level. Then they proceed with a discussion of her problem, fantasies, etc., as if she had understood fully his explanation. It is only at the end of the hour that she refers to her conviction that the machinery was to cure her by a kind of surgery or a kind of magic-influencing machine (Ekstein, 1963).

In other instances the superficial adjustment breaks down as the effectiveness of the anxiety in mobilizing her coping resources begins to fail and panic and disorganization make their appearance. Thus, in another hour with this patient she describes her experiences as she attempts to deal with a malfunctioning TV set in the following way:[2]

> . . . so I started fooling around trying to fix it. And I never could fix it so anyway I spent a whole hour trying to fix that channel. I kept on changing stations . . . finally I fooled around with the TV antenna in the back of the TV . . . I would try to fix it . . . there

---

[2] Permission to quote this excerpt from the tape recording of the therapy sessions has been generously granted by the therapist, Rudol F. Ekstein.

> were three little buttons that told you how to fix the TV and, but I didn't even understand what it really meant you know . . . I took a screw and started turning them to see if the TV would get fixed and the TV jumped out worse and got in line . . . the picture was low down . . . then you could see all the people large, big you know . . . but then it got shrinked up on the end of the picture . . . suddenly I started knocking. I was angry, I started knock, knocking . . . I ruined everything, and you know what I did, I ruined the television . . .

Thus we hear in this experience of how she initially attempts to cope with the situation rationally but as her anxiety mounts with lack of success she becomes increasingly panicked. Then as she becomes more disorganized the chaos within her is finally projected onto the television set and she suffers an acute psychotic episode.

One of the most striking features about the record are the seemingly unpredictable and extreme fluctuations in level of functioning which are reflective of the underlying shifts in ego states. The points of disorganization do not seem to occur at the expected points of stress and pressure; rather, they seem to occur in response primarily to a variety of inner impulses and fantasies that cannot be predictably related to stimuli in the environment, as for example the pressure of emotional stimulation. Although she does have difficulty in integrating her affective life and tends to isolate her feelings by means of a thin intellectualized veneer, she does so without marked interruption in her level of functioning. If the emotionally stimulating situation is fairly organized and structured for her she can function quite effectively. However, in a strange or unstructured situation she begins to respond in a more helpless, uncritical fashion, with little or no capacity to reflect about herself. Thus, for example, after several years of treatment she has reached a point where she travels alone by bus to a day care treatment center. However, in this situation she will indiscriminately beg for money or cigarettes from whomever she encounters irrespective of whether she is in actual need of it.

The schism between outer and inner reality testing is a very prominent feature of this girl's record and is most significant in understanding her behavior. Thus she may appear to be making a superficially adaptive adjustment with a seemingly appropriate comprehension of her environment; at the same time there may emerge primitive archaic features. She may then impose these upon her perceived reality, but in such a way as not to distort the accuracy of her perceptions so that neither she nor those with her recognize the entirely inappropriate nature of her inner life. For example, she readily makes promises which commit her to activities of which she is not capable. She will spontaneously promise to write a story for the therapist by the next session, which is externally appropriate but which good inner reality testing would tell her is impossible for her. Such unrealistic promises are frequent for her and are confusing to the naive recipient of them. For example, this child, after a year in treatment, would promise the volunteer occupational therapists to return the money she frequently borrowed. Subsequently she could not comprehend their distress at her not fulfilling the promise and they could not comprehend her lack of recognition of the obligation to fulfill it. However, there also do occur the more usual kinds of perceptual distortion in which she pays minimal attention to reality and where her behavior may begin to appear more flagrantly deviant as the primary thought disorder becomes more evident. As she becomes more and more preoccupied with primitive fantasies on a primary process level, reality percepts become increasingly subordinated to inner preoccupations and delusional misinterpretations of her surroundings may be accompanied by hallucinated objects projected onto her environment. Thus, with this girl there have been occasional episodes where the fantastic inner anxiety over her own impulses has created sufficient disorganization and regression in the level of ego functioning that a delusional and occasionally hallucinated creature makes its appearance, urging her to do evil or to destroy those around her who tempt her to do evil.

It is evident that such a method of evaluating the Rorschach reveals information about an isolated although important area of ego functioning—specifically, the ability of the ego to cope with reality, outer as well as inner. This in turn gives us much valuable information about the interplay of adaptive and defensive mechanisms and the critical and integrative functioning of the ego, particularly as we can explore the ways in which she fuses her perceived reality with her inner reality and creates for herself her own idiosyncratic actuality.

One brief clinical note about the youngster whose record has been evaluated. This schizophrenic girl, interestingly enough, presented somewhat of an initial diagnostic problem because of the effectiveness of certain adaptive aspects in her functioning. As long as she could function in a fairly structured situation, or when she could structure it herself by role playing a latency age child, she was able to give the impression of a dull, infantile, hysteric-like youngster. However, when this façade was penetrated either through projective tests or pressure of inner conflicts, or both, it became increasingly apparent that she was suffering from an extensive and flagrant schizophrenic reaction. Nevertheless, there occurred isolated and unpredictable islands of conforming behavior alongside markedly bizarre behavior. Progress in treatment was marked by the unpredictable nature of the shifts in level of functioning, as noted in the Rorschach, in preoccupation with inner or outer demands, and in the fluctuating insight into her own illness.

References

Ekstein, R. 1963. "The Opening Gambit in Psychotherapeutic Work with Psychotic Adolescents." *Amer. J. Ortho. Psychiat.* 33: 862–871.

———, and Wallerstein, Judith. 1954. "Observations on the Psychology of Borderline and Psychotic Children." *Psychoanal. Stud. Child.* 9: 344–369.

Fenichel, O. 1945. *The Psychoanalytic Theory of Neurosis.* New York: W. W. Norton & Co.

Hartmann, H. 1953. "Contribution to the Metapsychology of Schizophrenia." *Psychoanal. Stud. Child.* 8: 192.

Holt, R. R., and Havel, Joan. 1960. "A Method for Assessing Primary and Secondary Process in the Rorschach." In *Rorschach Psychology,* M. A. Rickers-Ovsiankina (Ed.). New York: John Wiley & Sons.

Holtzman, W. H., Thorpe, J. S., Swartz, J. D., and Herron, W. E. 1961. *Inkblot Perception and Personality.* Austin, Texas: Univ. of Texas Press.

Ittelson, W. H., and Kutash, S. B. (Eds.). 1961. *Perceptual Changes in Psychotherapy.* New Brunswick, N.J.: Rutgers Univ. Press.

Murphy, Lois B. 1962. *The Widening World of Childhood.* New York: Basic Books.

Rapaport, D. 1946. *Diagnostic Psychological Testing.* Chicago: Year Book Publishers.

Schafer, R. 1954. *Psychoanalytic Interpretation in Rorschach Testing.* New York: Grune & Stratton.

Sechehaye, M. A. 1951. *Symbolic Realization; New Method of Psychotherapy Applied to a Case of Schizophrenia.* Translated from French by Barbröw and Helmut Würsten. New York: Univ. Press. Monograph Series on Schizophrenia, No. 2.

3

Harvey Mindess

The Symbolic Dimension

Over the years, Rorschach interpretation has come to consist of a family of related techniques—a family in which determinant analysis is the favorite son and symbol analysis the neglected child. Studies dealing with the symbolic significance of Rorschach responses have appeared from time to time, but they constitute a tiny fraction of the literature. [For a representative selection, see Beck (1952), Brown (1953), Klopfer (1954), Lindner (1950), Phillips and Smith (1953), Schachtel (1943), and Schafer (1954).] This relative neglect of a potentially fruitful source of information is, to say the least, regrettable. While admittedly a subtle, intuitive art, the interpretation of Rorschach symbols can expose the subject's being as lucidly as any psychological technique. And while, like any art, it may be difficult to teach, it is not by any means impossible to convey the principles on which it operates.

In order to give substance to these views, this chapter will describe the qualities by which symbolic responses can be recognized, indicate the conditions conducive to their emergence, propose a procedure by which they can be interpreted, and discuss the merit of employing this procedure both diagnostically and therapeutically.

The approach to be presented here blends in several areas with previous papers on the topic, but it highlights the kind of symbol which has received least attention of all: the dramatic, poetic image —the symbol which portrays its referent with striking, immediate impact. In contrast to responses which have generalized symbolic connotations (e.g., "a smoldering volcano" as suggestive of emotions threatening to erupt), we will focus on responses which are more or less unique (e.g., "a diseased heart valve which won't last long," given by a patient who later committed suicide). Our purpose is both to supplement the existing literature which has concentrated on the general symbol and to provide, in place of a glossary of interpretations, a set of principles for dealing with the symbolic dimension of the Rorschach.

Recognizing Symbols

When is a response symbolic? The question, as stated, is misleading. Except at the two extremes (e.g., "a bat" to Card V; "the end of the world" to every part of every card), most Rorschach responses represent a combination of perceptive and projective processes, objective appraisals and subjective distortions of the blot material. The problem, then, is one of determining *how projective* any given response may be. Let us rephrase the question, therefore, and ask how we can distinguish subjective elaborations from objective descriptions of the blots.

Four main criteria should guide us. First, the *originality* of the response may be taken as an indicator of its subjective importance. The more unusual an idea is, the more justified are we in considering it symbolic. "A bat" seen on Card I is unlikely to have symbolic implications; "the Greek Winged Victory, a statue of a woman representing freedom," on the other hand, most likely has. Even the basic bat idea, of course, may be elaborated in unusual fashion—"a parchment bat" or "a female bat, a vampire"—in which case the response takes on symbolic connotations. Whether in the response proper, then, or in additional remarks about it, originality is a sign of symbolic content.

Second, the emotional *cathexis* of the response reveals its subjective importance. The more imbued it is with feeling or portent, the more it can be considered symbolic. "Two people on the sides" seen on Card I is less cathected than "two people tearing a child apart"; "clouds" on Card VII is less cathected than "storm clouds threatening a deluge." For that reason alone, the former images are, in all probability, less meaningful than the latter. Once again, though, a basically neutral idea may be given an emotional fillip which makes it more symbolic than it started out to be. (For example, on Card VIII, "two animals—yes, two fat and disgusting sloths.")

Third, the *imaginativeness* of the response is indicative of its subjective importance. The more fanciful it is, the more it is likely to have symbolic meaning. "A fountain in the center with vegetation all around," to Card IX, is hardly barren, yet it is less suggestive of subjective import than "Vapor shooting up into the air and in the background there are mountains, pure white, and golden gates, carved perfectly, and way back in the distance is a tower and that tower is the capitol of the world and it's so beautiful that it makes everything look bright."

Finally, the *repetition* of any specific response or general theme implies its subjective importance. Seeing, let us say, "slashing knives" just once may be symbolically significant, but seeing them three times on different cards is almost certainly portentous.

These four criteria—originality, cathexis, imaginativeness, and repetition—may serve as guidelines to the symbolically meaningful responses in a Rorschach record. The more a response displays these qualities, the more it may be considered symbolic; the less it displays them, the less likely it is to have symbolic meaning.

It is characteristic of the phenomenon of symbolism, however, that no rules are binding, no formulations absolute. The criteria we have just sketched out, therefore, are not infallible signs. At times an unusual, emotional, fantastic, or repeated response may not be particularly pertinent to the subject's inner condition, while at other times a banal remark or gesture, tossed off laconically or casually, may prove to be highly revealing.[1] The determination of meaningfulness is aided by principles such as those set forth above, but the truly intuitive Rorschach interpreter must sustain a questioning approach to each and every response.

Conducive Conditions

Since Rorschach records vary widely in their symbolic richness, it seems important to consider the conditions which are conducive to the expression of symbolic material.

The central condition may be defined as *ego permeability*. In this state the ego is open to the irrational, to the unconscious, to moods, emotions, impulses, to fantasies and intuitions. It is relatively nondefensive, or at least its defenses are such that they allow the expression of ego-alien material. This condition inclines the subject toward pathology, creativity, or both. It is indicative of both regressive and progressive tendencies, for it is volatile, not static, and reveals the presence of active conflicts needing resolution.

Ego permeability may be provoked by certain drugs, but it is also provoked by crisis situations in the subject's life. It is related, though not identical, to awareness of unresolved conflicts and unlived potentials. Some individuals, notably either latent psychotics or creative seers, appear to be characterized by the condition throughout their adult lives. Others, notably stolid or phlegmatic individuals, appear to experience it rarely if ever. Variations in ego permeability are likely, however, in the life cycle of most persons, with very early childhood, adolescence, and dramatic turning points in adulthood the most common times for it to flourish.

---

[1] I am reminded of an actual situation in which three psychologists shared a suite of offices. When it came time to pay the rent, each man made out a personal check for his share. On comparing them, they found that one psychologist signed his checks, "Dr.—," another signed his, "—, Ph.D.," while the third signed his with his name alone. On the surface, their choice of signature style might seem a trivial matter, yet the men involved found the differences significant in terms of their individual self-concepts and the figures they were attempting to cut in the world.

The "permeable" individual who projects profusely onto the blots may be a willing or unwilling host to his fantasy. He may feel inspired, fascinated, or besieged by his unconscious. He may revel in the outpouring of his imagery or, quite the reverse, may strain to stem the flow. It is important for the Rorschach worker to determine the quality of the subject's reception of his fantasy material, for its role in his psychic economy is shaped by his evaluation of it. The man who sees "a stiletto" in the phallic area of Card VI and, sensing its connotations, exults, "Haw, haw—that's rich!," is a very different character from the man who sees the identical thing but introduces it with an apologetic, "Well, I guess I shouldn't say this, but. . . ."

While a grudging admission of symbolic content indicates an uncomfortable awareness of ego-alien impulses, a delighted recognition of such content reveals a readiness to be inflated by such impulses. Many subjects, however, offer symbolic responses with no apparent reaction to them at all; they simply state that that's what the blot looks like and seem to entertain not even the dimmest awareness that their response is a projection of their own condition. Naiveté such as this betrays a corresponding lack of insight into one's inner processes.[2]

Without denying the primary importance of the subject's relation to his unconscious, the influence of the examiner on the subject's production of symbolic content bears comment too. Personal experience suggests that the examiner's set is more influential than we generally admit. Whether his interest in, or resistance to, irrational projections is communicated by his facial expression, body tonus, unregistered comments, or other unrecognized avenues, his personal need to collect such material encourages its expression just as his personal distaste for it discourages it. This observation should not be surprising. Most subjects, after all, have potentially available to them various levels of inner experience. While neither their conscious intentions nor environmental expectations are likely to be-

---

[2] Distressing as the social inference may be, it should be noted that this blandly unconscious type of projection is by far the most prevalent, even in the psychologically sophisticated strata of our society.

come all-powerful in determining what levels they express, both these factors must play some part in determining their test responses, just as they play some part in determining other forms of social communication.

Interpretation Procedure

Interpretation of Rorschach symbols—especially those responses which are relatively unique—is an intuitive operation. Its difficulty lies in its stark simplicity. It is aided by openness to poetic levels of thought and hampered by insistence on logical chains of deduction. The Rorschach worker must allow each symbol to speak to him—to reveal a new vista, bring to light some characteristic he may never have considered—if he wishes to learn the most from the material before him.

It seems peculiarly difficult, even repugnant, for many of us to adopt this intuitive stance. We have been trained to rely on statistics, on verifiable data, or at the very least on deductive logic to carry us to our conclusions. Symbolic material, however, will yield its secrets soonest to an investigation conducted on *its* level—to an inquiry, that is, which seeks not so much to explain as to receive, which wishes less to "pin it down" than to "get with it."

In this mode, an effective first step in interpreting Rorschach symbols is to conceptualize them verbatim within the context of the subject's personality. If a man, for example, sees "an old tree stump, withered and rotting," in Card IV, imagine first that he is somehow like this old rotting stump. If a woman sees "a strutting peacock" in Card III, imagine that she is like this bird. Of course, they are like many other things too, but one important facet of their inner condition is symbolized in these images. When a series of projections is interpreted in this manner, each adding something more to the feel of the person under scrutiny, a Gestalt begins to crystallize, a personality begins to take shape, and the individual as a functioning entity moves into view.

Since this approach, by its very nature, does not lend itself to theoretical discussion, let us study more examples which may help to make it clear. First let us dwell on a number of single responses which in themselves shed remarkable light on the individuals who produced them. Then we will proceed to scrutinize a set of responses which combine to portray, in great complexity, one person's inner condition.[3]

An 8-year-old boy whose mother still feeds and dresses him, and who sleeps in her room so she can be sure he's breathing, responds to Card II, "You're in a tunnel and it's all closed up." No technical gyrations are required to guess how this child must feel about himself.

A 30-year-old son of a wealthy, conservative family who has become a hippy—complete with beard, sandals, torn clothes, and no job—sees in Card I "a Wagnerian singer shouting vengeance at the gods because he is not one of them." Consciously, he might resist the interpretation that he experiences his social rebellion as a grandiose gesture of spite against the people with whom he has been unable to identify, but his projection spells it out in no uncertain terms.

A 40-year-old unhappily married woman who complains that her husband is hard, cold, superficial, and rationalistic, describes the so-called vaginal area of Card VII as "a lock without a key. A very dreamy sort of thing that you can't put your finger on because it's too misty." If she were to comprehend the implications of this image, if she could come to see that she has cast herself in the role of the elusive enigma, perhaps her contemptuous evaluation of her husband would be modified.

A 21-year-old girl—sensitive, idealistic, and withdrawn—responds to Card IX, "The center light green are like eyes which know all the evil in the world but cannot prevent anything." What more poignant expression of her condition could one ask?

---

[3] I have chosen unusually lucid responses for purposes of illustration. While such exceedingly vivid images are not as common as these collected examples may suggest, it is instructive to note that they do in fact occur.

A 50-year-old woman professor who suffered a psychotic breakdown several months after being tested remarked to Card VIII, "Everything seems to be held together, but the foundation is not solid." At the time it would have seemed far-fetched to attribute any predictive value to the remark, yet in retrospect it appears that she sensed her state of being more keenly than she realized.

A 45-year-old doctor, a devout Catholic accused by his wife of being sadistic, projects on the phallic area of Card VI, "A royal sceptre covered with dirty ice. It has a cross on top and a sword blade on the bottom." Whatever the validity of his wife's complaints, this response alone makes it clear that his sexual feelings are anything but warm and loving.

Finally, a 23-year-old man suffering from intense stammering, who professes no interest in sexual or competitive pursuits, sees in Card X "a house on poles or beams holding it up, with a man inside. Like in the jungle, built up off the ground for safety from the animals." It would be difficult to create a more fitting image of his relation to his instincts.

While the evidence of these responses is admittedly anecdotal, their correspondence to their authors' states of being is too obvious to be denied. They demonstrate the fact that Rorschach subjects may, without intention or comprehension of what they are doing, portray their inner selves in vivid symbolic projections. But the terms *inner selves* or *inner conditions* or *states of being* are too diffuse to define these symbols' referents. It would be more cogent to assert that Rorschach symbols such as these express important aspects of the subject's *unacknowledged self-concept.* They depict, in other words, his semiconscious experience of himself, the ways in which he feels but cannot quite admit.

Since single responses, however, fail to capture the complexity of an individual's self-concept, let us now consider a series of symbols from one Rorschach protocol to see how they articulate a portrait of a person's inner experience.

The subject was a girl, unmarried, 18 years of age, an only child, and a freshman in college. She sought treatment because she found herself crying unexplainably in class and felt that other students were looking at her and talking about her. On the WAIS, her verbal IQ was 122, her performance IQ was 103, and her full scale IQ was 115. She was eager to take the Rorschach and gave a total of 57 responses to the cards. This number was not indicative of the volume of her responses, however, because two or three of them were several paragraphs long. Her mood in taking the test was enthusiastic, absorbed, and highly emotional. Some of her responses made her laugh, others made her cry. We will not attempt to reproduce the entire record here, but will simply excise a series of symbolically meaningful projections to observe the creation of a psychic self-portrait.

CARD I

The Virgin's head, with brain tubes coming out and nerves all over.

Oh no! A bug underneath and another bug crushing over it like a bridge.

CARD II

Something screeching, screeching and crawling, like sounds coming from it.

Some kind of energy or liquid oozing out of these wings.

CARD III

Dancers, they're having fun! Way out dancers. I've never seen these kind of people before. A puddle of water between them, and infinite space in the background. There is nowhere. And the dancers look like they have leprosy. And they have webbed feet, so they're out of the ocean. Yah, that's where they're from. A new form of life of the future.

CARD IV

Oh wow! There's a bunch of clouds and mermaids behind the clouds, ballet dancers. There's a new land back there. On the top, some acrobats and dancers are arching their backs and praying to the sky. But there's conflict in this picture too: two gods or lords keep them from doing what they want to do.

CARD V

Fish, needle fish, swimming along, and pollywogs. They're trying to separate, like an amoeba trying to separate and enter a new life.

Ooooo! It's a creature zooming down and the wings are like jelly. It's making odd sounds and there's one eye that keeps staring.

CARD VI

Reminds me of the very dead center of a bug that's getting at you. The core of things, the depth of things.

There's some sperms in here, male and female sperms. Looks like it's travelling up and at the end there is something beautiful being born. Something fantastic, a beautiful butterfly, it's dainty, a happy butterfly. It's gonna have a happy life, but something, some clouds or vapor, are following it. Reminds me of birth and rebirth.

CARD VII

Oh, I saw something cute! Little girls, like angels in space, going up. They look like orphans, no home. These little angels are closing a book, but it's a butterfly at the same time. Right in the dead center, there's a bug and a crack. It's so old, it's falling apart, and way back in the depth is a new land, a sea with a new opening to it.

CARD VIII

Oh heck! There's another creature crawling in there. I hate that! I hate those creatures!!

But at the bottom there's kings, yellow and pink, and they're so happy. A dark deep yellow that shows he knows what he's doing. Trying to make contact with that butterfly, but it's too late. And there are humble people praying. But these are terrible animals for a king to have. They shouldn't look like rats.

CARD IX

Vapor shooting up into the air, and in the background there are mountains, pure white, and golden gates, carved perfectly, and way back in the distance is a tower and that tower is the capitol of the world and it's so beautiful that it makes everything look bright. And there's a beautiful bug with color coming out and that color is reflecting on the world and saying, "Boy, is something being accomplished here!" And in the castle are people, all one color, and all the people are equal, and there's no ruler, and they don't read, they just grasp knowledge by going places. They can see the whole world just by looking, and by gosh they are finding something new, in a new universe, the sky is white and pure, and there are the new people, a redwood color, and they're more like animals, and below is cotton, fluffy and floating, and this cotton is what sends the information for the world. Hahahaha! That's a happy picture!

CARD X

There's this test tube. These animals are staring into it. They have tentacles and keep touching that hot test tube. Oh wow! There's a head in the test tube, a man, a triangle man, and the animals are trying to get him out. He has a tall aerial on his head. People are living differently, but it's all connected. This test tube is producing all these animals, not animals, not creatures, not toys, but living things. Just things. They live on the moon. On the outside, attached to it. They were sent out from the test tube through a chute and they floated up to the moon, but they don't go inside because inside is some kind of fire. So they just stick to it and suffer and die and rot away. . . .

Symbolic profusion such as this is, as we all know, rare. It serves, however, to magnify the type of material which is frequently projected—less copiously, to be sure—onto the blots. In essence, it provides a scenario of the subject's inner life. We see the lushness of her fantasy, the lability of her emotions, the weakness of her self-control, the confusion of her thinking. We see, too, the visionary quality of her dreams, the exuberant idealism striving to supplant a sense of desolation and horror. We are presented, in short, with an awe-inspiring view into the very interior of her psyche.

With regard to specific images, her first response to Card I ("The Virgin's head with brain tubes coming out and nerves all over") expresses both her attempted identification with the holiest of attitudes and her disconcerted awareness of her mental and nervous processes going awry. It shows her wish to be all love and gentleness and her fear of losing her mind. Her next response to the same card ("Oh no! A bug underneath and another bug crushing over it like a bridge") reveals her pained view of the brutality of life. These three facets of her experience—a sense of life as brutal, a wish to be totally loving, and anxiety about a mental breakdown—are probably interrelated, the latter being a result of the essential incompatibility of the former two. In any case, they introduce us at once to the dissonance within her.

Her final response to Card X ("There's this test tube . . . This test tube is producing all these animals, not animals, not creatures, not toys, but living things . . . They floated up to the moon, but they don't go inside because inside is some kind of fire. So they just stick to it and suffer and die and rot away . . .") reiterates a theme which had found expression in several previous cards: the fantasy of creating new forms of life. It is remarkable that this theme was already presaged in the image of the Virgin, who of course accomplished just that feat. The fantasy itself, however, represents the subject's need for a creative rebirth, her need to be mother to herself, to develop new feelings, new values, a new orientation to life. Unhappily, at the time of taking the test at least, her prospects of success seemed dim to her. The creatures born out of the test tube cannot enter the moon; they "suffer and die and rot away." She was despairing of finding a haven wherein she could nurture herself. Yet a sensitive therapist, aware of her need, might very well have provided the sustenance she was seeking.

While the struggles and torments these responses reveal and the overall view the entire record provides can be abstracted into psychodynamic formulations, the uniqueness of their symbolic expression resides in its virtually palpable rendering of the texture of her being. Having explored its weird panorama, having absorbed its unearthly music, we are enabled to empathize with this girl's experience on an extraordinarily intimate level.

Utilizing Symbols Diagnostically and Therapeutically

It goes without saying that, just as the Rorschach itself is employed as only part of a battery of tests and interviews from which conclusions may be drawn, the symbolic material elicited by the blots is utilized only in conjunction with the more objective data they supply. Its specific contribution, though, derives from its naked immediacy, from its direct portrayal of facets of semiconscious experience.

Diagnostic clues may be gleaned from symbolic responses—e.g., the woman who saw "a strutting peacock" in Card III probably entertains exhibitionistic impulses, while the man who saw Card

VI as "a royal sceptre covered with dirty ice. It has a cross on top and a sword blade on the bottom," is probably engulfed in a morass of self-glorifying phallic aggression—but their essential content is less organized, less refined than our psychodynamic concepts. Translating symbols into rationally manipulable terms is analogous to transposing poetry into prose. It can be done, but it is a heavy-handed operation and in the process the lifeblood drains away.

For purposes of professional communication, it may nevertheless be useful to reduce symbolic material to psychodynamic concepts. Demonstrations of this procedure abound in such studies as those by Brown (1953) and Phillips and Smith (1953). In therapeutic work with the subject, however, there is no substitute for his unique imagery. An effective technique—dependent, of course, on the subject's ability to tolerate and comprehend his unconscious—is to select those responses which appear to be symbolically meaningful and direct his attention to them in the framework of a therapy session. Suggest that he attempt to conceptualize them as facets of his unacknowledged self-concept and encourage him to dwell at length on each of them. Have him associate to them and attempt to revive the feeling-tones they contain. The resultant expansion of his consciousness may be impressive to both the therapist and the subject himself.[4]

---

[4] Such a dialogue might go like this:

T: You remember you called this first blot *a parchment bat.* Now that's an unusual idea. Many people call it a bat, but a *parchment* bat is unique. What do you think it expresses?

S: I really don't know. It just looked that way to me.

T: Yes, I'm sure it did. But since it doesn't look that way to most people, the image probably has some particular relevance to you.

S: Well, I like parchment. Not that I've ever owned any, but the associations it carries are pleasant to me. Something ancient, rare and fragile. A treasured document, an esoteric text.

T: All right then, if that's what it means to you, I ask you: how does it relate to your self? How are you like such a piece of parchment?

S: Me? Like a piece of parchment? Well, by God, I guess you're right. I am a piece of parchment, in a way. So damn fragile and, and intellectual, and always mulling around with offbeat theories. Isn't that fantastic! I had no suspicion that I was talking about myself when I described the blot.

T: We rarely do.

Conclusion

Studies of Rorschach symbolism do not, at this juncture, all agree with one another on the best approach to be pursued. This essay is no exception. The intuitive, phenomenological procedure presented here is distinct from most other methods which have been proposed. Still, it agrees with many of the basic propositions previous investigators have put forth. It subscribes to Walter Klopfer's statement (Klopfer, 1954),

> An attempt to deal with the content of Rorschach reponses as symbolic is justified (only) under certain special circumstances. These conditions require that the individual constantly check himself by comparing the hypotheses formed on this basis with one another, with hypotheses derived from an analysis of structure, and with hypotheses formed on the basis of other tests and case history materials.

It accepts, too, Schafer's criteria for judging the adequacy of interpretations (Schafer, 1954) and Phillips and Smith's criteria for evaluating the importance of symbolic responses (Phillips and Smith, 1953). But rehashing their particular contributions or comparing its merits to theirs has not been its province.

At this stage in the development of the Rorschach technique, it seems as important to the present writer to open up fresh lines of investigation as to argue the validity of those which are already being followed. Accordingly, the goal of this chapter has been to present an approach to the symbolic dimension which might encourage other workers to expand their own interest and facility in dealing with Rorschach symbolism.

References

Beck, Samuel. 1952. *Rorschach's Test,* Volume III, *Advanced Interpretation.* New York: Grune & Stratton.

Brown, Fred. 1953. "An Exploratory Study of Dynamic Factors in the Content of the Rorschach Protocol." *J. Proj. Tech.* 17: 251–279.

Klopfer, Walter. 1954. "Interpretative Hypotheses Derived from the Analysis of Content." In *Developments in the Rorschach Technique,* Volume I, B. Klopfer et al. (Eds.). New York: World Book Co.

Lindner, Robert. 1950. "The Content Analysis of the Rorschach Protocol." In *Projective Pychology,* L. E. Abt and L. Bellak (Eds.). New York: Knopf.

Phillips, Leslie, and Smith, Joseph G. 1953. *Rorschach Interpretation: Advanced Technique.* New York: Grune & Stratton.

Schachtel, Ernest G. 1943. "On Color and Affect." *Psychiatry* 6: 393–409.

Schafer, Roy. 1954. *Psychoanalytic Interpretation in Rorschach Testing.* New York: Grune & Stratton.

Helmut Würsten

The Relationship between Piaget's Developmental Theory and the Rorschach Method *

Introduction

Responses to the Rorschach ink-blot test have been examined from many different theoretical viewpoints. The processes underlying Rorschach responses are many, including many cognitive functions, the individual's personal experiential and general cultural background, the entire range of affect, and many aspects of social relationships. Responses have been processed in innumerable ways by clinicians, educators, and statisticians.

Yet, despite the large number of studies—some of them very scholarly and frequently highly imaginative, creative, and thorough—analysis of Rorschach responses has not been able to provide a

* Professor Piaget, in reviewing the present article, stated that in general, it did not raise any fundamental objection and he felt that "it poses in fact an interesting problem of coordination. However, this coordination remains still somewhat vague, undoubtedly mostly because of the nature of the things involved here. Perhaps this study could be pushed ahead more by planning longitudinal studies which would reveal the eventual transformations in projective tests during changes from one stage to another. I am afraid that one might not find any correlation. On the other hand, if there should be some correlation, this would raise the delicate problem of the relationships between intelligence and the totality of the personality, a problem I would personally not want to tackle and deal with, as far as I am concerned."

valid assessment of the total personality of the individual studied. As Piotrowski and Lewis [1] state,

> The Rorschach method detects many traits pertaining to dynamic psychosocial interrelationships, but the total personality in the strict meaning of the word eludes it, as it eludes every experimental psychological procedure.

This is especially true, we feel, when dealing with children. To administer the Rorschach test to a child with the intent of sizing up his "total personality" seems to us not only overambitious, but also rather naive and unrealistic. That the Rorschach method can contribute a great deal to the knowledge we seek about a child, to the understanding of various aspects of his personality, is unquestionably true and has been demonstrated quite clearly. Like other "tests" or psychological procedures, the Rorschach method provides us essentially with samples: samples obtained of a certain individual, of a given age, at a certain time under specific conditions, of which the examiner is also a part. What we obtain are samples of behavior of a child whose personality is in the process of development and in constant flux.

A number of authors have investigated this experimentally, and we shall very briefly summarize a few of the essential studies done with children and their reactions to the Rorschach test. Ames herself states (Ames et al., 1952, p. 2):

> The developmental viewpoint suggests that the behavior of the child, as well as his physical organism, develops through a sequence of structured, patterned stages. It comes from within. The clinician is in danger of attributing too entirely to the child's own unique individuality in his life situation behavior which is actually merely characteristic of his age level.

She adds that it is probable that at some age, perhaps in the early twenties, individual response patterns become predominant over responses characteristic of a given age level. Changes with time in Rorschach protocols of an individual child cannot be accounted for

---

[1] Quoted in Ames et al. (1952), page 5.

solely by happenings in his environment. The influence of maturation is probably very significant in affecting the Rorschach performance, which reveals more of the general developmental status than of individual personality structure until adulthood (Ames et al., 1952, p. 285). Of course, the overall advantages and limitations of the Rorschach test have been discussed so well and so extensively by others that we shall not comment upon that aspect further.

Werner,[2] whose ideas on child development resemble Piaget's theory in many ways (the major reason for mentioning his work here in some detail), has stressed that "developmental changes take place in terms of a systematic, orderly sequence; a direction is implied." There is a regulatory principle, according to which development proceeds from a state of relative global and undifferentiated structure to a state of increasing differentiation, articulation, and hierarchic integration. An analysis of the type of operations underlying an individual's performance will provide us with a truer picture than an analysis of the accuracy of the performance. Werner defines organic development as increasing differentiation and centralization or hierarchic integration. The undifferentiated structural process is syncretic, diffused, labile, indefinite, and rigid. Differentiated and organized structures are discrete, articulated, stable, definite, and flexible. Although structural aspects are discussed in great detail, Werner is also aware of the importance of content. He states that one cannot deal with structure wholly without regard for content. Development proceeds from a state of relative undifferentiation through a state of individuation of parts to a state in which the individual parts are hierarchically integrated.

This developmental concept is given an operational definition in terms of the properties of Rorschach responses. The most mature type of percept is the one in which the subject breaks down a solid blot into parts and then relates the parts to each other in a meaningful whole. Levine, in his excellent critical review (1966, pp. 293–294), discusses the developmental maturity score applied to the Rorschach test and derived from Heinz Werner's viewpoint. This

---

[2] Quoted in Hemmendinger (1966), page 59.

score has shown age-related changes, differentiates levels of mental deficiency, and relates to a clinically ordered continuum of maturity in adult patients. Levine stresses the need for a closer tie between research with projective tests and theory. Thus, there are many normative studies, but the findings are not incorporated into any systematic theoretical framework as yet.

Hemmendinger (1966, pp. 58–76) discusses various attempts, including his own, to link Werner's concepts of child development and genetic theory with clinical theory. He reviews in detail the work of Friedman, who applied Werner's developmental principles to structural aspects of Rorschach location scores. Hemmendinger comments on the difficulty of dealing with "pure structure" without regard for content—in fact, an impossible task. He points out that some psychological determinants of structure are imaginal-motor-emotional in nature and states that it is often difficult to differentiate whether a subject is responding essentially to qualities of the blot or primarily to inner personal experiences that may result in a very unusual, even bizarre, response.

Dealing exclusively with the perceptual aspects represents, of course, an arbitrary and rather artificial approach. In his own study with 160 children, aged 3 to 10, Hemmendinger found that the basic principles of development were confirmed; namely, vague, undifferentiated *W*'s changed to increasingly better articulation, better integrated *W*'s, and to *D* responses. He states that his ontogenetic scale provides a developmental scale that can be applied to a wide variety of research problems in which change of function and/or performance is relevant.

Hemmendinger also considers the Rorschach a very useful tool for studies on thinking, especially the study of mechanisms of projection. He believes it would provide much more than a "sign" approach.

Gertrude Meili-Dworetzki concludes her extremely interesting and helpful research study (Dworetzki, 1939) by stating that, in regard to the child's general mental development, there is a progression from general and confused perception of the whole (syncretic perceptions) to much more distinct and analytic perception of the parts and, eventually, synthesis of the whole, with awareness of the parts. This development can be considered the manifestation of increasing flexibility or plasticity of mental structures. Each age level has its "type of perception," and this should be considered, first of all, in interpreting findings, instead of drawing conclusions immediately as to the child's character. The degree of complexity of the responses given, their particular form, will provide us with the perceptual level of the child. During the child's mental development, perception becomes increasingly more flexible, yielding its original rigidity, and, thanks to this greater elasticity, the child becomes capable of structuring the perceptual stimulus in an increasingly more varied manner. This supposes a breaking up and restructuring of what is being perceived. Color responses—their evolution from primitive, highly impulsive responses to, finally, well-integrated responses combined with form—also follow specific rules of development. Kinesthetic (movement) responses, for Hermann Rorschach an indicator of "inner life" of the subject, appear rather late in the child's mental development and are considered indicators of the psychological complexity and maturational aspects of perceptual and associative functions (Meili-Dworetzki, 1956).

Hertz (1960) discusses various research papers dealing with organization activity. This need to evaluate the organizational activity was taken up by various authors and eventually led to Klopfer's rating scale and Beck's Z-score. Thetford (quoted by Hertz) found in his work with children that the ability to organize relationships meaningfully increases with the child's chronological development and manifests itself to a pronounced degree in adolescent years. Hertz concludes that "in general, the organizational factor in the Rorschach helps gauge the intellectual level of the individual, the efficiency with which he functions, the influence of emotional factors and mental disturbance on the intellectual functioning." The organizational score should be considered and evaluated in conjunction with productivity.

Klopfer and his co-workers (1954) stress the difficulties of translating a child's Rorschach responses into a description of his personality organization and psychological processes. The risks are discussed, including the need to avoid the dangers of misinterpretation by having "a sound understanding of personality theory, a thorough comprehension of the psychological processes reflected in the Rorschach protocols—particularly in its structural aspects—and a sound rationale that connects the two."

It is difficult to give a systematic presentation of interpretation problems connected with age patterns. The experimental studies reviewed by these authors, involving children between 2 and 7 years of age, describe a sequential order that progresses from the magic wand perseveration of 3-year-old children to the level of confabulation typical at 4, and evolves to confabulatory combinations typical of children between 4 and 5 years of age. The significance of these age patterns is discussed by Fox (1956). In his rationale he combines psychoanalytic, Gestalt, and Piaget theory: Fox feels that all three theories complement and amplify each other. He states that the confabulatory pattern of generalizing part to whole is a function of the sparsely differentiated inner world of the child at this age level (2 to 4 years), of the fluidity of the inner organization, of the limited ability to postpone gratification, and of need dominance in perception. He discusses some aspects of Piaget's theory and its application to this particular level, feeling that in regard to the magic wand perseveration and confabulation, assimilation seems to be predominant. The child modifies and distorts the blot to suit his inner schemata and needs. In the confabulatory combination (4 to 6 years), however, accommodation predominates. It shows a higher form of mastery. The child is able to cope with requests of the examiner in a specific manner. However, there is lack of hierarchical organization in his thought processes, which represent prelogical syncretic thinking. The child also is not yet bothered by contradictions. Below 5 years the child produces mostly *W*'s. He moves from a need-and-fantasy-oriented mode of ideation at 3 years to a reality-and-object-oriented mode at 5 years. With maturation, he shows better ability to test reality on the object plane and shifts from being governed by the pleasure principle toward greater awareness of reality. However, the 5-year-old's thinking is still prelogical, concrete, and syncretic; assimilation and accommodation show more "regulation" [3] than actual equilibrium.

As children evolve and mature, their various psychological functions change, in both quantity and quality. In order to better understand how these changes manifest themselves in the Rorschach protocol of children (many psychological functions are being tapped by that test), it seems important first to find out what children think at certain ages, how they think, and why. We then might attempt to correlate some of these particular age characteristics with various aspects of the Rorschach responses. In order to understand a child's present developmental status at a given time, it is also important to know his background, how he arrived at that particular level and under what circumstances, i.e., what obstacles he encountered in his life and how he coped with them. What is the child's inner world like, and how does he view the outside world and react to it? Piaget is one of the few experimental child psychologists (he actually prefers to be considered an epistemologist), who, for about 50 years, have painstakingly explored the cognitive processes of children, from infancy through adolescence. He has not explored their reactions to the Rorschach test specifically but has studied children's thinking, their language, and their perceptual processes by means of most ingenious and fascinating experiments and a most effective clinical method. He has succeeded in relating all his observations to a solidly established theoretical system of interrelated and interacting functions and structures, units that develop in the direction of an increasingly stable and flexible total equilibrium. Although we do not by any means look to Piaget here for a clinical model of Rorschach interpretation, we have wondered whether some of his observations, ideas, and theories—important (we feel) to both experimentalists and clinicians—might not be used in understanding children's experiences with the Rorschach test, especially some of their predominantly cognitive processes mobilized by this test.

---

[3] The term "regulation" is not discussed further by Fox but will be expanded upon in the discussion of Piaget's theory.

We shall now present some of our general and more specific conclusions, show how and to what extent we feel Piaget's interactionistic theory can be related to the Rorschach test at the present time, and suggest some areas in need of research. In order to facilitate the discussion of some of our hypotheses, we intend to summarize very briefly the essentials of Piaget's theory as we came to understand it [4] (although it has been done most skillfully and in great detail by others).[5] We shall sketch only the essential, broad outlines as we perceive them and explore some specific concepts that appear to us to relate more directly to our topic, namely, the possible application of some of Piaget's theory to the Rorschach test, as we see it. We are thinking particularly of the concepts of structure, adaptation, and equilibrium, and the relationship of perception, intelligence and affectivity, and memory and mental images.

Our Conclusions

1. Piaget tells us that there are no pure cognitive actions or states, or pure affective ones, but always a combination of both, though in various proportions. This is applicable to the Rorschach test, as well as to a Binet test or any other structured or unstructured "test" used with children. We always deal with multiple factors, though in different proportions, depending on the task, the child's age, and other circumstances.[6]

2. Mental development occurs in a spiraling,[7] orderly succession of well-differentiated stages and periods, according to Piaget, and to a greater extent than has been presented by early and orthodox psy-

---

[4] As a former student and research assistant of his.

[5] See Flavell (1963), McV. Hunt (1961), and Wolff (1960).

[6] For instance, at times a Binet test (considered predominantly an intelligence test) administered to a very frightened, inhibited child may reveal more about his anxiety and inhibition than about his true cognitive level, his intellectual strong points, or his so-called "potential."

[7] Our term.

choanalytic theory,[8] in which one speaks of a dominant stage (for instance, anal or oral) but which may recur at various ages, simultaneously with other stages, either still in a dominant role (a fixation, sometimes) or now in a secondary role. It would seem easier to assess a more specific developmental level by using Piaget's concepts, especially in dealing with cognitive functions.

3. Piaget's total theoretical system is based on essentially very normal, healthy children. The principles derived from such studies should prove helpful, in general, in viewing a child's performance and behavior, first of all, from this very positive, constructive viewpoint, instead of searching predominantly for signs of psychopathology and maladjustment.

Knowledge of what a child thinks, how and why, would seem of considerable usefulness. Responses in the Rorschach considered pathological in adults may not be so at all in children of various ages, if one considers, for instance, the magic-phenomenalistic or animistic phase that is normal in young children; responses may not appear unusually rigid if one is well aware of the type of equilibrium that predominates at the intuitive or preoperational level.

4. Piaget views the child's behavior as the result of a continuous interaction between the organism and the environment in the broadest sense. In order to understand behavior, much needs to be known regarding the heredity, constitution, and environment of that particular child. A Rorschach protocol would seem much more useful if viewed in the light of this multiplicity of factors (and a total test battery).[9]

5. The fact that there is no pure cognitive act or state, nor a pure emotional one, should make us more cautious in separating "intelligence tests" from "personality tests" or other kinds of tests, or separating cognition from affect. Though from a practical viewpoint it is at times necessary to focus individually on these closely inter-

---

[8] Broadened considerably by recent modern ego psychology.

[9] This may, indeed, seem most obvious, even naive. However, psychological reports we review (from clinics and schools) seem frequently to underestimate or neglect these factors.

related functions, we should do this perhaps with greater awareness of the arbitrariness involved.

6. Since, according to Piaget's theory, personality emerges rather late in life (during later adolescence),[10] it would seem hazardous to consider a Rorschach protocol as a valid measure of the so-called "total personality," especially in the case of children. The child's personality is in a constant flux of on-going construction of inner and outer reality. We get only a sampling of some aspects of a child's personality, and this, too, depends on the particular conditions of the evaluation.

7. Piaget's theory revives the need for looking more closely at the child and his environment, instead of almost exclusively at the parents, in order to understand his particular behavior and especially his learning difficulties.

8. Since the rate and the level of mental development depend on multiple factors, but particularly on the aliment received, it would seem important to get a clear idea of the type and amount of "nourishment" (in its broadest sense) that the child received before attempting to explain his present status or to predict his future rate of development.[11]

9. Piaget's genetic viewpoint and periods include very broad concepts regarding the determinants of children's behavior. They include cognitive, perceptual, and affective factors, all interrelated, but do not limit themselves to a specific area only. The broadness of Piaget's hierarchical organization seems to make it easier to gain an appropriate and more objective perspective when viewing a child at a given time in his life. We consider Piaget's theory a very helpful genetic model.

10. Piaget's clinical method[12] is ideal for application to the Rorschach method (including testing the limits) and can be used

---

10 See section on emotional-social development.

11 This would seem of particular importance in the case of children evaluated psychologically at school, often, unfortunately, without the precaution of adequate background information.

12 See section on Practical Application.

much more effectively if considered in the framework of the multiplicity of factors and Piaget's hierarchical organization.

11. His theory provides a clear explanation of the gradual detachment of early stimulus dependency (Wolff, 1960, p. 170) and the subsequent construction of autonomy.[13] This seems directly applicable to the Rorschach test and the complex processes involved, especially as regards the complex interplay between perceptual and operational processes.

12. Piaget's ideas on the origin and development of need and interests encourages looking at a Rorschach record first from the viewpoint of healthy, normal ego production, before resorting to more complex, perhaps far-fetched, symbolic explanations involving deeply unconscious material.

13. Piaget's ideas of "reaction schemata" may, in the near future, provide a relatively simple explanation of behavior, which might otherwise be overlooked. It may at times replace a not necessarily justified symbolic explanation that emphasizes psychopathology perhaps more than need be. We feel that the concept of "reaction schemata" is likely to prove most useful and should be studied further experimentally.

14. "Regressive phenomena" may be pathological, indeed, but may also occur in the "service of the ego"—a healthy way of dealing with too complicated situations (for instance, from the cognitive viewpoint). It may be too difficult for a child to deal successfully with a particular question or ink blot, and his response of "I don't know," or "Nothing," may, indeed, be just that, and not necessarily or invariably (though in some cases possibly) indicative of negativism or serious defenses related to upsetting traumatic experiences.

15. Piaget's theory, in general, might add an element of caution in regard to overly subjective interpretations of Rorschach protocols, especially when dealing with children.

---

[13] See Hedda Bolgar's excellent and concise discussion of problems of autonomy (Bolgar, 1964).

Piaget's Developmental Theory

We feel that some aspects of Piaget's developmental theory can be viewed as a progressive spiral, forming essentially four interrelated, major periods, with several stages and substages. During the first period (birth to 2 years)[14] simple hereditary reflexes lead to simple habits, which are formed into circular reactions (defined as the child's tendency to reproduce an interesting result). Repetitive behavior implies pleasure in performance itself and a form of persistence. Simple motor units are thus formed, which are called "schema" or "schemata." Things, objects, and people are not considered as entities in themselves but only as functional elements. The ability to recognize a familiar object develops gradually; some identification and generalization become possible. Sensorimotor units introduce a certain permanence into the universe of the baby, the basis for all future operational constructions. Things, feelings, and experiences are assimilated to schemata of action. Those schemata become coordinated into larger, more complex, and more mobile action systems (which will be discussed a little further). These systems, in turn, become internalized as images and then, in turn, be-

---

[14] Although Piaget speaks of periods and age levels, we should stress that he has not been particularly interested in determining statistically very precise, exact age norms. The ages he mentions in his work (ages at which new periods begin, for instance) are to be taken as approximate and with the understanding that there is a certain amount of brief overlapping between two successive periods, but without prolonged lingering of former, earlier periods (as one finds, for instance, in psychoanalytic concepts of child development). We mention this since there has been a tendency, especially on the part of the statistically oriented experimentalist, to misinterpret Piaget's use of age norms or criticize him rather severely for not being more exact in this respect. What is much more important to Piaget than the actual age norms (and what has been well understood by scientists like Oppenheimer[15]) is the method —the descriptive approach leading to the discovery of a succession of qualitative changes in the child's thinking, a succession that Piaget considers irreversible. His findings have had the merit of stirring up immense curiosity and intensive research in various centers.

[15] J. Robert Oppenheimer, "Analogy in Science," address, Sixty-third Annual Convention of the American Psychological Association, San Francisco, quoted in *Developments in the Rorschach Technique,* Vol. II, p. x, Foreword.

come coordinated as intuitions during the preoperational (second) period (2 to 6 years). These particular intuitions (a form of practical intelligence, based on perceptual qualities) are gradually decentered during the third period (7 to 12 years, approximately) and are grouped into reversible and associative, concrete operations with concrete objects and materials. Finally, during the fourth period (12 years to adolescence) these units evolve further and are regrouped into the formal operations of adolescence and, eventually, adulthood.

Piaget demonstrates the continuity beween intelligence and purely biological processes and emphasizes that intelligence exhibits the same functions as all other biological processes of which it is a part. Verbal logical intelligence rests on practical or sensorimotor intelligence, supported by acquired and recombined habits based, in turn, on a system of reflexes in the anatomic and morphological structure of the organism.

Reflex schemata are automatic but require external stimulation and are modified as a result of exercise and experience. The stimulation provided by the environment may be conceptualized as the indispensable aliment for the exercise of the reflex, thus providing opportunity for learning. Schemata, at a more advanced level, need aliments, too, in order to maintain themselves. Stimulation and exercise of the schemata are essential for their maintenance. Aliment is found in the constant interaction between the organism and its environment (in a broad sense). The organism, in its perpetual interaction, tries to maintain an equilibrium with its environment and within itself. There is a perpetual adaptation on the part of the organism to a perpetually changing environment. Two complementary essential processes, assimilation and accommodation, assist the organism in this process of adaptation. Certain aspects of the environment are assimilated ("digested") to existing structures; and certain modifications (accommodations) may occur in the schemata themselves, namely, new forms and structures, new "inventions." New, increasingly more flexible and stable structures are thus created and permit progress on the developmental spiral. Action plays a significant part (as we shall discuss in more detail), especially at first, in the infant's direct contact with his reality, the world of objects, people, parts of his body, etc. Physical action, however, gradually changes from the very overt type to a less overt, less physical, more perceptual, and, eventually, more internalized type, namely thought. Eventually it results in planned, anticipated, rational thinking, depending essentially on thinking activity, rather than sensorimotor performance. Cognition, at all genetic levels, is a matter of real actions performed by the individual.

Motor action, and the subject's activity in general, are directly related to a need to function. Cognitive organs or structures, once generated by functioning, have an intrinsic need to perpetuate themselves by further functioning. Both biological and psychological organs are created through functioning and, once created, must continue to function. All action—be it motoric, thought, or feeling—represents a response to a need, which in itself is a manifestation of a disequilibration. However, this functional mechanism does not explain the content of the need, which is related to the organization of that particular period or stage. Piaget reminds us that the interest of the child depends on his acquired ideas and emotional inclinations.[16]

Needs incorporate things (and people) into the subject's own activity and thus attempt to assimilate the external world into the structures that already have been constructed. These structures, in turn, have to be readjusted and transformed, due to the pressures exerted by the environment. Piaget refers to this as a process of accommodation, and it manifests itself through all the periods. The mind thus attempts to incorporate the universe to itself. However, the modes of incorporation vary, and evolve from simple percepts and movements to the most advanced mental operations. Only those percepts and ideas can be incorporated by the child which he is ready to assimilate and accommodate to. It is therefore not surprising that, for example, human responses appear rather late[17] in the

---

16 For further discussion of these needs see Piaget (1967), Chapter I, "Mental Development of the Child," and Piaget (1962).

17 Ames et al. (1952), pp. 286–287.

hierarchy of Rorschach responses given by children. In order to perceive human figures in these ink blots (which do not claim to be particularly human-like), a certain amount of abstraction and conceptualization is probably required, and with it an ability to situate one's own person and body as one among many other objects in the outer world.[18] To conceptualize human beings in a rather abstract manner is probably a very complex process and, we suspect, requires fairly advanced intellectual organization. The balancing of these two processes, assimilation and accommodation, is referred to as "adaptation," adaptation in the sense of an on-going process, not a fixed state.

Logical, abstract operations derive from actions, from the coordination of actions, and not from objects themselves. Operations are more than just internalized actions. These actions must, first of all, meet certain requirements (for instance, be reversible and be capable of being coordinated into integrated structures, referred to as "grouping" or "group").

Structures are elaborated, step by step, and change in response to environmental intrusion. Cognitive structures need not be explained on the basis of "drive theory." They are self-activating; they derive from and are sustained by the "need to function" principle. What applies to cognitive structures seems applicable (to Piaget) also to personality and the self, both of which are governed by the same law of organization. No structure is completely innate or acquired, but a combination of both.

Structures, in Piaget's terms, are reversible systems with specific laws that are different from the laws of totality as described by the Gestalt theory. Specific structures characterize each stage or period of development. The variable structures represent the organizational forms of mental activity. Structures, like logico-mathematical structures, are not innate, but are acquired little by little. They all suppose a construction, an active interaction between the organism and the environment; genesis and structure, therefore, are indissoluble. In contrast, for instance, the concept of Gestalt is seen (by

---

[18] See, also, our discussion of *M* in relation to Mental Images, p. 138.

Piaget) as a predominantly irreversible system. Piaget's observations of children have led him to conclude that genesis emanates from a structure and culminates in another structure. All structures actually can be traced back to more elementary structures, none of which has an absolute beginning itself, but a more primitive structure at its base, also. For the time being, the research psychologist has to stop at birth, at the sensorimotor level, since previous to that he would be dealing with the neurological structures and predominantly biological problems, which also, of course, have a genesis.

Experiences are not just passively recorded by the child but, on the contrary, are very actively integrated into the various schema at their respective levels of development. Maturation is made possible through the organism's fundamental tendency to organize and integrate all experiences which can be assimilated. New experiences can be introduced into this organization so as to alter behavior and permit learning.

What occurred and was achieved at the sensorimotor level has to be relearned and conquered at the verbal level in a concrete-practical form, and again, later on, in a more formal abstract-logical manner at a higher level. Thinking, during these periods, has shifted from being extremely self-centered and perception-dominated to becoming increasingly flexible, reality-oriented, and independent of outward perceptual aspects. This shift may partially explain the change we find, for example, in children's responses involving color, like the change from impulsive, crude color responses [19] (which do not necessarily imply psychopathology in young children, as they might in older ones or adults) to beginning combinations of color and shape (*CF*), and eventually shape and color (*FC*), with ultimately an appropriate mixture of both in better organized, better controlled, and better integrated total responses.

Thanks to the emergence of intelligence, its socialized aspects in particular (for instance, being now less egocentric), what has been gathered by experience can be restructured and reintegrated, to create a more objective and much more stable universe in which many physical qualities have now acquired permanence.

---

19 Ames et al. (1952), p. 286.

Another concept which we feel needs to be discussed at some length here is Piaget's concept of equilibrium. The organism, in its evolution, passes through periods of variable unstable equilibrium, described by Piaget in great detail. Piaget compares its development with a continuous construction of a vast building that becomes more solid with each addition (Piaget, 1967, p. 4). He also compares it with the assembly of a subtle mechanism that goes through gradual phases of adjustment, in which the individual pieces become more supple and mobile as the equilibrium of the mechanism as a whole becomes more stable. Variable structures define the successive states of equilibrium, but a certain constant functioning assures the transition from any one state to the following one. The variable structures (motor, intellectual, affective) are the organized forms of mental activity. They are organized along two dimensions: intrapersonal and interpersonal (social). Each stage or period represents a particular form of equilibrium as a function of its characteristic structure. Equilibrium at any age may be disrupted by change in the external or internal world. Behavior consists, then, in making the necessary adjustments to reestablish an adequate equilibrium and moving gradually toward a more stable equilibrium than the previous one. Human activity thus consists of a perpetual readjustment of a perpetually disrupted equilibrium. This functional mechanism, however, does not explain the content or structure of the various needs, which are related to the organization of the particular stage that is being considered. As Piaget puts it,

> "The interest of a child at any given moment depend on the system of ideas he has acquired, plus his affective inclinations, and he tends to fulfill his interests in the direction of greater equilibrium" (Piaget, 1967, p. 7).

At each level the mind performs the same function, namely, to incorporate the universe within itself. However, the nature of this assimilation varies (perception, movements, reasoning, etc.). This eventually results in an increasingly more precise adaptation to reality. Some aspects of this progressive adaptation to reality can be observed in several ways in the Rorschach protocol of children as they grow older. We notice, for example, an increase in productivity (number of *R*); improved form level (especially a change from *F*— in the very young child at the prelogical level to *F*+ and original, creative responses); emergence of movement responses shifting from inanimate animal responses to animals in action and eventually clearly perceived humans also in action; greater awareness of feelings and incorporation of them in some of the responses (for example, *Fc* or *c* quality); incorporation of color into meaningful concepts.

Of course, no single aspect mentioned above represents, in itself, a valid or efficient measure of reality adaptation but may be of help when considered in relation to other items listed previously and, of course, in relation to the child's age. Minus form-level responses in young children, for example, would be considered as an immature but age-appropriate and nonpathological adaptation to reality. The Rorschach test may, at times, be of help also in evaluating some aspects of reality adaptation when dealing with intellectually very precocious children who, for various reasons, do not seem particularly precocious (or may, in fact, seem quite immature) in regard to their social-emotional behavior.

Piaget goes to some length in describing the characteristics of an equilibrium.[20] He mentions, first of all, stability (not to be confused with immobility) and shows how an equilibrium can be both stable and mobile. Secondly, an equilibrium is subject to external intrusion, which tends to modify it. An equilibrium is reached when such an intrusion is compensated by action of the subject. A third characteristic is that an equilibrium is something very active, not passive at all, and has to be prepared to deal with intrusions of many sorts.

The Concept of Equilibrium during the Intuitive Period (2 to 7 Years, Approximately)

This period is based on sensorimotor intelligence, but the child is not yet able to verbalize his thoughts, being still involved essen-

---

20 Analogous to Cannon's theory of homeostasis, we believe.

tially in actions and manipulations. His thinking is predominantly prelogical. In place of logic the child substitutes so-called "intuitions," characterized by internalization of percepts and movements in the form of representation of images. The child's thinking is dominated by the perceptual aspects of objects considered. These elementary intuitions are action or perception schemata, transposed and internalized as representations. They are not yet logical operations that can be generalized and combined one with the other.

These primary intuitions represent a rather rigid type of equilibrium. They tend gradually, however, toward a more articulated form which can anticipate the consequence of action and reconstitute previous states. This articulated intuition is still irreversible, however, but it is capable of attaining a more stable and mobile level of equilibrium than sensorimotor actions alone. As Piaget describes it (1967, p. 33):

> Compared to logic, intuition is a less stable equilibrium because of its lack of reversibility; but compared to preverbal acts, it marks a definite advance in equilibrium.

The Period of Concrete Operations (7 to 12 Years)

An operation is an internalized and reversible action; its origin is perceptual, intuitive, and motoric. Intuitions become transformed into operations as soon as they constitute groupings, which obey certain specific laws that Piaget has analyzed thoroughly and described in great detail. In such groupings all of the elements are interdependent and in equilibrium. Reversibility has been attained by the child by this time and permits achievement of a much more stable, more permanent equilibrium between the assimilatory activities and accommodations to schema.

Adolescence (From 12 Years On)

Transition from one stage to another brings about oscillations in the established equilibrium. Adolescent thought is characterized by the ability to construct theories and by interest in systems.[21] Thinking becomes more oriented toward the formal, abstract aspects, such as formulation of hypotheses. The logic of propositions replaces the logic of relations, classes, and numbers and permits a certain detachment from concrete reality, sometimes to the point of believing wholeheartedly in the omnipotence of reasoning and idealism. Piaget describes this as the metaphysical age *par excellence*. A certain adjustment is necessary to reconcile formal thought and reality, and thus a new equilibrium is created: the adolescent learns that the major role of reasoning is to interpret and predict, rather than to contradict and negate.

An equilibrium or equilibrated system is never static but always mobile, open. Each newly achieved equilibrium prepares for the next disequilibrium. Newly acquired concepts permit acquisition of new forms of information, etc. Each cognitive structure has its own dynamic aspects, so that once a structure has been achieved it becomes essential to utilize it and thus satisfy it through exercise. The "function-pleasure" seems to be Piaget's major formulation for his explanation of motivation.

Any equilibrium may be temporarily disrupted by external or internal factors. Adjustments take place, in the form of reestablishing a perpetually disrupted equilibrium. This disruption of equilibrium can be observed in actual process during Rorschach administration. It may manifest itself in prolonged response time, in "shocks" of various types, expressed verbally or through other outward physical manifestations, in disorganization of the blot material presented or inability to cope with it at all (blockage, refusals), in marked changes in form level, in overt anxiety or even panic, or, more subtly, in the form of various denials. The individual's adjustment to such a disruption gives us useful clues regarding his resourcefulness and his ability to deal with various aspects of inner and/or outer reality. It provides an opportunity to observe his recoverability in relation to a specific blot, or from one blot to the next, or from achromatic to chromatic cards or vice versa. This

21 At least in the case of the European, especially Swiss, children studied by Piaget.

steady progress toward an increasingly flexible and therefore more stable equilibrium also represents what Piaget considers the most profound tendency in all human activity.

Since both *perceptual and intellectual phenomena* play an important role in Rorschach responses, we would like to briefly present some of Piaget's observations and conclusions. For him, perception constitutes a special case of sensorimotor activities. Their development is interdependent, and each enhances the other.

Piaget distinguishes two kinds of visual perception:

1. Effect of the field or centration, which does not suppose any eye movement; the figure is visible upon one centration alone.
2. Perceptual activities, which suppose some eye movement and depend upon an active search on the part of the subject.

Perceptual activities develop gradually with age, reaching their asymptote at approximately 9 years. Perceptual activities, in general, render perceptions more adequate, correcting illusions and systematic distortions that are part of the "field effect."

An immediate perception is the product of a probabilistic sampling. In viewing a configuration, even a very simple one, one does not see all positions of it with the same precision or the entire figure at once. The systematic distortion (or illusion) remains the same at all ages but diminishes in intensity with age, being gradually corrected by perceptual activities.

The lack of active perceptual exploration in children under 7 explains their syncretic or global views, as described by Claparède (1951) and Decroly (see Claparède, 1951, p. 523). Young children tend to perceive objects essentially globally, without analysis of the parts or synthesis of their relationships. Piaget explains some of the results obtained by Dworetzki (1939), namely, the lack of differentiation of *W*'s, as based on a lack of exploratory systematic activity on the part of the child. Piaget does not feel that in such cases the laws of perception, as developed by the Gestalt theory, are applicable or explain these phenomena.

Perceptual activities continue to develop with increasing age, until they can accept modifications suggested by the intellectual processes that are becoming increasingly more operational (Piaget and Inhelder, 1966b). The restructuring of percepts by means of mental operations could explain the changes in *W* organization, their increasingly better form level and greater flexibility, which permits incorporation of more details into more clearly perceived, better integrated, and more meaningful *W*'s. Of course, affective motivations are present, as they are in all cognitive activities.[22]

Perceptual constancy appears early in life; constancy in one dimension (distance, rotation, form, etc.) seems present from birth (Bower, 1966). Various mechanisms of perceptual compensation can be observed between 6 and 12 months. However, operational constancies (substance, weight, volume, etc.), which involve relationships of parameters, are achieved only much later, from approximately 7 to 8 years on. The reasons for this, Piaget feels, are quite simple. In the case of perceptual constancy, the object is not modified in reality at all, but only in its appearance and only from the subject's own viewpoint. It is not necessary in this case to use logical operations in order to correct outward appearances. A so-called "perceptual regulation" is sufficient for that purpose.

In the case of the conservation (of substance, weight, etc.), the object is actually modified by the subject. Compensations have to be constructed in order to modify outward appearances (i.e., little pieces of clay mentally put together again to make the same quantity; or an elongated shape mentally changed back into a ball). Perceptual structures as such seem essentially irreversible at that stage: they are still present to some extent during activities such as perceptual comparisons and gradually change to increasingly more reversible processes, thanks to the impact of intellectual operations.

In his genetic study of perception, and especially in exploring "illusions," Piaget (1961) has found that these develop in at least three different ways: some remain relatively constant or diminish with age; others increase in importance with age; some increase up to a certain age (9 to 11 years, for instance, as we found in our own

---

22 To be discussed later. See section on emotional-social development.

research) [23] and diminish shortly after that. Piaget, in viewing these results with many other research findings, concluded that the space of the small child is less structured along horizontal and vertical coordinates than that of the adult because of a difference in the system of reference. With increasing age, there is a steadily broadening and more far-reaching frame of reference.

Piaget (1961), in his extensive experimental studies of perceptual mechanisms, found that operational structures of intelligence differ qualitatively from initial perceptual structures. Both constitute forms of equilibrium, totalities that have their own laws. It is unsatisfactory to try to explain both types of totalities by the laws developed by Gestalt theory. Many characteristics have been found by the Gestaltists, but what then became a series of enumerations and descriptions was mistaken for an explanation of the subordination of parts to the whole. It led to the mistaken conclusion that both intelligence and perception had the same structure, mostly because the characteristics ascribed to perception often also applied to intelligence.

Piaget's theory, on the contrary, is based on a continuous construction, beginning with the relationship between elements and units themselves. Perceptual activity leads to more advanced structures, as well as to new links between elements so far unrelated. Sometimes, by means of this activity and new centration, additional errors are created. This exploration leads to both synthesizing and analyzing processes. It is impossible to perceive the object in its totality (Piaget, 1961) for reasons that Piaget explains in great detail. A constructive process takes place to correct certain errors created by immediate and incomplete perception. This corrective method leads eventually to more objective perceptions (Piaget, 1961, p. 452). All centration is always part of the context of eye movements and always subordinated to an activity.

Speaking of constancy in the area of perception, Piaget states that the constancies of length are not explainable on the basis of inborn,

---

[23] Research undertaken at Prof. Piaget's suggestion and published as doctoral dissertation in *Archives de Psychologie;* see Würsten (1946).

ready-made mechanisms (though a certain amount of innateness cannot be excluded, of course), nor is this due to an automatic equilibrium of the physiological type. These constancies are the result of precocious perceptual activities, involving various compensatory mechanisms, which he explains in detail (Piaget, 1961, p. 297).

Differences between Perception and Intelligence

Perception is much more egocentric than intelligence, and very individualistic. Intelligence, on the contrary, attempts to achieve knowledge that is not exclusively dependent on the individual himself or valid for him alone. Perception is much more object-bound. In the area of perception, form and content are indissolubly linked. This is not necessarily the case in the field of intelligence (Piaget, 1961, p. 359). Intelligence becomes capable of generalization and abstraction. We can observe this in the Rorschach process, also. Young children appear to respond somewhat haphazardly to blot stimulation, on the basis of a vague resemblance of the blot or a particular aspect of it to a certain object. There is usually very little if any justification given for the answer. Things are seen in a certain way "because" (the child often cannot explain further). A little later, the child explains his interpretation or choice more clearly or defends it more strongly. He sees a butterfly, because it *is* a butterfly. Children below school age can be quite rigid and adamant about their answers, which appear rigidly perception-dominated. A few years later, a much more active comparison takes place, a sort of mental restructuring and a comparison with mental images of things as they are or as they are remembered. Intellectual processes take an active part in this restructuring of the perceived phenomena. "Good form," in the sense used by Klopfer, for example, manifests itself in increasingly better structured and organized responses, leading to higher form levels.

The term "good form" applies to both perception and intelligence, but in different ways. A good form, in relation to intellectual activities, imposes itself as a logical necessity, constitutes an obligation similar to moral obligation, as long as the individual reasons honestly, Piaget feels. By "honest reasoning" he means that the individual is willing to consider all the elements involved. Perceptual schemata differ from intellectual schemata, principally in that the latter are much more reversible. Perception depends constantly on the irreversible flux of exterior events and cannot go back in time. Each perception is modified by the preceding one. One can, of course, return to former perceptions, but in that case we are not dealing with the same phenomena any more, but rather with perceptual comparisons and mental operations of various types.

Partial isomorphism between perception and intelligence is meaningful only if considered from the genetic viewpoint (Piaget, 1961, p. 365). Perceptual activities introduce gradually an increasingly greater number of mobile relationships. On the other hand, the child's thinking remains, for a while, quite rigid and perception-dominated. It manifests itself in the Rorschach quite often by a tendency to perseverate, as found especially in young children and, of course, in children affected by certain forms of cerebral pathology, severe personality disorders (psychosis, for example), and mental retardation. The whole history of cognitive development is indicative of a gradual liberation of these rigid forms. It is a slow and laborious process.

The forms of intellectual operations do not derive from perception but, on the contrary, influence perceptual activities, perceptual comparisons. We perceive better what we can structure and restructure.

Perceptual relationships are rather distorting, while logical relationships are much more conserving. According to Piaget's interactionistic theory, there is a continuity from sensorimotor regulations to reversible operations, but the progress of perceptual regulations in the direction of semireversibility (Piaget, 1961, p. 384) is to be understood as a series of repercussions, rather than as a causal condition of the genetic series leading from action to operations.

Piaget maintains that there is an autonomous development of intelligence, beginning with sensorimotor activities, with continued enrichment of the perceptual structures, thanks to this development (Piaget, 1961, p. 386). Perception and perceptual activities are restructured by the emerging operations, not vice versa. A perceptual equilibrium is a concept involving active compensation on the part of the subject.

Perceptual schemata are elaborated, thanks to the perceptual activities of various forms and levels. These perceptual activities develop only partially in an autonomous manner, being motivated by the need for actions (sensorimotor schemata, operational schemata, etc.).

Intelligence, defined by Piaget (1962a) as a progressive formation of operational structures and the coordination of these operations, does not proceed from perception by simple extension of it. Perceptions do not constitute the source of our knowledge but assume the role of maintaining contact between operations or actions on the one hand and objects and events on the other. In order to construct reality, an extensive restructuring of experience is needed, combined with deductive operations that consist of interiorized and coordinated actions. Eventually, logico-mathematical knowledge broadens our reality by including it in the realm of all possibilities (Piaget, 1961, p. 444).

Piaget opposes the theory of "geneticism without structure" proposed by the empiricists and also the "structuralization without genesis" of the Gestaltists. He proposes, instead, a genetic structuralization in the sense that each structure be considered the product of a genetic phenomena and each genesis constitute the passage of a less evolved structure to a more complex one.

Mental Images

Mental images make their appearance with the onset of the semiotic function (a term more frequently used by Piaget now than the former "symbolic function") after the sensorimotor period. They result from an internalized imitation. Mental images at the preoperational level (until 7 to 8 years, approximately) differ from those of the level of mental operations. Piaget distinguishes two kinds: *Reproductive images,* which evoke already known, familiar, previously perceived phenomena; and *anticipatory images,* in which the child is able to imagine movements or transformations, as well as the results, without, however, having previously been part of this realization.

Mental images may deal with static configurations, movements, or transformations. If mental images were derived exclusively from perception, one would expect to find such reproductive images at all ages. Research, however, indicates that this is not so.

At the preoperational level, the child's mental images are almost exclusively static, and it is only at the operational level (after 7 or 8 years of age) that children succeed in reproducing movements by mental images. This could explain, at least to some extent, why animal movement responses appear rarely in very young children and only after a certain *MA* has been reached. It would partially also explain the rather late appearance of the more complex *M* response. Piaget explains that the mental image in itself is not sufficient for the development of operational structures. Later on, around 7 to 8 years of age, the image becomes anticipatory. This is not the result of an inner modification or of autonomy for mental images, but the result of other factors related to the formation of operations themselves. These operations derive directly from actions, not from the symbolism associated with mental images.

Anticipatory images are formed only through the help of operations. They are also indispensable for the reconstitution at the representational level of movements and transformations already known to the subject. A logico-mathematical framework seems necessary, not only for the interpretation of what is given in perception, but also for what is being evoked by the image. Conservations of various types suppose a system of quantitative compensations of which the image is incapable. The logico-mathematical frame of reference, once constituted, imposes itself upon the image and permits objective anticipations. It is thus a very important part of the construction of reality, involving a constant restructuring of the data provided by perception, which in themselves do not constitute true knowledge.

It is the function of the concept, not of images, to interpret and help comprehend. However, in order to evoke by thought what has been perceived, both verbal signs and symbolic imagery is needed. One cannot think without semiotic instruments (Piaget and Inhelder, 1966a). Language alone is insufficient. Images are thus symbols, since they constitute the necessary semiotic instruments in order to evoke and bring back what has been perceived (*ibid.*, p. 448).

The semiotic function emerges during the second year of childhood and is used primarily in evoking an absent object or past event. Piaget distinguishes several types, of which mental images and language seem to us to be the most important in the present essay. Mental images seem to be primarily an internalized imitation, which eventually becomes thought. Piaget (1967) states,

> "The image is neither an element of thought itself nor a direct continuity of perception. It is a symbol of the object, which is not yet manifested at the level of sensorimotor intelligence" [p. 90].

Semiotic function permits the development of two kinds of instruments: (1) symbols, and (2) signs (arbitrary or conventional).

The young child, who is presented by the outside adult world with a ready-made language that he himself has not invented, cannot use this instrument of expression and communication until much later. Meanwhile, he needs some means of expression, namely, a system of signifiers, constructed by him and based on his own needs. Symbolic play expresses some of this. It represents a symbolism centered on the self.[24] This symbolism deals with the multiple interests and needs of the child, conscious and unconscious conflicts, certain defenses against anxiety, etc.

---

24 Piaget does not use the term "egocentric" any more, because of the many misunderstandings it apparently caused, as explained by him in the *Six Psychological Studies* (1967, p. 49).

Distortions of reality that occur with mental images are not of the same order as those that are occasioned by illusions. As far as the genetic succession is concerned, images are third in order, being preceded by perceptions and imitations. The structural aspects of images appear to be related much more closely to imitations than perceptions.

Structure of Memory

In their most recent book, Piaget and Inhelder (1966b, pp. 63–66) discuss the progressive organization of memory in relation to age changes.[25] They consider primarily two aspects of memory: memory of recognition and memory of recall. Memory of recognition appears very early in human and animal life, even in inferior vertebrates.[26] Memory recall, however, does not appear before the capacity for mental images has developed. Memories of this type are dominated by the schema corresponding to the particular mental level of the child at that time. The memory-image then relates more to the particular schema, which conserves itself by means of its own functioning, than to the perceptual model. The image, which intervenes in the memory-image, seems to constitute an internalized imitation, which also involves a motor element. Piaget stresses the importance of motor elements and operations at all levels of memory functions.[27]

Piaget and Inhelder mention several of the many different theories proposed to explain the conservation of memories: Freud postulated that memories accumulate in the unconscious and either remain forgotten or are subject to recall under certain specific situations; Penfield has described the neurological aspects of memory storage.[28] It has been found, however, that although some memories

---

25 A major study of memory is in preparation by Piaget.

26 Also in some invertebrates, such as planaria.

27 Confirmed also by Luria.

28 Confirmed by Ray John.

are quite vivid, they may at times be actually quite faulty. This suggests a certain element of reconstitution and with it, of course, certain distortions.

Emotional-Social Development

Piaget has been criticized for giving little consideration to the role of emotions and values in the child's development. This, we feel, is a misconception and needs some correction. It is true that Piaget has focused experimentally primarily on the child's cognitive development, which now is frequently referred to as the "conflict-free ego sphere." He has not studied the affective development experimentally, but he has expressed his views in detail regarding the emotional-social aspects of the child's development (Piaget, 1962a, p. 135; 1967, pp. 3–64; 1943, vol. I. Unfortunately, his views have remained little known to the English-speaking public, mostly because they were not translated until very recently. Piaget tells us that all behavior supposes tools and techniques, namely, movements and intelligence. All behavior also supposes motives, values, and feelings. Affectivity is the energetic force of behavior, whereas structures define cognitive functioning. Both are indissolubly united in the functioning of the personality. Affectivity provides values and energy, but intelligence provides means and helps clarify goals. The source of all motivation is the inherent tendency of any schema to establish and maintain an equilibrium between assimilation of an aliment and accommodation to it. Global schemata differentiate when exposed to experience. These differentiated schemata integrate because of the organism's tendency to maintain a stable mental organization. The stability of the organism depends on how well the parts have established an equilibrium with each other and have been integrated into a whole. Piaget is not simply a developmentalist, but much more an interactionist.[29] The increased stability, flexibility, and integration of schemata with age seems to be an impor-

[29] Piaget's major interest has actually been in the field of epistemology.

tant aspect of mental development that tends toward an increasingly more stable equilibrium. This may manifest itself in the Rorschach protocol in the level of organization of a response, or in the actual, and at times directly observable, processes involved. The looser the organization of a response, the more tenuous the ties with reality are likely to be and the more fragile the tentative equilibrium reached. The looseness of such responses may not always be evident at first sight, and may actually be masked by quite adequate exterior appearances. It may come to the fore, however, during a more probing exploration, as in a carefully conducted inquiry or in testing the limits. The importance of such clinical exploration is, of course, self-evident.

The extreme looseness and bizarreness of some responses—leading, for example, to a diagnostic impression of possible psychotic disorder—may to some extent be explained on the basis of such defective ego functions as seriously impaired organization and integration of schemata with each other and within themselves. Such responses have to be viewed also as a function of the child's age, of course, and at times may reflect more the chronological immaturity than really serious ego impairment or personality disorganization.

Piaget's observations [supported very recently by Décarie's experiments (Décarie, 1965)] have led him to the conviction that there is a significant parallelism between the development of affectivity and intellectual functions. They represent two indissociable aspects of every action and state, but neither can explain the other. There is never a truly completely intellectual action nor a purely affective act or state. Affect plays an essential role in the functioning of intelligence. It can explain the rate of structure formation but not the cause of it.[30]

By 2 years of age the child has developed elementary feelings

---

[30] In a recent verbal communication to us, Prof. Piaget expressed some concern at the hastiness with which theories emerge and practical application takes place in regard to the affective life of the child without proper experimental controls. Such control studies, in the fields of psychology, psychophysiology, and neurology, seem especially necessary, since so little is presently known that can really be based on fundamental, sound experimental research.

(what is agreeable, disagreeable; pleasure, pain; success, failure); he is capable of joy and sadness, though still quite self-centered. He has preferences among people he knows and shows a beginning of like and dislike for people. It represents an elementary affective organization and the first affective fixations.

During the period of intuitive intelligence, interpersonal emotions develop, associated with socialization of action. Intuitive moral feelings emerge as a result of the child–parent relationship. A regulation of interests and values takes place, interests being the prolongation of a need. Interest (as a motivation) is a regulator of energy.[31] Interest also implies a system of values. Closely related are feelings of inferiority and superiority. The individual is gradually led to evaluate himself, and this may have considerable effect on his whole development (failures, real or imaginary; anxieties; etc.).

The active exchange of values leads to spontaneous feelings between one person and another and thus to likes and dislikes. A feeling of respect develops for people considered superiors. Respect represents a combination of fear and affection. The first moral feelings seem to originate here. Rules develop regarding acceptable and unacceptable behavior, especially in games. Moral feelings at that level are essentially heteronomous, subject to the external will of the respected adult but not generalized as yet. Respect is unilateral at that level, rather than reciprocal. A "moral realism" emerges gradually, in which obligations and values are determined by the rules of the game itself or the requests made, and this later will be modified and changed into a "moral relativism."

In order to explain how infantile feelings influence later affective development, Piaget invokes schemata of reaction (Piaget, 1962a, p. 135). These schemata are similar to the sensorimotor schemata but more complicated in nature. Permanence of such schemata explains the permanence of feelings, without having to resort to unconscious representations.

During the next period, that of practical intelligence (7 to 12 years), much progress in social behavior takes place. Instead of impulsive behavior, the child is now more capable of thinking, of

---

[31] Piaget refers here to Claparède, in his *Six Psychological Studies* (1967, p. 36).

internal deliberation before acting. He succeeds in gradually shedding his social and intellectual egocentricity. A morality of cooperation and reciprocity develops, as the child becomes more capable of understanding others and their viewpoints. As mental operations facilitate logical coordination, so does the will assist in the field of affectivity as a regulator of affective life. Mutual respect now develops, making it possible to submit to the rules of collective games. It is only at this age that the child begins to understand the implications of lying. Feelings of justice emerge. Mutual respect leads to a system of morality based on cooperation and reciprocity, which Piaget considers a higher form of equilibrium than the morals of simple submission.

Affective life is not purely intuitive now, as it was in earlier childhood. As emotions become organized, they emerge as regulators. The final form of emotional equilibrium is the will, which is the true affective equivalent of the formal operation in the cognitive sphere. The will is not energy itself but a regulator of energy and appears when there is a conflict of tendencies or tensions. "Will power involves reinforcing the superior but weaker tendency, so as to make it triumph" (Piaget, 1967, p. 59). Will is an affective regulator that has become reversible and, in this sense, is comparable to an operation. To quote Piaget (1962b),

> The act of will consists here simply in relying upon a decentration, upon something which is exactly analogous to the reversibility of the intellectual operations and which consists in subordinating the actual value, the desire, to a larger scale of value.

In adolescence we observe an ability of the self (which is rather primitive) to willfully submit to some kind of discipline from within and from without. This results in the development of personality.[32]

---

[32] Piaget distinguishes self and personality (1967, pp. 65–70). The self is seen as relatively primitive, like the center of one's own activity, and it is characterized by its conscious or unconscious egocentricity. "Personality, on the other hand, results from the submission, or rather the autosubmission, of the self to some kind of discipline. . . . Personality implies cooperation and personal autonomy. It is opposed, both to anomie, the complete absence of rules, and to complete heteronomy, abject submission to the constraints imposed from without."

Personality implies cooperation and personal autonomy. Personality formation (as Piaget defines it) begins in the middle to late childhood (8 to 12 years) with the development of rules and values, a hierarchy of moral tendencies and ideals. Piaget tells us that these factors all are integrated with the self into a unique system, to which all the separate parts are subordinated. To construct such a system, the ability for formal thought is required. Personality forms as a "life plan" emerges, which in itself also requires hypothetical-deductive thinking. Puberty, although a reality, represents only one aspect of changes that take place in adolescence. The adolescent's asocial behavior is, in a way, misleading. He is actually often meditating about society and wants to reform it.

Affectivity evolves parallel to intellectual processes. It is the incentive for actions that appear at each new period, since it assigns value to activities and distributes energy to them. Piaget states that affectivity, however, is nothing without intelligence. Intelligence furnishes affectivity with its means and clarifies its ends. There is conservation of feelings and affective values (as we find it in cognitive areas) due to moral feelings and the obligations they engender (Piaget, 1967, pp. 69–70). To quote Piaget (1967, pp. 69–70):

> It is erroneous and mythical to attribute the causes of development to great ancestral tendencies, as though activities and biological growth were by nature foreign to reason. In reality, the most profound tendency of all human activity is progression toward equilibrium. Reason, which expresses the highest form of equilibrium, reunites intelligence and affectivity.

Practical Application of Some of Piaget's Specific Concepts

We shall now attempt to draw some practical conclusions concerning the application of some of the concepts previously outlined. We do not anticipate at this point in any way to formulate a new method of Rorschach interpretation based on Piaget's theory—some rather extensive experimental work should precede such an attempt—but we hope to establish some useful guidelines, especially for clinicians working with children.

The Clinical Method

This method, used extensively by Piaget in his own investigations, seems to us the method of choice in exploring mental processes involved in the Rorschach responses. It consists essentially of giving a child considerable freedom in expressing his thoughts, feelings, and attitudes, in letting him experiment freely with the material at hand and, subsequently or whenever needed, conduct the interview or modify the experiment in such a way as to ferret out the basis for his particular statement. It permits exploration of the limits of his reasoning and the factors affecting it, gives him ample opportunity to qualify his responses (without, of course, becoming too directive and influencing his suggestibility), and can lead him subtly to follow a trend of thought a little further, by means of either logical deduction or free association. At times this method is particularly useful in exploring predominantly the flexibility or rigidity of certain concepts from a structural viewpoint, in order to test out just how perception-dominated a particular response seems to be; at other times we might encourage a child, for instance, to develop or expand a percept or an (inferred) action process a little further by inviting him to make a story or at least free associate some. All this supposes a very gentle, interested, friendly, unhurried, very supportive attitude on the part of the examiner, and a very nonthreatening general atmosphere. It represents an extension of our usual inquiry and can be combined well with the frequently used "testing the limits" procedure. It seems especially useful and, we feel, necessary in the case of children, in view of the arbitrariness of their responses and the variability of the meaning of their responses, according to age, for instance. The major merit of this method is to follow the child's production (his thinking, his feelings, etc.) while in action, in being much more interested in the processes involved here than in the final end product. It is sometimes advisable to use such a method to some extent directly after each card, or even each response, especially when dealing with hyperactive, flighty children who tend to forget where they saw certain things and why, what made them think of it, and what they might associate with it.

Cognitive Structures

Significant qualitative changes occur in the child's cognitive development, as clearly demonstrated by Piaget. The truism, based mostly on former developmental theories, that as the child grows older he can do more, is totally insufficient. Piaget explains when, how, and why changes occur in the child's thinking. The principles of adaptation, construction, operation, and equilibrium are all applicable at all levels and permit a comparison on a continuum.

Cognitive structures appearing in the Rorschach protocol can be analyzed from Piaget's viewpoint in terms of his principles of organization, flexibility, type of equilibrium, and level of reversibility. The rigidity of certain perceptual structures, for instance, is evident in children with various types of brain damage and can be studied in the Rorschach protocol from that viewpoint and by means of Piaget's clinical method previously discussed. Also, a similar percept may not have the same meaning or the same basis of origin, depending on the child's age. A "butterfly" may represent a most carefully analyzed, elaborated, and synthesized concept that includes *W* and *D,* a high form level and shading, movement and subtle details. Or "butterfly" may be seen haphazardly on the basis of a small detail or even only the vaguest resemblance. Children will say similar things at different ages, often on an entirely different basis, and we should remain well aware of this. Children's justifications often reveal the true determinant of their statements and the particular cognitive level that the child has reached, as well as affective factors involved here.

Since all structures are not just innate but acquired, and since they have been formed from interaction between the organism and the environment, it would seem essential for the interpreter of the

Rorschach protocol to become familiar with both the child's cognitive structure and his particular environment. Neglect of one or the other is likely to lead to very incomplete or even actually misleading, erroneous conclusions and recommendations.

Equilibrium

Piaget's concept of equilibrium is a dynamic one. In viewing Rorschach ink blots, our total psychological apparatus is involved: A problem is posed, calling for some solution. A stimulus is offered, inviting an adaptation to the disequilibrium that it caused. Children of different ages have different types of equilibrium. The Rorschach process seems to offer a good opportunity to view this adaptation in process. A certain assimilation will take place as the subject tries to fit the rather vague blot into his already acquired cognitive and affective schemata. The easier the blot or perception of the blot fits into such a schema, the less disrupted the equilibrium. The more flexible the equilibrium, the easier the adjustment and probably the easier for the subject to accommodate in as inventive and creative a manner as he can, allowing for differences in the blot (from the actual image the subject has of certain objects or phenomena) without letting it develop into major perceptual confusion, cognitive bewilderment, or emotional upsets. As clinicians, we are in a position to view a system of regulations at work here and very likely we can draw some useful conclusions from this as to the individual's ability to cope with complex new situations. It would seem worthwhile to explore this further experimentally.

Since Piaget states that "the interest of a child at any given moment depends on the system of ideas he has acquired, plus his affective inclinations, and he tends to fulfill his interest in the direction of greater equilibrium," it would seem to us of considerable importance to know something of that child's particular interests and, if possible, the basis for them. The younger the child, the more rigid his equilibrium, Piaget tells us. We need to keep this in mind in viewing a Rorschach protocol. It may well be that in the case of the Rorschach test, very young children of 2 and 3 are not really challenged by the procedure, being perfectly satisfied to say anything to any blot, regardless of any resemblances, in the manner of free association. When a child accepts the challenge, when a search begins in terms of perceptual comparisons with his vast reservoir of mental images, then very likely the disruption of a certain equilibrium is apt to take place. Probably very subtle and complex processes take place in this comparison, depending, of course, on the cognitive level achieved, how general the child's specific concept or image of a certain object (for instance, a butterfly) is, and how egosyntonic it is from all viewpoints, rather than almost exclusively or predominantly from the emotional viewpoint. Certain responses should be viewed in these terms and not interpreted on the basis of their face value alone. What may appear to be a disturbed answer, a bizarre or far-fetched one, may actually be much less so under the particular circumstances and with a particular child. Or, on the other hand, a moderately aggressive-hostile response may represent an unusual admission on the part of a very controlled, reserved, inhibited youngster, and it may be associated with considerable disruption in equilibrium and struggle in recovering from it. A careful use of Piaget's clinical method should prove very helpful in determining the true situation, and in understanding the processes involved.

Perception

Any percept is a result of an activity and should therefore not be viewed as a passive-receptive phenomenon. It involves an active search on the part of the subject. In viewing an ink blot, much more complex activities are involved than simple perception; namely, perceptual comparisons, mental images, and eventually, after a certain age, operations of various types and imagination, with the resulting restructuring of the data provided by perception. The child is subject to illusions and distortions. He proceeds by means of selective centrations to the point of neglecting other aspects. Piaget explains the syncretic and global view of children under 7 years of age as due to a lack of active perceptual exploration. This should be kept in mind as a first possibility in viewing Rorschach protocols of children, instead of trying to explain all formal aspects of the responses in terms of laws of the Gestalt theory. That affective factors play a role, even a very significant one, is fully accepted by Piaget. He stated clearly that affective factors in one way or another are present in all cognitive functions.

As the child becomes more capable of effecting various compensations in comparing ink blots with mental images and concepts he has constructed, he is likely to perceive more accurately, compare with a broader frame of reference, and arrive at more elaborated, more complete and more articulated, better constructed, and less subjective responses. These responses should not then, be viewed as just simple percepts (like the very immediate, uncorrected percepts of a young child in relation to a very briefly exposed stimulus), but rather as the result of a probably quite complex series of different activities.

A careful, skillfully conducted inquiry based on Piaget's clinical method can very likely help determine the degree of rigidity of these perceptual schemata and help determine how perception-bound that particular child really is.

Mental Images

Although Piaget and Inhelder (1966a), in their recent research, have not studied ink blots, their observations and conclusions seem to us to carry some implication for the present essay. The authors declare that the development of mental images, implying the growth of conservation abilities, is a very important part of the construction of reality. Operations are needed to form anticipatory images, which seem especially important in the reconstruction (at the representational level) of movements and transformations already known to the subject. It would seem to us that this evolution may well explain, at least in part, the relatively late arrival of *FM* and especially *M* responses in children and the predominance of *F* responses, even though action schemata have existed for a long time in the child's life, having started in infancy. We understand from their research that mental images differ from one level to another, seeming essentially static at the preoperational level but changing with the onset of mental operations. It is only after 7 or 8 years of age that they become anticipatory. It is also around that age that movement responses, especially human movement responses, make their appearance, though one can detect some of these at times at much earlier ages. It seems very likely to us that only after a certain operational level has been reached can movements of this type be reconstructed. We suspect that, thanks to the child's ability to form operations, the ink blot, or a part of it, can be successfully compared with an increasingly more vast, steadily enriched, refurnished, and restructured reservoir of mental images and memories. This selection and comparison very likely is subject to an interplay of multiple factors, of which perceptual, cognitive, and emotional aspects are essential. The development of anticipatory images of action represents a rather creative reconstruction, since no action is given perceptually or contained or implied in the verbal instruction presented. One might search for this kind of "action schemata" in the Rorschach response by means of the clinical method (without becoming too suggestive or directive, of course), especially when the diagnostic problem requires a careful scrutinizing of the level and quality of cognitive operations achieved in dealing with well-structured tasks and material (for instance, certain reasoning problems), as well as the much less structured situations of the ink-blot type.

We are fully aware of the very speculative nature of the above statements—just one more attempt among a great many others to shed light on the complex nature of *M*—and hope that this will be explored experimentally by others.

Memory

Rorschach responses occur partly in relation to selective memory functions. Piaget and Inhelder (1966b) inform us that the memory image relates more to the particular schema than to the perceptual model. This suggests to us that what children remember or cannot recall, in relation to the Rorschach test, should not be interpreted exclusively or even predominantly from a symbolic viewpoint or as representing primarily a manifestation of a defense mechanism. It may be, to a large extent, related to the child's mental and operational level achieved at that time and also the cultural background, the aliment to which he has been exposed.

Emotional-Social Aspects

Piaget's statement that affectivity and intelligence evolve parallel to each other and are mutually dependent suggests that Rorschach responses, especially of children, should not be viewed (as is still often the case, we believe) as representing essentially or predominantly one aspect, the emotional aspect of the personality. These responses are the product of both cognitive and emotional factors—an intricate interplay of them—though, of course, not always in the same proportion.

Piaget also stresses the changes of values in the child's affective development, and looking at the Rorschach responses from that viewpoint (whenever responses lend themselves to such analysis) might at times add some useful information. Piaget also invokes reaction schemata (1962a, p. 135), which he considers similar to, yet also more complex than, the sensorimotor schemata, to explain certain reactions of the child. Piaget in no way claims that these schemata are ready to be used diagnostically. They have not been sufficiently clearly defined or studied experimentally. Once clarified, however, we feel that they might prove extremely useful—perhaps be more precise, broader, and more inclusive than the present psychoanalytic categories of psychosocial and psychosexual development. They would not be intended as a displacement or replacement of these other approaches, such as psychoanalytic concepts relating to stages of child development, but might incorporate them and be combined successfully with modern ego psychology concepts.

Since both affective and cognitive development proceed in the direction of an increased equilibrium, one could eventually study these reaction schemata in regard to their reversibility, adaptability, and flexibility; explore the type and degree of affective regulation of which a subject is capable in the light of some specific situations, such as the Rorschach ink blots; and, it is hoped, be able to compare this with appropriate control studies involving specific and better defined situations. Perhaps in experimenting with the reaction schemata it might become possible to understand better what has actually become assimilated by the child and is now quite egosyntonic for him, from the cognitive as well as from the affective point of view, and also what the child might be defending himself against and what he has difficulties in assimilating or accommodating to. Such an investigation might lead to an expansion and better understanding of the developmental maturity scores studied by others.

Acknowledgment

We would like to express our deep appreciation to Alan J. Glasser, Ph. D., Associate Professor of Psychology, Long Beach State College, California, and Phyllis Maslow, M. A., Director of Research, The Frostig Center for Educational Therapy, Los Angeles, who reviewed our manuscript and offered very helpful suggestions.

References

Ames, Louise B., et al. 1952. *Child Rorschach Responses.* New York: Paul B. Hoeber.

Bolgar, Hedda. 1964. "Contributions Toward a General Theory of Mental Development: Piaget and Hartman." In *Science and Psychoanalysis,* Vol. VII. New York: Grune & Stratton.

Bower, T. G. R. 1966. "The Visual World of Infants." *Scientific American.* 215: 80–92.

Claparède, E. 1951. *Le Développement Mental.* Neuchâtel: Delachaux et Niestlé.

Décarie, Thérèse Gouin. 1965. *Intelligence and Affectivity in Early Childhood.* New York: International Universities Press.

Dworetzki, Gertrude. 1939. "Le test de Rorschach et l'évolution de la perception." Doctoral Dissertation No. 89. Geneva: Librarie Naville. (See also Meili-Dworetzki.)

Flavell, John H. 1963. *Developmental Psychology of Jean Piaget.* Princeton, N.J.: Van Nostrand.

Fox, Jack. 1956. "Significance of Age Patterns in the Rorschach Records of Children." Chapter IV in *Developments in the Rorschach Technique,* Vol. II, Bruno Klopfer et al. (Eds.). New York: Harcourt, Brace & World.

Hemmendinger, Laurence. 1966. "Developmental Theory and the Rorschach Method." In *Rorschach Psychology,* M. A. Rickers-Ovsiankina (Ed.). New York: John Wiley & Sons.

Hertz, Marguerite. 1960. "The Organization Activity." In *Rorschach Psychology,* M. A. Rickers-Ovsiankina (Ed.), Chapter 2, pp. 25–57. New York: John Wiley & Sons.

Hunt, J. McV. 1961. *Intelligence and Experience.* New York: The Ronald Press.

Klopfer, B., Spiegelman, M., and Fox, J. 1954. "The Interpretation of Children's Records." In *Developments in the Rorschach Technique,* Vol. II, B. Klopfer et al. (Eds.), Chapter 2. New York: Harcourt, Brace & World.

Levine, Murray. 1966. "Psychological Testing of Children." In *Child Development Research,* Vol. II. New York: Russell Sage Foundation.

Meili-Dworetzki, Gertrude. 1956. "The Development of Perception in the Rorschach." In *Developments in the Rorschach Technique,* Vol. II, B. Klopfer et al. (Eds.), Chapter 5. New York: Harcourt, Brace & World.

Oppenheimer, J. Robert. 1956. "Analogy in Science." Address, Sixty-Third Annual Convention of the American Psychological Association, San Francisco. Quoted in *Developments in the Rorschach Technique,* Vol. II, B. Klopfer et al. (Eds.), p. x. New York: Harcourt, Brace & World.

Piaget, Jean. 1943. "Le développement mental de l'enfant." *Juventus Helvetica,* Vol. I.

———. 1951. "The Principal Factors Determining Intellectual Evolution from Childhood to Adult Life." In *Organization and Pathology of Thought,* David Rapaport (Ed.). New York: Columbia Univ. Press.

———. 1961. *Les Mécanismes Perceptifs.* Paris: Presses Universitaires de France.

———. 1962. "The Relations of Affectivity to Intelligence in the Mental Development of the Child." *Bull. Menninger Clinic.* 26(3): 129–138.

———. 1967. *Six Psychological Studies.* New York: Random House.

———, and Inhelder, Bärbel. 1966a. *L'Image Mentale chez l'Enfant.* Paris: Presses Universitaires de France.

———. 1966b. *La Psychologie de l'Enfant.* Paris: Presses Universitaires de France.

Wolff, Peter H. 1960. "The Developmental Psychologies of Jean Piaget and Psychoanalysis." *Psychological Issues.* Vol. II, No. 1. New York: International Universities Press.

Würsten, Helmut. 1946. "L'evolution des comparaisons de longueurs de l'enfant à l'adulte." *Arch. de psychol.* XXXII: 1–144. (Doctoral dissertation)

Seymour L. Zelen

5

Rorschach Patterns in Three Generations of a Family *

Conceptualizations about personality and psychopathology have tended to represent the family as the basic social environment in which the individual develops (Bell and Vogel, 1960). The transmission of cultural, class, and familial patterns through the various generations of a family may be examined by comparing responses of each generation to standard stimuli under uniform conditions.

Such a study was undertaken with all the consanguine members of three generations of one family and with some of the available spouses. This family exhibited "sufficient pathology" to make it a noteworthy teaching case (Abt and Weissman, 1965). An attempt will be made in the following report to examine each member of the family and to place him within the framework of the family milieu so that the interaction of family forces and individual factors and the transmission of the pathological patterns will be made evi-

* The data for this article were obtained by direct interviews and testing. Originally one adult member of the family and then others came for therapy. The children, some of whom were not seen therapeutically, were volunteered by their parents. Those children who were old enough, as well as all the adults, had the nature of the project explained to them and participated voluntarily. Written permission was secured from each adult and from the parents for the children discussed herein.

THE JACK ARMSTRONG FAMILY

dent. No attempt will be made to explain the nature of the transmission of the pathology, whether it be class-cultural or learned family patterns, except that a learning orientation rather than a genetic hypothesis is posited.

The family will be evaluated generation by generation through a combination of life history and Rorschach to illustrate pathological responses. After the case histories of all three generations of this family have been developed, conclusions regarding family group phenomena both in life style and common Rorschach factors will be derived. Hypotheses concerning individuals and the family will be derived from the Rorschach and hopefully illustrated with Rorschach data, but they will not be limited to specific scoring items.

Rorschachs were administered and scored according to Klopfer.

General Family Background

The family to be discussed will be called the Jack Armstrong family. It consists of Jack and his wife Jane (generation I), their five children, now married with children of their own (generation II), and their grandchildren (generation III). All members of the family were interviewed within the same year. Economically they belong to the skilled or semiskilled worker level, with occasional forays into the "very small" business level. Socio-economically they could be classified as upper-lower (according to the Warner system) (Warner and Lunt, 1941). The entire family history is replete with much acting-out, impulsive behavior. There was much involvement with the law, but only on a minimal level of antisocial behavior. In the third generation there was an individual who attended college, but to this date there are no college graduates in the entire family. The family stock was white, Anglo-Saxon, Protestant American, with only one individual of the second generation venturing out of this mold, to marry a Mexican-American.

First Generation

The titular head of this family, Jack Armstrong, Sr., is 57 years old and has been married for 35 years. He is the older son of his mother's first of three marriages and his education is sixth grade. Jack and his brother grew up in a family which was pretty well dominated by their mother. He ran away from home at the age of 14 to join a carnival, and worked in the carnivals for a number of years. He gave up the carnival life about two years before he married and worked in the steel mills. Jack has many talents, none of which have been thoroughly developed. He can play many musical instruments, yet he never had any music lessons. He is an expert cabinet-maker, having for a short time had his own cabinet-making shop. He and Jane were married when he was 22 and she 20. Presently he states he is a door-to-door appliance salesman, but the income from his very desultory labors is minimal. He and his wife live primarily on her earnings as a cook.

Jack, Sr. has a history of uncontrolled outbursts of temper, during which he has quite often beaten his wife and children. He was forced into therapy by his grown children after they found him molesting his granddaughters. Apparently he had intercourse with four or five of them, who ranged in ages from 7 to 12 years. Parenthetically, Jack's father died in a "state institution" where he had been placed for "molesting children." Along with all this acting-out behavior, Jack, Sr. has also had an operation for ulcers.

Jane Armstrong, 55, the mother, came from a somewhat different socio-economic background than her husband. Her father worked as a mill foreman, but at one time he was president of the Chamber of Commerce of the small town where the family originated, and was elected mayor of the town. Jane graduated from high school and married Jack within a year after graduation. In Jane's family, according to Jane, her mother was the dominant parent. Jane's older unmarried brother is an intermittent patient in one of the state mental hospitals and carries the diagnosis of schizophrenia. Her "favored" younger brother died a few years ago of cirrhosis of the liver brought about by excessive drinking. He and his wife had numerous separations. Though he married, he never had any children. Thus, Jane with her five children represents the only biologically productive member of her family.

Upon careful physical and neurological examination, Jane was diagnosed as having essential hypertension. Three years before testing, Jane had a total hysterectomy. Upon being examined with psychological tests, she presented a markedly organic picture. The neurological examination, however, was negative. Recently one of the daughters mentioned that her mother had had Sydenham's chorea as a child.

Her children report that Jane was a fussy mother, that she was quite concerned with toilet training, and that she made strenuous, but sporadic, attempts at keeping the house clean. She tended to discipline her children by invoking the father's wrath. By and large, she did not seem to occupy the place of importance in her children's lives that her husband did. She was seen by her children as a relatively prissy woman who was fairly ineffectual when confronted by her husband's desires and demands or by the family in general. She was also seen as relatively inhibited in contrast to her husband and family. Altogether, she presents a picture of a neurotic masochist.

It will be seen from an examination of Jack Armstrong's Rorschach that his dynamics are like the eye of a hurricane. Around him, and apparently from him, flow currents that influence his entire family unto the third generation. The Rorschach illustrates his role and the type of model he provided for his children.

Rorschach Protocol, Jack Armstrong, Sr.

CARD I

5″

1. Well that looks to me like the rib section (laugh)—It has a spine and wall I would say it comes pretty close to an X-ray picture of some part of the anatomy. That's about

1. Spine, ribs. (Q) Openings, general shape of it. (Q) Because of its coloring. (Q) No multicolor—uniform. (Q) Can't say. I can't tell I wonder how they determine them.

all I can see. It has a—That's about it.

W Fk At
Add: That could be an urn supported on legs and a basin around it. Kind of support from there up. (Q) Contour lid on it. (Q) Supports here could be gargoyle. Outlandish piece of art. (Q) Nose forehead chin.
V (*W F Obj*)

CARD II
3″

1. Well that looks like two fellows in some kind of an athletic contest. Both wearing same type uniform . . . cause they don't have the right kind of faces—wearing a mask of some kind—theatrical. That's it, about all I can see there.

1. Like puppets—heads all out proportion—like Kukkla Fran and Ollie. A contest—opposing two hands. Symbolic. Faces exaggerated. Nose and chin. Would be doing some kind of dance. This indicates opposition when two hands together. (Q) Undeterminable.
W M (H) P
Add: The center part, the white part looks like some kind of a light with a red orange flame on the top and the rest would be background, of course.
(*WS C′ F, CF Fire*)

CARD III
12″

Well that looks like two men engaged in some kind of occupation . . . oh . . . wouldn't necessarily say men . . . some form of animal.

1. Frame of the man or woman (Q) I wouldn't know. Flatness gone. Hands not clear. Trying to do something. Feet, heels, costume legs, features here.
W M (H) P

Two people hanging from the ceiling or some contrivance. Can't determine what occupation could be. It is coordinated action of some kind, the fact they are off balance

2. More ape-like than human, something holding them up. This part of costume protrudes like a bouquet of flowers or something like that, clothing.

doing the same thing. Parts of it have to be filled in by imagination, the contour about it.

D FM(Fm) H

Add: V Two trees here, shadows, flower bed and on both sides (Q) Contour of a tree. (Q) Color (Q) The coloring, way it's layer cut—bare space area—shadows darkest at top like going uphill.

(*D_s F Bt*
D F, FC' BH)

CARD IV

7″

1. (Exclamation) That—looks like the lower extremities of a man sitting on a stump. Not so mature arms hanging down. A trampy sort of of fellow. That's about that, I am not too good at this I'm afraid. I don't have much imagination.

1. Feet, worn out shoes, baggy trousers —ground roots—upper part of body doesn't show—sagged down out of proportion—the arms—toes out of them—hand to heels, ragged at knees.

W M Hd, Cg, Bt

CARD V

5″

1. Well that looks like a butterfly—antenna on the head and the large wings busted up somehow, broken up, body looks normal could be a bat, more bat than a butterfly—legs sticking out the back, flying.

1. Antenna large—I mean thick—wings too large for a butterfly—wings broken up—not proper contour—out of shape.

W FM A P

CARD VI

6″

1. Uh, Oh well that looks to me like the pelt of some animal. Some freakish type of stretcher that protrudes above it. That's all I can see there.

1. Indians in the North Country have luck charms something like this. (Q) Coloring, lighter and darker, black streak up back. (Q) Underpart usually a little light, legs, neck part (Q) Fur out. (Q) Light and dark spots indicates how.

W Fc A Obj P
Add: Part of a charm attached.
(*D F Obj*)

CARD VII
7″

1. Well. It's disjointed. Reminds me of some types of statues I've seen, modern art (laugh). Two faces pointed one way and two faces pointed the other way, totem-like. The faces somewhat like a nodule. Fact I've seen things like that in nodules ("volcano bubble") some type of agate.

1. One on top of other, totem-like core of it, center, nothing in it. (Q) Distorted features of a human being.
W FC′ Hd N
Add: V Way its laid out, colored, way colors fade and become more prominent.
(*D FC′ Abst*)

CARD VIII
8″

1. Well now the lower part of that looks like a pansy with two chameleons looking standing on the pansy and holding supporting two other structures.
2. The top one looks like a large beetle and the two center parts look like cushions.
3. The coloring is pretty. That's all I can see there.

1. Coloring, pastel color of a pansy.
W FC, FM N, A P
2. Q. Short neck sharp nose, and legs, pink body. Q. Rough clawlike legs of a beetle, spiny body.
D F A
3. Q. Shape of it, lighter in the center gives it cushiony appearance.
D FK Obj

CARD IX
9″

1. Seems to be two characters lying side by side at the bottom. Their features indicate them to be men.

1. Head, shoulders, eye, nose, hair, neck with bloody part.
W M CF Hd

Hands seem to be supporting some kind of structure. I don't know what they are supposed to be. Egg-shaped head coloring at neck makes it seem lopped off.

2. And of course there are some reddish clouds above it.

2. Spreads out with change of color from center.
D KF Cl

3. And a fountain in the center. Another modern art study.

3. Center dark then blue spray.
D KF Fountain

CARD X
12″

That is something. Matter which way I hold it? I'll hold it the way you gave it. I like it better that way.

1. I can only think of flowers when I look at that. Coloring conducive of flowers, but not necessarily the contours.

1. I've picked up orchids which were soft and light blue.

What confuses me about those things is the coloring. Gives me one opinion and the contour gives me another. But the coloring is more convincing than the contour. And I like the color. I'd give more detail but . . .

Spinal coloring of the flower exclusive of white—stem—pistil where pollination is.
Rest is coincidental. Doesn't tell me anything.
W CF N

From the psychogram it can immediately be seen that his use of form is low, two *F* responses out of 16 for a 12½*F*%. Thus, his reality testing and ego controls are relatively poor. Nonetheless, the three additional *F*'s indicate his potential for increased control. It would almost seem that in this man ego controls are an afterthought. What an analysis of the psychogram does emphasize is the predominance of fantasy or inner life in this man. There are four movement responses, and there are three animal movement (*FM*) responses. When this is compared with the paucity of color responses (two *C*, with one of the two being a *CF*, plus two additionals—an *FC* and a *CF*), it becomes obvious that this man is driven by his inner needs and fantasies—that he is not oriented to responding to external cues and stimuli. Like many a schizoid person he may somewhat distort the outside world in a relatively free manner to meet his needs. The low number of color responses indicates an inability to maintain affect. Thus, under stress, Jack Armstrong would tend to discharge his impulses in a direct, motoric manner with cognitive awareness of reality hampered by his lack of ability to sustain an input of external and affect-laden cues. Conflict for Jack is intrapsychic and is reflected in the mild dysphoria indicated by the one achromatic response and three additional *C′* responses. Depression is not, however, the primary expression of his conflict. Rather anxiety, both free-floating and bound, as expressed in the number and variety of shading responses, is the predominant state in which Jack finds himself.

While his aspirations and desires are high, his poor reality testing does not afford him much opportunity of success. This would further increase his frustration. He does have a high capacity to delay gratification, but his chances for satisfaction are so small in relation to his needs that there is a constant buildup of frustration, leading inevitably to some acting-out behavior.

A content analysis of Jack Armstrong's Rorschach has as its predominant theme an inability to relate to people, considerable feelings of inadequacy about himself as a person and a man, and some fear of dependency. His initial response to Card I is "X-ray—anatomy," reflecting his basic anxiety, as well as an attempt to gain some security by keeping himself at a distance from the test situation. On Card II he begins by making a response of "two people," but almost immediately he places masks on them and in the Inquiry he changes the living-human quality even further by making them puppets. When he does see "nondistorted and vital" people they are "hanging down"—under tension—tenuously holding on. Likewise, the human response on Card VII is "Statues." On Card VI he makes special note of the phallic projection at the top by calling it "some freakish kind of stretcher" for the fur. This preoccupation with the phallus coupled with the immediately preceding response to Card V of "broken wings" graphically illustrates his feelings of inadequacy and some of his hostility.

It is worth noting that the number and variety of his additional responses (*five* compared to 11 originals) reveal the potential for greater imposition of reality controls as well as confirming the original impressions of a person given to mood swings with emotional lability. The additionals also confirm his hostility and primitive negativism.

Rorschach Protocol, Mrs. Jane Armstrong

CARD I
4″

1. Looks like a bat. 23″ Sometimes people see more than one thing. Do you turn it?	1. Spread, head, flying. *W FM A P*
2. Pair of hands with mittens on.	2. Shape of them. *D F Hd*
3. Could be—partly—a head—not very easily because this too straight. Don't see anything else.	3. Shape. *dr F Hd*
4. Could be part of a body and this the center—small waist and hips.	4. Looks like a dressmaker's dummy. *D F Hd*

CARD II
35″

1. Rabbit except face isn't quite right.	1. Ears and face, front leg and body (looks like) furry. *D Fc A*

2. Pair of candlesticks held. Just blot.	2. Held up—pointy. *D F Obj* Red at top.
3. Butterfly, when give it a passing glance.	3. Flying—wings spread apart. *D FM A*

CARD III
8″

1. French poodles	1. Head and front part of body—neck not rest—shape *D F Ad*
2. Bow tie	2. Shape—odd color *D F Cg*
3. Looks like monkeys with tails.	3. Upside down—head—tail hanging by tail. *D Fm A*
4. Dead limbs from a tree.	4. Tree limb that's been in a fire burnt wood—shape. Black gave me idea it had been in a fire. *D Fc, FC′ Bt*

CARD IV
5″

1. Looks like bear rug (on floor).	1. Outline head (side up?) hairy side up—looks like fur. *W Fc A Obj P* *Add:* could be feet with somebody hiding behind hanging rug, trousers —shoes— (*DW M Hd*)

CARD V
10″

1. Looks like a bat too (shape).	1. Flying ears—looks like body cut in two because of line—back feet. *W FM A P*

CARD VI
16″

1. Puts me in mind of a fish, that's been filleted open. (They all have center line.)

1. Head chopped off shape.
W F Ad

CARD VII
52″

1. No shape of anything. Unless this could be face over there.

1. Head looks like a little girl's face. Pony tail flying.
DM Hd P

CARD VIII
10″

1. Looks like lion or some animal standing on cliff looking over and this same thing.

1. Face and eye, two front feet and back legs, no tail—ready to spring. Rest of card cliff.
W FM A P

2. Could be like dirty snow in distance.

2. Greyish looking.
D CF Snow

CARD IX
45″
Rejection

Doesn't suggest anything to me.

(Q) Rejects—picks up—rejects.

CARD X
20″

1. They look like sheep and sheep heads—standing just on back legs.

1. Shape like it—sheep don't have tails —heads here.
D FM A

2. This could be chandelier and this could be green pine or vine hanging down.	2. Pine because it was green—shape that hangs down in middle—ornament. *D FC Obj Bt*
3. Puts me in mind of a caterpillar (top pink)	3. Knobby shape *Dd F A*
4. Animal's head (green top)	4. Whole sheep—head gave me idea—laying down because hadn't any legs. *D FM A*
5. Looks like head.	5. Mouth, tongue, eyes, mouth. *Dd F Hd*

When a man with Jack Armstrong's hostile hyperactivity has a wife like Jane, the resultant behavior disorders in their children are almost sure to follow, and the Rorschach illustrates this admirably. Jane is a flabby individual with little determination in her character. The high *FM* (five) in comparison to *M* (one) demonstrates the easy acceptance of her instinctual drives and her needs for more immediate gratification. She is realistic in her orientation to life with nine form responses (out of a total of 22 responses), but she tends to be a relatively banal person who lacks the resources to impose her reality orientation on her husband. For example, she produced five popular responses (no originals), but none of these involved an *M* or human response. Her own unresolved primitive impulses (5 *FM*) play into the hands of Jack, who exploits Jane for his own ends. She seems to lack organization and creativity. The sequence of initial responses to Card I were (1) *W,* (2) *D,* (3) *dr,* and (4) *D*. Out of all of her 22 responses, only one movement response was made. There was an "Additional" which was scored *DW,* and a rejection of Card IX, which requires some organizing ability to handle. Her anxiety (three *Fc*) can, especially after being brutalized by her husband, turn into depression. This inward turning of her own hostility results from her poor coping mechanisms, more particularly from an almost total lack of contact with the affective aspects of her personality (two responses out of a total of 22 which fall into the color determinants).

Jane's Rorschach itself does not directly demonstrate any organicity, but her Sydenham's chorea may have been so mild and occurred so long ago that it may well be compensated for and overlaid by later characterological development. These two people, making up the first generation, seem to have character structures which dovetail into each other. Jane seems to be the ideal foil for Jack, and he in turn seems to provide enough sadism and rejection to meet her infantile expectations.

The three texture responses would make her sensitive to her husband's demands, and her lack of imagination and inner life, coupled with the poor level of specification throughout her protocol, would permit her to rationalize his somewhat harebrained proposals as realistic and worthwhile.

Second Generation

The eldest child, Jacqueline Armstrong Smith, at the time of examination was 34 years old. Divorced from her second husband, she has six children, two by her first husband and four by her second husband. This woman, along with the father, dominates the family. Although she is only a year and a half older than her nearest sibling, she quite effectively controlled all of them. The father, during her childhood, would very often pair her off in fights against her nearest sibling, a brother. Jacqueline felt that she could win her father's approval only by winning these contests.

Rorschach Protocol, Jacqueline Armstrong Smith

CARD I
5″

1. Looks like butterfly—don't see anything.	1. *W*. Wings, head, body got little different figures in its wings. *W F AP*

2. Reminds me of something sexual-like (?) don't know.	2. Female—labia, uterus, tubes—not clear. *W F Sex*
3. Wonder why dots are here—looks like eyes. Don't know what I'm supposed to say—	3. Dark dots. *de F Hd*
4. Looks like ink blot.	4. Cause it is. *W F Abst*
5. Bug—top part—with feelers.	5. Looks like a crab or beetle with feelers. *D F A*
6. Birds.	6. Hens—shape of tail and body. *D F A*

CARD II

DK—10″

25″—Just not made right.

1. Female sex organs. Hole reminds me of that too.	1. No, because it's too big. *D F At, Sex*
2. Butterfly.	2. Looks like one—wings. *D F AP*
3. French poodles—or ponies—or dogs that have big chests.	3. With paws up sitting—with paws out. *D FM A*
4. Camel.	4. Just face—jaws, etc. *D F Ad* *Add:* Two little puppy dogs balancing on nose—back to back yet face to each other. (*D FM A P*)

CARD III

8″

1. Could be jitterbugging, but looks like two little boys in dancing school—except faces—.	1. Now—have hands on something like on chairs. *D M H P* *Add:* Or like skinny old Frenchmen

and penises seem to come out where knees are.
(*D F H*)
Add: Bow tie.
(*D F Cg P*)
All that stuff—the line helps more. (Not hole?)

2. What does it mean if see dog faces?

2. Looks like face of dogs up here.
D F Ad

3. Could this be a penis?

3. Just looks like it.
D F Sex

4. Every time see this reminds me of woman's sex organs. Spot of blood.

4. Red and looks like ran down, into a puddle.
D CF Bl, Sex

5. Something hanging by tail.

5. Monkey, tail and head and body.
D FM, FmA

6. Butterfly.
It's ridiculous!

6. Center—shape.
D F AP

CARD IV
23″

1. Looks like bear rug—just upper half. (Oh, this is dull.)

1. Center form doesn't fit—(up side?) furry—can see up and down of fur.
W Fc AObj P

2. Big animal on a little one—small body—or something under there.

2. Don't like it that way!
Dd FM A O

3. Foxes standing up. Why don't I see people—not just animals.
This is aggravating because not distinct.
Asks about why all have projections and then asks about upper inner detail.

3. Long nose, tail, body is slim.
D FM A

CARD V
5″

1. Bat.

1. *W*. Feelers, legs, no ears, (Q) He's just flying.
W FM A P

2. Chicken leg. What does everybody else say about these things. Why don't I see people? Faces.	2. Shape. *D F Ad*

CARD VI

Don't see anything, tired of this stuff. 100″	Don't see a damn thing—getting mad.
1. Sunfish. Every time crack reminds me of woman's sex organs "hole in wall" and butterflies remind me of that.	1. Angel fish—big fins. *Dd F A*

CARD VII

8″

1. Two old maids fighting with each other on top—sitting back to each other—head turned. (covers part of blot with hand)	1. Faces dirty—Looks like had them in mud or chocolate cake. *D M(m) HP*
2. Rabbit—both sides.	2. (Furry) No velvety because of shadows. *D Fc Ad P*
3. Arm leg body neck, but no head.	3. Shape of body—can see skirt—could even be running. *Dd M Hd*
4. Butterflies.	4. Flying. *D FM A*
5. Woman's vagina.	5. Shape—lips. *D F Sex*

CARD VIII

13″

1. Two skinny bears coming out for some water—after hibernating all winter.	1. Water—center blue (no color). *D FM A P*

2. Mountain lion getting ready to spring.

2. Standing on cliff.
D FM A P
Add: Spinal column
(*D F At*)

CARD IX
10″
Don't see anything.
25″

1. Big butterfly—tired of butterflies, and birds.

1. Green shape. Two butterflies face to face on a pole.
D FM A

CARD X
5″

1. Looks like a bunch of marine animals—starfish—sea horses—two bugs mad at each other arguing—could be tadpoles—cause have tails—crab.

1. Blue *D1* or crab green; top grey are the bugs arguing; sea horses on the bottom.
W F Ls

The six direct sex responses to be found in Jacqueline's protocol are illustrative of her preoccupation with sex and her masculine approach to sexuality. Almost immediately, the second response to Card I is a sexual response. The first response to Card II is "female sex organs." The very openness and freedom with which she deals with sexuality reveals her masculine identification. Likewise, the easy accessibility to her primitive impulses and the need for immediate gratification are illustrated by the predominance of the animal movement responses in her protocol.

Nonetheless, the identification with her mother is demonstrated by the high frequency of *F* and *FM* responses, similar to her mother's psychogram. The almost complete absence of any shading responses (just two texture responses out of 32) is unlike her father, but remarkably similar to her mother. Like both parents, she does not have easy access to her feelings and thus would not have the balancing influence of an external orientation in determining her behavior.

Behaviorally, she has tended to act out. Like all of her siblings, she was placed in Juvenile Hall. At the age of 16 she left the twelfth grade to marry her first husband, with whom she lived for a total of 18 months out of four years. She had two children by this man. Jacqueline, although of WASP background, married a Mexican-American. She found that she could dominate him easily. Later this was also given as one of the reasons why she left him. Again her behavior illustrates her ambivalence about her sexual role and her ambivalence about identification with her mother or father. Within two years she married a man of the same ethnic background as herself, remaining married this time for over ten years. During both marriages Jacqueline worked as a waitress or as a nurse's aid. Both her husbands were semiskilled construction workers.

Throughout much of her adult life she has had many extramarital affairs, some of them with members of her husband's family (such as his brothers) as well as friends. The sexual responses on the Rorschach and the free access to her "instinctual drives"—illustrated by the eight animal movement responses when compared with only the three human movement responses—indicate the small amount of gratification delay she possesses. Her life history as well as the number of sexual percepts on the Rorschach exemplify her basic personality conflicts around identification and castration. The second response to Card IV graphically illustrates her castration anxiety and the resentment of the feminine role. She sees a "big animal on a little one—somebody or something—under there," and on the Inquiry says "I don't like it that way." This response is located within the large, lower center detail. Further identification with the father is seen in her artistic abilities. She paints and plays the piano and violin.

Another side of her personality, however, was that inculcated by her mother. A little catechismic rhyme indicated this identification with a "prissy mother." She stated: "I was not supposed to drink, smoke, or swear—get a divorce, or dye my hair."

She secured a divorce from her second husband on rather innocuous grounds, but the relationship between them was strained considerably when she found that her husband was molesting her eldest daughter, a child by her first husband, as well as having an affair with her sister. After this second divorce she indulged in a great deal of sexual promiscuity, including considerable homosexual acting-out behavior.

Jacqueline's psychogram combined elements of both her mother and her father. Her Rorschach indicated her aggressiveness and sexual freedom, somewhat like her father, and her masochism and sexual confusion, somewhat like her mother. Considering Jacqueline's sexual identification problems it is worth noting the variety of her sexual behavior. Despite her problems, this woman was able to marry twice, albeit each time unsuccessfully. Jacqueline and her father typify the primitive vitality of this family, which, while not necessarily healthy, was quite vibrant.

If Jacqueline had problems in identification, her next closest sibling, Jack Armstrong, Jr., seems to have had similar difficulties. With a sadistic father and a rejecting mother, the man seemed to have very few growth options. Jack, Jr., whose nickname is Buddy, is a year and a half younger than Jacqueline.

When seen this man was 32 years old; he had been married legally only two years. He lived with his present wife in a common-law relationship for four or five years before marrying her. He has two children by this marriage, 3 and 4 years old, and has one previous illegitimate child by another woman. He left school at the beginning of the eighth grade at the age of 16 after a history of truancy, poor grades, repetition in grades, and inability to learn in school. Later in life he taught himself to read. The school considered him very aggressive, and he was finally expelled from school because he almost killed a classmate. When he left school he couldn't read a first grade reader. It should be remembered that this is the same "Buddy" who used to lose fights to his older sister until he was about 10 or 11.

His ambivalence over his masculine identification is further demonstrated in his life by his fear of marital commitment. On the Rorschach he made a response to Card II: "Steeple, but it's split";

on Card IV his first response was "Back or breast of a chicken—split open. . . ." Then he continued with response 2: "All have pretty much the same tops—not necessarily a steeple," which upon Inquiry he denied. Finally, his third response was: "A womb"; Inquiry: "Looks like a woman's vagina that's gotten old and sloppy—outer and inner lips." Again on Card III, the humans are seen as people of both sexes: "Breast and also penis." He would not decide between them. Referring again to Card IV, the so-called "father card," Buddy splits the massiveness of the card (split-open, little chicken), denies the phallic aspects of the card (not necessarily a steeple), and winds up with a depreciated womb. On Card V he sees the figure in the center as "the lower half of a woman"; Inquiry on this response yields: "Legs of a woman—back view—knock-kneed—see her butt—bent over and can see her shoulders." These Rorschach responses graphically illustrate his ambivalence toward his father, his passivity, and his feelings of masculine inadequacy. Furthermore, his feelings in relation to women are demonstrated by two of his responses to Card IX; his second response is "the inside—not the outside—of a pregnant woman" and his fourth response is "Green, looks like something slimy. Something you get on your hands and can't get it off. Something I can't stand is slimy things on my hands." Hatred, fear, and guilt in his relationship to women is quite evident. Finally his own negative self-concept is made abundantly clear by his spontaneous opening remark upon being presented Card IX: "Why is it all animals are brutes? I don't feel myself as a brute."

Rorschach Protocol, Jack Armstrong, Jr. (Buddy)

CARD I
8″ Don't see anything.
12″

1. Butterfly.	1. Upper *D* (Q) Wings. Like. (Q) Floating in air. *D Fm A*
2. Woman in middle—legs and hips	2. Like she bent back.

breasts longated stomach—navel. Out of proportion.
Kind of fine head, small head.

Broad hip, calf of leg and breast. Gay Nineties dress at top—full at breast.
D M H
Add: Hands at top.
(*D F Hd*)

CARD II
10″ You are supposed to see some thing.
17″

1. At bottom—a womb.

   1. Color and shape.
   D FC At

2. At top looks like I've seen it in a colored medical book—internal organ—lungs or kidneys.

   2. Lungs—shape and color.
   D FC At

3. Steeple, but it's split.

   3. Belfry. Shape.
   D F Obj

I have a tendency to lean toward sex.
Is there a time element?

CARD III
8″

1. Two people—at first going to say cradle—but now—pulling something apart. Guess they'd have to be hermaphrodite. Should be something to tell whether it's a man or a woman, but now they appear the same.

   1. Two women. (Q) Well, of both sexes. (Q) Breast and also penis.
   W M H P

2. Bow in middle.

   2. Bow on a dress—like entire bodice—coming clear to puffed sleeve.
   D F Obj P

3. Light—dizzy feeling—amoeba in background.

   3. Not amoeba but rather an embryo—an unborn monkey. (Q) (dizzy feeling) fighting feeling—looks like they're fighting. I want to get away from it.
   D F A

CARD IV
40″

1. Back or breast of chicken split open. Wings and pretty definite spinal column of a small chicken. Used to work in slaughter house.	1. *W*. Just laying there with no flour on it, before they throw it onto a frying pan. *W F Food*
2. All have pretty same tops. Not necessary a steeple.	2. Denied steeple—Looks like gargoyle. *D F Obj*
3. A womb.	3. Looks like womb like a woman's vagina that's gotten old and sloppy, outer and inner lips. *D F At (Sex)*

CARD V
15″

1. A butterfly.	1. Whole thing—Flying, extending legs and stretched out. *W FM A*
2. A bat.	2. Whole thing. Flying. *W FM A*
3. Top—all the same—(?) Lower half of woman.	3. Legs of a woman—back view—knock-kneed—see her butt—bent over and can see shoulders. *D M Hd*

CARD VI
20″

1. Totem pole—top part.	1. Wings and pole—saw them up in Alaska. *D F Obj*
2. Bottom part is like a bearskin hide.	2. A stretched hide (Q) up (Q) fur side of a grizzly bear—kind of shades. *D Fc AObj*
3. Lungs—in middle—about halfway down.	3. Lungs—shape. *D F At*

4. Can't explain bottom part—looks like on bat's wings—what am I thinking of?—my wife? There's something there.	4. Hooks (Q)—Shape *d F Ad* *Add a:* Eagle's head—shape (*D F Ad*) *Add b:* Middle looks like column down to lumbar region. (*D F At*)

CARD VII
30″

1. Backbone with either wings or skin stretched out.	1. Part of an animal (Q wings or skin) Have to be skin. (stretched) Had been stretched—not in here. *D F AObj*
2. Ice—gets dark and gets to edges where have snow with dirt on it and then have part where it *started* to melt and *froze* again.	2. Snow with dirt and ice. (Q) Icicles hanging downing—hard at edges. (Q) Sort of transparent, really more like translucent. *D FC′* (*Fm*) *Dirt*

CARD VIII
7″

1. Two wolves or bears coming up either side. Have to be bears with blunt nose. Everything is closing in at top.	1. Shape—climbing up. *D FM A P*
2. Two other animals at top—coyotes.	2. Coyotes—baying, nose, head tail, two back legs together, one front leg down and other front leg out reaching. *D FM A*
3. Backbone.	3. Skeleton of backbone with ribs and part of old fur left on it. *D F At*
4. Bats in middle of blot.	4. One bat blue—wings and hooks. *D FC A*

5. Butterfly at bottom of blot.

5. Shape—pink color helped.
D FC A
Add: (V) looks like fur coat pink and orange. *D.* kind of sickening.
(D FC Obj)

6. Design of some club in Alaska—bears on either side.

6. *W* Like emblems. Shape.
W F Emblem

CARD IX

Why is it all my animals are brutes. (Q) Bears, coyotes, I don't feel myself as brute.
Getting prettier.
20″

1. Blood at top—spattered.

1. Dark orange—person with skin off—then blood is there.
D CF Bl

2. Halfway down—would be more like inside—not outside of a pregnant woman.

2. Just same idea for this. Don't think much of pregnant women. (?) Because of pouch just belly-part.
Dd F Hd

3. Red at bottom kind of—heads facing in opposite directions—with trunks joined together—more like babies.

3. Eyes—head looks like older people but bodies are those of babies.
(?) Not yet born—no sense of life—shape.
D F H

4. Green—looks like something slimy, something get on hand and can't get it off—something I can't stand is slimy things on my hands.

4. (Slimy Q) Green is just slimy.
D CF Slime
Add: Hands, thumbs and fingers reaching back.
(D M Hd)

CARD X

10″

1. Looks like a bunch of slimy worms and crabs.

1. (?) *W.* Where—all over—
(a) Blue on outside—crabs.
D F A

	(b) Grasshopper or snail with antenna. *D F A*
2. Thing at bottom looks like grasshopper.	2. Shape. *D F A*
3. Or rabbit.	3. The shape. *D F A*
4. Pink would be lungs with the heart —two hearts in the middle.	4. Color and shape because lungs are irregular inside. *D FC At*
5. Orange thing is one of those balances that goes around on steam engine.	5. Shape. *D F Obj*
6. Yellow on the outside—looks like flower—now—bird of paradise.	6. Color and shape—paradise flower comes up out of pod. *D FC Bt* *Add a:* Top—part—grey could be trachea. (*D FC′ At*) *Add b:* Also looks like two animal bugs—seem to be eating—TB bacillus looks like that also. (*d F A*)

This man is not totally maladjusted nor inadequate, as might be thought after a perusal of some of his pathological responses. He has an occupational history of semiskilled and skilled labor. He seems invariably to rise to a foreman or supervisory position, but becomes uncomfortable, and then seems to fail on the job or he quits. It is obvious that at the time of testing he did not like himself nor did he think much of himself.

Buddy reports that he can't really form attachments and that he never really loved anyone, not even his own children. The illegitimate child is never seen by Buddy, yet the mother of this child still continues to be a friend of the family and comes to visit his sisters quite often.

Once again this behavior is substantiated by the Rorschach protocol.

Buddy reports that he drank heavily from the age of 15 to 29 but that at age 29 he got into a car wreck where he had a slight concussion and some retrograde amnesia. He stated that he was drunk at the time and that this caused the accident. After the wreck he quit drinking completely. Today he says he "can't seem to get enough of pop, cake, and candy." His dependency needs are further illustrated by the food response to Card IV, which also illustrates some of his oral sadism (split-open chicken—"with no flour on it, before they throw it onto a frying pan"). This sadism is similar to his father's. Like his father, he reports that he suffers from many digestive problems. Similarly, he turns his anger against himself by biting his nails and scratching himself to the point where he bleeds. His covert hostility to his mother and women in general, so well illustrated in previously mentioned Rorschach responses, was also expressed behaviorally by bedwetting until the age of 9.

Overall, Buddy exemplifies the impulsive-compulsive neurotic whose six color responses considerably exceed his two shading responses and who has an overemphasis on animal movement. All of the factors lend considerable psychodynamic credence to his acting-out behavior. When this is coupled with the further loss of control indicated by a "snow—icicle" response on Card VII and the "slime" response on Card IX, the picture of an impulsive, acting-out individual with poor ego controls is fairly complete. With Buddy, the Rorschach demonstrated admirably the value in the use of content as a dynamic diagnostic.

The second daughter and third sibling is Maggie Armstrong Jones, age 31. "Maggie" was a nickname given her by her older sister, and she reports that she prefers this to her given name. She was put under the care of her older sister, Jacqueline, at quite an early age, and at the present time verbalizes open rivalry with her. It was probably as much a result of her rivalry with this sister as the realization of her need for help that brought her into therapy. She married at the age of 17, remained married for six years, and had two children by this marriage. After obtaining a divorce from her husband at the age of 23, she remained unmarried until the age of

30. During most of this time she lived in a house trailer, on the property of her parents or her older sister.

Rorschach Protocol, Maggie Armstrong Jones

CARD I
7″

Response	Inquiry
1. Witches.	1. Looks like it. *D F H*
2. These look like legs (in the center).	2. Shaped and look like heels at the bottom. *D F Hd*

CARD II
10″ ∧ ∨

Response	Inquiry
1. Looks like two men standing on their heads.	1. Standing on their hands, not heads. *D M H*
2. Two monkeys dancing.	2. Hands touching; seeing their backs. Furry because of raggedy edges. Fat (Q) because they're broad. Head bent in—can't see head too well. (Q) Dancing. *WK* (*M*) *A*

CARD III
8″

Response	Inquiry
1. Looks like women. Reminds me of some kind of a table that they're both reaching over.	1. (Q Women) High heels and bust-line. Head, neck, bottoms, arms. *D M H P*
2. Red thing in the middle. (don't know why) reminds me of a pelvic area.	2. Pelvic bones, seemed to be shaped backwards for pelvic bone. *D F At*

CARD IV
5″ Bah, 16″

1. Don't get much out of that except a monstrosity.	1. Whole thing, it's so—it's a blob—could remind me of a monster, great big feet, dinky arms and frog's head. Now that's a monster. *W F A*
2. Reminded me of a bug or insect—or maybe a frog at the top.	2. Looking down at frog eyes at the front. *Dd Fc Ad*
3. Feet	3. Shaped like feet, heel and toes. *D F Ad*
4. Snake—inside of one after it's been skinned.	4. (Q) Shading in the skin. *d Fc Ad*

CARD V
1″

1. Butterfly—no a	1. Whole thing. Wings, tail, feelers, flying. *W Fm A*
2. Bat	2. Whole thing. Wings are back like it's flying. *W FM A P*
3. Shape up here of a man's head with ears.	3. Ears on the side. (Q) Shape. *D F Hd*
4. These things remind me of turkey legs after they've been cooked.	4. Shape—skinned, no feathers on them. *D F Ad*
5. Looking down—area reminds me of a hawk—with its head down and mouth open—bill or beak.	5. Beak is curved and the mouth is the space in between. *DS F Ad*

CARD VI
12″

1. This reminds me of the vagina area.	1. Shading. *D Fc Sex*

2. Up here reminds me of an eagle or some kind of large bird.	2. Design on an Indian blanket—shading, colored vision—just wings. *D FC′ At*
3. Top—reminds me of a child's rag doll type face.	3. Like doll face I made when I was eleven—Shape. *D F (Hd)* *Add:* Totem pole. *(D F Obj)*

CARD VII
6″

1. Clouds	1. Whole thing, different shadings—dark and light. *W KF Cl*
2. River	2. Light part in the center. *Dd Fk Geo*
3. Icicles—even though upside down.	3. Shape and little things on the end like thawing—dot of water. *de F Ice*
4. Cliffs.	4. Rough outline reminded me of when I was a kid and we played in caves. *Dd F Ls*
5. Something about it reminds me of a lamb. Don't know what.	5. Rejected.

CARD VIII
5″

1. Intestines.	1. Color, like in a book. *D CF At*
2. Looks like animals with white rings on their faces—raccoons.	2. Nose, eye, feet, tail. Peering, looking for something. *D FM A P*
3. Backbone with ribs, in the center.	3. Shape, spaces between the ribs. *DS F At*
4. Kite.	4. Whole thing looks like the design of a Chinese kite, the colors. *W CF Obj*

5. Pine tree—slope of it.
5. Shape. (Sloping Q) Swooping down.
D F Bt

6. Orange.
6. Color inside, pulp.
D CF Fd

7. Two people standing.
7. Points to *d* at top.
Heads.
d M H

CARD IX
2″

1. Witches again—with long fingernails. Witches look like they're both pregnant.
1. Shape, fingernails, pregnant.
D F (H) P

2. Muddy water.
2. 'Cause it's all smeary. (Q) Colors.
D CF Water

3. Two caves inside of cliff.
3. Shape of space. Seen going in one side, other side shaded.
DdS FK (FC) Ls

4. Pink at the bottom reminds me of liver.
4. Color, it's sickening.
D CF At

CARD X
2″ Pretty 8″

1. Reminds me of sea horses.
1. I see it upside down.
D F A

2. Crabs.
2. D_1, have arms.
D F A P

3. Cherry bough.
3. Cherry at each end—stems and place connected on to bough; color.
D FC Bt

4. Pelvic area.
4. Shape.
D F At

5. Top grey looks like backbone.
5. Shape; dark background and white bone.
D FC′ AT

6. Katydids.
6. Color and wings; seem to be perched.
D FC′ FM A

7. Spiders.

7. Look mean.
D Fm A

8. Rabbit in the middle.

8. Ears, eyes, nose and white around the nose—head.
D F Ad

9. Looks like rivers; don't know why, just the shape.

9. Looking down from above.
D FK Ls

10. Whole thing reminds me of autumn.

10. Don't know why, just does—colors maybe.
W CF Abst

11. Branches and tiny leaves—things at the top.

11. New thin branches and leaves. Looks wintery—. (Q) Color and shape.
dr FC′ Bt

The dependency needs and the hostility in this inadequate passive-aggressive woman are evident quite early on the Rorschach by her response to Card II, where she sees two men standing on their heads in a *W*. Likewise, to the same *W*, she sees monkeys (not humans) dancing with their hands touching. On Card V she uses the small *d*1 in the bottom center, including the space, as an open bill or beak of a hawk, an indication of some oral aggression.

Her poor feminine identification is demonstrated on the Rorschach by her responses to Cards VI and VII. On Card VI there is a longer reaction latency than to any other card. All her responses to this card center around the upper (phallic) portion of the card. She ignores the larger, lower mass. As a reaction against her own impulses to deal with the phallic aspects of the card, she opens with a response of "vagina," but in the course of responding, this area is also seen as "eagle," a "rag doll face," and finally a "totem pole." To the so-called mother card, VII, she demonstrates considerable anxiety with first a *KF*, then an *FK* followed by *C′*, Icicle response. Lastly she sees the lambs, but on the Inquiry she rejects this aspect of her tenderness. As almost a dynamic carrying of "coals to Newcastle" she sees the conventional witches on Card IX as pregnant and having long nails. With both her parents as well as her older sister rejecting the feminine role and her older brother obviously so filled with hatred for women, is there any doubt that she too would reject any but the superficial trappings of femininity? To her, marriage is a caretaking institution, in which she would like care to be taken of her.

During the interval between her two marriages, Maggie formed two strong heterosexual attachments: one to a man considerably older than herself and one to a man her own age whom she apparently babied. In addition to these two liaisons, she also had many minor affairs. At the present time she is married to a semiskilled steel worker and is superficially engaged in maintaining her marriage. At the same time she has renewed an extramarital affair with one of her earlier lovers and has begun a new affair.

All this sexual acting-out is a defense against her own dislike of her femininity. Like so many other members of her family, she seems to have learned that acting-out is a good immediate defense against anxiety. But she cannot handle affect, and she thus tends to be an impulse-ridden individual whose defenses against her own impulses are rather brittle projections. She develops considerable anxiety when confronted with the first all-color card (Card VIII). The determinants used to this card in sequence are: *CF, FM, F, CF, CF,* and finally *M*. It seems that the vitality and energy developed by Maggie are, once again, of a superficial quality, and are really expressions of her acting-out defenses. Nonetheless, this woman, like so many other members of the family, expresses herself artistically. She too plays musical instruments and writes poetry—of a dubious quality. As mentioned earlier, one of Maggie's guiding lietmotifs is her rivalry with her older sister Jacqueline. Maggie has attempted to obtain for herself the primary friendship of people who were her sister's friends, both male and female. For example, she made strenuous efforts to win her sister's girl friends and she made even greater efforts to woo her sister's lover and her sister's husband for herself, eventually having an affair with her brother-in-law. It is hardly unusual that Maggie would do this, since unconsciously she would be obtaining the sexuality of her sister, and thereby make herself more feminine.

If Maggie is in many respects an imitation of her sister Jacqueline, she also has elements in common with Buddy. A striking example of this is the similar response she made to the *D*1 green center portion of Card IX. Buddy called it "slime"; Maggie called it "muddy water" and upon Inquiry finds it "all smeary."

The third daughter, and fourth child, is Catherine Armstrong Post, who was a 29-year-old divorcee at the time of this study. Her family nickname is Katie. During 13 years of marriage she left her husband periodically, occasionally for as long as a year or two. She has two children by this marriage. For the nonce she has married an old "boyfriend." She now has, and has had for some time past, a number of heterosexual liaisons characterized by a high degree of upward mobility, almost all of them being with professional men. While married, her first husband had a number of extramarital affairs, and she says that she did not allow herself to be outdone by her husband in this respect. It should be noted that her present husband, like her former husband, is a skilled worker even though her lovers remain professional men. This woman's work history is quite good. She has been steadily employed in hospital work as a nurse's aid and has even risen to supervisory responsibility, but, like her siblings, she behaves in such a way that she loses her supervisory position. Operating under considerable tension (two *Fm* responses), with realistic but brittle controls (57*F*%), she has little sensitivity (no *c*) to others. Like her sisters, she is obessed by a failure to make an adequate feminine identification, and thus she also acts out (sexually and otherwise) to resolve her conflicts (three *CF* responses). The long response latency to Card IV and the anxiety it provoked indicated a great deal of unresolved conflict with her father. Two other individual responses are of special significance. On Card VII she saw "Jackasses braying at each other" (*D*4). In the Inquiry she said: "Mom and daddy yelling—shut up—. Like children's animals —not real." Finally to the, by now, well-designated green center *D*1 on Card IX, like her brother and sister, she said: "Makes me feel like I have to void," and upon Inquiry responded by saying it was the blend of colors in the green.

The fifth child, John Armstrong, aged 27, is the baby of the family. He is called "Boo" by his sisters. His ties to his sisters are quite strong and as a child he was treated as "their baby" by Maggie and Catherine, who protected him from the father. Nonetheless, John did not escape paternal wrath. At the present time John is working as a plasterer but cannot seem to hold a job. He is an excellent craftsman, having risen to a foreman's position, but his own self-defeating impulses often lead him to give up the job or in some way cause him to be dismissed from this supervisory level. John is quite an aggressive man and came for therapy because he was dissatisfied with his life. He felt he was doing poorly on his job in that he lacked reading ability (like Buddy) and that his performance was inadequate. Only later did his marital unhappiness come out. John's speech is characterized by a frontal lisp.

He first ran away from home at the age of 11, winding up in Juvenile Hall. He ran away a number of times following this and eventually made his way in the world at the mature age of 14. As a boy, John presented many problems in school and did not learn well. His formal education ended in the sixth grade. At the age of 17 he enlisted in the army and became a cook. He married at the time he entered service, to a 16-year-old girl, and at the time of this study was still married to her. He seems to be maladjusted sexually, as are so many members of his family, and has a great deal of overcontrolled hostility, which he tends to act out periodically. Unlike the rest of his family, however, he has not acted out sexually since his marriage. He seems to be much more socially isolated than his sisters and resembles his brother much more in this respect. Presently, he has difficulties with his neighbors because he starts doing favors for them but never finishes the job.

Rorschach Protocol, John Armstrong (Boo)

CARD I
11″

1. I don't know—it looks to me that would be a butterfly. My brother-in-law told me about it. (Q) I don't know—nothing much.

1. It looks like it, mostly the form and shape.
W F A

2. It looks like a—the shape of a body there.	2. Flanks, hips, breast. *D F H*
3. At the top, it could be a woman's womb, or something.	3. Womb, woman's privates; shape. *D F Sex*

CARD II
19″

1. Here we go—hold it up or down? Or does it matter? (laugh) O.K. a—these look like heads of a teddy bear—or a mule—nostrils of some kind of animal.	1. Head to shoulders; teddy bears, two, fighting over a bottle. *D FM Ad*
2. Down here it looks like—a womb—	2. Looks kind of bloody, but mainly form and color. *D FC Sex*
3. Looks like two arrows together, on the top.	3. Just look like arrows. Form. *D F Obj*

CARD III
8″

1. Looks like one of those fancy dogs—what do you call them? It's shaved off in spots.	1. The head, neck, and back. Sitting up. *D FM A*
2. And a bow tie in the middle. I don't see too much of anything there. That's all.	2. Looks like it. *D F Cg* *Add:* Lion, long tail moving. (*D F M A*)

CARD IV
14″

1. Looks like a flower. (laugh)	1. Orchid; beat up. *W Fc Bt*
2. Might be the legs of a monster or something—other than that, I see nothing.	2. Huge person, feet, part of leg. *D F Hd*
3. Might be a backbone, up the middle.	3. Turkey or chicken. *D Fc At*

4. Possibly a butterfly or sea shell.	4. Sea shell. Shape. *D F A*

CARD V
3″

1. Now there's a butterfly (looked at back of card)—yep, butterfly—nothing else. How do you analyze these?	1. Very distinct, all. *W F A P*

CARD VI
7″

1. At the top I could possibly see another butterfly, with antennae and eyes.	1. Distorted, just form. *D F A*
2. This reminds me of a backbone of a chicken or turkey. I've done a lot of eviscerating.	2. Seen a lot of them. Like coagulated blood. *D Fc At*

CARD VII
4″

1. This slit at the bottom might be another womb—but other than that I see nothing.	1. Woman's womb, private parts. *D Fc Sex*
2. Well, maybe an elephant. I have no perspective whatsoever. I'd never be an art critic.	2. Two of them doing tricks, trunk up, foot out. *D FM A*

CARD VIII
3″

1. More backbone—	1. Dark, a chicken maybe. *D Fc At*
2. And a gila monster.	2. Walking along; ready to jump (pronounced g). *D FM A*

3. I don't know—I can see another one of those wombs on the bottom here. Nothing else.	3. I don't know why I see it. Puffy. *D Fc Sex*

CARD IX
15″

1. (At arm's length) Looks like the back of a skull—nothing else.	1. Human, I guess, back—can't see it well now. *DS F At*
2. Looks like, don't know why, but it looks like a hand, there for a minute.	2. Thumb is all. *Dd F Hd*
3. I see a face of a man upside-down. Profile, I should say. Nothing.	3. Shape. *de F Hd*
4. There's a distinct face of a man with a beard, or something out from his nose; deep-set eyes.	4. Two of them. Don't know who. Some leader, I guess. *D F Hd*

CARD X
11″

1. I expect to see something, under water or sea, like marine life. Crabs, lobsters, different species.	1. Whole, not sure if color necessary. *W F Ls*
2. A sea horse there.	2. Shape. *D F A*
3. Wishbone of a chicken.	3. Form. *D F A*
4. I see something—can't make it out. Looks like the face of a woman, with her hair blown.	4. Don't know who. *de Fm Hd*

"I heard about the Rorschach from relatives who just took it; supposed to see butterflies and sex?"

Of all the siblings John appears to be the best adjusted. Much of this can be ascribed to the help he has received from his wife. The Rorschach, however, reveals more dynamic reasons. Out of the 28 responses he made, six were texture responses, indicating his great sensitivity to other people and their needs and his evident attempts to meet these needs in others. Likewise, his responses to color were not *CF*'s, but rather two *FC*'s. Once again he is able to control his affect. On the other hand, his total lack of human movement and his use of animal movement determinants indicate the ready availability of his primitive impulses. Only by use of good ego controls, embodied in a 54*F*%, is he able to maintain himself.

His aggressiveness and his sexual inadequacy are evidenced by a number of responses dealing with fighting and weapons. This is his method of demonstrating masculinity. Likewise, the heightened number of sexual responses would indicate an almost prurient interest in women, particularly since all his sexual responses were of the "womb." He did not respond at all to the phallic aspects of the blots. All in all, the man seems to be a passive-aggressive person, his passive-aggressiveness being best illustrated by his never finishing jobs he has volunteered to do for his neighbors.

Summary of the Second Generation

Given parents like Jack and Jane Armstrong, the development of psychopathology in their children would be a prediction with a high probability of occurrence. The behavioral evidence of this psychopathology in this second generation of the Armstrongs has been repeatedly demonstrated. The evidence on the Rorschach substantiates and further elucidates this picture. More particularly, for the second generation of Armstrongs, the obvious overall similarities in the Rorschach profiles is striking. It seems quite evident that despite differences in sex, age, and position in the family they all made similar identifications with the father. A median test was performed to test the independence of the samples using the Davidson Rorschach signs of adjustment (Davidson, 1950).

It was hypothesized that if the protocols of these five siblings were different from each other (drawn from independent samples), they would have a significantly different number of Davidson signs. A

TABLE 1 *Davidson Rorschach Adjustment Signs* [a] *for Individual Family Members*

	JACK, SR.	JANE	JACQUELINE	JACK, JR.	MAGGIE	KATE	JOHN	MICKEY ♂	NELLIE	PAUL JAY	TERRY	DINA LEE	MISTY	LINDA ANNE	RACHEL	GAIL	FRANK	JUDY-JO
1. *M* greater than *FM* or *M* equal to *FM*	x			x	x						x	x				x		
2. 3 or more *M* (including additionals)	x		x	x	x			x				x						
3. Sum *C* more than *Fc* plus *c* plus *C′*				x						x		x			x	x		x
4. *F%* between 30 and 50		x			x							x	x	x				
5. *Dd* plus 5%, 10 or less				x	x					x	x	x	x			x		
6. 4 or more *P* (less than 30% *R*)		x	x		x	x		x	x					x				
7. *R* between 20 and 40		x	x	x		x	x	x						x				
8. *FC* more than *CF* or *FC* equals *CF*		x		x			x							x	x	x		
9. 2 or more *FC*				x	x	x	x							x	x			
10. No pure *C*	x	x	x	x	x	x	x	x	x	x	x	x	x	x	x	x	x	x
11. % *R* for VIII, IX, X between 35–60				x	x	x	x	x	x	x		x			x	x		x
12. *FK* plus *Fc* 2 or more	x		x		x		x							x	x			
13. *W*:*M* equals approximately 2:1			x									x						
14. *A%* 50 or less		x		x	x	x	x		x		x				x			x
15. No color shock	x	x	x	x	x	x		x	x	x	x	x	x	x	x	x	x	x
16. No shading shock	x	x	x	x	x	x		x	x	x	x	x	x	x	x	x	x	x
17. No refusals	x		x	x	x	x	x	x	x	x	x	x	x	x	x	x		
Total no. signs	7	8	9	13	13	9	8	8	7	7	7	11	6	10	10	9	3	6

[a] This is a 17-item check list (Davidson, 1950) for rating psychological adjustment from individual Rorschach psychograms. Scores range from 0 to 17, with higher scores representing more signs of adjustment.

TABLE 2 *Davidson Rorschach Adjustment Signs for Generations and Sexes*

	GENERATION								
	I MALE	I FEMALE	I TOTAL	II MALE	II FEMALE	II TOTAL	III MALE	III FEMALE	III TOTAL
1. *M* greater than *FM* or *M* equal to *FM*	x		0.5	0.5	0.33	0.42	0.25	0.29	0.27
2. 3 or more *M* (including additionals)	x		0.5	0.5	0.66	0.58	0.25	0.14	0.20
3. Sum *C* more than *Fc* plus *c* plus *C′*			—	0.5	—	0.25	0.25	0.57	0.41
4. *F*% between 30 and 50		x	0.5	—	0.33	0.16	—	0.43	0.22
5. *Dd* plus 5%, 10 or less			—	0.5	0.33	0.42	0.50	0.43	0.47
6. 4 or more *P* (less than 30% *R*)		x	0.5	—	1.00	0.50	0.25	0.24	0.27
7. *R* between 20 and 40		x	0.5	1.0	0.66	0.83	0.25	0.14	0.20
8. *FC* more than *CF* or *FC* equals *CF*		x	0.5	1.0	—	0.50	—	0.43	0.22
9. 2 or more *FC*			—	1.0	0.66	0.83	—	0.29	0.15
10. No pure *C*	x	x	1.0	1.0	1.00	1.00	1.00	1.00	1.00
11. % *R* for VIII, IX, X between 35–60			—	1.0	0.66	0.83	0.50	0.57	0.54
12. *FK* plus *Fc* 2 or more	x		0.5	0.5	0.66	0.55	—	0.29	0.15
13. *W*:*M* equals approximately 2:1			—	—	0.33	0.16	—	0.14	0.07
14. *A*% 50 or less		x	0.5	1.0	0.66	0.83	0.25	0.43	0.34
15. No color shock	x	x	1.0	0.5	1.00	0.75	1.00	1.00	1.00
16. No shading shock	x	x	1.0	0.5	1.00	0.75	1.00	1.00	1.00
17. No refusals	x		0.5	1.0	1.00	1.00	0.75	0.86	0.80
Total no. signs	7	8	7.5	10.5	10.33	10.40	6.25	8.32	7.29

chi square of 0.20 resulted which was completely nonsignificant between the 50th and the 70th percentile level of confidence. While this result does not indicate that these Rorschach protocols are similar, it does strongly reject the null hypothesis that they are independent.

TABLE 3 *Chi Squares for Independence of Samples*

GENERATION	X^2	*Df*	*P* LEVEL
Overall	3.17	2	> .20–.30
II	0.20	1	> .50–.70
III	0.09	1	> .70–.80

The emphasis, but not necessarily overemphasis, on form (*F*) is evident. Likewise, there seems to be considerable support for the hypothesis that these people have a basic narcissistic impulsivity, based on their strong primitive impulses (the use of animal movement, *FM*) with only the relatively brittle controls of reality (elevated *F*). They have limited tolerance of frustration—anxiety (even that represented by texture responses, *Fc*) in most of these cases is low. When this is linked with the almost uniformly small but significant amount of inanimate movement (*m*) present in the protocols, the displacement of the expressions of affect to pseudo-affect and acting out became quite understandable. In three of these five siblings there is an almost total absence of any of the dysphoric determinants from "*k* to *c*" on the psychogram.

The emphasis on animal movement, particularly true of Jacqueline and John but also prominent in the other siblings, serves to illustrate the orally demanding nature of their defenses with its demands for praise and special considerations. Again, these profiles with their brittle, façadelike defenses would explain the explosive aggressiveness and the sexual acting out of these siblings. These people present a façade of a spurious interest in life, but they are basically dependent and conventional like their mother. Likewise, their apparent sensitivity seems to be part of their frantic efforts not to have to face their own emptiness.

When the males and females of this second generation are compared on the Rorschach, the female profiles are considerably more homogeneous. The two brothers are different on a number of categories with Jack, Jr.'s Rorschach profile being more similar to his sisters, particularly in the use or rather minimal use of shading (*Fc*).

One of the most striking similarities in the Rorschachs of the Armstrong siblings is in the content category. Here these five people produced 22 sexual responses, for an average sexual response of 4.5 per protocol. This hyperaccessibility of sexually laden associations demonstrates quite clearly the almost "polymorphous perverse" behavior of this family. Likewise, the slime–mud–voiding response found in three of these five siblings is more than coincidence.

Third Generation

In this generation there are sixteen individuals ranging in age from 3 to 18 years. Of these, eleven were examined. Three children of the older brother, Buddy, were not available for assessment, and two children of the younger brother, John, were too young for meaningful projective evaluation. Each child will be discussed within the context of his family unit, after which each individual and his behavior will be related back to his parents and/or grandparents. The children of Jacqueline, Buddy, and Maggie have all had considerable difficulties. As a group, they have been school behavior and learning problems, truancy and juvenile problems; they have been arrested for car theft and shoplifting, taken drugs and used alcohol excessively; and, finally they, like their parents and grandfather, have acted out sexually. The other group of children, those of Catherine and John, are too young to get into any noteworthy difficulty and somehow the family climate in the latter two families is less hectic and disturbed. A good clinical prediction would be that the grandchildren from the two youngest children of Jack and Jane will not use antisocial or asocial acting-out defenses, but would rather develop along neurotic lines. At the present time this hypothesis cannot be verified, but it would be interesting to follow it up in five or ten years.

The oldest grandchildren are the son and daughter of Jacqueline Smith by her first husband, the Mexican-American she married at 16. Although this man continues to live in the same small city as his ex-wife and children, he has not visited them since the divorce, and they grew up into late adolescence not knowing about their real father nor their Mexican-American heritage. It was only when the oldest boy, Mickey, became eligible for the draft and his sister, Nellie, applied for a marriage license that they found out what their real surname was and about their ethnic background.

Mickey was arrested for car theft and was in trouble with the school authorities throughout high school but was able to go on to the local junior college for a semester. This represents the present educational high-water mark of the entire family.

Incidentally, during his last year of high school Mickey had an affair with one of his mother's homosexual partners, from which an illegitimate child was born. The Oedipal aspects of this affair seem quite evident. Mickey assumed no responsibility for this child, but Jacqueline, his mother, often acted as a babysitter for her grandchild even after this particular lesbian relationship terminated. After one semester of college, Mickey quit and married a 15-year-old girl. He is currently working in construction.

Rorschach Protocol, Mickey Smith

CARD I

6″ ∧ Should I lay it down?

1. Looks like a pelvic girdle. What if you see more than one thing? That was my first impression. But I stick to that.	1. Whole outline except for that (outer *Ds*) Looks like an X-ray of a pelvic girdle. (Q) Cause it's black. Got light and dark spots. (Parts?) Just the general outline. *W̸ Fk At*

CARD II

5″ ∧ ∨

1. Looks like the same thing. The lungs are included. Two little things up there are not big enough in proportion.
   (Lays card down)
   (Picks card up) Maybe they're kidneys.

1. Too small for lungs, probably kidneys. (Some confusion over positional location of parts) (Q) Same thing. Other than general outline—nothing specific.
   W F At

CARD III

8″ ∧

1. Looks like a spider, I guess.

1. That's legs, two eyes, teeth.
   W̸ F Ad
   (use up to here)
   Add a: Now that I come at it, looks like a little bow. (Q) (Describes shape.) (How looking at it?) Little bit above.
   ∧ >
   Add b: Little like two chessmen—knights, except that isn't supposed to be here. (What?) Lesbian shape. (Q)
   Add a: D F Obj P
   Add b: dr F Obj

CARD IV

9″ ∂

16″ Don't especially know what it looks like.

1. It looks like an otter.

1. Looks like it's got arms out head, ears, eyes—Sorta looks like he's cut off—not finished. It just that it's flat and got a head like that.
   W̸ FM Ad

CARD V

7″ ∧

1. This looks like a bat with antenna.

1. Feet, most perfect thing about it—looks like sorta wearing the antennas—like you put them on—the wings feet shaped perfectly. Wings just look scribbled—wings crooked —(How see?) Flying, looking down. *W F* (→ *FM*) *A P*

CARD VI

8″ ∂

16″ ∧

1. Looks like a bear rug with a long neck.

1. Anyway—laying down, flat. Somebody took a bear rug, cut it to make it unusual—don't see no feet. (Side up?) Outside (Why?) That's the way a rug should lay. *W F A Obj* (→ *P*)

Add: Cartoon of a cat—just the head. (?) Whiskers. (?) Like looking down on a cat. (*D F Ad*)

CARD VII

21″∢

1. Sorta looks like two crazy looking dogs balanced on their noses—or something.

1. Not noses—chins. (Q) Tail, short feet, eyes, nose, mouth. (Kind?) Two terriers. (Describes a hairy dog—by head.) Both look pretty mean—you can see their teeth—way eyes look. (Hairy?) The dogs don't look hairy —The kind I was thinking of do. *D FM* (*m*) *A*

CARD VIII

19″

1. Looks like two raccoons trying to climb a tree. (Continues to look at card.)

1. Eye, snout, two feet—one back here, don't see the other. (Q) Could be a skunk—nothing especially—just looks like a raccoon.
D→W FM A P

CARD IX

Don't you get tired writing?

13″ ∂ Looks like an inkblot.

22″ V

1. What if I see something in a section of it—then it looks like an elephant's head—but the rest don't look like nothing.

1. Big ears here, top should be rounded more—here's his trunk—head sorta shaped funny. (Q) Trunk and ears.
D F Ad

CARD X

18″ V That looks like a bunch of things.

1. V That looks like a man jumping from a parachute.

1. Don't see umbrella—man holding onto a string—jumped out of a plane. (Q) Looks like legs, air and hair.
D M H, Obj

2. V This reminds one of a shot—hypodermic needle.

2. There's the plunger—where it fits.
D F Obj

3. Two big caterpillars.

3. These two—(Q) The way the bottom is shaped—fuzzy and two eyes.
D F A
Add: This there looks like a wishbone. (Q) The way it's shaped.
(*D F Ad*)

4. Two elephant heads—holding up trunks. That's it.	4. Not so much elephant heads as you can see the trunks and see the eyes. Check where trunk comes out. This in here is supposed to be the neck. *D FM Ad*

Mickey's Rorschach psychogram abundantly illustrates the pathology of his parents. There is a total absence of responses which could be scored on the right or affective side of the psychogram. He does not even have a single texture response. On testing the limits he was only able to use color to help define form. His form percent was 54, with three additional *F* responses. His overreliance on objective reality is quite clear, considering that the only other major determinant he used was animal movement. When his brittle ego controls break, all that is left for him functionally are his primitive impulses. It seems that all he has to defend himself against these primitive impulses are stereotyped, banal, and constricted intellectual defenses. Like most of his family he subjects himself to considerable failure by aspiring too high.

It may well be that Mickey's paucity of resources is the result of a failure to establish identity with either his stepfather or his mother.

Nellie, the oldest daughter of Jacqueline, had an equally checkered life. While still in her early teens she was engaged in sexual intercourse by her stepfather. This pattern of sexual behavior persisted for about two years until her mother, investigating other sexual acting out by her husband, discovered it. Earlier she had been molested but not sexually assaulted by her grandfather, Jack Armstrong. Nellie's relationship with her stepfather has elements of incest and recalls the oblique Oedipal problems of her brother Mickey. Nellie repeatedly ran away from home. Both she and Mickey were drunk on numerous occasions, with an occasional arrest by the police. As a teenager, she found periodically that she could not live with her mother and intermittently moved out to live with relatives. She did not finish high school, leaving to work as a clerk in a chain variety store. Very shortly thereafter she married and had a child.

Rorschach Protocol, Nellie Smith

CARD I

1″ What if you don't see nothing.
3″

1. Butterfly

1. Whole thing—all except the—. (What?) Mean here in the center. Looks like somebody cut holes in it. (Parts?) See wings—center part is the body. (Kind?) I don't know a big one.
WS F A P

CARD II

(Takes card herself, without waiting)

7″ V Doesn't look like anything to me.

(Anything now?)
Add a: Almost everyone has one of these. Looks like one of these pens.
(*d F Obj*)
Add b: Right here looks like an opening with blood coming out. (Kind?) Beats me; looks like a blood vessel opening. (Blood?) That stuff right here (Q)—red and all splattery.
(*D CF At*)

CARD III

5″

1. Looks like butterfly in the middle of something.

1. Looks more like a bow. (What?) The wings—
D F A
(Else?) No, looks like it's lost its body.
Add a: (Why bow?)
Well, it's shaped the same in here.
(*D F Cg*)

Add b: These look like ladies—look like they're holding something. (Q) Have busts and heads, sorta fuzzy. (Else?) No.
(*W M H P*)

CARD IV
8″

1. Looks like two boats.

1. (Q) Cause they look like boats—old. (Q) Cause all tore up—holes on each end.
D F Obj

2. Looks like a tree's growing behind it.

2. Here—awful fuzzy though. Little limbs. Looks like it's dying or burned. (Q) Cause it's hanging down—all black and all leaning together. (Burnt?) Cause they're black.
dr FC′ (Fc) Bt

CARD V
1″ ∧ ∨

1. Looks like a butterfly.

1. Looks most like it, of any of the others. That looks like its antlers. Don't know what type it is. (Parts?) Just looks like wings—and butterflies have these things coming out and they have to have antlers or else they couldn't communicate. (See it?) Laying down.
W FM A P

CARD VI
8″ ∧ ∨ > Golly!
21″ ∨

1. Looks like an out-of-shape bat.

1. Only thing I could think of. (How much?) I see two halves. The cen-

ter—(See wings?) Not easily—sorta here. Wings and a head.
D F A
Add: Here—a bird—head wings here, has whiskers too—Maybe a duck (Why?)
(*D F A*)

CARD VII
8″ >

1. Looks like smoke.

1. Mostly all of it—except in here. (Q) Because, well, it's black and grey and it's going straight up.
W C′F (mF) Cl
Add a: Know what else it looks like —girls heads with ponytails sticking up. (Q) It has ponytails has nose and mouth. Looks like they're giving each other dirty looks. Here it looks like a dog. Bottom parts—paws. They're half girl and half dog—(Where would you see?) I wouldn't. (Q) Paw—hind end, sitting down.
(*D M→FM(H)*)

CARD VIII
11″

1. There a—squirrels on both sides of it. Looks like they're walking up to a mountain—I don't know.

1. Here and here. They only have three legs—(Q) Cause have legs, head and a long tail.
D→W FM A

CARD IX
4″

1. This looks like something inside your body—I studied it before—not sure what—all bloody though.

1. Whole thing. (Q) Don't know—We studied it in school and just looks like something we studied. (Q) Its

shape. Blood vessel—Blood here, it's red.
W CF At, Bl

CARD X
15″ V V Λ
Mostly this looks like ink blots.

1. Blood coming down.

1. Here. (Q) It's red and has little blue in it.
D CF Bl

2. At end, it looks like a pen, fancy pens you write letters with.

2. Here. (Q) Oh, the writing end. (Q) Looks like it spattered a bit.
D FC′ Obj
Add: This looks like a little rabbit, two eyes—something hanging down. (Q) Yeah—stuck to it. (Q) Has head, ears, nose like a little rabbit.
(*D F Ad→P*)

Like her brother Mickey's, Nellie's Rorschach reveals considerable constriction. She made only eleven responses, with 64% of her responses using the form determinant and 46% being classified as animal responses. When the Rorschach protocol is examined sequentially, Nellie opens up to Card I with a space response; she rejects the first color card, II, and finally is able to settle down to work. Noteworthy are her additional responses to the "rejected" Card II. The small, usual, upper center *d*1, she calls a pen, and follows this with a second response to the large, usual detail *D*1, the lower red-black mixture, seen by Nellie as "blood coming out of an opening—splattery." The obvious preoccupation with sexual symbols is by now a family trademark, as is the acceptance of the masculine symbol and the rejection of the feminine.

The remaining children of Jacqueline are the result of her marriage to Jay Smith. At the time of assessment, they ranged in age from 10 to 14. The oldest, a son called by the family PJ (his name is Paul Jay), was a chronic school behavior problem; he had been expelled on a number of occasions. Since the assessment, PJ has gone on to the use of marijuana and LSD and has been arrested for the possession and use of narcotics. While he is not behind in his school grade, his progress has been marked more by social promotions than by real academic achievement.

PJ's Rorschach shows more balance than those of his older brother and sister. His "*M:* sum *C* ratio" is 2:3. He makes use of three animal movement responses, but his main resource is in the intellectual, objective perception of reality, indicated by 62.5% use of form.

The last three children of Jacqueline and Jay are Terry, a 13-year-old son; Dina Lee, an 11-year-old daughter; and Mistinguette (Misty), who at the time of assessment was 10. Terry is a behavior problem in school; he has stolen bicycles and been placed in Juvenile Hall and is a conspicuously poor reader. He seems to be a relatively withdrawn youngster with few resources to cope with life. Dina Lee was an attractive 11-year-old at the time of evaluation and since then has grown into an even more attractive teenager. As of this time she has not been reported in any particular difficulty and may well be the best adjusted member of her family. The youngest child, "Misty," has not exhibited any behavioral acting out, but by the age of 12, two years after her testing, she had changed her religious affiliation three times, from Methodist to Pentecostal to Roman Catholic.

Buddy's children were not evaluated. Apparently Mrs. Armstrong, Jr. had objections and the examination was not pushed.

Linda Anne and Rachel Jones are the two daughters of Maggie Armstrong Jones. They were 14 and 12 at the time of assessment. Their mother and father had divorced when both children were relatively young. Since then and until quite recently their home was a small house trailer, to which her mother frequently invited men friends for the night. Linda Anne was sexually molested by her grandfather, Jack Armstrong; has been arrested and placed in Juvenile Hall for shoplifting; has been promiscuous with eight to ten young men; and has used marijuana and LSD repeatedly. She was brought into therapy by her mother because her behavior under LSD frightened her mother. Rachel, her younger sister by approximately two years, has had numerous school problems, none of which seemed to be serious to the school authorities. These school problems were, however, troubling to her mother, and the school authorities reported the mother as a problem rather than the child. It should be noted, almost as an afterthought, that Rachel, like her sister and cousins, was sexually molested by her grandfather.

Rorschach Protocol, Linda Anne Jones

CARD I
85″ ∧ ∨ ∧

1. ∂ ∧ Looks like < > ∧ light inside of a pumpkin. And looks like a light shining through ∨ ∧ > ∧	1. Kinda mean looking mouth—only it's covered up—not all of it *DS FC′(Fm) Obj*

CARD II
10″ ∧ ∨

1. Looks like a butterfly's wings only they're too far apart.	1. Shape, that's all. (? Black) Yeah but the color makes it stand out, but if it were black I'd still notice it. *D F Ad*
2. > ∧ ∨ ∧ Looks like two dogs with big old noses together.	2. Shape, part of dog. *D FM A*
3. ∨ Looks like a dog, but it's a scottie dog.	3. Shape—ears eyes and nose, ears are fuzzy. *D F Ad*

CARD III
5″ ∧

1. Looks like a person.	1. (*D*) Bending down touching something. (? Sex) Women because she has breasts. *D M H P*

2. > V Looks like a sea horse.

   2. Red side detail—except tail too long and head turn down too much.
   D F A

3. Butterfly.

   3. Center red. (?) Wings. (? more) Shape and color.
   D FC A P

4. Looks like hamsters—cheeks with mouth full.

   4. Cheeks look like they're full.
   D F Ad

CARD IV
6″ ∧

1. Looks like a boot.

   1. Shaped like a boot and it's black and most boots are black.
   D FC′ Cg

2. Looks like a dead candle—fallen over. > V ∧

   2. Just kinda drooping down—wax falling over.
   D F Obj

CARD V
10″ ∧ V ∧

1. Looks like a bat—only wings wrong way.

   1. Wings mostly wings down instead of going up—flying.
   W̸ FM A P

2. > This way looks like a big bird with a big old long beak and its wings are way up here (mouth open).

   2. Just top part—looks like an eagle flying.
   D FM A

3. > Alligator head with mouth open (center).

   3. (*DS*) head. Looks like jaws.
   DS FM Ad

4. ∧ Side. Alligator with mouth open.

   4. He looks like a meaner one. His mouth opens too but not very wide.
   D FM (Fm) Ad

5. V Butterfly except for part over here.

   5. Whole thing. Feelers and—only head should come together a little bit.
   W̸ FM A P

CARD VI
6″ ∧ ∨

1. Looks like a pussy cat with its head down—like in cartoon with a big old nose.
   1. Just head. Cutest—nose sticks out. Laying down flat—with his head flat —side fur on head—looks fluffy and furry and straggly.
   D Fc FM Ad
2. ∨ Skinned rug—tiger rug.
   2. (*D*) (? up) Fur side.
   D Fc AObj
3. ∂ ∨ Looks like fire—kinda.
   3. Flame like it rushes up.
   D mF Fi

CARD VII
3″ ∧

1. Looks like a girl with her pony tail up and her hand back up this way. (demonstrates)
   1. Shape, looking at herself in the mirror—just posing.
   D M Hd P
2. ∨ Looks like a cat's tail with all its coloring.
   2. (colors?) Different greys.
   D FC′ Ad
3. ∨ Looks like eye of an elephant with its trunk down there.
   3. Eye and trunk. (Q) Shape.
   Dd F Ad
   Add: Goblin—staring real mean—teeth showing—grinning real mean.
   (*D Fm(H)*)
4. ∨ Dog with a raccoon's hat on and that's its tail there.
   4. Dog, nose and eye wearing hat and tail of raccoon hat.
   D Fc A

CARD VIII
2″ Oh that's pretty
12″ ∧ ∨

1. That looks like a butterfly.
   1. (*dd*) Shape and colors
   Dd FC A
2. > ∧ Looks like animal walking.
   2. (*D*) Shape, legs mostly.
   D FM(Fm) A P
   Add: It looks like a cat only its ears are back. He's mean looking.

CARD IX

24″ ∧ ∨

1. That looks like head of a hippopotamus.	1. Ear, eye, nose. *Dd F Ad*
2. That looks like fire.	2. Color. *D CF Fi*

CARD X

2″ Oh how pretty.

12″ ∧

1. In the middle looks like rabbit's head and ears.	1. Ears, head. *D F Ad*
2. ∨ That looks like lungs—those two.	2. Grey upper center shape and side by side and looks like ribs. *D F At*
3. Those look like sea horses.	3. Shape. *D F A*
4. That looks like head of sea horse.	4. Shape. *Dd F A*
5. Looks like feelers in the center.	5. Shape. *D F Ad*
6. Reminds me of spiders—the legs you know.	6. (D_1) All the legs *D F A P* *Add:* Wishbone. (*D F Ad*)

In the third generation the overall homogeneity of the Rorschach patterns breaks down. In a large measure this may be ascribed to the greater variability in psychological age, maturity, and character formation among these young people. But the variability introduced by the different non-Armstrong spouses also plays a part. Nonetheless, one can easily identify the characterological referents of the impulsive, acting-out behavior. This is particularly true of the older grandchildren, where the development of basic character structure has led to the formation of a more comprehensive life style.

Jacqueline Smith's six children break down into two groups on the basis of Rorschach patterns. When these two groups are examined the differentiation is seen to be simply sex; the boys have a Rorschach pattern similar to their mother while the girls have a different pattern, reflecting better adjustment. For the Smith boys the number of determinants used is limited; each one used only four, with a heavy emphasis on the use of form (*F*), similar to Jacqueline. Altogether only six determinants were used, with animal movement (*FM*) the only determinant other than form to have any extensive use. In addition, the total number of responses was very limited, with a mean of 13.66 responses being produced.

Both the boys and the girls of the Smith family had high (perhaps unrealistically high) levels of aspiration. The *W*:*M* ratio for the boys averaged 4.5:1. Surprisingly, the girls' ratio averaged 5.22:1. Terry, the youngest son, seems to be the most inadequate. His total record is coarctated; he made 12 responses, eight of which were form, with three additional form responses. Of the four remaining responses, two reflect his anxiety (*Fc*), with just one human movement (*M*) and one color-form (*CF*). With such limited resources, there can only be a limited and pathological repertory of responses on Terry's part.

Mickey, the oldest son, used no color or shading determinants whatsoever. He also made a limited number of responses, 13, with major emphasis on maintaining reality contact (seven *F* and three additional *F* responses).

The girls of the Smith family seem to have fared better in terms of their coping resources. Not only did the girls use more determinants than the boys (9:6), but they showed greater resiliency in the ability to produce additional responses (21 additionals for the girls to 7 for the boys). Moreover, where the boys indicated great discomfort and quite inadequate techniques in handling affectively laden material, the girls demonstrated greater comfort and a wider latitude of responses when dealing with stimuli tapping their emotions. As a corollary to this ability to cope with their emotions, there was less over dependence on reality testing, a greater willingness to listen to other voices than that of external-realistic cues.

When the Rorschach protocols of the two Jones girls are compared with their Smith cousins, the differences are rather prominent.

The two Jones girls used more determinants than did the Smith children; the use of form (*F*) was considerably less, and there was much more emphasis on the extratensive, emotion-tapping side of the psychogram for the Jones children than for the Smith children. Along with the more extensive use of color as a determinant, almost as a corollary of the greater ease and familiarity with the emotional components of their makeup, there was a more controlled use of color. Instead of the *CF* responses of the Smiths, the Joneses tended to use more *FC*. Both Jones children used the animal movement (*FM*) more frequently than the Smiths.

On the other hand, when the Smith children are divided by sexes, the Rorschach profiles of the girls in both families are more alike than those of the sisters and brothers of the Smith family. Sex differences seem to be holding up. It is important to note that the children of the Smith family have Rorschach protocols that are closely related to their mother's Rorschach. Likewise the greater variability to be found in Maggie Armstrong Jones' protocol seems to have correlations to her daughters' Rorschachs.

The rest of the children of the third generation of Armstrongs are quite young and as such have not had too much opportunity to get into difficulties. They range from Gail and Frank Post, aged 9 and 8, respectively, to Judy-Jo, Anne, and James Armstrong aged 6, 5, and 3. Anne and James Armstrong, the two younger children of John and Manon Armstrong, were not given Rorschachs, since they were only 5 and 3 years old. Thus, discussion will center around the three older children of the two nuclear (but related) families. Both Gail and Frank Post appear to be reasonably well adjusted, although Gail does show some signs of stress and tension as reflected by one small *m* and the two additional *K*'s. The pressure of one *Fc* and one *C'* in Frank's Rorschach indicate some anxiety but also demonstrate his sensitivity. For an 8-year-old boy, Frank's Rorschach profile is quite mature. The relatively low *F* percentage of 22% is mitigated by two additional *F* responses, so that while he may be more involved with his impulses (not atypical for an 8-year-old), he can test reality a little more extensively during a second opportunity. Gail's

Rorschach profile may be mildly constricted, with an overemphasis on form responses, but the overall balance indicates some ability for affective living and even greater capacity for introspection and intellectualized control. The similarities between the Rorschach profiles of Gail and her mother are once again striking and illustrate the identification between mother and daughter.

The one child of John Armstrong who will be discussed is, as of the present, a fairly intact little girl. Judy-Jo does not see herself as closely integrated into the family as her younger sister and brother, nor as strongly desired. These feelings may well be a function of sibling rivalry and also reflect that her parents see her as older and expect more impulse control of her. Observationally, she is more compliant, less rebellious, and gets along better in the family. "Cookie," as the younger sister Anne is known, seems to have a more secure relationship in the family and seems, therefore, more capable of self-assertion, but both children have a feeling they are being pushed and pressured. Judy-Jo's Rorschach reflects her relative inability to cope with her primitive impulses, and seems to reflect a conforming yet warm, affectionate child. Her ability to produce human movement and animal movement additional responses indicates her positive potentials, and the fact that they are "additionals" rather than original responses reflects the pressure of her repressions. Unlike her cousins, her Rorschach is not similar to the Armstrongs (her father), and this may be a reflection of the sex differences and the profound influence her mother has had upon her characterological development up the present.

Summary

The presence of psychopathology has been amply demonstrated both behaviorally and on the Rorschach in all three generations of this family. The feelings of inadequacy and rejection, the processes of sadism and castration, were so severe in Jack and Jane Armstrong that maladjustment was the rule rather than the exception. The failure of the Armstrong children to make adequate identifications, both male and female, led to further pathological functioning on their part, influencing in turn the third generation.

This entire family was, to say the least, asocial, self-defeating, and sexually promiscuous. It might well be posited that family processes in the Armstrongs were breaking down despite the superficial vitality and talent they displayed.

The Rorschach not only clarified the individual personality structures, but made possible comparison of these three generations. The obvious similarities of the Rorschach psychograms and even of responses to individual cards were quite striking and palpably beyond chance. It is almost possible to conclude that any nondamaged member of the Armstrongs resulted because of the more adequate model and functioning of the non-Armstrong spouse.

On the whole, these people were impulse-ridden, orally demanding, dependent individuals with a spurious façade of integration and vitality. They were constricted, conventional people who had very low frustration tolerance and few defenses for coping with frustration. They were hostile, resentful people who seemed to be fearful of expressing their anger (except in explosive outbursts) because they would lose whatever narcissistic gratification they were getting. Thus, this led to a displacement of affect and considerable acting-out behavior.

In some ways the Armstrongs are typical of us all, but hopefully it is suggested that many of us may have grown beyond this type of "all-American boy" toward maturity.

References

Abt, L. E. and Weissman, S. L. 1965. *Acting Out*. New York: Grune and Stratton.

Bell, N. W. and Vogel, E. F. (Eds.). 1960. *A Modern Introduction to the Family*. Glencoe, Ill.: The Free Press.

Davidson, Helen H. 1950. A measure of adjustment obtained from the Rorschach protocol. *J. Proj. Techniques,* 14: 31–38.

Sobler, Dorothy T., Holzberg, J. D., Fleck, S., Cornelison, Alice R., Kay, Eleanor and Lidz, T. 1957. The prediction of family interaction from a battery of projective tests. *J. Proj. Techniques,* 21: 199–208.

Warner, W. L. and Lunt, P. S. 1941. *The Social Life of a Modern Community.* New Haven: Yale University Press.

PART TWO

New Approaches

Fred Cutter
Norman L. Farberow

6

The Consensus Rorschach

The consensus Rorschach is a term applied to a protocol elicited from two or more people who are asked to reach agreement in their responses to ink blots (Farberow, 1968). Beyond this minimal definition, any number of conditions can be specified under which agreement is sought.

In the literature to date, the consensus protocols have been obtained before or after, or without, standard individual Rorschach administrations. This latter procedure is the only alternative where the identified patient is dead or absent, as in suicide and AWOL. The psychologist may be present as a participant-observer in any variation of the standard role, or he may structure the group into a form of self-administering consensus while he leaves the room, followed by an individual inquiry. Additionally, the psychologist can await a signal to return or observe through a one-way mirror. Each subject may be given a complete set of Rorschach cards, or they may all be asked to share one. The groups can consist of an entire family regardless of number, spouses only, or parent–child or sibling subgroups. Other combinations can be formed according to the purpose of testing, such as with peers, friends, roommates, employees, patient–staff, and so forth. Even the number of ink blots administered can be varied significantly depending upon the situation.

Blanchard (1959) reported on the process between gang members using only four blots, while Loveland, Singer, and Wynne (1963) examined the quality of the relation apparent in families using as few as two ink blots.

Any group can be selected to serve as the social context whose influence on the subject requires examination. Beyond the family, both primary and parental, there is the possibility of investigating status influence, social class (rich–poor), degree of education, age, sex, marital status, and other groupings. Within total institutions, such as mental hospitals or prisons, the study of recidivism can be facilitated by relating the behavior of the subject to his relevant staff on the one hand and his inmate group on the other. The information available from a consensus Rorschach with both groups would permit the study of discrepant expectations in the roles assigned by the subject's different reference groups. The selective accommodations of the individual, apparent in the consensus Rorschachs, allows for better explanation of postinstitutional or enigmatic behavior.

The consensus protocols allow an analysis in terms of the process, the product, or the polarity elicited in the course of the testing (Wynne, 1968). A process analysis emphasizes the interaction between the members, such as occurs in group therapy, and attempts to examine the ways in which the members react to each other (Blanchard, 1959; Levy and Epstein, 1964; Loveland, 1967). The product, or content analysis, examines the meaning of the responses in terms of the nature and structure of the group (Bauman and Roman, 1964). The content also can be examined for variations between individual Rorschachs and the responses obtained in the consensus period. Examination of polarities focuses on the manifestation of controversies in which conflicting expectations are expressed by members of the group (Cutter, 1968, 1968a).

Because each subject has more than one possible social context and its associated role, the serial effect of repeated consensus Rorschachs was investigated in a variety of reference groups, particularly relevant to the given subject's problem behavior (Cutter and Farberow, 1968). This serial approach makes it possible to examine the range of expectations apparent in all the contexts and the discrepancies between them as well. For example, a sex offender should be evaluated in a consensus Rorschach with his family, with his fellow patients, with his sex partner, if possible, and with staff members. The range of expectations to which this person is subject will then be externalized. Where discrepancies occur, the psychologist will have clues to adjustment problems and the specific social context in which these will emerge.

The variety of results, thus far, augur well for future developments, but it is clear at this point that not all the possibilities have been identified nor explored. The consensus Rorschach procedure is still too new for standardized rules and conditions.

The consensus Rorschach has been used in a treatment situation by Walter Klopfer as a means of sensitizing patients to discrepancies in their private behavior (individual Rorschachs) as compared with the manifest acts in family groups (consensus), such as with wife, mother, etc. Klopfer has also adapted this technique to orient teachers in the problems of their individual students by having children first respond individually to each card and later work out a consensus. The individual and group responses occur in a class setting with all students present throughout the procedure (Klopfer, 1968).[1]

The remainder of this chapter presents the literature on the consensus Rorschach to date, describes our present theory in more detail, including clinical applications, and suggests implication for further research on the basis of our present experiences (Cutter, 1968a).

Review of the Literature

The Rorschach of consensus was first reported by W. H. Blanchard (1959). He elicited individual Rorschachs of gang members for

---

[1] A short private communication, July 26, 1968.

comparison with a total gang protocol called the "group process" Rorschach. Blanchard reports clinical and Rorschach impressions of three gang members in a white group and four gang members in a Negro group. Both gangs had participated in a rape. In the white group, the gang leader quickly demonstrated his dominance by getting the other two members to accept his definitions of three out of the four ink blots given. In the Negro group, four boys participated in the group process Rorschach, with a clearly manifested struggle between the leader and a relatively "nice" member of the group. The struggle appeared to be in terms of who would dominate the others, and was focused in the choice between the response of "male homosexuals" on Card III by the leader, versus "two ladies" by the nice boy.

Blanchard felt the material documented an hypothesis of the presence of homosexual impulses in leaders of gangs, triggered by the presence of gang members. At the very least, his publication demonstrated the greater usefulness of data reflecting group processes over the collection of individual responses in classic testing procedures in examination of role relationships. Thus, of most interest was his description of the interaction between the leader and a member for dominance of the consensus. In the present context, this rivalry is interpreted as reflecting an area of group conflict, shared by all the members but expressed primarily by the two persons verbalizing the opposite polarities (Cutter, Farberow, and Sapin, 1967). Thus, in the white gang a response of "blue brassiere" to the central blue area of Card X by one of the subordinate members is rejected vehemently by the leader and others. The conflict appears between a subordinate member versus a dominant and reality-oriented leader. In the second gang, the competition can be construed similarly, with the group sharing the conflict. However, in the Negro group, the roles are reversed, with the leader asserting the more sexually aberrant response of male homosexuals, and a subordinate urging the socially more acceptable two ladies. In the context of a California youth authority reception center, the dominant preoccupation in any inmate is not to reveal damaging information. In two gangs incarcerated for rape, it would therefore appear highly significant that sexual responses of any sort would emerge. Its occurrence in the group process Rorschach demonstrates the group's need to externalize all aspects of a dominant conflict.

Bauman and Roman (1964) have described their approach under the rubric "interaction testing" (Roman and Bauman, 1966). In their procedures they gave the standard individual administration followed by an interaction session to couples in which one member was receiving psychiatric care in a Day Treatment Center. The couple was required to agree upon a mutually acceptable response and one member, previously selected by the group, had to record. The authors do not report direct results with the Rorschach in their initial publications. Instead, they describe their system using the Wechsler-Bellevue similarities and comprehension subtest items from both Form I and Form II. However, since their method has implications for consensus Rorschach, it will be described here. The authors have also indicated they are collecting consensus Rorschachs using the same system for analysis which they developed with the Wechsler. Essentially they rated each agreement response as dominance, combination, emergence, or reinforcement by contrasting the individual and interaction testing. They also scored the quality of interaction responses in comparison to individual answers.

While the partner with the highest IQ tended to dominate agreement, the effects of sex, patient status, and role of recorder were also significantly related to dominance. The authors noted a trend toward pooling of resources so that the task efficiency of "normal" couples was not only consistent but effective enough to differentiate them from couples with a neurotic member and also from couples with a psychotic member. The authors conclude that decision-making processes studied by them are significant in discriminating normal from pathological, and hospitalized from discharged, patient groups. They also note that negative emergence scores are the most discriminating in terms of identifying pathological marital interaction.

Loveland, Wynne, and Singer reported their preliminary experiences under the title "The Family Rorschach" (1963). Their administration procedures consisted of eliciting an individual and consensus protocol in much the same fashion as the other researchers, with the exception that each member of the family had his own set of inkblots, and the consensus was obtained after the examiner left the room. The authors describe their experience with a family of three in which the 25-year-old son is a schizophrenic patient. All were in family therapy at NIMH. The consensus Rorschach elicited evidence of mother's disruptive and impairing effect with respect to father's and son's effort to communicate with each other and with her. They see its value as a standardized sampling procedure for studying how family members interpret reality to each other.

Later, Loveland (1967) extended this approach under the name "relation Rorschach." She reports collecting verbatim recordings of interactions for approximately 150 groups of two or more members. These included patients and their therapists, spouses only, and families and family subgroups, including preschoolers. With increasing experience there developed, she reports, "stable inferences" from card to card, and she recommends the use of one card only to elicit a 10-minute transcription of interaction in arriving at consensus. An additional 5 minutes is permitted for families having difficulty. Loveland asks each participant to indicate all the things that were agreed upon in a written individual inquiry following the "relation Rorschach." This protocol yields three kinds of information: (1) each person's grasp of the consensus; (2) the clarity of the written over the verbal exposition; and (3) those consensuses where the individual had unspoken reservations.

Interestingly, Loveland offers a rationale for the use of the Rorschach rather than tasks, examples from life, or other projective and objective tests: (1) the Rorschach test is engrossing without being traumatic for the participants, even with repetition; (2) the ambiguity of the stimuli permits projection, not only of the individual, but of the subculture of the group being tested; (3) the extensive experience of Rorschach psychologists and the background knowledge of the Rorschach ink blots permits the investigator to make use of relatively known materials to study human relations. Loveland's system for analysis attempted to assess three qualities of interaction:

(a) Clarity and vividness of the speaker's verbal communication.
(b) The grasp of meaning and the imagination, sensitivity, appropriateness, and accuracy of understanding of the assignment, to each other, and the ink-blot interpretation.
(c) Relations—the affective stand the participants take to each other, the task, and the ink blots.

Each aspect is then rated on a four-point scale:

1. Unusually sensitive, imaginative, realistic interaction which facilitates group movement in the direction of the task.
2. More ordinary objective transactions which are adequate in the situation.
3. Transactions which tend to constrict, hamper, distract, or otherwise limit consensus.
4. Transactions which preclude, distort, or disrupt consensus.

Loveland reports a pilot study of reliability using 12 spouse protocols with two other judges as "significant at .03." The judges had graduate training in psychology and had been trained in making these ratings. The total ratings tended to differentiate parents by severity of psychiatric diagnosis carried for their offsprings, i.e., schizophrenic from neurotic, neurotic from medical, and volunteer.

Levy and Epstein (1964) report their use of consensus Rorschachs with a family preceded by individual testing. They believe that the Rorschach protocols thus obtained throw light on how the family achieves equilibrium. They conceptualize this continuous process as consisting of efforts by each member to "level off" his individual response from a highly personal and expressive percept (either good quality or poor) to one that is more compatible with the emerging consensus in the family context. The quality of the consensus response may be better than the individual's or worse; the comparison permits an inference about the price the individual pays for his participation in achieving consensus. "Maladaptive functioning" on the individual Rorschachs by both parents and one child produces psychopathological areas on the consensus. In this case, the individual's typical mode of achieving equilibrium fails in the group protocol and consensus fails to emerge, or emerges in poor quality.

Singer and Wynne (1963) have described the stylistic consistencies of family members which impair communication. The critical aspect they have emphasized is the style of communicating in which the pattern of handling attention and meaning was most predictive. Singer was able to match Rorschach protocols of patients to those of members of the patient's family. They report a detailed guide for differentiating the families of schizophrenics from those of non-schizophrenics in terms of how they handle attention and meaning.

This introduction and overview of consensus Rorschachs illustrates the previous attempts to organize the wealth of new data obtained and indicates the need for continued efforts toward conceptual ordering of the human events it elicits. In the following sections we shall describe our own theoretical approach more fully and some of the implications for further research.

Theory of Content Polarities and Consensus

Our rationale for analyzing the protocols of consensus Rorschachs had its origin in prior efforts to deal conceptually with the individual Rorschach records of symbiotic partners (Cutter, Farberow, and Sapin, 1967). The very first example we examined, and all those subsequent to it, were striking for the degree of similarity or relatedness of content, phrases, and styles of attending in the responses. We can illustrate with a mother and her adult schizophrenic son who later hanged himself. Where she saw people pulling, he saw them as hanging on. Where she saw a rug hanging on the wall, he saw a stingray with a barb hanging by its side for protection. The entire protocol of both are given in Table 1. We hypothesized that individual responses by two people to the same ink blots could be construed as end points of a dimension describing a range of expectations in role behavior. This hypothesis assumes the individuals are not only symbiotic partners but also belong to a natural grouping such as the family, work, play, school, therapy. We hypothesized further that the total content of the pair approximated the array of expectations to be found in the repertoire of roles usable by this group. We mean by this statement that differences between roles can be detected by variations in degree of the dimensions definable by Rorschach responses of partners. We can illustrate this last by reference to Table 1.

The 20 corresponding responses of this pair define 20 expectations incorporated in various degrees into each of the roles available to the members in their group, e.g., husband, siblings, and the associated roles of father, brother, son. Using these 20 expectations or dimensions, we can describe a mother and son role for this family. The mother role can be inferred as: maker, diminisher of others, concerned with time, controlling environment and others in it; does so with certainty that her efforts are valid and that she herself is adequate; and communicates her wishes by negation, default, or action but not by direct statement. The son's role is inferred as: attempts but never succeeds in quite knowing the nature of his world, inadequate, defective, unable to think, holding on to whatever little things he gets, derives contempt wherever he looks, feels useless, ignores time, and needs protection.

These role descriptions are simply a summary of the endpoints of the dimensions defined by mother–son responses to the same ink blots. Other roles for other members of their group would be describable by means of the same array of expectations. However, differentiations would be found in terms of degree for each dimension. The father in this family was already dead at the time the mother was given the Rorschach. Her son had died the year before. However, the father's role would be describable by reference to the same array of expectations listed in Table 1, but at intermediate points to the mother and son. This will be illustrated later in Tables 4 and 5 which describe a family of four.

We employed the same rationale in looking at the content polarities apparent in consensus Rorschach protocols. The process of identifying a content polarity is simply one of linking the two contents expressing the polar opposites within the group. The process

TABLE 1 *Content Polarities of Symbiotic Partners Illustrating Role Dimensions*

SOURCE	CONTENT POLARITIES (RORSCHACH RESPONSES) MOTHER	SON	INFERRED DIMENSION	MUTUAL EXPECTATIONS MOTHER	SON
I	1. Two little hands	Pieces cut out	Percept by	Diminishes	Damages
	2. Bat	Mask	New situation	Conventional	Mysterious
	3. That's all I can make—	—All I know	Coping	Maker	Knower
II	4. Rising sun	Butterfly	Time orientation	Concerned	Ignores
	5. Uses form only	Poor form, odd, long	Coping	Adequate	Inadequate
III	6. Pulling at something	Hanging on something	Coping	Pulling	Holding
	7. Ribcage	—pieces	Nutritional source	Inside her	Outside him
IV	8. Head of hippo	Boots	Self-orientation	Superior	Inferior
V	9. Another bat	Could be bat	Epistemology	Certainty	Doubt
VI	10. Animal skin	Sting ray	Vitality	Animal object	Live fish
	11. Skinned	Intact	Wholeness	Takes apart	Holds together
	12. Hung up to dry	Whip hanging for protection	Coping	Processed	Protected
	13. Eyes—mouth (laughter) —little black dots	Barb, close to body	Coping	Sense organs	Limb

VII	14. Ears, paws of rabbit	Face, chest, hair	Coping	Animal detail	Human detail
	15. Not an animal	Two ladies	Communication	Assertion	Denial
VIII	16. Two animals	Two mice	Affect	Activity	Static
	17. Going opposite direction	Fur	Affect	Ambivalence	Internalized
	18. Feet, head	Legs, no tail	Communication	Assertion	Denial
IX	19. I don't see anything—describes construction	I don't know, I can't think	Coping	Maker	Knower
X	20. A crab but not with that long thing	I don't know I can't think	Communication	Denial	Assertion

TABLE 2 *Consensus and Content Polarities in Rorschach Protocols Derived from Surviving Family*

		FIRST WIFE DAUGHTER SON	VICTIM (49 at death 2/21/63)	
AGES (Divorced 1957)		54 24 18	39	43
DATES OF RORSCHACH:		4/22/66 (Consensus)	(Individual) 7/24/50	(Individual) 3/23/56
CARD	CONSENSUS	CONTENT—POLARITIES	RESPONSE	RESPONSE
I	Vertebrates	Wasp—pumpkin, frog (biology)	Bat, figure of, me in Carlsbad Cavern—frightened	Hawk, person, turkey carcass
II	Smokey the Bear	Aegina rocket—vagina, entrance part	Two dogs fighting, red is blood, rib, red—suffering	Dogs—bears fighting
III	Two skeletons	Two cannibals over pot, ritual fire around them—two natives banging a drum	Two animals facing, two men in tux with high heels	Animals, bird, and kangaroo
IV	Beaver, a squirrel pelt	Eyes—teeth	Butterfly, bull's face, two swans	Hide, carcass; little baby held on a stick
V	Butterfly	No content polarity	Butterfly, hawk flying	Bat, Carlsbad Caverns
VI	Candle holder	Worm—copper sculpture you stick on church with symbolism	Torch with symbol of man on top—into light, through darkness	Looking in a crevice; person on end of a rod
VII	Two some-thing	Two hindu dancers, weird gyrations Two bunny rabbits—two people about to kiss	Where open is—could be me, get above all this	Something I saw in Carlsbad Caverns, icicles hanging down

VIII	Two animals	Two bears—two lizards	Gophers, bears, ads for Golden State ice cream, rats	Dish of ice cream melted, two bears, California flag
IX	Flowers	Mushroom shaped; bomb blast atom bomb, hydrogen bomb—grass	Person coming out, red stop, green go, yellow caution	Water color laid down; mountains, clouds, coral sea
X	No consensus	"I'm just a poor old thing" Floral setting, towers	"All my thoughts have been about getting better" Black day, yellow fright, red tears and sorrow caused for self and family	"Someone had a nice time of it." Animals, dogs, spiders Crabs, head of rabbit

consists of scanning the protocols for disagreement in whatever affective degree, regardless of who it was that verbalized the disagreements. Where several controversies are expressed, difficulty may occur in aligning the relevant extremes. Usually the decision is then based on sequence, in that one definition is typically challenged by a second, and several alternatives may build up a general concept to oppose the first response.

Content polarity also includes nonverbal behavior or process statements, such as exclamations, verbal asides, styles of attending, and sequence. Each content polarity identified contributes to a profile of the expectations within the roles available to members of that group.

As an illustration of some actual content polarities, we can look at an example from the consensus Rorschach of a mother, age 43, daughter, 24, and son, 18, taken in 1966, three years after the father's suicide by hanging. On Card III, the controversy is between "two cannibals over a pot with a ritual fire" versus "two natives banging a drum." The poles of the controversy are apparent in the phrases: (a) cannibal—natives; (b) over a pot—banging on drums. The dimensions implied exist in the degree of cannibalism and the degree of noisemaking assumed in any role taken by a member. The clinical meaning inferred from these content polarities is that each member of the group is faced with a conflict between aggressive versus nonaggressive expectations when it comes to carrying out an assigned role in the family context. In addition, they are also in conflict about the degree of ritual versus noisemaking encountered in fulfilling these roles. There are, of course, other conflicting expectations but these are identified by additional content polarities. Table 2 abstracts from the verbatim protocols of this surviving family's consensus, including content from two prior individual Rorschachs of the father taken 10 and 16 years earlier.

A consensus achieved by the group for any one ink blot, no matter how superficial, common, or inadequate its form quality, can be viewed as an expectation that is binding on all the members, precisely because it reflects the least common denominator acceptable to each. To the degree that a member finds such a consensus unacceptable, either privately or later, to that degree is his membership diluted or its expectations not binding; which is to say, the degree of alienation from this group in particular is reflected.

In the example used in Table 2, the three members of the family agreed upon two skeletons for Card III. Sixteen years earlier the father saw two men in tuxedos, but in his second Rorschach eight years later, his content was unrelated to his family's subsequent consensus. The husband's two earlier responses of "two animals facing" and "two men in tuxedos with high heels," retain both aspects of the family's conflicting expectations—degree of aggressiveness (cannibal—native) and degree of ritual (over a pot—banging on drums)—but at ambiguous or ambivalent levels for sex roles, respectively. The later response of animals, birds, and kangaroos appears to be unrelated to the content in the consensus Rorschach of Table 2.

In the interim between the two Rorschachs, the husband had been divorced by his wife and was in the process of remarrying. During his first marriage he was in constant distress from his wife's conflicting expectations within the roles available to him as father, husband, male, or worker.

Table 3 illustrates the clinical application of the consensus Rorschach for the protocols seen in Table 2. The primary question of why this 49-year-old veteran elected to kill himself can now be approached but not completely answered, especially in the absence of an opportunity for a consensus Rorschach from his second wife and stepdaughter. However, some of the similarities and changes between his first and second Rorschach and the consensus obtained from his first family yield some clues of the motivation for his suicide at age 49 rather than at age 42.

Table 3 juxtaposes selected individual Rorschach responses from Table 2 that reflect a personal reaction to family-imposed conflicts. These latter are derived from the content polarities found in the consensus Rorschach of the surviving first wife and children. These selected responses document preexisting self-expectations in the victim that are manifested in the actual completed suicide incident.

This can be illustrated by reference to Card VI. The family agrees on "candle holder" while arguing over "worm" versus "copper

TABLE 3 *Clinical Replication of Data Presented in Table 2*

<table>
<tr><td>The suicide of this 49-year-old victim was triggered by his second wife's threat to obtain a divorce. Why didn't the first wife's divorce action trigger any form of self-terminating behavior at the age of 42?</td><td>Table 2 indicates a shift toward resolution and away from ambivalence around family imposed conflicts and expectations. This qualitative emancipation is correlated with the divorce.

Card I: The victim retains his original ambivalence to the family conflict of victim-predator. On Card IV, his efforts to resolve a different conflict succeeds, but at the price of a regressive victim self-expectation. To the family's conflicting expectations for an adequate male, the victim responds equally bad on the two Rorschachs (see Cards VI and VII). However, at age 37 he puts a good face on it all and tries for a positive image. At age 42, he is more defeated and together with the alienation from family, is less distressed at the discrepancies between his own achievement and their expectations.</td></tr>
<tr><td>This 49-year-old veteran hung himself in a garage after removing the car, closing the door, and writing a note "ill health." He died between 10 A.M. and 2 P.M., while his second wife was away. At the time he was on pass from a Veterans Administration hospital. She had announced her intention to file for divorce a few weeks earlier. A 12-year-old stepdaughter had publicly ridiculed him recently.</td><td>Card VI: Conflict in expectations for male behavior exists in family between symbols of "worm" versus "spiritual or light." Victim's effort to take "light" role fails. By second Rorschach he adopts "worm or victim" role.

Card VII: Family conflicted about proper expression of heterosexual feeling between "cute" and "weird" gyrations. Husband affectively blocked and responds with autistic continuations of imagery in Card VI, i.e., he becomes an icicle hanging in Carlsbad Cavern.

Card I: Family conflict in expectations for each member in terms of predator-victim with the patient eventually accepting the victim image (see Card IV, 1956).</td></tr>
</table>

sculpture." Every member of this group is expected to be a "light giver" in all roles available to them. In addition, they incorporate a conflict between "bearer of light" and "worm." The father adapts to these family expectations by attempting to maintain the "light giver" image at age 37. At age 42, he has shifted to the image of an object, i.e., "man on end of a rod." "Looking into a crevice" and the Card IV response of "body held on a stick" further amplify this shift toward an object or "wormlike" self-expectation.

The suicide of this patient is described in Table 3, where it is related to the content he gave to Card VII on the two individual Rorschach protocols. His family responds to this ink blot with the minimal agreement of "two something." It is clear they disagree about the content. The polarity consists of "weird gyrations"—"kissing." This family imposes a conflicting expectation about proper expression of heterosexual impulses. The husband adapts to this conflict at age 37 by an autistic continuation of his light role, "symbol of man," on Card VI. He literally denies an improper feeling, i.e., "get above all this." At age 42, he responds to the same conflicting expectations by accepting a passive, frozen role and the threatening context of "Carlsbad Caverns"; i.e., a shift to the victim role following failure to be "proper" as a husband. This second Rorschach was taken while his wife was initiating divorce proceedings.

The data in Table 2 show a shift away from the markedly ambivalent feelings about his role as father and husband. By the time of the second Rorschach, and his first wife's divorce, he appears to have accepted a victim expectation and was no longer as concerned, nor conflicted, about living up to the role of capable provider or adequate father. While the content in the second Rorschach is rather depressed and otherwise pathognomonic, it is marked more by surrender rather than conflict. It is this acceptance that permits him to go on living, first as a patient and then as the supported husband of an affluent widow.

In general, the concept of consensus and content polarities refer to group-imposed agreements as well as conflicts in expectation. Each member's acceptance of these expectations and the degree of resolution where conflicts occur can be inferred from his individual

TABLE 4

H.H. CA-50 MALE 1-6-68	A.H. CA-45 FEMALE 2-19-68	W.H. CA-15 FEMALE 2-12-68	J.H. CA-13 MALE 2-12-68
CARD I 5″–90″	5″–180″	5″–75″	20″–30″
1. Small sort of bat, yet has crab-like claws with eyes and tail.	1. Butterfly.	1. ∧ Sort of looks like a bat.	1. ∧ I guess it looks like a butterfly.
2. Also makes me think of an airplane.	2. Crab. Just.	2. ∨ Looks like something over in a pagoda. Something that might be on a pond in Japan.	
3. Irregularity around edges makes me think of clouds.	3. Insects in general. Beetle-type insects.	3. ∨ Or a table with something on it.	
4. Also see map of a country with the lakes and the mountains.	4. Figure of a person without a head. Costume out at side. She is standing with feet close together and her hands up here.		
	5. > Dog on top, a poodle-type dog with cone-like cap on, as if in stage act.		

INQUIRY			
1. Profile. Outer shape.	1. Pincher-like things in front. Symmetry of thing.	1. The color. This part could be the body with wings.	1. Well, wings and smooth like a head up here and feelers and part of body sticking out.
2. Outline. (Q) Engine.	2. Same as #1.	2. It is kind of stocky and short. Looks like it could be a temple. I have seen them in that shape.	
3. (*W* response). Curved and peaks. (Q) Mostly the edge detail. Also the whiteness in center make it seem more like clouds. They were broken up.	3. Just pinchers. (Q) *W*.	3. Legs here. This could be something on it. (Lower position of blot).	
4. Outline. White spots are the lakes.	4. Just central part. I feel I have to account for all this out here. A play. Very fanciful.		
	5. Tail, back, head is turned so you don't see the nose. I have to account for this, so see it as a hat.		
	(Asked to limit to not more than 5 responses).		

(continued)

TABLE 4 *(continued)*

H.H. CA-50 MALE 1-6-68	A.H. CA-45 FEMALE 2-19-68	W.H. CA-15 FEMALE 2-12-68	J.H. CA-13 MALE 2-12-68
CARD II 12″–75″	10″–180″	20″–65″	25″–40″
1. I think of missile blasting off. It leaves a fiery trail.	1. Head and shoulders of two animals. They are mythical animals. Too long for nose and too short for a proboscus. See ears and front paws. Look more like bears than anything else, with long funny noses.	1. $\wedge \vee <$ Could be two animals fighting. Blood and everything.	1. $\wedge \vee < \wedge$ Looks like two sitting people with their hands touching each other.
2. Could be capsule out in space.	2. Two seals with heads and body thrust upward as if balancing an object. (Upper *D*.)		
3. Could be two animals nose to nose.	3. Old-fashioned lamp with tassle hanging down from the middle.		

INQUIRY			
1. Shape and fiery trail.	1. Looks more like bears. If I did not have to work this into picture I would say bears.	1. Just the general shape and the blood make me think of fighting. Can sort of see feet and tail. Just general shape.	1. Heads (red). These look like hands. Body here and feet coming down so it looks like they are sitting.
2. White against black. It is center section.	2.		
3. (*P*) Two dark objects. Little dogs or bears. (Q) Just profile of head. I saw ears and nose.	3. (*S*) Tassle is here (lower *D*).		
CARD III			
5″–90″	5″–90″	15″–70″	30″–50″
1. Two people dancing.	1. Two people bowing to each other.	1. $\wedge <$ Could be fish.	1. $\wedge \vee \wedge$ There are two people and they are facing each other and they are holding onto something. I don't know what it is.
2. Again I could see the insect or two crab types with the tentacles.	2. Two monkeys dressed in clothes but bowing to each other.	2. $\vee$ Frog. Small body could have dissected it or something. Red could signify blood I guess.	

(continued)

TABLE 4 *(continued)*

H.H. CA-50 MALE 1-6-68	A.H. CA-45 FEMALE 2-19-68	W.H. CA-15 FEMALE 2-12-68	J.H. CA-13 MALE 2-12-68
3. Possibly someone wearing dark glasses.	3. Bow tie.		
4. Possibly a bow tie on a white shirt.	4. Stomach with esophagus coming up from it (side *D*).		
INQUIRY			
1. (*P*) (Q) Way legs are flexed would not be normal stance. They are off balance.	1.	1. Could be fin and tail (side *D*).	1. Well, the heads and these definitely look like arms. Legs here and have shoes on. It looks like a drum they are beating on.
2. Tentacles with mouth here.	2. They are so scrawny that I thought of monkeys.	2. Eyes and shape of his head. (Q) Just half of it (frog).	
3. Elongated glasses on a face.	3.		
4. (*P*) Color.	4. (Side *D*.)		

CARD IV

8″–60″	6″–100″	15″–60″	25″–60″
1. Reminds me of an animal that has been skinned and put out to dry—like a muskrat.	1. Looks like a bear skin rug.	1. ∧ < ∨ Looks like a dragon.	1. ∧ ∨ I see a dragon with wings and a
2. Flying squirrel.	2. Couple of giant legs and feet. 3. Looks like a crocodile—just the head. 4. Witch doctor dressed in a fantastic skin or tribal costume because of appendages that are out.	2. ∧ Or could be a piece of ash from the fire. 3. ∧ Could be a person sitting on a log with his feet up.	2. Looks like a real fat kind of Chinese person.
INQUIRY			
1. Profile or outline.	1. Looks like the head of bear flattened. The ragged outline and gradation in color.	1. Cause of general shape. Looks like his feet were up.	1. Wings on the side. Big head with spikes coming out and two tails and looks like has spikes coming out a little bit.
2. Profile (Q) Furry aspect of outstretched legs.	2. Usual.	2. The way it is folded up here—the shadow. It is floating away. It is not heavy.	2. For face, I see slits for eyes. Lots of wrinkles. Big feet and small arms.

(continued)

TABLE 4 (*continued*)

H.H. CA-50 MALE 1-6-68	A.H. CA-45 FEMALE 2-19-68	W.H. CA-15 FEMALE 2-12-68	J.H. CA-13 MALE 2-12-68
	3. Usual.	3. Because it was folded up again. Looks like shoes. Looks like sitting on something at top. Looks like eyes and big nose.	
	4. The arms here as if in a pose like this (demonstrates).		
CARD V 8″–90″	3″–105″	10″–60″	10″–30″
1. Butterfly.	1. A bat—the overall impression.	1. ∧ Looks like a bat.	1. ∧ ∨ A bat.
2. And a bat.	2. Elaborate costume as in a stage production.	2. ∧ Or could be a rabbit behind a hedge.	
3. Possibly an airplane.	3. Three people with one in middle supporting the two leaning in from the sides.	3. ∨ < Could be an airplane.	

4. Possibly twins back to back. Twin people with curly hair reclining on small sort of couch or chair.			
INQUIRY			
1. Profile	1. Slender body with outstretched wings.	1. Because of general shape and the color.	1. Wings at side. Reminds me of ears bat has and body sticks out at bottom.
2. Same idea.	2. Person with hat and the costume here.	2. Because of ears. And looks like a rabbit's feet. Since I can't see the whole rabbit it would have to be behind something.	
3. Same again	3. Legs here. The rest is obscured. I guess I see such fantastic things that I have to relate to stage play or something like that.	3. General shape—the wings (*W*).	
4. Could almost see eyes and nose. Could almost see breast or could be arms folded. (Q) I could see it there on top.			

(continued)

TABLE 4 *(continued)*

H.H. CA-50 MALE 1-6-68	A.H. CA-45 FEMALE 2-19-68	W.H. CA-15 FEMALE 2-12-68	J.H. CA-13 MALE 2-12-68
CARD VI 10″–55″	8″–120″	8″–55″	40″–45″
1. Again little skinned animal stretched out to dry. 2. Also Zulu native with feathers around his neck.	1. Suggests a skinned animal. All flattened out. 2. Totem pole. 3. Central post part looks like a bed post or table leg that has been turned on a lathe. 4. Birds in flight. Looks feathery there near the top. 5. Whole thing looks like a bellows, possibly a bagpipe.	1. ∧ Looks like an X-ray. 2. ∧ Could be a bearskin rug. 3. > Airplane coming out of a cloud. 4. > Or a ray gun.	1. ∧ ∨ < ∧ A fur rug.
INQUIRY 1. Right. The profile. (Q) Duplication of pairs. I can see four feet.	1. The sort of thing you see tacked up on the wall of a den.	1. Because it is light and dark.	1. From picture it doesn't look like it has very much depth. It looks soft (Q) I don't know. Just the way the ink—it looks smooth.

2. Profile thing here. (Q) Zulu. The fact that neck was real long compared to the body. (Q) Lower part could be the body.	2. The upper part. I think I have seen totem poles with wings. This suggested it.	2. Could be like a bear head and like a big thick skin opened up. (Side?) This is fur that I am seeing.	
	3. Turned on a lathe.	3. Like a rain cloud because of color and wings (top *D*).	
	4. These birds are going this way and these are going this way. The way they stick their necks out in flight.	4. It is the shape. This could be handle and this could be fire coming out of it.	
	5. Handle of bellows (top *D*) and the rest is part that opens up.		
CARD VII			
10″–70″	25″–115″	10″–35″	25″–55″
1. Reminds me of England and Ireland. Map in pairs sort of.	1. Two faces—sort of panting faces.	1. Looks like two rabbits on top of a hedge or something.	1. ∧ Two oriental dancers—women dancers.
2. Pair of camels standing on their heads.	2. Couple of dogs balancing on their heads. Paws sort of up in the air.		2. ∧ Rabbits with their heads on backwards.
3. Oh! Two people with coonskin caps looking at each other.	3. Looks sort of like upside down maps of North and South America.		
	4. Two rabbits crouched backside to backside.		

(*continued*)

TABLE 4 (*continued*)

H.H. CA-50 MALE 1-6-68	A.H. CA-45 FEMALE 2-19-68	W.H. CA-15 FEMALE 2-12-68	J.H. CA-13 MALE 2-12-68
INQUIRY			
1. Outline.	1. Facing each other. (Panting?) Something about full cheeks.	1. The shape. Their ears and tails.	1. Head and a hat and their hands and body. (Q) Hats, I think.
2. Feet and hump on their back.	2. Usual		2. (Usual)
3. Profile and coonskin cap. Face, here.	3. (Upside down?) I was seeing this as North America and this as South America.		
	4. Just happen to be back to back (lower *D*).		
CARD VIII			
7″–80″	15″–190″	10″–80″	15″–40″
1. Two pink animals like guinea pigs, maybe.	1. That's prettier! Two animals walking.	1. ∧ Well, like a mountain with two animals going up the side of a mountain.	1. ∧ Two porcupines.
2. Medical symbol for the A.M.A.	2. Horseshoe crab.	2. ∧ Cavern with stalactites and stalagmites.	2. ∧ Chest bones—the chest.

3. Color makes me think of modern art—an abstract.	3. Looking down on a marshy piece of land. Lot of waterways show up. 4. Some suggestion of backbone with ribs coming off that. 5. Colors of bottom part suggest an animal at the zoo. The back end is a brilliant color. I don't know the name of the animal, but anyone who has been to the zoo will know what I mean.	3. ∧ Could be rocket taking off. 4. ∨ Could be a dish of ice cream with drips coming off it.	
INQUIRY			
1. Here are the feet and here is the tail.	1. Looks like tiger-like animal.	1. Because of their shape. Have to be going up something because it is vertical.	1. They have feet and ridges along the back. That is what made me think of porcupines.
2. Whole outline here.	2. (*W*) General configuration.	2. Color and everything sort of jagged.	2. Reminds me of ribs and this is the spinal column.
3. Mostly color.	3. Blue and gray in particular.	3. Color. Pink could signify fire.	
	4. Usual.	4. Because of color could be sherbet and drips because of shape. Dish is here (blue).	

(*continued*)

TABLE 4 *(continued)*

H.H. CA-50 MALE 1-6-68	A.H. CA-45 FEMALE 2-19-68	W.H. CA-15 FEMALE 2-12-68	J.H. CA-13 MALE 2-12-68
	5. It isn't the shape. It is the colors. It's a drill. The colors are so outlandish for the animal.		
CARD IX 15″–100″	20″–165″	15″–80″	40″–75″
1. Sort of centerpiece dish. Vase of small sort.	1. Looks like beginning of a pretty water color.	1. ∧ ∨ Could be a volcano.	1. ∧ > ∨ An African—yes an African with a big headdress on and either a fiddle or a bass.
2. Again with all the tentacles it makes me think of a lobster because of color.	2. Could be two people fencing (upper *D*).	2. ∨ Could be a thumb tack pounded into some wood.	
3. Thunder clouds (green)	3. > Oh! I see a violin.	3. ∨ Could be a chair—sort of like a stool.	

4. Pair of faces. Only predominate thing is large nose and shock of hair.	4. V Feels like I am having to work hard on this card. Little like a kidney—like the rounded sections. 5. Λ Vase—a bowl-like vase on a standard.		
INQUIRY			
1. Base here and vase here (*W*).	1. My best perception came toward end when I could see something in the whole thing.	1. Guess because of color.	1. Big things on top of what looks like a head. Looks like a piece of wood running down. This looks like the body of it. Down at the bottom is the spike they have to rest it on.
2. The pink color up here. All the tentacles are up here in front, and the tail.	2. Suggestion of very slim rapier blades that are fenced with.	2. General shape with pointed thing into something. Could be wood.	
3. Color and the shape. It was the shading.	3. Usual.	3. Top of chair (lower *D*) and it rotates around. Top looks sort of soft. (Q) The folds, like all billowy.	
4. There is the nose and here is shock of hair. Here is face and jaw here.	4. (Lower *D*) Shape. The rounded sections. 5. (*W*) I think this is the clearest perception.		

(continued)

TABLE 4 (*continued*)

H.H. CA-50 MALE 1-6-68	A.H. CA-45 FEMALE 2-19-68	W.H. CA-15 FEMALE 2-12-68	J.H. CA-13 MALE 2-12-68
CARD X			
8″–80″	15″–280″	10″–65″	25″
1. Pair of sand crabs (blue).	1. Somebody dancing with an elaborate shimmery costume.	1. ∧ Could be a microorganism colony.	1. ∧ < Two sand crabs.
2. Two people looking at each other. Looks like they may be chewing same piece of candy or toffee.	2. Couple of crabs on each side (laughs).	2. ∧ Could be birds.	2. Two lobsters.
3. Looking down at a coastline (pink).	3. Parts look like a flowering shrub. Very pretty flowers.		
4. Butterfly cocoon—larva ready to hatch.	4. A pyramid-like tower. ∨ ∧ Like at Disneyland. The tower of Sleeping Beauty.		
5. Frogs with long legs stretched out.	5. ∨ Torch.		
6. Governor that goes on a steam engine.	6. Also looks like thistles (side blue).		
	7. Two peculiar animals on bird legs supporting this		

	tube-like thing between them.		
	8. Very ornate cherub-like faces. See on buildings (pink).		
INQUIRY			
1. Color and spidery outline.	1. Legs (lower *D*) and head up here (top *D*). The rest of this color was part of costume.	1. Sort of the color and the shape. They are all unusually shaped.	1. (Brown) Looks like they have a hard shell and feet coming out the front.
2. See mouth, head and hair. Doesn't go beyond the chin.	2. Usual.	2. I guess because of shape. A lot of little things.	2. Two lobsters. Looks like they have hard shells and antennae. (Q) It is a man with a mustache and he looks angry and he has long hair (pink) Eyes (blue).
3. In fact, like an island, all the way around.	3. Very delicate. The colors are so pretty (side brown, yellow and gray). I said shrub because this is more like wood (gray).		

(*continued*)

TABLE 4 *(continued)*

H.H. CA-50 MALE 1-6-68	A.H. CA-45 FEMALE 2-19-68	W.H. CA-15 FEMALE 2-12-68	J.H. CA-13 MALE 2-12-68
4. Actually four of them (tan and upper green) (Q) Color. Fact that reddish, pinkish.	4. This could be door (lower *D*) and tower up here.		
5. The legs stretched out.	5.		
6. The two masses that would fly out.	6. (Side *D*) Well, soft center with prickly part surrounding the center.		
	7. (Top *D*) Two hind legs with tail hanging down. Massive heads. Buffalo-like.		
	8. This would be head and face part.		

Rorschach protocols and by analyzing his contribution to the consensus process. The degree to which his individual content overlaps the consensus protocols helps to determine how much of an identified member of the group he is and therefore how vulnerable he is to its influence.

A subject who responds to one aspect of a content polarity is different from another member who responds to both or none. The member who describes both poles can be viewed as ambivalent in response to his group's conflicting expectation; the member who responds with only one aspect has made a choice. He is not ambivalent about the choice, even though he may still be preoccupied with the group-imposed conflict. Another member who responds orthogonal to his group shows no conflict and presumably has resolved the conflict. He may therefore be much less involved in terms of sharing their expectations, but he will also be under much less duress with respect to those same social expectations. Alternatively, the member who does not respond at all to the conflicted areas can be viewed as blocked and be considered more alienated from his group's concerns.

Another case may serve to illustrate the method further. Table 4 presents the individual Rorschach protocols of each member of the "H" family, which consists of husband, age 50, mother, age 45, daughter, age 15, and son, age 13.

A consensus protocol was obtained a few weeks later, a condensed version, which is presented as Table 5. The last column lists the content polarities expressed toward each ink blot by the family as a whole. No attempt has been made to identify the polarity in terms of the individual; rather, the conflict is viewed in terms of the problem it presented for the group. The agreements of this family are reported under the heading "Consensus." The reader can infer individual differences in the acceptance or rejection of the group expectations by referring to the individual protocols in Table 4. The question which now needs to be asked is: Considering the amount of time and effort required to administer, transcribe, abstract, and organize the information, have the efforts yielded something not otherwise known? In answer, we offer several observations.

TABLE 5 *Abstract of Family Protocols*

CARD	POSITION	AREA	CONSENSUS	CONTENT POLARITIES
I	∧	*W*	Any flying thing	Airplane—Butterfly, bat, beetle [Whole—Part]
II	∧	*D*-1	Bears, dancers	Bears—Oriental dancers
		DS	B-70, lampshade	Rocket—Old-fashioned lampshade
		D-2		Blood—Tall hats
				Fighting (daughter)—Kissing (father)
				Nose—Feet
				Pushed up—Crouching pose
III	∧	*D*-1	African people	African—Skinny animal sort
			French poodles	Poodle—Frog
			Frog, bow tie	Frog—Fly eyes
	∨		Fly magnified	Fly eyes—Crab with pincers
	∧	*D*-2	Bow tie	Stomach with esophagus—Bow tie
IV	∧	*W*	Rug, giant, ash Dragon	Animal skinned and stretched out—Ash of a folded newspaper, curled
				Giant—Crocodile, or alligator
				Feet and tail—Head and wings
				Disneyland castle (mother)—"Kids dominating us" (father)
V	∧	*W*	Butterfly, three people	Two people stretched out—Russian dance team
			Rabbit with reflection	Resting—Practicing yoga
				Dance—Off balance
				Hedge—Lake
VI	∧	*W*	Skin stretched out	Ray gun, fire coming out—Map, like U.S., Texas
				Bellows, bagpipe, birds flying (mother)—Man's face, beard and crown (father)
VII	∨	*W*	Scotty dogs	Kissing—Fighting or tugging on newspaper or magazine
	∧	*W*	Two girl dancers, oriental	Head dress—Coonskin cap
				Rabbits with heads on backwards—Dogs standing on head
				Lions with manes and paws—Camels with hump back

(*continued*)

TABLE 5 (*continued*)

CARD	POSITION	AREA	CONSENSUS	CONTENT POLARITIES
VIII	∧	*D*	Skeletons	Rib cage—AMA seal
	∨	*D*-1	Animals	Horseshoe crab—Porcupine
				Ice cream or sherbet—Crescent rolls
IX	∧	*W*	Ornate goblet	Disagreement over man's face
	∨	*W*	Base fiddle, guitar	Base fiddle—Piano bench
			Piano bench, tack	Fur, soft—Thumb tack
X	∧	*D*-1	Crabs, blossoms	Crabs, with pincers—Blossoms
		WS	Man's face with mustache	Butterfly cocoons—Face with big mustache
		D	Microscope	Microscope—Two buffaloes standing on hind legs
				Govenor on steam engine (*m*)—Ball attached to strings (*m*)
	∨	*WS*	White-faced goat	Japanese Geisha girl, face missing—Face, he's mad, with mustache
				Pink tight dress—Caterpillar with suction cups
				Microscope—Pencil
				Syringe—Pencil sharpened
				My little governor—Wishbone or seed of maple tree, falls down
				Triangle-shaped face, old man's, devil—White-faced goat
	Number of:		Consensus: 32	Content polarities: 39

1. The family as a whole handles the ink-blot experiences differently than when each individual member responds to the cards alone. Note the reversal of sheer verbal output for the mother and the son on the two occasions. This conclusion may seem self-evident, but clinical judgments are often offered on the basis of one individual Rorschach performance. It is apparent that the behavior in the consensus situation is influenced by the number and quality of others present in the group, as well as by an interaction factor

illustrated by Bauman and Roman (1968). While the nature of this interaction at the present remains obscure, the advantage of the consensus Rorschach lies in providing a standard sample of such behavior for continuous and intensive study.

2. This particular family arrives at consensus relatively fast, in terms of time (30 minutes). Considering the great number of potential disagreements possible with four people as contrasted with a smaller group of two, the faster consensus may be interpreted as a sign of strength and adequate communication within the family. Experience has shown, thus far, that the more psychopathology apparent in one or more of the members, the fewer the responses, the lower the quality, and the less originality of consensus as well as the longer it takes to achieve these. Relatives of psychotic patients, for example, have been observed to engage in prolonged controversies, consuming anywhere from 5 to 15 minutes over the definition of any one response. In one example, Card III was vehemently perceived as "open heart surgery" by two adult daughters, while the mother and the eldest daughter insisted it was a "carcass of a human being." In this particular family, the son had committed suicide after a prolonged series of schizophrenic episodes and inadequate adjustments.

3. The mother in the "H" family (Tables 4 and 5) suffers from more ambivalence than the other members. These conflicting expectations occur in the qualities of all roles she attempts, be it wife, mother, woman, nurse, etc. Her conflicts are manifested by the ambivalence she shows to most of the content polarities found in the consensus protocol. For example, the family expresses (see Table 5) the following four content-polarities: (a) African–skinny animal (Card III); (b) stomach–bow tie (Card III); (c) giant–crocodile (Card IV); (d) pincers–blossoms (Card X). The mother's individual protocol shown in Table 4 indicates that these four group-imposed controversies were especially distressing for her.

The four dimensions implied by these content polarities are: (a) natural versus artificial gestures; (b) underlying versus superficial needs; (c) movement versus static or, alternatively, action versus intellectualization of impulses; and (d) predatory versus decorative intention. These four areas of conflicting expectations distress and baffle the mother in all the social situations she normally encounters and in which she attempts to take a feminine role. While these conflicts are soluble for most women, the mother in this family group has not yet resolved them.

4. The father's main area of conflicting expectations occurs in terms of a bat–airplane, which suggests a dimension of impulsiveness and some associated defensiveness. For him these defenses are denial, intellectualization, and externalization onto mechanical sources; the latter are perceived with great intensity. The father also experiences profound doubts about his sexual adequacy. He literally and figuratively anticipates impaired sexual performances. The content polarity given for Card X documents the above inference. The family debates a "governor on a steam engine" versus "balls attached to strings," both described as whirling around and actually verbalized by father and son. Later on in the same card, the father inquires, "Whatever became of my little governor?" He is answered with another polarity, "It looks like a wishbone," or "A maple seed, falling down from a tree."

5. The daughter, age 15, gives only one ambivalent response to her family's array of content polarities. This occurs on Card IX, where the family debates "fur—thumbtack." On her individual Rorschach, she gives the response of a thumbtack pounded into some wood and follows it with a chair response. The dimension suggested here seems to be one of impulse control with the conflicting expectation about self-control expressed in any role she attempts. We infer a volatile teenage daugher with a high level of conflict over behavior controls. In this context the father and daughter expressed opposite poles of kissing–fighting polarity on Cards II and VII. These preferred expectations will be manifested in her role as daughter, girl friend, and eventually wife, in relation to her father, boy friend, and husband, respectively. If she acts out sexually, it would be motivated by feeling sexual inadequacy, similar to that which her father projects. The inference is of something more intense than a generalized feeling of uncertainty that is expected from teenagers.

6. In the family context the son's relatively high frequency of verbalization serves to externalize what the other members are feeling but may be reluctant to say or unable to recognize as their own until he makes the statement. Conversely, the mother makes her statements by proxy. When alone she has much to say; in the group she waits until all have spoken before offering what she thinks has been omitted. There are a number of typical and sometimes poignant examples where her suggestions are rejected or are used without acknowledgment.

7. The consensus Rorschach protocols of the "H" family provided a direct experience with them as a group. It was possible to come away with some kind of knowledge of the sort of people they are in their most typical social environment, namely, an encounter with each other. The consensus experience recorded and summarized allows the psychologist-reader to achieve this awareness in a natural manner despite the use of that unnatural method, the Rorschach test. This is possible because the consensus approach forces the participants to do what comes most naturally to them in the here and now and with each other.

The content-polarities system of organizing the Rorschach information permits a sort of thematic condensation of each individual's content. With the reduction of detail, there is an immediate advantage in terms of attempting a content analysis with several related people. Further precision is introduced by making comparisons between the same ink blots. Finally, more stability of meaning accumulates as two or more people interact to agree upon a specific content for any blot. This provides a kind of built-in series of checks and balances that saves the Rorschach analyst from imposing too much of his own apperceptive background upon the responses. This danger is always present when interpreting content, whether it be dreams, TAT, or overt behavior. In the consensus Rorschach context, the observer can look at any array of content and employ a relatively objective approach to comparisons and subsequent interpretations—all of which is facilitated by the content-polarities system for abstracting a verbatim protocol.

Choice of Reference Group for Consensus Rorschach

The preceding framework is the conceptual approach we use to order the Rorschach protocols. However, each identified subject belongs to a variety of social groups to which he accommodates in varying degrees in terms of the roles he is expected to play. The expectations of some of these reference groups are more relevant than those of others in explaining enigmatic behavior. The question of which group to use must be faced at the outset.

Traditionally, the Rorschach protocol is obtained in a dyadic situation, i.e., patient and examiner. Interpretation of behavior in the testing context is then extrapolated to behavior with other individuals and groups, such as family, significant others, authority figures, and school. The protocols obtained in a consensus administration represent a radical departure from the older method. Behavior manifested in a consensus protocol is more like the actual behavior to be found in the social situation represented by the group participants, since they share the quality of existential encounter. Indeed, every group and its respective encounters can be considered as unique.

While the family is the group with the most ubiquitous if not profound impact, there are many other possible groups that can be studied appropriately. Indeed, the question occurs, Will consensus Rorschach with different groups yield different results? While we can easily accept that manifest differences will be present from one consensus group to another, and that some similarities will persist, it is important to know what order of behavior continues.

To study this question a serial consensus Rorschach procedure was administered to a 42-year-old male alcoholic patient with three friends, three roommates, his wife (on two occasions, separated by six months), and a high–low status pair (Cutter and Farberow, 1968). An abstraction of all the protocols is presented in Table 6.

At the start the subject was known to be an alcoholic with periodic binges that disrupted home and work. His Japanese wife's

TABLE 6 *Abstract of Serially Administered Consensus Rorschachs to an Alcoholic Patient and Five Groups to Which He Belongs*

INDIVIDUAL	FRIENDS	ROOMMATES	WIFE	STATUS	INDIVIDUAL (10 DAYS LATER)	WIFE (6 MONTHS LATER)
I	(Bat)	(Bat)	(Bat)	(Bat)		(No Consensus)
Wild bat.	Deteriorated bat/Devil's mask.	A. Bird, what's/P-38 left of one. B. Animal/Fossil.	Animal/Crab.	Clean/Came off a dirty place.	Bat.	Flying mammal/ Spider head.
II	(Sheep)	(Pelvis)	(Wooley bear)	(Butterfly)		(Bear)
Tigers and shadow.	Two ovaries, vagina/Sheep fighting, blood off their paws.	A. Shadow/Reflection. B. Two dogs, bloodhounds/Skin cut in half. C. Bad kidneys/Skeleton. D. Two bears/Two birds.	Puppy/Mouse.	Furry/ Wounded.	Two animals, fancy, dog or bear wounded.	Teddy bear/ Bear in funny papers.
III	(Two women)	(Two women)	(Two women working)	(Two women working)		(Two women)
Two people conversing.	A. Women/Men (Working)/(Tug of war). B. Backbone/Hearts. C. TV monsters/Two dancers.	A. Vase/Bow tie. B. Two women/Two guys (Working)/(Trying). C. Wash bench/Beating drum (Laundry)/(Slaughter).	Shoes/Breast.	A. Crab/Human. B. Cremated/ Boiling.	Two women working.	Working/Dancing.
IV	(Cow hide)	(A hide)	(Lobster)	(Hide)		(No consensus)
Man riding a motorcycle sure got big feet.	Flying dragon/X-Ray of spine.	Cross section of a flower/Antenna, face of a grasshopper.	Snail, squashed, sick/Hide.	Bug/Snail.	Hide of bear.	Lobster/Snail.
V	(Butterfly and ladies)	(Butterfly)	(Butterfly)	(Butterfly)		(Bird)
Butterfly in flight.	No content polarity.	No content polarity.	No content polarity.	Bat/Flying mammal.	Bat flying.	No content polarity.

VI	(Microscopic sewage water)	(Indian totem pole, etc.)	(Skin)	(Missile)		(Hide)
Buffalo skin/ Stretched out.	Cheeks of an ass/Mouth of a grasshopper, open.	A. Hide/In ground, going down. B. Insect going through a bubble, drill sting going in/Brush and water coming out.	A. Butterfly/ Bird. B. Dolls/Dragon fly.	No content polarity.	Indian design on top of hide.	No content polarity.
VII	(Poodle)	(Wig)	(Scotty dogs)	(Vaginas)		(Puppy dogs)
Inlet you would see on a map.	A. Lock/Hasp, post. B. Penis/Vagina. C. Cracker. (Animal/Poodles on head).	A. Hairline/Wig. B. G. Washington/Little Iodine. C. Cloud/Smoke. D. Harbor/Lake. E. Dogs/Rabbits. F. French poodles/Scotch terrier.	Puppy dog/Harbor.	A. Scotty/ French poodle. B. Standard/ Larger size. C. Dogs/Harbor.	Inlet or harbor map.	Island map/Two puppy dogs.
VIII	(Animal and sex symbol)	(Animal)	(Animal)	(Animal walking)		(Animals)
Opposum, crossing the creek and this would be his reflection.	Cat/Mangy rat. (Evil)/(Cute). (Up X-mas tree)/(In pit). (Climbing tree)/(Crossing river).	A. Egyptian Cleopatra boat/ Flowers in Japanese garden. B. Emblem/Coat of arms. C. Girl's mask/Skull bone.	A. Land/Water. B. Wild/Walt Disney.	Wolverine/Bufalo. (Crawling)/ (Walking).	Varmint crossing a stream.	Crossing stream/ In water.
IX	(Wooded area and violin)	(Flower)	(Man at work)	(Man working)		(Baby)
Man in a pool of water and he's pushing an object out of the water.	A. Old witch/Fu Manchu mustache. (Faces)/(Masks). (Blowing on a pipe)/(Violin). B. Sand or desert/Wooded area with a stream.	A. Alligator/Dragon. B. Guy/Woman. C. Cross section of flower/Chinese design.	No content polarity.	A. Animal/Bug. B. Reflection/ Cloud form. C. Blooming flower/explosion.	Little man working.	Little man/ Baby.
X	(Blue brassiere)	(Goat)	(Aquarium)	(Marine life)		(Aquarium)
Sea view under water like an aquarium.	Inlets/Water life.	A. Tower/Napkin, oriental. B. Nanny goat/Mary's lamb. C. Moon people/Sea life. D. Goat peeking/Billy goat.	Fish/Crabs.	Native/Foreign	Sea life.	Sea life/Bug eating.

shy, passive demeanor masked negative feelings toward men in general and her husband in particular. Her softly mumbled pidgin English presented communication problems to everyone, and especially to her partially deaf husband. What light did the series of consensus Rorschach protocols throw on the function of "alcoholism" and the assignment of roles in this pair?

From the individual Rorschach administration it was possible to write a thumbnail sketch of his self-image: "Wild, irresponsible, dependent, passive; impulses are denied, rationalized, and dissociated; intoxication permits return of the repressed impulses and subsequent self-denigration."

From the consensus procedures it was noted how he related to the different social groups. With his friends he takes a relaxed, passive role, going along with whatever consensus appears to emerge. Even when they agree on the conventional "hide" for Card IV, he represses his highly original and irresponsible reaction of "a man with big feet riding a motorcycle" in order to agree with his friends. With his roommates he becomes more active and attempts to dominate their emerging consensus, even while attempting to maintain affective distance. With his frustrating wife the subject "loses his cool" by attempting to play a dominant but yet inappropriately chivalrous role. With a high and low status pair, the subject tries to gain approval of the high status partner. On the second consensus Rorschach with his wife, the patient is more relaxed and his efforts to dominate are blocked more openly by his wife, especially on those ink blots where he earlier expressed free-swinging self-images.

We infer a great effort to maintain a proper Victorian husband role opposite the traditional submissive role of his Japanese wife. However, his effectiveness is sabotaged by his own conflicting needs for impulsive and irresponsible activities. This is further aggravated by his wife's negativistic but indirect and devious attacks on his masculine role. "Alcoholism" for this pair functions as a positive release valve for him and as justification of contempt and skepticism for her. Eventually the subject's behavior deteriorates in relation to his wife. Additional areas of conflict in self-expectations versus that expected by others are: victim–aggressor; affectively close or detached; and responsible–irresponsible. Alcoholic binges permit return of the repressed side of these conflicts as frustration accumulates.

The overt failure to achieve consensus on Card IV with his wife is especially poignant from the perspective of marital conflict since collateral information by means of the semantic differential indicates this is the card they evaluate most similarly with the smallest obtained distance index (Osgood and Suci, 1952). In contrast, in a control (renal dialysis) couple's rating, the distance index was equal for the same ink blot, but they achieved consensus by virtue of the wife's willingness to accept the dominant role of her husband, even though her objective experience with his prolonged illness is one that emphasizes his inadequacy as a husband, breadwinner, male, etc.

The alcoholic subject and his Japanese wife both expect a traditional male role which is perceived to be in conflict with his prevailing self-image and preferred role. She does not accept his dominance but, at the same time, expects him to assert traditional male adequacy.

The changes observed in the consensus Rorschach in these different social contexts can be conceptualized as adaptations to variations in the particular group's conflicting expectations for him: (a) with friends he expects to be irresponsible; (b) with roommates he expects to maintain affective distance; (c) with his wife he expects to be a victim; (d) with a high–low status group he expects to be inadequate. A smaller quality persists which might be considered as character, or self-expectations. In terms of content polarities this is the conflicting expectation regarding work and play imposed by any group, to which he reacts with the self-image of happy-go-lucky irresponsibility. However, among specific groups his self-expectations vary, as indicated above.

The consensus Rorschach procedure can be applied to any relevant reference group and to more than one for any particular patient, as in the serial procedure just noted. Of particular interest to us and to the social psychologist concerned with the influence of total institutions is the consensus protocol of relevant staff and other inmates in explaining problem behavior, e.g., recidivism or management problems.

Experience has shown that the consensus Rorschach approach is sufficiently novel as to pose a perceived threat to some staff and administrators in terms of legal involvements, or confrontation with irrational and inimical motivation by staff. Despite this, the consensus Rorschach approach also offers a vehicle for selective intervention in the reference group most relevant to an identified patient and problem, precisely because it externalizes the influence of others on the identified subject. Some clinical or administrative decisions affecting a patient can be enhanced by a consensus Rorschach among relevant staff, inmates, peers, and relatives. At the very least such a procedure will permit the communications among these parties to improve. In such a context the consensus Rorschach procedure becomes a technique of small group or subcultural innovation.

Implications for Further Research

The history of the Rorschach test is a record of the attempt to relate individual differences as projected into the protocols with external criteria of behavior. The Rorschach of consensus, in contrast, is a direct measure of how a group arrives at, or fails to reach, agreement. When people who are socially related are compared on individual protocols, striking similarities are to be noted in content, phraseology, and styles of attending. Indeed, Singer was able to match identified schizophrenics to their families strictly on the basis of pattern of attention in responding to the Rorschach (Singer and Wynne, 1963). While she specifically cautions the investigator to avoid seduction by content, she is speaking of comparisons between individually derived protocols. In consensus responses the content is more determined by the task and the investigator is less dependent on his own apperceptive mass. Still, the question remains, What are the connections between the individual responses and the consensus reactions? Five testable hypotheses can be formulated based on preliminary experiences (Cutter, 1968a).

1. Any consensus record by a group will tend to be shared by an absent member of the group such that individual protocols elicited at different times, before or after, will contain recognizable elements of the group's consensus.

2. Similarly, any content polarity found in the responses of a consensus protocol will tend to be manifested by the responses of an individual belonging to this group, regardless of when the individual Rorschach is taken.

We are not postulating a perfect isomorphism between individual and consensus protocols. However, we do anticipate a large proportion of common elements between any consensus protocol and the standard Rorschach for each member.

3. A corollary hypothesis is that intensity of group memberships will affect the degree of communality. Members whose involvement is minimal will manifest this attenuated membership by lesser proportions of common elements than those who are known to be intensively involved.

4. Time differences between protocols will tend to attenuate common elements only where membership is otherwise diluted. If degree of membership can be held constant, then the length of interval between administrations will not affect the proportion of common elements.

5. The number of consensus responses will diminish the more disturbed the identified patient appears to have been. The sheer process of achieving agreement is a direct measure of the reference group's capacity to function, and provides a criterion for judging the effectiveness of the relevant social environment to which an identified patient is expected to adjust.

The consensus process exposes the group expectations to which the members must then react. Proper behavior on the part of the individual can be explained as some kind of member adaptation to ambivalent or conflicting group expectations. These group-imposed conflicts provide a measure of group mental health and can be used as a direct reflection of the identified patient or at least his social environment. In view of the known difficulties in establishing measures of mental health, the use of any existing mode for judging Rorschach quality would predispose for failure. However, positive results would be even more impressive.

We hypothesize an association between the patient's mental status and that of his reference group and are optimistic of establishing positive correlations because our epistemology presumes the association is between individual behavior (in Rorschach space) and group behavior in the same field (consensus Rorschach). We contrast this approach with the more traditional clinical judgment versus Rorschach signs where the epistemology itself precludes significant results.

We hypothesize these five connections whether or not the identified patient participates or is absent from the consensus process of his group. We would expect to find the same degree of evidence for equivalence in samples where the identified patient has and has not participated in his group's consensus. Despite the explicit instruction to achieve agreement, many groups are unable to do so, or often not on all of the cards. The number of agreements that do occur reflects a group capacity that may be inversely associated with other manifestations of problem behavior in one or more members. Here the theory of psychopathology used is relevant. We consider problem behavior as an individual adaptation to conflicting group expectations in the repertoire of social roles available to group members. The individual's unique adaptation to his group's conflicting expectations or "double-binds" makes problem behavior a shared experience. The occurrence of psychopathological symptoms is by definition, then, a response to conflicting demands from the reference group, i.e., the group to which the identified patient belongs and is most vulnerable (Bateson et al., 1956).

Aside from conflicting demands, groups also have negative roles in their available repertoire which they need to assign to accommodating members who, in turn, provide group catharsis by taking their roles. Identified mental patients tend to accept and even to seek these negative roles (MacGregor, 1965; Vogel and Bell, 1960).

Given this point of view about mental illness, the concepts of consensus and content polarity yield observations of relevant and typical group processes which may help in explaining problem behavior.

While individual members can adapt their assigned roles to their unique needs, every role in a specific reference group reflects certain expectations in terms of qualities common to all the roles but varying in degree for each member. By expectation, we mean a quality of social behavior that can be manifested in any role but which can vary in degree between different roles or different subjects taking the same role. In the "H" case (see Tables 4 and 5) a natural–mechanical polarity is apparent on Card I where agreement occurs about "any flying thing." All roles in this group share in common an expectation that the actor be active, flighty, or impulsive. Additionally, a natural–mechanical conflict in modes of action is imposed on all the roles available to this group. Each member adapts to these expectations uniquely: the father is ambivalent, the mother is polar with emphasis on natural, the daughter is also ambivalent but leans to the natural and resolves by reference to the foreign or fantastic, the son is uncertain and inhibited but clearly prefers a natural orientation. The group-imposed conflict must be handled by each member in every role he takes. Eventually his preferred or usual adaptations are challenged by a new expectation or another group-imposed conflict. Problem behavior is most likely to emerge in a subsequent transition stage. These inferences are also testable and indeed are derived from our clinical experiences to date (Cutter, 1968a).

Beyond agreement there is the question of quality. A consensus on bizarre, confabulated, or poor form quality is clearly different from that about a popular or well-formed definition. Evaluation of the consensus response can be made with reference to knowledge and experience with individual protocols. This permits the psychologist to make a judgment about the quality of the group's collective efforts and subsequently to relate these judgments to individual Rorschach responses. The total provides a much more complete explanation for observable symptoms, such as problem behavior by any one member.

TABLE 7 *Tentative Analysis Form for Consensus Rorschach Data*

NAME: ________ GROUP: ______ NO. (N): _____ PRESENTING PROBLEM: ________

DATE: ______ DATE: ______

CARD NO.	POS.	LOC.	NO.	CONSENSUS	DET. AND F	P/O	NO.	CONTENT-POLARITY	NO.	IDENTIFIED SUBJECT CONTENT	ADAPT.	DET. AND F	P/O

Sum of consensus (C): ______ Sum of content polarities (CP): ______

Ambivalent (A): ______
Polar (P): ______
Resolved (R): ______
Omitted (O): ______
In consensus (C): ______

T = _____ C/CP = _____ A/P = _____ O/CP = _____ R/CP = _____

DATE: ______ PSYCHOLOGIST: ________

So far we have not attempted any extensive or large-scale scoring procedures. Table 7 is a preliminary data analysis sheet which juxtaposes the consensus and content polarities of the group with the individual content. Several aspects lend themselves to a scoring procedure, but not all of these appear equally promising. For example, the total time consumed in arriving at consensus for all ten ink blots or per ink blot would seem to be a valuable index of group effectiveness. Yet the boredom or anxiety of the test administrator is uncontrolled and operates differentially to decrease the total time of some cases and not of others. With proper evaluation a time index might be usable. However, we think it tends to be pseudo-objective and not as useful as other possible indices.

Other sources of scoring indices are the number and quality of consensus, the content polarities, and the ratio of the consensus to the content polarities. There will be controversies in any group struggling to achieve agreement. The identification of these in terms of content polarities permits their tabulation as an index of group effectiveness. The ratio of content polarities to achieved consensus provides a convenient index between the number of potential conflicts and the degree of agreement. Potential conflicts generally outnumber agreements. Our preliminary impression of the ratio yields a rather small range between 1.0 and 4.0, with the larger scores occurring in groups that can be presumed to be more closely involved, e.g., families versus friends.

Clinically, the identified subject's individual Rorschach can be viewed as his preferred, or usual, adaptation to the specified reference group's conflict of expectations, imposed on all members. This premise permits the psychologist to categorize the individual's responses to the same ink blots as ambivalent (*A*), polar (*P*), resolved (*R*), omitted (*O*), and sharing in the consensus (*C*) with respect to the group's content polarity. If we tabulate the number of *A* and *P* reactions and express these as a proportion of the total number of content polarities, the ratio of *A* to *P* appears to vary from 0 to 3.0 in our samples thus far. The lower values, indicating minimal ambivalence with respect to group conflicts, occur more frequently in nonclinical subjects and those with lesser involvements in their reference group. Conversely to the above, the occurrence of *R%* (*R/C-P*) is a measure of freedom from group-imposed conflicts and consequently can be interpreted as lack of membership in the reference group. The range found thus far is 2% to 54%, with the lower percents found in clinical or uninvolved subjects.

Conclusion

In this chapter we have reviewed the literature on consensus Rorschach and described our own evolving approach and theory to date. Some suggestions for clinical use and testable hypotheses for interested researchers have been presented. The consensus Rorschach approach appears to reflect our changing *Zeitgeist,* building upon more sophisticated views of human behavior with its attendant social problems. The way seems open to further intensive efforts in the study and influence of consensus Rorschach upon enigmatic behavior.

References

Bateson, G., Jackson, P. P., Haley, J., and Weakland, J. 1956. "Towards a Theory of Schizophrenia." *Behav. Sci.* 1: 251–264.

Bauman, G., and Roman, M. 1964. "Interaction Testing in the Study of Marital Dominance." *Fam. Proc.* 3(1): 230–242.

———, and Roman, M. 1968. "Interaction Product Analysis in Group and Family Diagnosis." *J. Proj. Tech. Pers. Assess.* 32(4): 331–337.

Blanchard, W. 1959. "The Group Process in Gang Rape." *J. Soc. Psych.* 49: 259–266.

Cutter, F. 1968a. "Role Complements and Changes in Consensus Rorschachs." *J. Proj. Tech. Pers. Assess.* 32(4): 338–347.

———. 1968b. "Consensus Rorschach: Introduction." Paper presented at Western Psychological Association meeting, San Diego, California, March 29.

———, and Farberow, N. L. 1968. "Serial Administration of Consensus Rorschachs to One Patient." *J. Proj. Tech. Pers. Assess.* 32(4): 358–374.

———, Farberow, N. L., and Sapin, D. 1967. "Explaining Suicide by Rorschach Comparison with Survivors." Paper presented at the California State Psychological Association meeting, San Diego, California, January 27.

Farberow, N. L. 1968. (Chm.) Symposium: "Consensus Rorschach in the Study of Problem Behavior." Presented at American Psychological Association meeting, New York, September 3, 1967. *J. Proj. Tech. Pers. Assess.* 32(4): 326–357.

Levy, J., and Epstein, N. B. 1964. "An Application of the Rorschach Test in Family Investigation." *Fam. Proc.* 3(2): 344–376.

Loveland, N. 1967. "The Relation Rorschach." Mimeographed paper, 31 pp., National Institute of Mental Health, Bethesda, Md.

———, Wynne, L. C., and Singer, M. T. 1963. "The Family Rorschach: A New Method for Studying Family Interaction." *Fam. Proc.* 2(2): 187–215.

MacGregor, R. 1965. "Competition, Compromise and Collusion." Paper presented at Eighth Institute for Research in Clinical Psychology, Lawrence, Kansas, April.

Osgood, C. E., and Suci, G. J. 1952. "A Measure of Relation Determined by Both Mean Differences and Profile Information." *Psych. Bull.* 49: 251–262.

Roman, M., and Bauman, G. 1966. "Interacting Testing: Progress Report and Manual for Administration Scoring." Mimeographed, Yeshiva University, Division of Social and Community Psychiatry, Albert Einstein College of Medicine, New York, July.

Singer, M. T., and Wynne, L. C. 1963. "Thought Disorders and Family Relations of Schizophrenics. III. Methodology Using Projective Techniques." *Arch. Gen. Psych.* (February) 12: 187–200.

Vogel, E. F., and Bell, N. W. 1960. "The Emotionally Disturbed Child as a Family Scapegoat." In *A Modern Introduction to the Family,* N. W. Bell and E. F. Vogel (Eds.). New York: The Free Press of Glencoe, pp. 382–397.

Wynne, L. C. 1968. "Consensus Rorschachs and Related Procedures for Studying Interpersonal Patterns." *J. Proj. Tech. Pers. Assess.* 32(4): 352–356.

Robert R. Holt

7

Artistic Creativity and Rorschach Measures of Adaptive Regression *

There is no great genius without a tincture of madness.
—Seneca (ca. 50 AD)

Perhaps it is a sign of democratization that what was once discussed as the study of genius is today the psychology of creativity. Implicitly, it is being recognized that original, creative work is not the exclusive function of the rare genius, but that it is at least potentially within the reach of most of us. In any event, the last decade or so has seen a great emergence of research on the creative process and on creative personalities, much of it using relatively permissive criteria of what is creative. It is tempting to see this phenomenon as a reaction against the conformity and stereotypy of modern life, against the many pressures felt, particularly by intellectuals, to get into step, suppress dissent, and integrate with the group. In an other-directed society there is bound to be a wistful admiration for

* Preparation of this paper was supported by a Public Health Service Research Career Program Award (MH-K6-12, 455) from the National Institute of Mental Health. I am also much indebted to a number of friends and colleagues for giving kind permission to cite unpublished data or for helpful suggestions about the revision of this paper: Drs. Henry Bachrach, Bruce Derman, Erika Fromm, James Gray, Mark Oberlander, Fred Pine, Maryrose Rogolsky, and John J. Sullivan.

the inner-directed original—the person who deviates but manages to do so in a socially valued, constructive way.

The Psychoanalytic Theory of Creative Thinking

Despite all of the research interest, attested by many symposia, books, grants, and now a *Journal of Creative Behavior* (Vol. 1, 1967), there has been, relatively speaking, a dearth of theory for psychologists to go on. The dominant theoretical orientation of most psychologists—some theory of learning or reinforcement growing out of behaviorism—has little to offer. In such a desert, the little spring of ideas welling out of psychoanalysis looks like a major oasis. The first of Freud's relevant ideas to attain wide notice, the theory of sublimation, has not led to a great deal of research, and what there is has, if anything, tended to disconfirm it, so I shall not discuss it further.

Adaptive vs. Maladaptive Regression

Freud mentioned a second idea in a couple of his works (1905, 1915) without ever elaborating it to any great extent: he noted that the type of thinking he considered characteristic of the unconscious—the primary process—did penetrate into consciousness in humor, art, and other creative mental functioning as well as in psychotic thinking. One of his pupils, Ernst Kris (1952), developed this idea, which he called ego-controlled regression or *regression in the service of the ego.* A lifelong student and devotee of the arts, Kris centered his work for decades on artists and their work, being interested, for example, in series of paintings or sculptures produced as their creators went into or emerged from psychosis, which he studied in relation to whatever parallel clinical observations were available. "Schematically speaking," Kris wrote, "we may view the process of artistic creation as composed of two phases . . . inspiration and elaboration. . . . The first has many features in common with regressive processes: impulses and drives, otherwise hidden, emerge. The subjective experience is that of a flow of thought and images driving toward expression" (1952, p. 59). But we must distinguish creation, "in which the ego controls the primary process and puts it into its service . . . [from] the psychotic condition, in which the ego is overwhelmed by the primary process" (p. 60).

Kris was making two distinctions: the first was between the passive inspirational phase when creative ideas emerge into consciousness and the primary process is particularly evident, and the active elaborational phase when the ideas are systematically worked out and the secondary process plays a larger role. Second, he was distinguishing between two types of regression, which may more succinctly be called maladaptive (as in psychosis) and adaptive (as in creativity). But if the former is a pathogenetic process and the latter promotes the finest kinds of human achievements, why should they both be called *regression?* On the way to an answer, let us examine first the definition of this term. In the 1914 revision of *The Interpretation of Dreams,* Freud inserted a description of three kinds of regression: "(*a*) *topographical* regression, in the sense of the schematic picture of the ψ-systems . . . ; (*b*) *temporal* regression, in so far as what is in question is a harking back to older psychical structures; and (*c*) *formal* regression, where primitive methods of expression and representation take the place of the usual ones" (Freud, 1900, p. 548).

Of these three, topographical regression need not concern us, since it involves the topographic model of the psychic apparatus which was superseded by the structural model of *The Ego and the Id* (1923; see also Gill, 1963, and Arlow and Brenner, 1964). The central idea in regression is a figurative temporal retrogression, an undoing or reversal of evolution as an explanation of pathology. This concept Freud had learned from Hughlings Jackson, who used it with brilliant success in explaining a number of neurological symptoms. The regression in neurosis as Freud presented it did not, of course, imply that literally childish behavior typically emerged. Rather, he thought that as mature modes of gratification, defenses, and modes of adaptation became unworkable, the person fell back on earlier forms of each of these, determined particularly by the nature of earlier libidinal fixations.

The third type is the one that mainly concerns us. Formal regression means merely that the secondary process is replaced by the primary. When Freud concluded the above passage by saying that "all these three kinds of regression are, however, one at bottom," he no doubt had in mind his belief that the primary process (attributed to the *Ucs.*) was the genetic antecedent and seedbed out of which the secondary process (of the *Pcs.-Cs.*) grew. Though I have serious reservations about this hypothetical genetic series (Holt, 1967b), it seems reasonable to follow Freud's terminology in calling it a regressive change when the nature of thinking shifts toward the primary process pole, which is in a number of respects less highly evolved, socialized, and differentiated.

Definition of Primary and Secondary Process

What, then, is meant by the primary and secondary processes? These terms embody one of Freud's greatest discoveries, originating in his efforts to make sense out of the fascinating ambiguities of the dream. Once he had achieved the basic insight that dreams are allegorical fulfillments of unconscious wishes, he was able to figure out the principal modes of disguise used in the dream work, which so effectively conceal the wish-fulfilling nature of manifest dreams. He then saw the similarities in all forms of disordered or primitive thought: the speech of psychotics, the myths of preliterate cultures, the play of children, even the implicit processes that produce neurotic symptoms and character attitudes. His great insight was that all of these bizarre forms of psychic functioning were not the product of random error but represented a second system of ideation [1]

[1] It is true that primary and secondary processes are considered by many psychoanalysts to refer to affect and action as well as cognition; but for present purposes the narrower definition will suffice.

(which he called the primary process) operating on different principles from the familiar, waking, logical variety (secondary process). Once the special principles governing the primary process had been discovered, it was possible to see the meaningfulness in disordered thought, and thus to understand and interpret dreams, symptoms, and the like.

These principles were, first, that primary process is *wishful,* taking short-cuts to immediate gratification without regard to reality; second, that it has a limited number of distinctive *formal properties:* displacement, in which one content—often a symbol—is substituted for another; condensation, in which one thought product or image may stand for several others, often incorporating various elements of them; a kind of false reasoning that has been called autistic logic (Rapaport) or predicative reasoning (von Domarus); and a general disregard for the usual standards of fidelity to reality and rationality, so that mutually contradictory propositions may stand side by side unresolved, the restrictions of space and time may be flouted, impossibilities be blandly imagined, and normal expectations violated. The secondary process, defined by contrast, is purposive, effective, realistic, orderly, logical thinking. Though Freud assumed that it makes up the main part of the conscious thought of normal civilized adults, it is transparently an ideal conception, which is rarely attained. Similarly, the primary process is also a complex *ideal type,* in Max Weber's term, defined in terms of a cluster of variables or attributes which are never present simultaneously at their maxima.

It was characteristic of Freud that he set these concepts forth in dichotomous fashion, even attributing them to different systems or making them the principal defining characteristic of the systems *Ucs.* and *Pcs.-Cs,* later of the id and ego. Yet he went ahead to discuss them in such a way as to make it clear that there are in fact no distinct dividing lines. Recall his statement, "The ego is not sharply separated from the id; its lower portion merges into it" (1923, p. 24). This must mean that primary and secondary processes are not sharply differentiated either, nor are their component mechanisms.

Gill (1967) and I (Holt, 1967b) have come to the conclusion that Freud described a continuous series of condensations and of displacements ranging all up and down the continuum from primary to secondary process. The same is true for the involvement of motivation in thought: by insensible stages, we can proceed from the most "neutralized" kind of logical thinking motivated by highly derivative ego-interests, to more and more pressured, tendential, purposive thinking, to frankly drive-dominated ideation that seems completely in the service of the most immediate gratification of the crudest instinctual motives. Finally, the basic criteria for primary and secondary process are contained in what Freud (1911) called the two principles of mental functioning, taken conjointly: The more thinking is directed toward immediate pleasure and away from pain or unpleasure, the more primary it is; and the more it disregards reality and logic, the more primary it is.

Despite the fact that primary and secondary processes theoretically represent the ideal endpoints of complex sets of continua, it is convenient to continue to follow the custom of psychoanalysts and speak as if there were two distinct, sharply differentiated processes.

The Development of a System for Scoring Primary Process Manifestations

A Pioneering Empirical Study: The Work of Myden

One of the first attempts to put the psychoanalytic hypothesis of a relation between creativity and adaptive regression to an empirical test illustrates the need for an explicit scoring system. Myden (1959) studied the personalities of creative people by testing a creative group and a noncreative but equally successful group with a battery of projective tests, from which he reported quantitative results from the Rorschach only. Each group was made up of 16 men and 4 women, with ages ranging from 30 to 55 (median 41 years) and no significant difference between the samples as to age or socioeconomic status. Without mentioning names, Myden says that all of the members of his creative group are well known "to those familiar with the cultural life of America"; they include dramatists, composers, choreographers, stage designers, painters, poets, novelists, and lyricists. No noncreative subject was an amateur in any of the arts; "All had achieved success by their own efforts . . . [as] heads of corporations of international importance, attorneys, educational specialists . . . physicians and surgeons. . . . In each group, three Ss had undergone some form of psychotherapy."

Myden makes a convincing case that his samples were well and meaningfully matched and that the most noteworthy difference between them was in their demonstrated capacity for creative work in the arts. He scored his Rorschachs in two ways: he followed the system of Piotrowski for the conventional scoring of locations, determinants, etc., and to test his psychoanalytic hypotheses he scored each protocol for manifestations of primary process, anxiety, passivity, and sexual ambivalence. Of the latter group of variables, he discusses his scoring criteria for primary process only and gives them in only the most general terms.

> In analyzing the Rorschach for evidences of primary process, Schafer's suggestions were followed. . . . where the primary process dominates, the secondary concept tends to be organized around drives and fears rather than reactions that exist in reality. He [Schafer, 1954] adds that attention will be limited, and aggressive and libidinal images will dominate. . . . Primary processes in Rorschach responses are characterized by uncontrolled discharge, autism, fluidity, and minimal selective and reflective capacity. [Myden, 1959, p. 141]

Myden used Chi square to test the null hypothesis that each of his groups contained equal numbers of subjects above and below the combined median. The first thing that strikes one about his data is that there is a large difference in total productivity: the median R of the creative group is 40.5, and that of the noncreative subjects is 23. Though Myden exaggerated this difference in discussing his findings, he neglected to test it; a Chi square computed from his table of raw data is 8.1, $p < .01$. It would seem prudent to hold R constant in any subsequent analyses, but Myden failed to do so; moreover, because of a peculiar feature of his tables of raw data ("Numbers in each row do not derive from the same protocol") it is impossible to convert his figures on *M,* sum *C,* etc., to percentages of *R.* Therefore, one does not know how seriously to take his apparent finding that the creative subjects produced more *M, C,* and *c,* more categories of content, and more sexually ambivalent responses, since all of these scores are undoubtedly correlated with *R.*

The chief finding of interest in the present context involves responses scored for primary process: the median for the creative subjects is 6, for noncreative subjects it is 1. Chi square (recomputed with the Yates correction) for the difference in distributions is 20.5, which is highly significant; when Chi square is 10.8 with one degree of freedom, $p = .001$. Moreover, it is possible to compute the *mean* percentage of primary process; for the creative group, it is 21 percent; for the noncreative group, 8 percent. It seems likely, therefore, that creative subjects produced substantially more regressive responses than their controls, even allowing for the difference in general productivity. Myden's argument that the regression is in the service of the ego hinges on his finding that both groups had median $F+$ percents of 85.

Despite this apparently positive finding, the study is quite vulnerable to methodological criticism. Its worst defect is the failure to guard against criterion contamination: since the same examiner administered the Rorschachs and scored them, there can be no guarantee that he did not inadvertently influence his results, both in the gathering of the data and in the scoring. He made no attempt to test the reliability of his scoring; the only bit of internal evidence that the data were not completely malleable is the fact that one predicted difference did not emerge: the creative subjects failed to produce more evidence of passivity than the noncreative subjects.

Myden is appropriately modest in presenting his findings as exploratory:

> The study itself represents a mere first step in what is essential to the progress of the scientific understanding of human thought, namely the development of hypotheses which are then subjected to rigorous testing procedures.

Unfortunately, however, there is no way for another investigator to take this next step and replicate the study with more rigorous testing procedures. Even if he gathered parallel data without criterion contamination, which would be difficult, the independent investigator would have no way of knowing whether he was using Schafer's very general guidelines for the identification of primary process in the same way that Myden had. Anyone who has done much research with Rorschach data knows that even well-trained and experienced testers do not agree as often as would be desirable even on the scoring of some traditional determinants, especially when the sample of responses is not routine and stereotyped. The situation is far worse when new scores are introduced, especially if these require clinical judgment.

Problems in Developing a System of Scoring Adaptive vs. Maladaptive Regression

For the psychoanalytic theory of thinking to become useful in research, an explicit and detailed method of measuring manifestations of the primary process was essential. Moreover, the method had to include a way of assessing the degree to which such regressive thought products are adaptive or maladaptive. Many discussions of the primary process state that it "has to do essentially with mental energies" (Arlow and Brenner, 1964), and it is true that most of Freud's theoretical discussions and approaches to definition do emphasize cathexis or psychic energy, its degree of binding, inhibition vs. free discharge, and like considerations. Since this energy is not in any way directly measurable or observable (see Holt, 1967a), the fact that primary process is defined in terms of it seems to be a formidable obstacle. Yet as Gill (1967) has demonstrated, Freud did fortunately discuss many concrete examples of what he meant, so that the concept may be made adequately operational.

About fifteen years ago, it struck me that the Rorschach test ought to lend itself quite well to assessing the primary process. Why should the Rorschach, as compared to other tests, stimulate primary process along with the usual secondary process? Briefly, for three reasons (or hypotheses): First, the test requires the subject to produce a series of concrete, visual images as the core of his responses, discouraging abstract thought (which is exclusive to the secondary process). Freud argued that "Thinking in pictures . . . stands nearer to unconscious processes than does thinking in words" (1923, p. 21). Second, the strange, ambiguous, unfamiliar nature of the blots and the open-endedness of the task facilitate an imaginative, fantastic approach, as Rorschach himself noted. Third, the mystique of the Rorschach, its reputation for uncannily piercing through one's conscious defenses and revealing inner secrets to the trained examiner, arouses anxiety about self-revelation and thus stirs up primary process material.

Content Scores

The earliest stage in the development of a method for scoring the signs of the primary process that show themselves in Rorschach responses was reported fifteen years ago (Klopfer, Ainsworth, Klopfer, and Holt, 1954, pp. 547–549). The first categories distinguished were based on content, following the suggestion of Hartmann (1950) that the degree of neutralization was indicated by the direction or aim of thought. Neutralization was of interest because Rapaport (1951b) and Kris (1952), as well as Hartmann, proposed that the more neutralized the energies of thought are, the more the latter approximates the ideal of the secondary process. On the assumption that overt content of a libidinal or aggressive sort in an objectively neutral testing situation indicates the "drive-domination" allegedly characteristic of the primary process, I set up a check list of drive categories. These came to include seven types of libidinal content (oral-receptive; oral-aggressive; anal; sexual—i.e., directly phallic or genital; exhibitionistic-voyeuristic; homosexual; and miscellaneous —including urethral, narcissistic, and birth-relevant) and three of aggressive content (emphasizing the standpoint of the subject or aggressor, emphasizing the standpoint of the object or victim of the aggression, and results of aggression). Each of these ten types was subdivided into two "levels," of which Level 1 is more blatant, more id-like, while Level 2 is more socialized. Thus, the distinction in the aggressive categories hinges on the lethality of the implied attack, murderous aggression being Level 1.[2]

Formal Scores

The first attempts to apply the above scheme as a "neutralization index" quickly led to the realization that the main defining characteristics of the primary process were being unnecessarily ignored. With the help of Dr. Joan Havel, I began defining a second series of scores for formal aspects, which grew to a present total of 40 categories, of which three-fifths are classified as Level 1. These include 8 forms of condensation, 6 of displacement, 5 of symbolism, 4 of contradiction, and about a half-dozen types of autistic reasoning. Many of them are outgrowths of Rapaport's (1945–1946) "verbalization" scores.

Control and Defense Scores

It soon became apparent that a total measure of primary process was not likely to be particularly meaningful without a consideration of the subject's defensive organization, particularly his degree of control over his own regressive thinking. This part of the system includes 44 varieties, many of which are subdivided according to the degree of their effectiveness. The categories are grouped into 15 types of remoteness, 4 contexts (cultural, esthetic, intellectual, and humorous) each of which is subdivided into successful and unsuccessful attempts, 11 pathological defenses, 4 types of overtness, 3

[2] These and other scores are discussed in a little more detail in Holt (1960), and fairly fully with concrete examples in Holt and Havel (1960). Mimeographed copies of the recently revised, unpublished, 150-page scoring manual (Holt, 1968) may be obtained from the Research Center for Mental Health, New York University. Most of the scoring symbols and terms are explained in an appendix to this chapter.

sequence scores, several types of adaptive transformations, and a few measures of delay and reflection on the response.

Ratings of the Total Response

In order to make the distinction between adaptive and maladaptive regression, it became necessary to have each response rated on four scales after the decision has been made that each of the above categories does or does not apply.

Defense Demand (*DD*) conceptualizes the dimension that is dichotomized in the distinction between Level 1 and Level 2; it is a six-point scale of the response's shock value as an interpersonal communication. A *DD* of 1 is given to responses that would not raise an eyebrow at a polite tea party; a *DD* of 6 implies the maximum need for some kind of controls to mitigate the intrinsic shockingness of both the content and the formal deviations contained in a response.

Defense Effectiveness (*DE*) is also rated on a six-point scale from +2 (completely successful control and defense in a wholly acceptable response) through 0 (only moderately successful attempts at control) to —3 (disorganized responses with only pathological attempts at defense). Three main considerations enter into this rating. First, one considers the *form level,* which is itself rated according to Mayman's (1960) unpublished scoring manual (see also Lohrenz and Gardner, 1967). Mayman distinguishes eight categories, ranging from the sharpest, most accurate (*F*+) to the most arbitrary (*F*—) perception of definitive forms, plus two degrees of nondefinitive form (vague and totally amorphous) and a "spoiled" score (*Fs*) for basically acceptable responses that are more or less ruined in their elaboration. To each of these scores there corresponds a beginning or trial *DE* rating, which is modified upwards or downwards depending on the nature of the Control and Defense categories that have been scored.[3] The scorer makes a further modification (if necessary)

[3] This procedure, with trial *DE* ratings assigned for each of Mayman's scores, is a recent innovation that seems to have improved the scorer reliability of *DE,* which had varied greatly from one study to another.

after considering the *affect* accompanying the response, on the assumption that when a response is under good control it should not cause any disturbance and may be positively enjoyable, whereas anxiety or other negative (or inappropriate) affects indicate disruption of cognitive functioning and the probability that the regression is maladaptive.

Finally, there is a rating scale for the *creativity* of the response, which is a rather loosely defined combination of statistical infrequency and "richness" (e.g., sensitive use of determinants, good verbalization). This five-point rating replaces the usual distinction between popular, unscored, and original.

Administration

It became evident to those who tried to apply the above scoring principles that not all Rorschach protocols could easily be scored. A truly verbatim record is essential, since the nuances of wording often determine several aspects of a response. Moreover, it turned out that an important control category was whether the primary process material emerged in the spontaneously given response or only later in inquiry; therefore, it is highly desirable that the subject be given a chance to discuss every response in the inquiry. My colleague Dr. Fred Pine suggested the major innovation in administration: the addition of an *affect inquiry.* For the great majority of responses, it is quite difficult to gauge the accompanying emotional response of the subject from the usual sort of protocol, even with good observational notes. It proves to be a simple matter to ask the subject directly to tell what his emotional reaction was at the time he gave each response, and this has turned out incidentally to be a valuable source of clinically useful material. I usually preface the general inquiry period by saying, "Now I want to go back over your responses with you and make sure that I saw them just as you did. I'd like for you to point out just where you saw each one, what about the blot made it look like that, and how you felt about it—whether at the time you found the idea pleasant, unpleasant, or neutral." Then it suffices in the detailed inquiry to remind the subject, after discussing location and determinants, "How did it strike you?" or "Did you have any particular emotional reaction to it?" It is important not to convey the impression that every response *ought* to be experienced as freighted with affect.

A Scored Sample Response [4]

Let me conclude this brief introduction to the scoring method by applying it to a response. Suppose a woman says, on looking at the first card, "Ugh—a horrible vampire bat! It looks almost as if it was Dracula or something, flying right at me." In the inquiry, she points out the usually seen details and adds that it makes her think of other horror stories and movies.

The conventional scoring, which my system does not supplant but supplements, is *W FM A P;* and by most systems, form level would be considered *F+*. In Mayman's scoring, however, all popular and near-popular responses are *Fo* (for "ordinary," acceptable accuracy).

On my scoring sheet I first record the response number, then the form level, *Fo,* followed by the Creativity rating; as a popular, not remarkably elaborated, response, this would get the lowest score, 1. Next, the drive content is scored. In this instance, the concept of a vampire bat, a blood-sucker, is an oral-aggressive threat, which would be scored *L* 2 *O–Ag* (libidinal, Level 2, oral aggression).

Next, we consider the response again, asking whether or not there is any formal manifestation of the primary process, like condensation, symbolism, or contradiction. There *is* something autistic about the response: it is treated as if the subject had lost sight of the fact that the bat was only her interpretation of an ink blot and was considering it as magically aimed at *her;* this we score as a Self-Reference (*SR* 1). But it has a control in the way she verbalized it: by use of the words "almost as if," she gains some distance and does not commit herself to the deviant idea. The relevant score is *R-cond:*

---

4 Adapted from Holt (1966), pp. 10–11.

remoteness, conditional. Other applicable control scores are: *R-(an)*, *R-fic s+*, and *Cx E+ weak;* that is, the orality and aggression are less threatening because they are attributed to an animal rather than to a person, and the response gains additional remoteness from the appropriate reference to a specific fictional character; the subject also invoked an esthetic context, but weakly.

Finally, we must rate Defense Demand and Defense Effectiveness. *DD* is 3, near the midpoint of the scale given by the manual. To estimate *DE,* we start with the assumption that a response with such good form accuracy must be potentially near the top of the scale, or +1.5, but since strong negative affect is expressed, it moves down a notch to +.5. The controls scored change the rating a notch upward to +1. The scorer still has the option of raising or lowering the rating one point for considerations that are not specified by the manual but that his clinical judgment tells him are relevant. By reference to scored examples in the manual, we find that this response has the same general feel as others that are rated +1, so that becomes the final score. It is still on the positive side of the zero point, indicating that the primary process manifestations that came into awareness were coped with well enough so that the response can be considered an adaptive rather than maladaptive regression: the product of *DD* and *DE* is +3.

Measuring Adaptive vs. Maladaptive Regression

It should be evident even from this very brief sketch that the scoring system yields a bewildering variety and number of specific scores, which may be summarized in several ways. Thus, one may be interested in the proportion of a record that contains any primary process material; that leads to the *total percent pripro* (an abbreviation for *pri*mary *pro*cess). Or, since Level 1 scores are most clearly primary process in nature, one may compute a *percent Level 1,* or even more specifically, *percent Level 1 Formal* (the proportion of *R* containing any material given Level 1 scores for formal aspects of primary process), etc. The first technique of incorporating the controlling and defensive aspects of the system into a single measure of adaptive vs. maladaptive regression was worked out by Dr. Leo Goldberger (1961; see also Holt, 1968); it will be described below. More recently, researchers have made extensive use of a score for which the formula may be expressed:

$$\frac{\Sigma\,(DD \times DE)}{PPR} = \text{adaptive vs. maladaptive regression}$$

That is, for each response, multiply the *DD* rating by the *DE* rating; take the algebraic sum of the resulting positive and negative numbers, and divide by the number of primary process responses (*PPR*). The theoretical limits of this quantity are +12 to −18, the positive numbers presumably indicating primary process material with good control, the negative ones disruptive breakthroughs.[5]

Reliability of Scoring

A detailed presentation of the issue of reliability and of representative results would occupy a great deal more space than is available here; some data have been presented elsewhere (Holt and Havel, 1960; Holt, 1966). On the whole, the level of agreement among independent scorers is about the same as has been reported for conventional Rorschach scores. It varies greatly from category to category and is of course much better for overall indices than for specific scores. *Total percent pripro* consistently yields reliabilities better than .90; *mean DE* has been quite variable but generally poorer—fairly typical figures are those of Blatt et al. (1969), who report relia-

---

[5] A disadvantage of this score is the fact that it is independent of the *amount* of pripro in a record. If the numerator is the total number of responses, the quotient is more sensitive to variations in the amount of primary process, but empirically this measure has not worked out as well as the formula in the text above. Multivariate analyses need not, of course, be limited to a single overall measure; sum Σ *(DD* $\times$ *DE)/PPR* may usefully be supplemented by *percent Level 1* in a multiple regression system or some approximation to it (like ranking subjects on both variables, adding ranks, and reranking totals). For groups of subjects small enough to rank, Goldberger's method may be the best available.

bilities of .73 for *DE* and .85 for adaptive regression (*mean of DD* × *DE*).

The remainder of this paper will be devoted to a review of the presently available evidence bearing on the construct validity of Rorschach measures of adaptive regression, as shown in studies of creativity.

Empirical Studies of Creativity and Primary Process in the Rorschach

Two principal approaches to a *criterion measure* of creativity have been used in research that attempts to test Kris's (and Freud's) hypotheses. The first is to select groups of people who are in other respects as well matched as possible, but who differ in their creative behavior, usually as judged by expert evaluation of their creative products. The second is to administer tests of creativity to an unselected group of available subjects; that is, to ask them to be creatively productive in certain specified ways and then to evaluate their products according to explicit criteria. The two approaches are in one sense the same; the former has in its favor the fact that it usually enables one to work with people who differ more widely on the judged continuum of creativity, while an advantage of the latter approach is that the judgmental operations going into the criterion are more explicit and the result is a more nearly continuous distribution along the continuum. (Other advantages of this approach will be discussed below.)

The Work of Cohen

An experimental study of the relation between artistic creativity and adaptive regression as measured in the Rorschach was carried out by Cohen (1960). He used the method of extreme groups, selecting 20 advanced undergraduate art majors at Michigan State University who were judged "highly creative" by their professors, and 20 others randomly selected from the remainder of the art students. Each group was made up of 10 males and 10 females. He administered Rorschachs to them individually, and scored them both conventionally and by an early edition of my primary process manual, before the introduction of the *DE* rating. Instead, at that time, adaptive regression was measured with the aid of a cumbersome system of "Defensive Contribution" (*DC*) ratings: an arbitrary quantitative weight was assigned to each type of form level, to each specific Control and Defense score, and to manifestations of affect when they were discriminable. Some weights were positive numbers, some negative; they were summed algebraically for each response. The resulting total *DC* for a response was multiplied by its *DD* rating, and such products were summed across responses for the Adaptive Regression score.

Cohen's results were, first, that none of the 28 traditional Rorschach scores (e.g., *W, M*) discriminated between the groups. Second, he found significantly more total pripro in the creative group, but the difference disappeared when the number of responses was partialled out. That is, the more creative subjects did produce more primary process, but they did so only to the extent that they were generally more productive of responses. Third, however, the measure of adaptive regression was significantly higher in the creative group.

Not content with this positive support for the hypothesis, Cohen looked further into his data and discovered that the entire effect was carried by the defensive contribution weights from Mayman's form-level scores—the *DC* weights from affect [6] and from Control and Defense scores made no difference one way or another. Might it not be, then, that primary process and adaptive regression had nothing to do with it, and it was merely that the more creative subjects saw more sharply and accurately than their less creative peers? No; the average form level was significantly superior for the creative group *only* on responses containing primary process material; there

[6] This study antedated the affect inquiry, so that scorable expressions of affect were probably too scanty to make any difference.

was no difference between the groups on the average form level of *non*-pripro responses.

The Work of Rogolsky

Rogolsky's (1968) design was in a number of respects similar to Cohen's, with children as subjects. She too separated her subjects into creative and noncreative groups, by having the drawing of 228 third-graders evaluated by professional artists. She then studied further the top and bottom 15 percent, giving Rorschachs to 57 subjects in all. Using the ninth edition of the pripro manual, she attempted to differentiate her groups by means of the currently recommended measure of adaptive vs. maladaptive regression: *mean* $DD \times DE$. There was no significant difference, nor did the groups differ on Cohen's measure of form level in pripro responses. Rogolsky noticed, however, that popular responses seemed to be functioning as an indicator of good control. Therefore, for one control variable she used the number of populars; for another, a form-level score based on *all* responses, using numerical equivalents of form levels as given in the primary process manual (see Appendix). To measure the amount of primary process, she used both total percent pripro and mean *DD*. The multiple correlation between creativity and ranked scores on the four variables was .62 ($p < .01$) for boys, only .29 (N.S.) for girls, and .43 ($p < .05$) for the entire group. The control dimensions contributed more than the measures of amount; as a matter of fact, in the male sample, the number of populars correlated .56 ($p < .01$) with creativity. This seems a paradoxical result, until one reflects that popular responses are defined by adult norms; thus, in a latency age sample, giving many populars may be a measure of maturity rather than of stereotypy.

The Work of Dudek

In an attempt to highlight the specific nature of creative talent, Dudek (1968) studied successful painters ($N = 19$, including 3 sculptors) and writers ($N = 22$) whose work had found critical as well as popular acclaim, comparing them with 19 other members of the same professions whose work was not considered creative, and with 22 occupationally successful but noncreative persons (including 9 businessmen, 6 professionals, and 3 housewives) matched for high productivity of *M*. Even within the group of successful artists she was able to make finer discriminations, thanks to four literary critics who evaluated the work of 14 writers and divided them into a superior 8 and a relatively inferior 6.

Contrary to some of her hypotheses, Dudek found no differences among her groups on mean *R, M, W,* sum *C,* or *F%* (all scored according to Piotrowski), after she had eliminated two highly atypical cases (both of whom happened to be superior, successful writers) who produced 136 *R* and 50 *M,* and 182 *R* and 53 *M*. There were no differences in the quality of *M* either, and no significant trends involving the dilation or introversion of the experience balance.

Dudek's positive findings came in the realm of what she calls "regressive responses" and affective reactions. To test Kris's hypothesis she scored the Rorschachs by her own adaptation of the condensed published version of my manual (Holt and Havel, 1960). She used Level 1 categories only, with the following further restrictions: "Only responses falling into the following categories were scored as regressive content or primary process thinking: 1) responses reflecting crude, direct or primitive expression of drive, 2) responses using confabulatory thinking, and 3) responses showing autistic secondary elaboration." In contrast to Myden (1959), she notes that regressive responses in her creative group were "often bizarre." Her further discussion does not indicate just which categories she used, but her examples suggest that scoring criteria were freely modified in an idiosyncratic way. Although the reliability of the Piotrowski scores is given as 88 percent agreement with another scorer on 13 percent of the records, there is no indication that Dudek checked the reliability of her primary process scoring. In some early editions of the primary process manual and in the published condensation, there was a category of affective responses (since abandoned). Dudek scored "affective expressions," tallying them separately from primary process responses.

She found, first, that the successful artists produced a mean of 7.3 regressive responses (out of 34 *R*), whereas the unsuccessful artists and the nonartists gave means of 4.1 and 4.2 (out of 39 and 35 *R*, respectively). But since only three of the unsuccessful artists gave more than a single regressive response each, 47 percent producing none, the averages are not particularly meaningful, and Dudek tested the significance of the difference by means of Chi square, splitting distributions near the mean and obtaining a Chi square of 6.9, $p < .01$. (If one dichotomizes the distributions in such a way as to maximize the theoretical values, pitting zero or one regressive response against more than one, the difference is even more significant, the p value being much less than .001.) The combined groups of artists had significantly more subjects who gave much primary process than the nonartists had ($p < .01$), and the successful artists can be even more significantly differentiated from the nonartists. Dudek presents no figures on any differences in production of regressive responses by her six "superior" and eight "inferior" successful writers. She adds:

> Although the successful group produced a large number of affective expressions (mean of 13.0 in the successful artists and 7.4 in the unsuccessful artists), the difference between the two groups minutely missed statistical significance (Chi square = 3.68 [$p = .06$]). The difference between successful artists and high-*M* nonartists, however, was significant ($p < .05$).

On the issue of whether the regression involved was adaptive or not, Dudek offers only her own impressions that

> artists who projected regressive content gave it frequently in a body of responses that were essentially sound. The content of the responses seemed to be taken as a matter of course and did not result in a flood of incapacitating anxiety. The shifting from a regressive to a normal level seemed to be easy and smooth and the full tone of the record was generally positive and constructive.

She reports her impression that her control subjects

> seemed to show a disintegration of defenses and of the synthetic faculties under the force or intensity of their own energy.

Dudek's findings, like those of Myden, are challenging in that both found at the extreme of demonstrated creativity a significant tendency to produce large amounts of primary process, but neither presents any quantitative findings on controls. Moreover, since both used idiosyncratic criteria for scoring primary process (and reported no data on the scorer reliability of their methods), the findings cannot be compared directly with those of any other studies.

A Second Type of Criterion: The Work of Guilford

The remaining studies have used the second type of criterion, tests of creativity—principally those of Guilford (1950, 1967) and his group. Guilford and collaborators have analyzed creative processes into a number of discrete, logically separate functions, have devised many ingenious tests of those functions, and then have refined and ordered their measures with the aid of factor analysis. Some of these tests have been used in numerous recent researches (e.g., Barron, 1955; Getzels and Jackson, 1962).

Since the first appearance of tests of flexibility, such as Brick Uses (Wilson et al., 1954), which measured the first of the creative-thinking abilities to be isolated by his Aptitudes Research Project, Guilford has made a major change in his theory of intelligence, resulting in what he calls the Structure of Intellect model. About 40 independent intellectual factors had been discovered, and they did not seem to fit easily into any of the existing schemes, such as hierarchical models calling for more general (e.g., *g*) and less general factors. Guilford noted first that there were three sets of factors with parallel properties, differing only in the kinds of content dealt with—figural (measured by spatial or visual-perceptual tests), symbolic (tests composed of numbers and letters), and semantic (those involving verbal meanings). Recently, he has added a fourth category of content, which he calls behavioral: it is the kind of information involved in understanding the emotions and behavior of other people. These different types of *content* make up one dimension of a cubic model; the other two dimensions deal with *products* and *operations*.

There had already been "some tradition for classifying the intellectual factors . . . according to the supposed kind of operations involved," Guilford (1967, p. 62) remarks. Cognition, memory, and evaluation (or judgment) were familiar types of operations, and with the study of creative thinking it became apparent that there should be a parallel set of abilities involving a type of operation that Guilford called "divergent production." Tests for these creativity factors "are all of completion form, and the examinee makes a good score for the number and variety of his responses and sometimes for high quality." Other, similar tests existed, in which the subject "has to generate his own answer to each item, but . . . it must satisfy a unique specification or set of specifications." Since, "in accordance with the information given in the item, the examinee must converge upon the one right answer," Guilford calls this fifth type of operation *convergent production.* Finally, a third way of classifying abilities which is orthogonal to the other two became apparent: according to the product—units, classes, relations, systems, transformations, or implications. The model has proved its heuristic value in giving the specifications for previously undemonstrated abilities; the Aptitudes Research Project has repeatedly set out to produce tests to fit an empty cell in the model and has succeeded in finding the predicted factor.

All of the operations are used in most types of creative work, Guilford (1967) tells us. Nevertheless, the kind of operation that is most distinctive to the generation of something original is divergent production. The model implies that there should be at least 24 factorially independent abilities within the realm of this one operation (six products times four contents), of which 16 have been demonstrated. "At least," because any particular art or science may also entail a number of specific abilities; for example, a painter needs to have special abilities to work with colors which are beyond the purview of the Structure of Intellect model. One great value of this approach is that it conclusively lays to rest the notion that there is any unitary "creativity" or creative ability. Further, it provides us with a useful framework in terms of which to analyze an activity and predict the types of abilities it requires.

The Work of Gray

Only one study to date has included a systematic sampling of creativity factors. With the aid of Professor Guilford, Gray (1967) chose six tests, one for each type of product, within the semantic content domain, as given in Table 1.

TABLE 1

DIVERGENT PRODUCTION OF	FACTOR	NATURE OF TEST
Units	Ideational fluency	Number of titles listed for a story outline
Classes	Spontaneous flexibility	Listing uses for a brick and a lead pencil
Relations	Associational fluency	Writing synonyms of words
Systems	Expressional fluency	Constructing a variety of four-word sentences, given four initial letters
Transformations	Originality	Number of clever plot titles for a story outline
Implications	Semantic elaboration	Naming possible jobs for which a symbol might stand

To control for "general intelligence," Gray obtained the Scholastic Aptitude Test scores of his subjects, 100 male undergraduates at Fordham University. He administered both forms of the Holtzman Inkblot Test, obtaining a total of nearly 9,000 responses. It is perhaps understandable that under the circumstances he scored only for primary process, omitting Control and Defense scores and the overall ratings (except for *DD*). Since he gave the two forms a month apart, he is able to present the first test–retest reliability coefficient for a primary process score: .85 for total Defense Demand. (Scorer reliability for total pripro was .86.)

His results were in some ways quite similar to Cohen's. The amount of primary process (not percent, since the number of responses is held constant in the Holtzman technique) correlated .23

with his composite creativity criterion ($p < .05$). Since pripro was also somewhat related to SAT scores ($r = -.15$), he partialled the latter out, and the r rose to .28 ($p < .01$). Gray noticed, however, that the protocols with more pripro scores were longer, so he also partialled out the number of words and the number of responses in all Guilford tests. With these measures of productivity held constant, the correlation fell to .06—completely insignificant. Once again, then, the more creative subjects brought forth more ideas in responding to the ink blots and thus produced more primary process, but not in a higher concentration than in the less creative subjects' responses.

In retrospect, it seems to have been a mistake to have added all the test scores together for a composite criterion measure. The tests were, after all, designed to measure orthogonal (uncorrelated) factors, so that when they are put together the result is not so much a measure of "overall creativity" as of whatever extraneous variance they share. In his attempt to partial out verbal productivity, Gray seems to have hit upon the main component of this composite criterion (the correlation between the criterion and "productivity"—a simple count of the total number of answers on all creativity tests—was .81). But Gray also reports results from a more promising approach, in which he correlated his total pripro measure with scores on each of the six Guilford tests separately. All of the correlations are negligible (from .00 to .18) with one exception: Expressional Fluency and primary process correlated .28 ($p < .01$).

Let us then take a closer look at the test of Expressional Fluency, the writing of as many different four-word sentences as possible, the first letters being specified. Guilford (1967, p. 151) gives as an example some answers to the item W . . . C . . . E . . . N . . . : "We can eat nuts"; "Who colored Eve's nose?"; and "Why cannot elephants navigate?" But notice that each of these is scorable for primary process! [The first is clearly *L 2 O* (Level 2 oral); the second, *Ag 2 R wk* (aggression, Level 2, results, weak), since coloring someone's nose is a mild prank, surely a very restrained form of hostility; the formal score *Ctr R 2* would also apply, since the humor of the sentence lies in its contradiction of expectations—coloring noses is an inappropriate, unlikely activity. The last sentence is another example of the contradiction score *Ctr R* 2.] When rather stringent constraints are placed on the production of sentences—they must be grammatical, they must use four words, all beginning with specified letters, and no word is to be used more than once—but there is *no* requirement as to content, nonsense being as acceptable as sense, anyone who operates under the self-imposed further constraint to stay within the realm of the secondary process will be left behind by those who are free to use their primary processes. It is therefore easily understandable that this particular test should be the one to be best correlated with the tendency to give primary process responses to ink blots.

The Work of Pine and Holt

First Study

With a rather similar design but a much smaller number of subjects, Pine and Holt (1960) were able to test Kris's major hypothesis. The criterion of creativity in this study was a composite [7] of 9 scores

[7] Retrospectively, it is possible to justify the pooling of these tests into a single criterion, because it happens that most of the scores seem to fit Guilford's criteria of divergent production of semantic transformations. "Consequences" is explicitly allocated to this factor; another he describes as follows: "Cartoons presents cartoon pictures adapted from magazines, with [the subject] to write the punch line for each one." This factor, he says, "is the ability known for some time as the originality factor. . . . An originality test should emphasize either (1) ability to produce responses that are statistically rare in the population, (2) ability to produce remotely related responses, or (3) ability to produce clever responses" (1967, pp. 153–154). To some extent these criteria touch on some of Pine's criteria for TAT Literary Quality, and they surely fit the Fantastic Animal originality score (though the latter may be primarily a figural test), and the Science Test. As to Rorschach originality, Guilford mentions as "a potential source of measurement" for this factor, "an unusualness score" for the Rorschach. It seems likely, therefore, that compositing all these scores emphasized the one factor many of them may have had in common: divergent production of semantic transformations. Moreover, since Freud described the primary process in the first instance as a collection of techniques by which the semantic meanings and figural content of the day's residues were transformed into the manifest dream, there is good reason to expect that this factor might be closely related to measures of primary process.

from 7 tests, two of which were Guilford's Brick Uses and Consequences Tests, most of the remainder having been devised by Pine. Nine TAT stories were scored for their literary quality (Pine, 1959); the Rorschach creativity score was the one described above, but the average rating given only to those responses containing no primary process was used, to prevent contamination. Each subject drew "a Fantastic Animal," making it as out-of-the-ordinary as possible; these were rated for the drawing ability and the originality shown in them. Raters also judged the humor of captions supplied by subjects for 15 cartoons in a Humor Test, and the quality of theories devised by subjects to account for two supposed surprising discoveries, in a Science Test. All ratings had satisfactory interjudge reliability.

Individually administered Rorschachs were reliably scored by the seventh edition of the primary process manual, and adaptive regression was measured by the Goldberger technique, as follows. First, the measure of *amount* of primary process was the *weighted total percent pripro,* in which double weight is assigned to Level 1 scores (more clearly regressive responses). The *control* score was the ratio of well-controlled responses containing much pripro to poorly controlled responses; that is, the number of responses with high *DD* ratings *and* good *DE* ratings was divided by the number of responses with poor *DE* ratings regardless of *DD* (those with good *DE* but low *DD* not being considered). Parenthetically, since this score considered Defense Demand a measure of the intensity of pripro expression, as well as Defense Effectiveness, it might be looked on itself as a measure of adaptive vs. maladaptive regression; it is very nearly the same as $DD \times DE$. Goldberger's method of computing *adaptive regression* is a reranking of subjects taking into account both the amount and the control score, so that at one extreme are subjects who are high on both the proportion of primary process responses in their Rorschachs and on the effectiveness with which it was controlled; in the middle are subjects who expressed least; and at the other end are those who expressed a great deal but ranked low on control (maladaptive or pathological regression).

Once again, the amount of primary process was not significantly related to total creativity in either the 13 male college freshmen or their 14 female classmates from the New York University School of Education. The control measure was significantly related to the composite criterion in both subsamples (rho = .80, $p < .01$, males; rho = .52, $p < .06$, females), but the correlations with adaptive regression provided two surprises: because they were so high (for the boys, rho = .90) and so low (for the girls, only the insignificant .28). It was pleasing, if not unexpected, that a number of the specific creativity test scores were significantly correlated with the males' Rorschach control scores (TAT .74; Fantastic Animal: drawing ability .69, originality .55; Guilford Consequences: originality .59) and their adaptive regression scores (the same tests yielded rho's ranging from .49 to .83; and Brick Uses, flexibility .48). But none of these subtests worked as expected for the girls; the only significant correlations involved the *amount* of pripro and TAT literary quality (.59) on the one hand, the score on one of the Science test items on the other (.64). The authors note that the adaptive regression score used here was not meaningful in the female sample (see Holt and Havel, 1960, p. 314) and cite additional data demonstrating that in this small group of college girls creativity was consistently more strongly related to the amount of primary process material than to measures of control.[8] Incidentally, in the total sample, adaptive vs. maladaptive regression (Goldberger measure) was essentially unrelated to intelligence as measured by the Ohio State Psychological Examination: the correlation was only .17.

Second Study

Because of the surprising findings with adaptive regression, Pine (1962) took the first opportunity to test out the hypotheses with a new sample. A true replication was not possible, but it happened that a group of 50 male members of Actors Equity (mostly unemployed) were studied at the Research Center for Mental Health a

[8] In this connection, see L. H. Silverman (1965) for a discussion of reasons why the Rorschach responses of a creative woman may contain much primary process with few controls, and negative as well as positive affect.

few years after the original experiment, and the following data were available on them: 47 subjects took Guilford's Brick Uses test; TAT's were available for 29 subjects (and were again rated for literary quality); in place of the Fantastic Animal, figure drawings were made by 36 subjects (and were rated for drawing ability); and all subjects took the Rorschach, which was scored as before both for creativity and for the various pripro measures. Whether scores from these slightly different tests of creativity were treated separately or were put together into a composite criterion, the findings were uniformly negative: none of them related to *any* of the three Rorschach measures. Pine (1962) points out the possibly extenuating fact that in this sample all subjects were pursuing an artistic profession into which presumably whatever creativity they had was channeled, while we lacked anything remotely resembling a criterion measure of creativity in the theater. In terms of Guilford's model one would expect actors to be creative with behavioral content much more than with the semantic and figural tests we used.

Some New Data

Pine and I were upset enough by the giddy plunge from .9 to .1 that neither of us examined the data any further for quite a while. A few years later, however, I had a great deal of information about these 50 subjects punched on IBM cards, including 88 variables derived from the primary process manual and the results of an intensive personality assessment. The latter comprised 78 scores from a variety of objective tests, and 73 clinical ratings by staff members of the Research Center,[9] based on dossiers which each contained an autobiography, notes on (or transcriptions of) several interviews, a Wechsler-Bellevue, TAT, and Rorschach (with conventional scoring only). With the help of a computer, a large correlation matrix was prepared, which contained some findings of interest and relevance (see Table 2).

[9] I want to express my thanks and indebtedness to the many staff members whose work made possible the results reported in Tables 2, 3, and 4.

TABLE 2 *Correlates of Creativity Tests in 50 Unemployed Actors Studied at the Research Center for Mental Health, 1959–61*

	Measures of creativity				
	BRICK USES		RORSCHACH	BARRON-WELSH	
MEASURES OF PERSONALITY	FLEXIBILITY ($N = 47$)	FLUENCY ($N = 47$)	CREATIVITY ($N = 50$)	ART SCALE ($N = 39$)	
Rorschach Pripro Scores					
Mean $DD \times DE$	—.22	—.19	—.08	.12	
Mean *DE*	—.02	—.01	.12	*.32*	
% Content	*.32*	.09	**.43**	—.02	
Mean density of pripro	**.42**	.11	.24	—.00	
Sum of *L* 1 *O*	*.34*	.17	**.41**	—.09	
Sum of misc. libidinal 1 scores	**.40**	.13	*.37*	—.19	
Sum of *L* 2 *M*	**.51**	.25	.13	.03	
Sum of *Ctr L* 1	*.35*	*.29*	.27	.09	
Sum of *V S* 2	*.31*	*.31*	.24	—.05	
Sum of *Au El* 2	**.47**	*.34*	*.36*	—.00	
Sum of Remoteness —Geographic	**.43**	*.37*	**.51**	—.06	
Sum of Remoteness + scores	**.43**	.02	*.34*	.04	
Sum of Context + scores	**.63**	.23	**.53**	—.03	
Other Tests and Measurements					
Hypnagogic imagery	**—.53**	**—.45**	*—.37*	—.19	($N = 32, 33$)
DPI *OA* (oral aggression)	.25	.02	*.33*	*.32*	($N = 49, 38$)
Jenkins:					
Cholinergy	*.39*	.19	*.31*	—.17	($N = 43, 45$)
Emotional spontaneity	*.36*	*.36*	.27	—.01	($N = 43$)
Kinesthetic empathy	*.33*	*.35*	*.37*	.13	($N = 43, 45$)
Vistorexis	*.31*	.17	*.36*	.22	($N = 43, 45$)

(*continued*)

TABLE 2 (*continued*)

	Measures of creativity				
	BRICK USES		RORSCHACH	BARRON-WELSH	
MEASURES OF PERSONALITY	FLEXIBILITY ($N = 47$)	FLUENCY ($N = 47$)	CREATIVITY ($N = 50$)	ART SCALE ($N = 39$)	
Stroop Color-Word Interference	.25	.31	.22	.23	($N = 40$)
Wechsler-Bellevue total IQ	.15	–.12	.05	.04	
Staff Clinical Ratings					
Ego autonomy (composite)	**.44**	.17	*.39*	*.34*	
Loose thinking	*–.35*	.10	**–.43**	**–.47**	
n Understanding, creativity	*.31*	.06	**.43**	.01	
Positive work attitude, responsible	*.38*	.16	*.35*	.26	
Suggestible	–.27	–.15	*–.30*	*–.33*	
Counterphobic, hypomanic	*.32*	*.32*	.08	.01	
Inhibited thinking	*–.33*	.12	–.26	–.27	
Undoing (as defense)	–.21	*–.30*	–.21	–.22	
Creativity Tests					
Brick Uses:					
Flexibility	x	**.62**	**.54**	.27	
Fluency	**.62**	x	**.41**	.11	
Rorschach Creativity	**.54**	**.41**	x	.10	
Barron-Welsh Art Scale	.27	.11	.10	x	

NOTE: $N = 50$ for all Rorschach variables, staff ratings, and others except as specified. In the case of the special tests and measurements, parenthetical figures indicate N for significant correlations only. Figures in *italics* are significant at the .05 level; in **bold face** at the .01 level (two-tailed). DPI stands for the Dynamic Personality Inventory (Grygier, 1955).

Interrelations of the Criteria

Note, first of all, that the Brick Uses variables and the mean creativity rating from the Rorschach (this time based on *all* responses) form a well-intercorrelated cluster, in which Fluency seems a little less central than Flexibility. That makes good sense, in view of the fact that the total number of Brick Uses given (Fluency) measures the simplest kind of divergent production, that of units; the Flexibility score, the frequency of shift from one type of use to another, measures the production of semantic classes.[10] The Barron-Welsh Art Scale is rather weakly related to Flexibility and not at all to the other two measures of creativity. This is hardly surprising, since it has no intrinsic validity as a measure of creativity: it is based on the expressed likes and dislikes of a group of professional artists (most of them painters) for a group of abstract linear designs. It measures, then, the tendency to evaluate visual materials in the same way as a group of creative artists; Barron (1953) presents evidence that it is a measure of complexity of personality. In Guilford's terms, it uses figural, not semantic, content and an evaluative operation, not one of divergent production. (Note that all four of these measures of creativity are unrelated to a standard measure of general—mainly cognitive—intelligence.)

Any single score from one test must be factorially impure, however, and the only moderate loadings of the two Brick Uses scores on two orthogonal factors (approximately .5) make it easily possible for the two scores to be as highly correlated as in fact they are in the present sample. Empirically, Brick Uses Fluency has markedly fewer personological correlates than Flexibility. With no way to get a factorially pure score out of it, Fluency acts like little more than an attenuated measure of the same underlying construct, and so it will not be further discussed.

The patterns of correlates in Table 2 for the experimentally independent Flexibility and Rorschach creativity ratings are strikingly

---

[10] In addition, it may be relevant that the *scorer* (not the subject) must make qualitative evaluations of responses both for Flexibility and for Rorschach creativity.

similar, supporting the inference that both are measures of the same construct, a different one from that measured by the Barron-Welsh, though all three are significantly related to a clinical measure of ego autonomy (as defined by Rapaport, 1951a, 1958; see Kafka, 1963). The emphasis in the Barron-Welsh seems to be more on an independent rejection of loose thinking and resistance to influence by others, while high standing on the creativity measures characterizes well-organized, emotionally well-balanced persons with strong intellectual interests and openness to experience. What appears in the table as "*n* Understanding, creativity" is a combination of highly correlated clinical ratings of Murray's needs for Construction (creative) and Understanding; it is the best criterion rating we have of *motivation* for creativity (as distinguished from ability or capacity to function creatively). The correlation of .43 between this rating and the mean rated creativity of Rorschach responses is a rather impressive construct validation of the later rating.[11] The Rorschach instructions, while clearly calling for divergent production, do not directly suggest that responses need be original or creative in any way. In such a bland and permissively open-ended situation, a person who spontaneously produces richly elaborated, ingenious, clever, and nonpathologically unusual responses must do so out of an internally generated need. Without some *talent* for divergent semantic production (indicated by correlations with Brick Uses Flexibility), of course, the motive alone could not produce responses of high quality.

Correlations between Creativity and Measures of Primary Process

Consistent with what Pine (1962) reported, the creativity measures show no relation to the currently most-used measure of adaptive re-

---

[11] There is some possibility that this validity is partly spurious. The clinical raters had access to the unscored Rorschach protocols, along with a large body of other qualitative data, and they may have been affected by the same qualities of the responses that were rated as part of the pripro scoring. The same caveat applies to all the correlations among Rorschach variables and staff ratings to be reported below.

gression, $\Sigma\ (DD \times DE)/PPR$, nor to most overall measures of the amount or control of primary process. Nevertheless, the proportion of responses containing scorable (i.e., drive-dominated) content—the *percent content*—was higher in the more creative subjects. The significant correlation with *density of pripro* is interesting; subjects who shifted a good deal from one category to another in talking about a brick (thus scoring high on Flexibility) were the ones who when discussing a Rorschach percept tended to say many things about it, any one of which would qualify for a pripro score, hence producing a high "density" of scores per response. Density is a measure of amount that is logically independent of the percent pripro, which measures the proportion of responses containing *any* scorable material.

Among the specific content scores, only three types of libidinal content were related to any measure of creativity, while no such correlations with measures of aggressive imagery appear. This finding is theoretically interesting, since L. H. Silverman's (1963) work, demonstrating how the arousal of aggressive ideation brings about maladaptive regression (various kinds of disruption of cognitive functions), might suggest, if anything, a negative correlation between creativity and aggression. There is another variable in the matrix that was designed to measure a person's preferential production of either aggressive or libidinal imagery independent of the total amount of such drive content; it is the proportion of all scorable content (libidinal plus aggressive) that is libidinal. This score was insignificantly related to Flexibility (.20) and to Rorschach creativity (.14); hence it does not appear in Table 2. It seems best, therefore, to interpret the correlations in Table 2 without specifying anything about aggressive content, since the latter seems unrelated to the creativity scores used, one way or another.

The nature of the specific libidinal content in the correlates of creativity suggests some speculations, which will be reserved for the discussion section.

Table 2 calls for a few more comments, about the remaining Rorschach primary process categories that proved to be significantly related to the measures of creativity. They fall into two groups:

some specific formal manifestations of primary process and some control categories. It is difficult to say why just these three formal scores should relate to creativity, and undoubtedly there is some degree of chance involved, since certain others yielded correlations just below the .05 level of significance. *Ctr L* 1 means outright logical contradictions: for example, asserting mutually incompatible things about a percept, such as that it is both beautiful and ugly. *V S* 2 stands for slips of the tongue, and *Au El* 2 refers to a rather benign and acceptable form of autistic elaboration, of the kind called *fabulation* by Rapaport et al. (1945–1946) and Schafer (1954) but more elaborated into a story-like fantasy than many of the brief responses they scored *fab*.[12] What do these three have in common? Perhaps a kind of cognitive looseness that might plausibly be related to associative flexibility—a willingness to let ideas slip out freely without much censorship even if it involves some self-contradiction, misspeaking, and wandering from the assigned task (of merely saying what the blot areas look like) into a story-telling vein of fancifulness. Or it may be that the underlying attitude is one of not taking the nature of the situation as a *test* terribly seriously, so that the subject lets down the bars of the usual standards of logic, language, and relevance in the service of allowing fancy to roam. Which rather closely approximates a description of adaptive regression!

In the final group of correlates, *R-Geographic* means giving a response a setting that is geographically remote from that of the test-taker. It is interesting and somewhat unexpected that this device seems to be such a favorite one of persons who come out high on the measures of creativity used here; [13] the other correlates of this score

---

[12] Dr. Erika Fromm, who is currently studying hypnosis as an adaptively regressive state, reports (in a personal communication) an impression that the hypnotic state is especially conducive to the emergence of *Au El* 2.

[13] There may be a linguistic clue to the relationship in the word *exotic*. Literally, it means geographically remote, *outlandish*, but both of those words connote the fascinatingly strange, unstereotyped, and glamorous. Perhaps an ideological or attitudinal dimension of creative personality includes a preference for the unusual, including the imported over the domestic. In *Ulysses*, Joyce pedantically underlines the banality of Mr. Bloom (in contrast to the creative hero, Stephen) by noting his preference for the cisatlantic over the transatlantic.

suggest that (at least in this sample) it is generally a positive sign of ego strength. The same is true of the other two control scores, Sum of Remoteness plus scores and Sum of Context plus scores. Both are composites of individual categories that occur rather infrequently. Of the 17 specific ways of reducing threat by giving a response remoteness (other than geographic) I arbitrarily assigned plus signs to five because they struck me as being adaptive ways of handling the problem of control and defense; they include, for example, appropriate references to fictional or religious characters. Finally, as mentioned earlier, a response may be made more acceptable by being put into a cultural, esthetic, intellectual, or humorous context: invoking a relevant custom or social role, one of the arts or sciences, or making a joke. Any of these maneuvers can be carried out appropriately and smoothly, or in a strained and awkward way that simply does not come off; therefore, context scores are subdivided into effective (+) and ineffective (—). Not surprisingly, it is the effective use of these means of control that characterizes the more creative members of the sample of actors.

Discussion

Orality and Creativity

The significant correlations between the two best criteria of creativity in Table 2 and *L* 1 *O* (the more primitive, or Level 1, manifestations of orality) can best be discussed in the context of other available information about the correlates of the oral scores, which have been collected together in Tables 3, 4, and 5.

At the time I published a good many of these data on orality (Holt, 1966), I was struck by what I thought was a consistent pattern: the more direct oral responses seemed to be given by the more creative men, who were outstanding for general competence and for an active, self-reliant, achieving orientation; whereas subjects who gave many socialized and innocuous oral responses (*L* 2 *O*) had some

TABLE 3 *Correlates of Level 1 (Direct, Unsocialized) Oral Responses in Two Studies*

p	*r*	VARIABLES
		Holt (1966: 50 actors)
.01	.41	Rorschach Creativity rating
.05	.34	Brick Uses: Flexibility
.05	.33	Creative, intellectual interests (Scale *CI,* DPI)
.05	.39	Seeks and enjoys sensuous and/or sensual experience (*n* Sentience, clinical rating)
.05	.32	Enjoys visual pleasures (Vistorexis scale, Jenkins)
.05	−.32	Has vivid imagery (clinical rating)
.05	.37	Cholinergy (Jenkins)
.05	.35	Ego autonomy (composite of several clinical ratings)
.01	−.37	Passivity (Scale *Wp,* DPI)
.05	−.34	Orderly and thrifty (*n* Order, *n* Retention; clinical rating)
.05	−.33	Defensive and guarded (clinical rating)
.05	−.33	Suggestible and dependent on others to take initiative (clinical rating)
.05	−.33	Prone to separation anxiety re paternal figures (clinical rating)
.05	.33	Achievement drive (Scale *Pa,* DPI)
.05	−.32	Feels sexually inadequate (clinical rating)
.05	.31	Interest in objects of phallic symbolic significance (Scale *P,* DPI)
.05	.30	Initiative, self-reliance (Scale *EI,* DPI)
		Holt (1960: mixed group of 96 normal and pathological subjects)
.05		15 subjects who performed best on all parts of Stroop's Color-Word Interference test had more *L* 1 *O* than 20 who performed worst.

specific cognitive competences of a noncreative sort. Even in the realm of interests, a significant correlate of *L* 1 *O* is a test measure of creative, intellectual interests, while *L* 2 *O* is associated with the breadth of interests generally. Both oral scores (Levels 1 and 2) are good correlates of ego autonomy and related variables including notably *Cholinergy* as measured by Jenkins's multifactor test, "How Well Do You Know Yourself?" Jenkins (1962) defines this variable as "a resilient tendency to feel energetic, happy, enthusiastic, secure,

TABLE 4 *Correlates of Level 2 (Indirect, Subtler) Oral Responses in Several Studies*

p	*r*	VARIABLES
		Holt (1966: 50 male actors)
.05	—.37	Embedded Figures test, total time
.05	—.33	Reading time for colors, noninterference series (Stroop Color-Word Test)
.05	.38	Enjoys nonmusical auditory sensations (Auditory orexis, Jenkins)
.05	.36	Has a strong desire for sexual stimulation (Sexorexis, Jenkins)
.05	.28	Enjoys visual pleasures (Vistorexis, Jenkins)
.01	—.39	Has vivid imagery (clinical rating)
.01	.43	Cholinergy (Jenkins)
.01	.38	Ego autonomy (clinical rating composite)
.01	—.52	Self-punitive, disillusioned (clinical rating)
.01	—.40	Has narrow range of interests (—.32 with R held constant, $p < .05$; clinical rating)
.01	—.38	Passively aggressive (clinical rating)
.01	—.37	Easily feels depressed, ashamed, inferior; turns hostility against himself (—.27 with R held constant, N. S.; clinical rating)
.05	.36	Expresses self naturally, enthusiastically (Emotional Spontaneity, Jenkins)
.05	—.32	Feels unloved and unwanted (clinical rating)
.05	—.31	Has diffuse and conflictful identity (—.24 with R held constant, N. S.; clinical rating)
		von Holt et al. (1960: 27, 23 college students, mixed)
.05		Positively related to solving the Hanfmann-Kasanin test, in each of two independent samples
		Rogolsky (1968: 32 third-grade boys)
.01		Artistically creative boys had more *L 2 O* than uncreative boys
		Blatt, Allison, and Feirstein (1969: 50 male graduate students)
.10	.25	Inefficiency in problem-solving, with percent *L 2 O*

or optimistic," which closely approximates the psychoanalytic conception of the satisfied oral character.

As further data have accumulated, I have been more struck by the convergence of correlates than by any persisting trend of a dif-

TABLE 5 *Correlates of Oral Responses Combining Levels 1 and 2 in Two Studies*

p	*r*	VARIABLES
		Gray (1967: 100 male college students)
.05	.22	Composite creativity criterion, six Guilford tests, with sum *DD* for all oral responses
		Sullivan (1963, unpublished data: 44 Peace Corps trainees)
.01	.42	Social Value (Allport-Vernon-Lindzey), with total oral responses divided by total number of primary process responses
.01	.42	*n* Nurturance (Edwards PPS), with same measure of oral responses

ferentiation.[14] I had exaggerated the unrelatedness of *L 2 O* to creativity, for Brick Uses Flexibility did turn out to be weakly correlated with this subtler measure of orality, $r = .28$, $p = .05$, and in a personal communication Rogolsky told me of her unpublished finding that her artistically creative schoolboys gave significantly more *L 2 O* than her generally matched but uncreative group. (She says that she found *no L 1 O* responses in her entire sample.) A measure like Gray's that combines *all* oral responses (weighting them according to their Defense Demand) was at least as strongly related to his composite criterion of creativity as the much more reliable measure of total primary process (Table 5). Unfortunately, this measure was not corrected for productivity and Gray (1967) does not give its correlation with the number of words per protocol, so there is no way

---

14 Apparently I was too much impressed by the unexpectedly low and insignificant correlation between Level 1 orality and Level 2 orality in the actor sample—only .23, despite the similarity in meaning between the contents scored *L 1 O* and *L 2 O*. I should have recalled that in a larger normal sample (121 subjects, mostly male college students) the correlation was .26, and it was .28 in a sample of 81 schizophrenics, both reliable at the .01 level (Holt, 1966). These are certainly not impressively large, and as coefficients of internal consistency they are poor indeed. In the near future, I am going to pursue this matter by more intensively studying the interrelations of all types of oral responses, and by seeing to what extent some of the correlations reported here might be enhanced if oral aggressive types of response were segregated from the more receptive types. Incidentally, the other oral score in Table 2—the Oral Aggression scale from Grygier's (1955) Dynamic Personality Inventory—is unrelated to either *L 1 O* or *L 2 O* (*r*'s about .1).

of knowing to what extent the finding would hold up if the latter variable were partialled out. As to the association of *L 2 O* with measures of the cognitive control of field articulation (of which both the Embedded Figures Test and the Color-Word Interference Test are measures; see Gardner et al., 1959), I was overlooking the fact that in 1960 I had reported a significant relationship between a complex measure of general efficiency (or cognitive flexibility) from the Color-Word Interference Test and the *other* oral measure, *L 1 O*. Likewise, both *L 1 O* and *L 2 O* are correlated with various measures of openness to and enjoyment of sensory intake from the outside, which is apparently rather antithetical to an inward focus on vivid imagery—note the negative correlations between both oral measures and a clinical rating of the vividness of imagery (Tables 3 and 4), and the strong negative correlations of the creativity scores in Table 2 with the incidence of hypnagogic imagery, as determined by a focused interview.

Note also that oral optimism (Jenkins's Cholinergy), emotional spontaneity, the enjoyment of visual pleasures (Jenkins's Vistorexis), and flexible cognitive control (Color-Word Interference) are correlates of creativity (Table 2) as well as of orality (Tables 3 and 4).

It appears, therefore, that despite some shift in the phenotypes from sample to sample, there is a good deal of stability on the inferential level of personological genotypes. That is, if we look behind the face meaning of the various test scores and clinically rated traits and attempt to interpret them, several hypotheses are available to account for the correlations between the kind of creative function tapped by original and well-elaborated Rorschach responses and by the spontaneous flexibility score of the Brick Uses test on the one side, and Rorschach images of mouths, breasts, food, sucking, biting, and the like on the other. Both of these types of test responses may entail, first, an attitude of receptivity toward the world of sensory information and, second, a flexible mode of cognitive processing. Underlying this openness and this freedom, I hypothesize further, are a sense of security and basic trust in the world and in oneself (self-reliance, ego autonomy), which may be ultimately rooted in a gratifying relationship with the mother in the early oral stage of development, as Erikson (1963) has taught. Conversely, if a person has learned from bitter[15] early experience that the world is harsh, barren, and frustrating, he may develop any of several kinds of defensive organizations: e.g., rigid, narrow compulsiveness; passive, dependent inadequacy with fear of abandonment; self-punitive, depressed inferiority and withdrawal. Any of these patterns (suggested by the correlates of oral scores in Tables 3 and 4) can plausibly interfere with a free intake of information such as is required for quick performance on Embedded Figures or Color-Word Interference or for absorbing visual impressions to be used in the graphic arts, and with flexible processing of material taken from memory storage. An orientation of receptive openness to the world expressed in oral responses to the Rorschach blots seems to enable a person to keep looking at complex visual stimuli undisturbed by the emotional stimulation of color they contain until their many sensory attributes can be registered separately; the Witkin Embedded Figures, the Color-Word Interference, and the Hanfmann-Kasanin tests all require the subject to disregard the affective pull of color and deal with it, if at all, purely in terms of the cognitive information it conveys.

Table 3 contains one finding, not as yet discussed, which stands in surprising conflict to the general trend of the correlations involving the oral scores. Blatt, Allison, and Feirstein (1969) studied problem-solving efficiency in 50 male graduate students at Yale, using the John-Remoldi PSI apparatus (John, 1957). This machine presents the subject with a circular array of nine lights, each controlled by one or more buttons, plus a center light which is not *directly* controlled by any button. Complex relations exist among the buttons and lights; the task is to learn how to turn on the center light in the most efficient way. The main measure of efficiency is the number of unnecessary information-yielding button pushes. This measure correlated highly ($r = -.40$) with adaptive regression as usually measured, and even more so with mean *DE*: $r = -.46$. But the correlation with *percent L 2 O* was .25 ($.10 > p > .05$), a reversal of the expected direction!

---

[15] How readily the oral metaphor comes to mind! The infant spits out what is bitter, acting hurt, as if his faith in the goodness of the world had been betrayed.

We cannot understand this finding unless we remember the lessons Guilford has taught about the independence of intellectual abilities. Blatt's description makes his test sound factorially complex, but its content is clearly figural and not semantic (whereas the creativity measures discussed here are almost entirely semantic), the product in question involves a system of relations and implications, and the operations seem to emphasize convergent production rather than divergent production (as well as all the others—cognition, memory, and evaluation). Since it is so much more complicated than tests that have proved related to oral responses and particularly since it differs from them in requiring the subject to learn a figural *system* in which color is not involved, it is probably uncorrelated with Embedded Figures, the Color-Word test, and the concept formation test of Vigotsky, Hanfmann, and Kasanin. Openness to sensory experience does not seem to be critical, and if the subject's attention can easily be caught by the purely sensuous properties of test materials he may do badly in such an abstract-mechanical task. This kind of analysis of Blatt's criterion of problem solving would have been more convincing if done before knowledge of his results; but at least it is hard to see how a positive correlation between his measure of efficiency and oral responses could have been predicted, and the negative one seems equally plausible if not more so.

Some further remarks about orality will be made in the next section, after we consider the implications of the fact that creativity is correlated with other types of libidinal content.

Other Pregenital Themes and Creativity

Among the correlates of Flexibility and Rorschach Creativity in Table 2, "Miscellaneous libidinal Level 1 scores" refers to three separately coded but infrequent and positively intercorrelated types of response: *L* 1 *E-V* (exhibitionistic-voyeuristic—chiefly nude figures), *L* 1 *H* (overtly homosexual or hermaphroditic responses), and *L* 1 *M* (a miscellany including menstruation, urine, and childbirth). Two points might be made: first, this is a group of socially rather unacceptable topics, which it would take considerable cognitive and emotional freedom to let oneself visualize and report; and second, it may not be coincidental that a disposition toward creativity is found in male actors whose Rorschach responses suggest that they have fantasies of sharing the physical sexuality and creativity of women. The latter interpretation is supported by the correlation with *L 2 M,* which includes uterus, ovaries, and embryos, as well as narcissistic responses.

Both Myden (1959) and Dudek (1968) report several similar findings with nonactors. The successful creative artists in both studies tended strongly to produce sexually ambiguous responses of the type that would probably be scored *L 1 H, L 1 M,* or *L 2 M.* Dudek also calls attention to the fact that her artists saw many "emblems" and other indications of a desire for status, an essentially exhibitionistic "need to be recognized and acknowledged as an artist."

These results take on special interest because of certain clinical findings reported by psychoanalysts who have treated creative persons, particularly writers: an unusual prominence of oral material, especially defense against oral masochism (Brill, Bergler, Kris), and pregenital fantasies generally, especially of a bisexual or homosexual nature (Freud, Kris—all as cited in Kris, 1952, Ch. 13). Thus, in analyzing A. E. Housman's report of how he usually wrote his poems, Kris notes the prominent oral themes in the manifest content of the introspections and concludes that in the unconscious process, "the path leads from anal activity to homosexual passivity and thus another well-known meaning of creation is evoked—that of giving birth to a child" (Kris, 1952, p. 301). Nevertheless, Kris added that it was his "impression that . . . the pregenital layers constitute nothing specific" that would enable one to predict which persons would be likely to experience creative inspiration.

Conclusions about the Relation between Adaptive Regression and Creativity

Let us take stock now, from a problem-centered, rather than a method-centered, point of view. How does the psychoanalytic hypothesis look in the light of the data reported here? The weight of the evidence seems to me impressively positive, in light of the many limitations of the pieces of research that have been done. True, the Rorschach primary process scores that have shown statistically significant relationships to measures of creativity have varied from study to study, but then so have the populations sampled and the kinds of creative functions considered as criteria. With so much error variance on both sides of the equation, it is remarkable that so many positive findings have come through: not only is there something to the hypothesis, but the phenomenon seems to be a rather strong one to show up so persistently.

Let us take a quick glance at some other recent tests of the hypothesized relationship between creativity and adaptive regression as measured by other means than the Rorschach.[16] Orgel (1955; see also Adelson, 1960) found that college girls who were rated creative in their writing reported dreams that more frequently (than their controls') departed from realistic conceptions of space, time, action, and causality. Moreover, girls who were rated as more creative writers reported dreams with more direct and uninhibited references to sex than girls rated uncreative. Child (1965) used a questionnaire method to measure adaptive regression and found it related to his measure of good esthetic judgment. D. K. Silverman (1963) induced children to paint and to speak freely as they did so; later, she had each child's several paintings rated by artists for creativity and scored his recorded verbalizations for primary process using a method based on mine, though deviating from it in a number of major respects. Her main finding was that within subjects, fluctuations in the degree of artistic excellence of paintings were related to changes in the amount of controlled primary process in their concomitant verbalizations. Wild (1965) found that art students were able to shift their Word Associa-

---

[16] A study using the Rorschachs administered to a sample of outstandingly successful (although chronically alcoholic) painters by Roe (1946) also deserves mention here. Hersch (1962) reanalyzed them according to the developmental scoring scheme of Werner's students, and supported the interpretation that a controlled regressive process was characteristic of painters as compared to both schizophrenics and a mixed normal control group. This is a perceptual regression, however, and not in any way a measure of primary process.

tion and Object Sorting test responses more in the direction of unregulated thinking than were teachers or hospitalized schizophrenics matched for sex and age; the art students, all of whom "were actively producing works of art at the time of testing," also tended to give more original responses to these tests under normal conditions, and those who were rated as more creative by their art teachers gave higher shift scores.

It may be taken as rather well established, therefore, that people who produce material that is judged creative (either in the course of their spontaneous artistic work, or in response to tests that call on them to be cognitively flexible or original) tend to have readier access to and better control over primary-process modes of thought, and are less threatened by drive-laden and unrealistic ideation than are people who are less able to be creative, in the sense that term has had in the research reported.

Access to primary process may be a necessary, but surely not sufficient, condition for artistic creativity. Indeed, I believe that many a moderately gifted painter of the surrealist school had as much access to archaic imagery as a Bosch or Brueghel, yet failed to produce works of lasting greatness. To be an artist at all, one must have a minimal degree of talent and skill at the basic disciplines of the craft; to be productive and original, one must have in addition some openness to the unconscious sources of creativity: an ability to tolerate in awareness fantasies, images, and scraps of ideation that may be shocking in their sexual or destructive content and in their departure from logic and realism. But to attain the highest reaches of artistic achievement, something more is necessary—something not yet approached by any of Guilford's factors nor by the hypotheses of the psychoanalysts. One must be able to open the door to the unconscious, yes, and to keep a firm grasp so that it can be closed again; but once granted that the door can open, what is there waiting to come through by way of communication probably matters a great deal more than the width of the aperture.

Here we have come full circle to the question with which this paper began—the relationship between creativity and genius. I still believe that it makes sense to study the types of cognitive and affective processes involved in creative work within the normal range. It just seems necessary to emphasize the discontinuities as well as the continuities between "the normally creative" and "the truly great." Likewise, we should beware of generalizing glibly about creativity at large or *"the* creative process" from researches that employ limited criteria, as they must. Brief reflection about the lives and works of the outstanding creative minds of our culture is enough to remind us that "universal geniuses" are excessively rare. It is not uncommon for an Einstein to have a modest competence at the fiddle, and to be unconventional in his dress and political views, but even he could hardly be said to have been creative in every department of his life. For this reason, Guilford's approach has a good deal to be said for it. He and his group are trying to analyze the many kinds of cognitive function involved in creative work of all kinds, and to develop specific tests of them which are interrelated and sorted out by means of factor analysis. There is no reason to think that any combination of such tests will pick out persons who will necessarily produce work of universally recognizable creative merit, but that is not a crushing criticism. Even standard intelligence tests, the best products of our oldest psychometric tradition, are generally agreed to be ineffective in making meaningful distinctions within the top one percent of the general population, yet they remain of great value and usefulness. Researches in intelligence and creativity suffer from the fact that both concepts are ultimately grounded in *social evaluations* of behavior (or, even more remotely, of the products of behavior): they are defined, not analytically and psychologically, but by means of evaluative criteria entirely external to the person and his ways of functioning.

A fruitful approach in future research on creativity may be to accept this limitation and to follow the general lead of research on cognitive style: after a specifiable and measurable cognitive function has been selected for study because it seems one of the necessary if not sufficient conditions for creative work in some area, investigate its generality and its personological correlates, including the kinds of Rorschach primary process scores associated with it. In this last area, I believe that we shall not learn as much by efforts to get one all-purpose measure of adaptive regression as by a more microscopic analysis of specific impulse-defense configurations, or specific kinds of formal properties of primary process and controls thereof.

Conclusions about Measuring Primary Process in Rorschach Responses

Finally, let us take a look at the status of the primary process scoring system and its construct validity. In line with the just preceding remarks, I believe that there is bound to be a ceiling on the replicable validity of any one overall index of adaptive vs. maladaptive regression and that the research reviewed here supports this judgment. Since we have rather clear indications that certain kinds of drive content are a good deal more relevant than others to the kinds of creativity studied, and since some specific sorts of formal variables prove to be related to cognitive flexibility or to perceptual problem solving, it becomes difficult to defend the practice of lumping together all manifestations of primary process and trying to get an average measure of the effectiveness with which they are all controlled. The results in Table 2 surely suggest that a more narrowly conceived index combining certain content scores, certain formal scores, and certain types of control would make a more plausible predictor of cognitive flexibility than *mean* $DD \times DE$.

Nevertheless, there is accumulating a considerable body of research evidence for the construct validity of this last index and for Goldberger's measure of adaptive regression, even though neither has held up well as a predictor of creativity. First, a group of studies suggests that it measures an openness to unusual types of experience when such openness is adaptive. Allison (1967) found this index to be significantly ($p < .05$) related to reported experiences of religious conversion in 20 theological students. Bachrach (1968) found a correlation of $+.79$ ($p < .01$) between *mean* $DD \times DE$ and independent measures of empathy in recorded samples of psychotherapeutic sessions with 22 therapists in training. Using several measures of tolerance for unrealistic experiences (Klein, Gardner, and Schlesinger, 1962), Feirstein (1967) found that their composite was correlated .49 ($p < .05$) with this measure of adaptive regression. Using Goldberger's method of measuring adaptive regression, Bergan (1965) found it strongly related to the vividness of imagery in 14 college men's dreams ($p < .01$), and with a similar sample of women, found it positively related (at the .05 level) to the intensity of waking auditory imagery and to the accuracy of pitch judgments (which were themselves highly correlated variables).

Second, another group of researchers have in various ways supported the interpretation that adaptive regression characterizes good psychological adjustment (see Schafer, 1958). Oberlander (1967) found a rho of .74 between *mean* $DD \times DE$ and the flexibility of autonomic nervous system functioning, as measured by the reactivity of the pupil in a sample of "11 young adult volunteers." Using the MMPI to measure thought disorder, Derman (1967) found that Goldberger's index significantly differentiated subgroups of 32 male college students who were classified as "ambulatory schizophrenics" and normal, respectively. In his studies of maturity in Haverford college students, Heath (1965) found that *mean* $DD \times DE$ discriminated in the predicted direction between the 12 best-organized and the 12 least-organized upperclassmen ($p < .05$), and a few years later the 10 most and 10 least organized upperclassmen ($p < .05$), in both cases as rated by faculty and fellow classmates. In the larger of these two samples this measure of adaptive regression was highly and significantly correlated with a number of test measures of adjustment (e.g., MMPI general maladjustment $-.43$, $p < .05$; incongruence of self-image $-.66$, $p < .01$) but few of these correlations held up in other samples studied in this country and abroad (personal communication). At best, therefore, adaptive regression as measured by either Goldberger's method or by *mean* $DD \times DE$ is likely to be an unreliable index of adjustment, sensitive only to gross differences or to smaller ones under unknown parametric conditions. It may be a measure of the *direction* of regression (adaptive or maladaptive), needing to be supplemented by measures of its amount, as in Goldberger's index.

In conclusion, while the trend of the research to date supports the validity of Rorschach scores of adaptive regression, I believe that further progress in our understanding both of the tool and of personality will come from the development of more differentiated indices. Fruitful ideas for these in turn are more likely to spring from phenomenological studies of psychological processes (Martin, Schachtel, Lyons, Mayman, and Holt, 1967) than from general theoretical considerations.

Appendix. A Glossary and Index to Special Terms and Symbols in the Primary Process Scoring System

CONTENT VARIABLES Manifestations of primary process taking the form of drive-dominated imagery.

Ag 1 *O* — *A*ggressive drive-imagery, Level *1* (sadistic, castrative, or lethal), from the standpoint of the *O*bject aggressed against (e.g., people being smashed, penis about to be severed).

Ag 1 *R* — *A*ggression, Level *1, R*esults (e.g., mutilated body, gangrenous flesh).

Ag 1 *S* — *A*ggression, Level *1, S*ubject (emphasis is on the aggressor; e.g., witches tearing a man apart).

Ag 2 *O* — Level *2 A*ggressive content, *O*bject-oriented (e.g., boy being spanked, frightened people).

Ag 2 *R* — Level *2 R*esults of *A*ggression (e.g., blood, torn leaf, peg leg).

Ag 2 *S* — Level *2 A*ggression, *S*ubject (e.g., charging lion, people fighting, volcano, pirate).

L 1 *A* — *L*ibidinal drive-imagery, Level *1* (raw, primitive, unsublimated), *A*nal (e.g., buttocks, feces).

L 1 *E-V* — *L*ibidinal, Level *1, E*xhibitionistic-*V*oyeuristic content (e.g., nudity).

L 1 *H* — *L*ibidinal, Level *1, H*omosexual and sexually ambiguous (e.g., hermaphrodites, homosexual acts).

L 1 *M* — *L*ibidinal, Level *1, M*iscellaneous * (e.g., menstruation, birth, urine).

* Distinguish from *Miscellaneous Libidinal Level 1 Scores:* the sum of all *L 1 E-V, L 1 H,* and *L 1 M.*

L 1 *O*	*L*ibidinal, Level *1, O*ral (e.g., mouths, breasts, nursing).
L 1 *O-Ag*	*L*ibidinal, Level *1, O*ral-*Ag*gressive (e.g., worms eating eyes out, vagina with teeth—also scored *L* 1 *S*).
L 1 *S*	*L*ibidinal, Level *1, S*exual (e.g., genitalia, sexual acts).
L 2 *A*	Level *2 A*nal content (e.g., mud, sewer, rear ends or tails).
L 2 *E-V*	Level *2 E*xhibitionistic-*V*oyeuristic (e.g., eyes, masks, showing off).
L 2 *H*	Level *2 H*omosexual (e.g., ambiguity or uncertainty *re* sex of figures, transvestism).
L 2 *M*	Level *2 M*iscellaneous (e.g., ovaries, embryo, narcissism).
L 2 *O*	Level *2 O*ral (eating, kissing, food, drunkards).
L 2 *O-Ag*	Level *2 O*ral-*Ag*gressive (e.g., sabertooth tiger, man being bawled out).
L 2 *S*	Level *2 S*exual (e.g., sweethearts, wedding ring).

FORMAL VARIABLES Manifestations of primary process in the figural, logical, linguistic, and structural properties of responses.

Au El 1	*A*utistic *El*aboration, Level *1* (Rapaport's and Schafer's confabulation).
Au El 2	*A*utistic *El*aboration, Level *2* (e.g., relatively realistic thematic elaboration, like Rapaport's fabulation).
Au Lg 1	*A*utistic *L*ogic, Level *1* (e.g., so small it must be a bug; also, *Po* and *DW* responses—Klopfer's confabulation).
C-a-c 2	*C*ondensation, *a*rbitrary *c*ombination, Level *2* (e.g., dog climbing on a butterfly).
C-arb 1	*C*ondensation, *arb*itrary color, Level *1* * (e.g., green rabbit).

* This category, *C-co,* and *Sym-C* exist in both Level 1 and Level 2 versions. The list of formal variables is not complete in this respect.

C-co 1 *C*ondensation, *co*mposition, Level *1* (e.g., men with breasts, cat with wings).

C-ctm 1 *C*ondensation, *contam*ination response, Level *1* (e.g., bloody island).

Ctr A 1 *A*ffective *Contr*adiction, Level *1* (e.g., he is sad but happy).

Ctr R 2 *Contr*adiction of *R*eality, Level *2* (e.g., people flying through the air).

Ctr L 1 *L*ogical *Contr*adiction, Level *1* (e.g., a benignly evil god).

D-clang 1 *D*isplacement, *clang* association, Level *1* (e.g., she's sent him on some mission—missile, he looks launched).

S-R 1 *S*elf-*R*eference of a magical, Level *1* kind: (e.g., eyes looking at me).

Sym C 2 *C*olor *sym*bolism, Level *2* (e.g., the red represents anger).

V S 2 *V*erbal *S*lip, Level *2* (e.g., an ant hill with people —I mean, ants).

V Q 1 *V*erbalization, *Q*ueer, Level *1* (after Rapaport; e.g., a figure pulling together—it's not funny, it's just laughter).

CONTROL AND DEFENSE VARIABLES Indications that the regression is either adaptive or maladaptive, in the way the response is given. (Partial listing.)

Cx C+ *C*ultural *C*onte*x*t, successful,* where cultural sanction is given to impulse expression (e.g., soldier with a gun).

Cx E+ *E*sthetic *C*onte*x*t, successfully* invoked (e.g., a nude statue).

Cx H+ *H*umorous *C*onte*x*t, successful* (appropriate use of humor).

Cx I+ *I*ntellectual *C*onte*x*t, successful* (e.g., saggital section of fetal brain).

---

* Unsuccessful forms of these controls are also scored, with minus signs, as well as a middle category without sign.

Del	*Del*ay: scorable aspect of response emerges only in inquiry.
O-pot	*O*vertness, *pot*ential (the drive-action is not overt but implicit; e.g., lion; but if attacking or charging, score *O*vertness, *beh*avioral).
R-an	*R*emoteness achieved by attributing content to an *an*imal—warmblooded (also *R-(an)* for cold-blooded animals with which it is harder to empathize).
R-cond	*R*emoteness through use of *cond*itional mood (e.g., he'll get well unless he starves).
R-fan+	*R*emoteness through making something a *fan*tasy, successfully* (e.g., a monster you might see in a nightmare).
R-fic s+	*R*emoteness, *fic*tional, *s*pecific character appropriately used* (e.g., the three witches from Macbeth).
R-fic n+	*R*emoteness, *fic*tional, *n*onspecific and successful* (e.g., a witch).
R-fig+	*R*emoteness through use of a *fig*ure of speech, successful* (e.g., it has the carrot-like shape of Kentucky).
R-geo+	*R*emoteness, *geo*graphic (e.g., a Spanish bullfighter).
R-rel+	*R*emoteness, *rel*igious, appropriate and successful* (e.g., Christ on the cross).
Refl +	*Refl*ection on response (e.g., half-man, half-woman —that's a crazy idea!).
S C 1-*O*+	*S*equence, *C*hange from any Level *1* response to one immediately following that is unscorable or secondary process. (There are several Sequence scores of this general type.)
Va–	*Va*gueness: S complains he can't really see it after giving response (e.g., flesh, almost breasts—it's not clear). (Also 9 other types of pathological defenses are scored.)

* Unsuccessful forms of these controls are also scored, with minus signs, as well as a middle category without sign.

RATINGS OF THE RESPONSE Quantitative scales applied to the whole response.

Cr *Cr*eativity, scaled from 5 (most original, clever, creative) to 1 (popular responses, without richness or elaboration).

DD *D*efense *D*emand, scaled from 1 (most innocuous, quite acceptable as an interpersonal communication) to 6 (most shocking, calling for greatest efforts to couch it in ways that might soften its interpersonal impact).

DE *D*efensive *E*ffectiveness, scaled from +2 (completely successful response: accurately seen, without affective disturbance or inappropriateness, and well defended) through 0 (only moderately successful response) to −3 (disorganized responses with only pathological attempts at defense, rare except in psychotic records).

Form Level Accuracy and definitiveness of form perceived (scored according to Mayman, 1960; categories may also be given the following quantitative weights).

+2 *F+* Sharp, convincing forms, easily seen when pointed out.

+1 *Fo* Ordinary level of accuracy: popular and near-popular forms.

0 *Fw+* Reasonably plausible (weak), but not clearly convincing forms.

−1 *Fw−* Forms that bear only a slight resemblance—on only one or two points.

−2 *Fv* Vague, nondefinitive forms—things that intrinsically lack specific shape.

−3 *Fa* Amorphous responses, in which form plays *no* role; usually abstract concepts.

−3 *Fs* Spoiled form responses: a basically good response with some arbitrary and unacceptable specification.

−4 F− Arbitrary forms, definitive but not matching the blot area.

SUMMARY SCORES Not for individual responses but for the record as a whole.

Adaptive Regression Either a ranking by Goldberger's method (explained in text, p. 289) combining measures of amount of pripro and control; or *mean DD* × *DE* (which see, below).

% Content Number of responses receiving any libidinal or aggressive scores (or both), Level 1 and/or Level 2, divided by the total number of responses (*R*).

% Formal Number of responses receiving any formal scores, Level 1 and/or Level 2, divided by total *R*.

% Level 1 Proportion of total *R* receiving Level 1 (more direct or blatant, less socialized) pripro scores, Content and/or Formal.

% Level 2 Proportion of total *R* receiving Level 2 (more sublimated and intrinsically controlled) pripro scores, Content and/or Formal.

Libidinal Balance Number of responses given any *L 1* or *L 2* (libidinal) scores, divided by number of responses given any libidinal and/or aggressive scores (= sum Content).

Mean Form Level Algebraic sum of quantitative weights for all form level scores, divided by *R*. (May be computed for pripro responses only, as in Cohen's index, or for secpro—i.e., secondary process, all other—responses separately.)

Mean Cr Sum of Creativity ratings for all responses, divided by *R*. (May be computed for pripro and secpro responses separately.)

Mean Density Total number of formal and content *scores* given, divided by *PPR;* the average frequency of the scorable varieties of pripro per scored response.

Mean DD Sum of all Defense Demand ratings divided by *PPR*.

Mean DE	Sum of all Defensive Effectiveness ratings divided by *PPR*.
Mean DD × DE	Algebraic sum of the products of *DD* and *DE* ratings, response by response, divided by *PPR* (or, sometimes, by *R*).
Oral DD	Sum of all *DD* ratings given for oral scores, Level 1 and Level 2 (Gray's score).
PPR	Number of pripro (primary process) responses.
Total % pripro	Proportion of all responses (*R*) containing *any* primary process, Level 1 and/or Level 2, Formal and/or Content.

References

Adelson, J. 1960. "Creativity and the Dream." *Merrill-Palmer Quart.* 6: 92–97.

Allison, J. 1967. "Adaptive Regression and Intense Religious Experiences." *J. Nerv. Mental Dis.* 145: 452–463.

Arlow, J., and Brenner, C. 1964. *Psychoanalytic Concepts and the Structural Theory.* New York: International Universities Press.

Bachrach, H. 1968. "Adaptive Regression, Empathy and Psychotherapy." *Psychotherapy: Theory, Research and Practice.* 5: 203–209.

Barron, F. 1953. "Complexity-Simplicity as a Personality Dimension." *J. Abnorm. Soc. Psych.* 48: 163–172.

———. 1955. "The Disposition toward Originality." *J. Abnorm. Soc. Psych.* 51: 478–485.

Bergan, J. R. 1965. "Pitch Perception, Imagery and Regression in the Service of the Ego." *J. Res. Music Educ.* 13: 15–32.

Blatt, S. J., Allison, J., and Feirstein, A. 1969. "The Capacity to Cope with Cognitive Complexity." *J. Pers.* 37: 269–288.

Child, I. L. 1965. "Personality Correlates of Esthetic Judgment in College Students." *J. Pers.* 33: 476–511.

Cohen, I. H. 1960. "An Investigation of the Relationship between Adaptive Regression, Dogmatism and Creativity Using the Rorschach and Dogmatism Scale." Unpublished doctoral dissertation, Michigan State University.

Derman, B. I. 1967. "Adaptive vs. Pathological Regression in Relation to Psychological Adjustment." Unpublished doctoral dissertation, University of Georgia.

Dudek, S. Z. 1968. "Regression and Creativity: A Comparison of the Rorschach Records of Successful versus Unsuccessful Painters and Writers." *J. Nerv. Mental Dis.* 147: 535–546.

Erikson, E. H. 1963. *Childhood and Society,* 2nd ed. New York: Norton.

Feirstein, A. 1967. "Personality Correlates of Tolerance for Unrealistic Experiences." *J. Consult. Psych.* 31: 387–395.

Freud, S. 1900. "The Interpretation of Dreams." *Standard Edition,* Vols. 4 and 5 (1953). London: Hogarth.

———. 1905. "Jokes and their Relation to the Unconscious." *Standard Edition,* Vol. 8 (1960). London: Hogarth.

———. 1911. "Formulations on the Two Principles of Mental Functioning." *Standard Edition,* Vol. 12 (1958), pp. 218–226. London: Hogarth.

———. 1915. "The Unconscious." *Standard Edition,* Vol. 14 (1957), pp. 166–215. London: Hogarth.

———. 1923. "The Ego and the Id." *Standard Edition,* Vol. 19 (1961). London: Hogarth.

Gardner, R. W., Holzman, P. S., Klein, G. S., Linton, H. B., and Spence, D. P. 1959. "Cognitive Control: A Study of Individual Consistencies in Cognitive Behavior." *Psychological Issues,* No. 4. New York: International Universities Press.

Getzels, J. W., and Jackson, P. W. 1962. *Creativity and Intelligence.* New York: John Wiley & Sons.

Gill, M. M. 1963. "Topography and Systems in Psychoanalytic Theory." *Psychological Issues,* No. 10. New York: International Universities Press.

———. 1967. "The Primary Process." In *Motives and Thought—Psychoanalytic Essays in Memory of David Rapaport,* R. R. Holt (Ed.). *Psychological Issues,* No. 18/19, pp. 260–298. New York: International Universities Press.

Goldberger, L. 1961. "Reactions to Perceptual Isolation and Rorschach Manifestations of the Primary Process." *J. Proj. Tech.* 25: 287–302.

Gray, J. J. 1967. "An Investigation of the Relationship between Primary Process Thinking and Creativity." Unpublished doctoral dissertation, Fordham University. See also Gray, J. J. 1969. "The Effect of Productivity on Primary Process and Creativity." *J. Proj. Tech. Pers. Assess.* 33:213–218.

Grygier, T. 1955. *The Dynamic Personality Inventory.* Sutton, England: Banstead Hospital Management Committee.

Guilford, J. P. 1950. "Creativity." *Am. Psychologist.* 14: 469–479.

———. 1967. *The Nature of Human Intelligence.* New York: McGraw-Hill.

Hartmann, H. 1950. "Comments on the Psychoanalytic Theory of the Ego," *Essays on Ego Psychology,* pp. 113–141. New York: International Universities Press.

Heath, D. H. 1965. *Explorations of Maturity.* New York: Appleton-Century-Crofts.

Hersch, C. 1962. "The Cognitive Functioning of the Creative Person: A Developmental Analysis." *J. Proj. Tech.* 26: 193–200.

Holt, R. R. 1960. "Cognitive Controls and Primary Processes." *J. Psych. Res.* 4: 105–112.

———. 1966. "Measuring Libidinal and Aggressive Motives and their Controls by Means of the Rorschach Test." In *Nebraska Symposium on Motivation, 1966,* D. Levine (Ed.), pp. 1–47. Lincoln: University of Nebraska Press.

———. 1967a. "Beyond Vitalism and Mechanism: Freud's Concept of Psychic Energy." In *Science and Psychoanalysis, Vol. XI,* J. H. Masserman (Ed.), pp. 1–41. New York: Grune & Stratton. Also in *Historical Roots of Contemporary Psychology,* B. Wolman (Ed.), pp. 196–226. New York: Harper & Row, 1968.

———. 1967b. "The Development of the Primary Process: A Structural View." In *Motives and Thought—Psychoanalytic Essays in Memory of David Rapaport,* R. R. Holt (Ed.). *Psychological Issues,* No. 18/19, pp. 345–383. New York: International Universities Press.

———. 1968. "Manual for the Scoring of Primary Process Manifestations in Rorschach Responses." New York: Research Center for Mental Health, New York University. (mimeographed)

——— and Havel, J. 1960. "A Method for Assessing Primary and Secondary Process in the Rorschach." In *Rorschach Psychology,* M. A. Rickers-Ovsiankina (Ed.), pp. 263–315. New York: John Wiley & Sons.

Jenkins, T. N. 1962. "Measurement of the Primary Factors of the Total Personality." *J. Psych.* 54: 417–442.

John, E. R. 1957. "Contributions to the Study of the Problem-Solving Process." *Psych. Monographs.* 71, No. 18 (Whole No. 447).

Kafka, H. 1963. "The Use of Color in Projective Tests and Dreams in Relation to the Theory of Ego Autonomy." Unpublished doctoral dissertation, New York University.

Klein, G. S., Gardner, R. W., and Schlesinger, H. J. 1962. "Tolerance for Unrealistic Experiences: A Study of the Generality of a Cognitive Control." *Brit. J. Psych.* 53: 41–55.

Klopfer, B., Ainsworth, M. D., Klopfer, W. G., and Holt, R. R. 1954. *Developments in the Rorschach Technique,* Vol. I., *Technique and Theory.* New York: World Book Co.

Kris, E. 1952. *Psychoanalytic Explorations in Art.* New York: International Universities Press.

Lohrenz, L. J., and Gardner, R. W. 1967. "The Mayman Form-Level Scoring Method: Scorer Reliability and Correlates of Form Level." *J. Proj. Tech. Pers. Assess.* 31(4): 39–43.

Martin, R. M., Schachtel, E. G., Lyons, J., Mayman, M., and Holt, R. R. 1967. Symposium: The Role of Experiential Data in Personality Assessment. *J. Proj. Tech. Pers. Assess.* 31(4): 3–30.

Mayman M. 1960. "Form Level Scoring Manual." Topeka, Kansas: Menninger Foundation. (mimeographed)

Myden, W. 1959. "Interpretation and Evaluation of Certain Personality Characteristics Involved in Creative Production." *Percept. Mot. Skills.* 9: 139–158.

Oberlander, M. I. 1967. "Pupillary Reaction Correlates of Adaptive Regression." Unpublished doctoral dissertation, University of Chicago.

Orgel, J. 1955. "A Comparative Analysis of the Manifest Dream Content of Students Rated as Imaginative and Unimaginative in Creative Writing." Unpublished B. A. thesis, Bennington College.

Pine, F. 1959. "Thematic Drive Content and Creativity." *J. Pers.* 27: 136–151.

———. 1962. "Creativity and Primary Process: Sample Variations." *J. Nerv. Mental Dis.* 134: 506–511.

———, and Holt, R. R. 1960. "Creativity and Primary Process: A Study of Adaptive Regression." *J. Abn. Soc. Psych.* 61: 370–379.

Rapaport, D. 1951a. "The Autonomy of the Ego." In *Collected Papers of David Rapaport,* M. Gill (Ed.). 1967, pp. 357–367. New York: Basic Books.

——— (Ed.). 1951b. *Organization and Pathology of Thought.* New York: Columbia Univ. Press.

———. 1958. "The Theory of Ego Autonomy: A Generalization." In *Collected Papers of David Rapaport,* M. Gill (Ed.). 1967, pp. 722–744. New York: Basic Books.

———, Gill, M. M., and Schafer, R. 1945–46. *Diagnostic Psychological Testing.* (Rev. ed. by R. R. Holt, 1968.) New York: International Universities Press.

Roe, A. 1946. "Painting and Personality." *Rorschach Res. Exch.* 10: 86–100.

Rogolsky, M. M. 1968. "Artistic Creativity and Adaptive Regression in Third Grade Children." *J. Proj. Tech. Pers. Assess.* 32(1): 53–62.

Schafer, R. 1954. *Psychoanalytic Interpretation in Rorschach Testing.* New York: Grune & Stratton.

———. 1958. "Regression in the Service of the Ego: The Relevance of a Psychoanalytic Concept for Personality Assessment." In *Assessment of Human Motives,* G. L. Lindzey (Ed.). New York: Rinehart.

Silverman, D. K. 1963. "Adaptive Regression and Creativity: A Study of Children's Verbalizations While Painting." Unpublished doctoral dissertation, New York University, 1963. (*Dissert. Abstr.* 1965. 26: 1812.)

Silverman, L. H. 1963. "On the Relationship between Aggressive Imagery and Thought Disturbance in Rorschach Responses." *J. Proj. Tech. Pers. Assess.* 27: 336–344.

———. 1965. "Regression in the Service of the Ego: A Case Study." *J. Proj. Tech. Pers. Assess.* 29: 232–244.

Sullivan, J. J. 1963. "Personality Correlates of Rorschach Primary Process Scores of Peace Corps Volunteers to Somalia." Unpublished data (by kind permission of author), New York University School of Education.

von Holt, H. W., Jr., Sengstake, C. B., Sonoda, B. C., and Draper, W. A. 1960. "Orality, Image Fusions and Concept-Formation." *J. Proj. Tech.* 24: 194–198.

Wild, C. 1965. "Creativity and Adaptive Regression." *J. Pers. Soc. Psych.* 2: 161–169. Also in *Personality, Selected Readings,* R. S. Lazarus and E. M. Opton (Eds.). 1967. Baltimore, Md.: Penguin Books.

Wilson, R. C., Guilford, J. P., Christensen, P. R., and Lewis, D. J. 1954. "A Factor-Analytic Study of Creative-Thinking Abilities." *Psychometrika* 19: 297–311.

Gertrude Baker

8

Post-Diagnostic Use of the Rorschach *

Introduction

Psychological tests are frequently used in pretreatment planning and in guiding the psychotherapist in making decisions during the course of psychotherapy. A much less common practice is the sharing of the test results with the patient himself through a discussion of the implications of his test responses. The extent to which this process of test interpretation can be useful as a treatment technique has not been explored broadly enough.

The main purpose of this chapter is to present illustrative materials that hopefully will help to describe the process of discussing a subject's psychological test responses with him. An earlier short paper on this topic (Baker, 1964) is republished as an appendix to this chapter. It contains an outline for use as a guide for the test discussion and some remarks seeking to justify the use of tests in such a manner.

* From the Psychology Service, Brentwood Hospital, Veterans Administration Center, Los Angeles, California.

General Considerations

Discussion of test responses with the subjects who give them has at least a twofold function. It can serve as a therapeutic measure for the benefit of the subject, and it provides a useful adjunct to the assessment process itself by providing supplemental information. Following the discussion period, the examiner is in a far better position to make valid interpretations and predictions, utilizing data from both the tests and the discussion interview.

Therapeutic Possibilities

In order to evaluate the use of tests in this manner as a treatment technique, many individuals skilled in test interpretation and psychotherapy will need to try it with a wide variety of subjects. For a discussion to be therapeutic, the subject must get something from it that he can work with and use. Experience to date indicates that what subjects gain depends upon both their test data and those aspects of the data they are willing to look at and work with.

It is not possible to judge immediately at the end of a discussion how much has been accomplished. If a subject seems to get nothing else at all—and this would be rare—he at least gains the experience of spending some time with another individual who is willing to help him take a frank look at himself and who shares with him impressions gained from his performance. Mostly, however, any constructive responses to the discussion come gradually and over a long period of time, after the subject has had time to absorb and process the content of the discussion. Some of it will undergo considerable change and distortion according to the needs of the subject, of course. But more frequently self-perception is improved, accelerating the process of change in well-motivated individuals.

Patients will start off with questions about "my diagnosis," seeming to feel that this is the sophisticated and correct way to join up with the psychiatrist and psychologist in viewing themselves. It can be a good reeducational experience for them to learn that the aim is not to label them but to view them dynamically. Their attitude and cooperation improve and their own conception of the role of the clinician in giving help changes when they observe that making an analysis of their problems is not an easy or a casual process.

Many patients, particularly the chronic, hospitalized variety who are accustomed to overprotection, are shocked at being told that test information can be shared with them and that, in fact, this information belongs more to them than to anyone else. This reaction may be partly due to reluctance to take responsibility for themselves. But it also probably stems from having built up the expectation that the hospital staff regard clinical data as something to be concealed from patients. How many patients have sought information, only to be rebuffed, and how many patients will sneak a look at their charts if they get a chance? To share data is to give the patient responsibility for himself, and this is usually therapeutic.

Guilt is often reduced, since a more dynamic view of the development of the character structure is gained; and this frees energy for more constructive pursuits. A good test discussion forces the subject to examine the effects his own characteristic ways of behaving have upon others and how others respond to him. Attention is focused on his own needs and on whether his behavior is appropriate for the accomplishment of need satisfaction. Conflicting or irreconcilable needs frequently show up beautifully on tests and can be identified and explored.

Conventional psychotherapy can, of course, accomplish all these objectives, but the comprehensive overview made possible in two or more hours of looking at the tests is unique in itself and offers an integration and framework that cannot be attained in the same time in psychotherapy. Test discussion is by no means a substitute for psychotherapy, but where it has preceded psychotherapy it has appeared to accelerate the process of therapy. And where it has occurred during psychotherapy—usually when a plateau seemed to have been reached or where the process seemed blocked—it usually improved motivation and led to further growth. Ideally, if the examiner is not also the therapist, the therapist should be present for the discussion, but this is not essential as long as the therapist is fully informed of the test findings prior to the discussion and receives a report of the important aspects of the discussion interview. If the tests turn up any areas of conflict or disturbance that have been overlooked by the therapist, the relationship between patient and therapist could be damaged if communication is not full and complete.

Improvements in Assessment

While some of the data subjects bring to test discussion require as much interpretation as projective test responses themselves, both the behavioral response to the discussion process and the factual or historical data subjects contribute lead to a more secure use of projective test responses. When discussions are long and thorough or when several interviews of an hour or two are required to cover the tests, subjects frequently exhibit shifts in their ways of viewing themselves and significant others. These shifts are often in a direction that appears to add validity to the original test interpretation, suggesting that the subject has been influenced. However, they also frequently seem to be the result of recall of historical events, sometimes long-forgotten, which have been triggered by the test interpretation. As a result of these recollections, new relationships may be seen for the first time or the original interpretation may be altered or expanded. Frequently, other test data whose significance had originally been obscure become meaningful.

Most therapists have had the experience of reviewing for themselves a subject's tests following a period of psychotherapy and discovering meanings from responses that had gone uninterpreted in the original test analysis. This improvement in insight into the test responses as the result of having more information probably differs little from what occurs as the result of test discussion with the subject. There simply is a shorter waiting period for the help that added historical and behavioral data can give when use is made of projective test responses.

In making predictions for response to psychotherapy or other kinds of behavior, such as performance in psychiatric residency, it is possible to achieve much greater accuracy if the test discussion is also part of the data. Subjects who seem quite defensive or immature during the obtaining of the test protocols may work very well with confrontations concerning these factors. A valid judgment regarding the prognosis for growth and change cannot be made without observation of the subject's response to confrontation with the signs of his own defensiveness or other characteristics.

The importance of showing a subject the test signs of his needs has been mentioned. One of the most significant of all needs that subjects have, the need to change, is best assessed during the process of the discussion. This period, in which the subject and his tests are the focus of so much attention, is an ideal situation in which to observe how much indulgence the subject directs toward his own pathology and how much real interest he has either in changing or in maintaining the status quo.

Other supplementary impressions to be gained include the following. Additional indications of quality and degree of ego strength are usually revealed. Is there a low or a high threshold for becoming illogical, paranoid, or otherwise defensive in this interpersonal relationship? The application and strength of resistances may show up well only in the discussion phase. Likewise, the ease with which the subject can relax what otherwise look like strong defenses can be assessed. Distinctions between suppression and repression become clarified. The response to test discussion is far superior to the test indicators themselves in determining the degree of rigidity—just as the "work sample" in industry is superior to the conventional aptitude test.

Kinds of Subjects Suitable for Test Discussion and Goals

Role of Diagnosis

Except in cases of extreme pathology, diagnosis is rarely the clue to whether a discussion of tests will be useful to the subject. Psychosis is not a contraindication for discussion. In fact, during the time that the psychotic individual's defenses are weakened by his disturbance he is likely to give test protocols that are very revealing of the causes of his conflicts, and he may be quite open and ready to consider why he is disturbed. Many acutely psychotic patients are under great pressure to communicate, and a long, supportive discussion session can be very therapeutic to them under these circumstances. On the other hand, some mildly neurotic individuals who are highly defensive not only profit little from test discussion but experience an increase, at least temporarily, in their defensiveness.

Brain damage can be a contraindication for discussion if memory is severely affected, simply because what is said is not well comprehended and is soon forgotten. But brain-damaged individuals who have at least fairly good recall can derive considerable comfort and help from an honest discussion of their test performance. They seem to feel accepted if their impairments are realistically acknowledged and are treated as if they do not need to be denied. In addition, a discussion of their emotional needs, past and present, can help them in reorienting themselves and adjusting to the changes that have taken place. For instance, a perfectionist who acquires brain damage which prevents the exercise of his compulsive defenses in the manner to which he is accustomed needs to have this pointed out to him as graphically as possible. Of course, he probably also will need continuing help in making his readjustment, but starting realistically with the tests can be very meaningful to him.

Patients with mild to moderate memory defects can be shown their test performances and given suggestions for helping to compensate for such loss. One patient who suffered a moderate memory loss following carbon monoxide poisoning developed the bad habit of confabulating. His judgment was much better than that of most patients who confabulate, so when he did this on paragraph recall it was called to his attention. He was instructed that when he could not remember he should admit it truthfully, since trying to cover up by making up something gave him an appearance of unreliability. His wife reported later that he was handling his memory problem in a more acceptable manner.

Because more questions have been raised about discussing test results with homosexuals and paranoids than for any other diagnostic categories, they will each be treated separately in other sections. More than any other subjects, they seem to look upon diagnosis as a crime they are charged with, so special attention will be given to choice of language in the test discussion.

The discussion can be especially useful to subjects with character disorders, particularly to those whose style is to act without thinking and to look very little at what they do. They are forced to look and to think during the discussion, and, although they may offer considerable protest, the tests sometimes intrigue them. This will be mentioned further in connection with the MMPI. Patients with neurotic character disorders are often ideal subjects, whereas the greater the trend in the sociopathic direction the more likelihood there is that listening and participation will be limited.

Psychosomatics vary greatly. In these cases it is wise to pay more attention to ego strength than is necessary in the psychological disorders since any exacerbation of the physical disorder through the arousal of anxiety could, at times, have serious consequences. Very supportive short sessions with plenty of followup give added safety. And while in every case it should be implicit that test discussion is undertaken only in collaboration with a patient's physician, it is particularly important with psychosomatics to use a team approach, making sure that everyone is informed regarding the treatment process. Frequently the psychosomatic is almost as unwilling as the conversion hysteric to look for a psychological cause for his disease. A tactful discussion of their test findings has helped such individuals to begin to look for psychological factors, and this helps to pave the way for a less resistant acceptance of psychotherapy.

Sources of Illustrative Materials

The examples discussed here come from a variety of sources—records of inpatients, outpatients, applicants for psychiatric residency, and residents accepted for the first year of residency (Baker and Ferguson, 1964). All will be treated as "subjects," and the exact status of any subject will not necessarily be identified in every case. Most of the materials are well aged and most have had the advantage of followup. Identifying data have been carefully eliminated, and it is doubtful whether more than a very few of the subjects themselves would recognize their own materials if they should read this chapter.

In some instances, reports written at the time of the testing and discussion will be quoted from, and on other occasions the test protocols will be quoted from directly. In quoting from protocols, for the sake of brevity some nonessential words will be deleted; but care will be taken not to make any deletion which might weaken any interpretation suggested or change the general meaning.

All interpretations made in this chapter should be regarded as hypothetical and subject to either revision or discard. It is important to maintain this emphasis on the hypothetical nature of test interpretations when discussing test data, and it is by no means necessary that the interpretation be correct if this attitude is maintained. An incorrect interpretation can elicit from the subject valuable discussion and information which will then lead to a revision of hypotheses and usually a more valid appraisal which the subject is often quite willing to accept because he has participated in its formation.

Various clinicians are likely to differ in their use of test materials, particularly in the interpretation of data from projective techniques. All clinicians operate with biases stemming from their particular training backgrounds and the populations which they have studied. Furthermore, populations contain variations dependent upon culture apart from individual characteristics, and these variations are not well studied or understood. Still other problems make the process of assessment an uncertain business at best. But hopefully, this chapter will help to support the position that these difficulties and weaknesses do not preclude clinicians' discussing test data with subjects who produce the data, to the enlightenment of both subject and clinician.

Choice of Tests

Any test is potentially useful, and experience has demonstrated that there is no "best" battery of tests for all subjects. Subjects are likely to be curious about any test they take, but they vary considerably in the interest they show in different kinds of techniques. Experience in this regard will be described as some of the tests are discussed here.

On the assumption that no one would attempt a discussion of a subject's tests without possessing some skill in test interpretation, this chapter is not designed to perform the function of a manual for the use of the tests that will be mentioned. The basic manuals for each test will be referred to; but the reader is not being proselytized to follow any particular system, nor should he look to this chapter for all his guidelines. Hopefully, clinicians who discuss tests with their subjects will introduce their own styles, experiment in various ways, and report on their results.

Protection of Test Validity

This is perhaps the stickiest problem confronting the clinician who uses tests in this manner. It is much less a matter of concern with the projective techniques than with some of the other more rigorously standardized tests, and the intelligence tests need to be used with the most care. However, most subjects respond well to being told in the beginning that it will be necessary to withhold certain kinds of information, such as the correct responses to intelligence test items, the meanings attached to projective test scores, etc. This becomes reasonable to them when it is explained that standardizing test instruments is a very laborious and expensive procedure and that it is unethical to do anything to damage the effectiveness of any test. This can be used as a valid reason to avoid discussing an intelligence test altogether if it seems desirable to leave it out of the discussion, but with some intelligence tests useful discussion can take place without invalidating the instrument for future use. This problem will be taken up in relation to each test or technique mentioned below.

Wechsler Intelligence Scales [1]

Because of the variety of tasks offered by these tests, they afford an opportunity to observe many kinds of behavior. Even the test scores themselves can be discussed without in any way giving out information regarding right and wrong answers. This is approached through the profile of scores, with the variability among scores as the focus in order to point up areas of efficiency and inefficiency or differences in aptitude. Vocational counsellors have, of course, used this approach for many years.

For purposes of assessing personality traits, the more fruitful area is that of the behavior itself while taking the test, and this only very indirectly involves scores or whether answers are right or wrong. For instance, regardless of whether the test score reflects any lack of aptitude or efficiency, some types of task arouse more resistance, anxiety, irritability, enthusiasm, effort, etc., than others. Being required to concentrate on Arithmetic or Digit Span may lead to severe anxiety; or, on the other hand, such impersonal tasks may be where some socially withdrawn individuals show their greatest efficiency. Comprehension, with its emphasis on right and wrong social behavior, may activate compulsive behavior expressed in overlong answers, hostile behavior expressed in facetious replies, signs of irritability expressed by the subject belligerently repeating all questions before replying, and a variety of other behaviors.

---

[1] Wechsler, D. (1944, 1955).

The repetition of questions can signify a number of habitual defensive maneuvers which most subjects can profit from recognizing. For instance, the subject may repeat the question with an air of helplessness, as if each question is one more burden imposed from outside (and this may have little bearing on whether the correct answer is forthcoming). Or it may be repeated belligerently and in the form of a question, so that it has the effect of being thrown back at the examiner. When this was pointed out to one subject and the examiner's feelings in the face of such behavior were discussed, the subject confessed that his wife had complained that he always repeated questions and said that he guessed he would now have to learn to stop, for he had never realized before why he was doing it. Sometimes the repetition of the question is only for purposes of stalling for time while thinking of the answer.

Some subjects indicate in this way and in other ways, such as by immediately beginning to talk before they have had time to formulate a reply, their feelings that they are being pressed to produce at once and that they are not going to be allowed to proceed at a comfortable pace. These anxious and sometimes hostile individuals can be confronted with the fact that all this extraneous verbalization puts a burden on the listener and the recorder, thus helping them to see that their discomfort is not just something that they bear alone, but also something which serves to plague others and interfere in interpersonal relationships.

One way of showing dependency is to ask the examiner for answers to the questions. If this occurs repeatedly and after reasons for not giving out answers are carefully explained as indicated above, it may be considered a form of passive-aggressive behavior with which the subject can be confronted. Following such a confrontation, some subjects have observed that they were unaware of the frequency with which they demand help and they have generalized from the tests to other situations in which they behave similarly.

Some individuals cannot seem to wait to finish a task. They resent being given something to do or are threatened by it and they wish to dispose of it as rapidly as possible. This attitude shows up on the Block Design in their manner of working. Instead of building the designs block by block and following the pattern in a workmanlike manner, they try to jam the blocks together all at once. This leads to errors, confusion, and delay, often with subjects who really have no impairment in their capacity to break down the patterns and follow them. Confronting such subjects with their manner of working and its various implications in respect to attitudes toward work can be quite helpful. For example, a college student who did this and with whom it was discussed reported to his therapist that he had begun to examine his study habits and realized that he was approaching his course work with the same kind of inefficiency and negativism. He had complained that studying did little good, although no intellectual reasons had been found for his poor school achievement.

Still other subjects get along fine as long as the designs require only four blocks, often putting the easy designs together with lightning speed. If the chevron design does not slow them down and yet they react to the first of the nine-block designs as if it is very difficult, then they are suspect of overreacting emotionally as soon as the going gets rough or challenging. In some settings, such as psychiatric hospitals, this is a frequent observation and one which should more often be shared with the one who has the problem.

In discussing tests with the psychiatric residents or other professionals who later will have access to the tests and learn about them in more detail, there are many other possibilities for use of the Wechsler materials. For instance, certain errors in word definitions are often revealing, such as "recalcitrant" for *reluctant* in the case of a particularly hostile, defensive individual. Or idiosyncratic solutions to the proverbs often give clues to character structure. For example, to the proverb, "One swallow does not make a summer," a subject who was overly preoccupied with becoming a financial success replied, "One instance of good fortune does not necessarily . . . mean that the total outcome will be favorable." To be sure, pointing out the significance of such responses can produce defensiveness, but it is truly remarkable how many of the residents have accepted and attempted to work with such revelations of attitudes.

Still other examples could be given, but those mentioned above serve to demonstrate the fact that intelligence tests, which have been regarded by clinicians as clinically useful, are valuable instruments in the discussion phase of testing.

The Minnesota Multiphasic Personality Inventory [2]

Because of the emphasis of this test on diagnosis and because subjects tend to be impressed with any extremes which may show up on the test and to become too literal about the profiles, it may not always be desirable to include the MMPI in the discussion battery. At the same time, for the very reasons for leaving it out of the battery in some cases, it may prove extremely useful with certain kinds of subjects.

In interpreting the MMPI profile, the diagnostic terminology which accompanies the pathology scores is to be avoided. Most subjects do not ask what the abbreviations stand for. If they do ask, it can be explained that they were used in the construction of the test as diagnostic categories but that experience with the test has shown that the scales tell something about ways of behaving and feeling and that a sophisticated use of the test requires thinking of the scales in this way. This explanation usually serves to turn interest away from diagnostic labeling. Drake and Oetting (1959) supply a good choice of vocabulary to attach to the scales. Words and phrases like "rationalizing," "shyness," "social insecurity," "indecisive," "conflict with family," "social adjustment," "lack of sensitivity to the reactions of others" are all readily grasped by most subjects. A high *Pa* score interpreted as representing too much concern about what others think makes good sense to the subject who gives it.

Experience with the MMPI has been most frequently gratifying in the case of character disorders. Two examples are cited below for illustrative purposes. They are both men who asked whether they might learn about their test results.

---

[2] Hathaway and Meehl (1951); Drake and Oetting (1959).

Figure 1 shows the profile of a 37-year-old male who entered the hospital with the complaint that his alcoholism was causing him to lose jobs, and he stated he wished to be cured. In group therapy he was verbal and aggressive, readily expressing hostility toward other members with whom he disagreed or whom he did not like. He had attended several group sessions before the test discussion, always expressing concern about being "an alcoholic."

Tests discussed with him were the Saxe Sentence Completion, Draw-A-Person, and MMPI, in that order. He used the discussion of the sentence completion to ventilate some hostility, which was already rather apparent in the completions, but this did not yield very much that was new. The Draw-A-Person was handsomely executed, but an effort to discuss the ostentatious sexiness of the female was met with defensiveness. He was, however, at least mildly impressed when the drawings, which were on opposite sides of the same sheet of paper, were held up to the light and the difference in size of the figures pointed out (the female figure was 9 inches high, while the male figure was less than 7 inches high). But he did not want to explore the significance of this size difference, so the MMPI was turned to.

He clearly was impressed with the mysterious looking profile, seeming to feel that this clean-cut line must contain the clue to his personality. Probably he also found some appeal in the nonverbal character of such a representation of his personality. As the significance of the heavy black lines at T-scores of 70 and 30 and the meaning of a standard deviation were explained to him in simple terms, he became rather excited, and, pointing to the peak at *Pd,* demanded to know, "Where did I fly off the handle here?" The categories within the "normal" range were explained first, and he became very restless, hardly listening, and focusing all his attention on the high peak at *Pd*. By the time it was reached, he had built up a good deal of suspense, and when it was explained that this was a score which showed difficulty in getting along with others, hostility, and resentment of authority figures, he pushed back his chair as if this were all he needed to know and became very reflective and serious. Like a man confessing his sins, he told of numerous incidents in which he had

FIGURE 1 *MMPI profile for male subject, age 37.* (Reproduced by permission. Copyright 1948 by The Psychological Corporation, New York, N.Y. All rights reserved.)

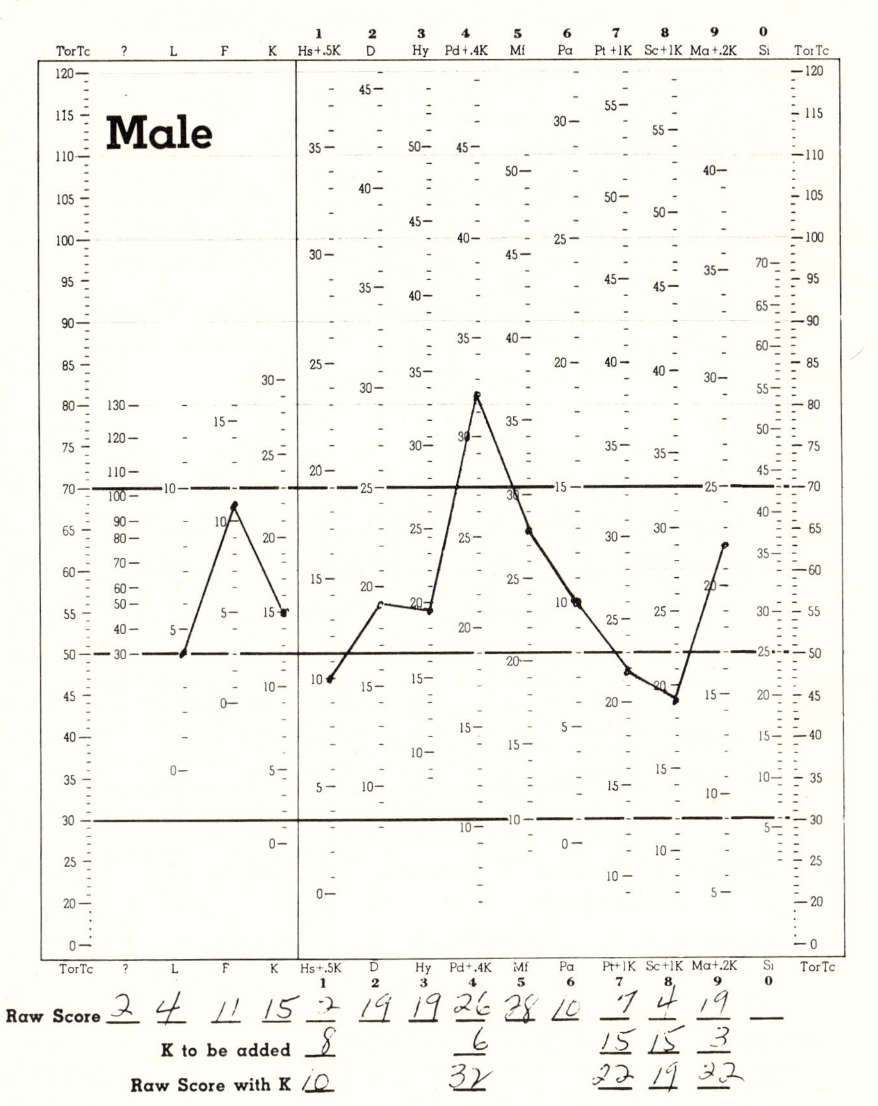

been fired from jobs for inappropriate, hostile outbreaks, giving details in respect to his own behavior and what was said to him by the authority figures who fired him. He made no further mention of his "alcoholism."

A day or two later this man asked to be discharged from the hospital, saying he was ready to leave and that he knew he would have no trouble getting a job and holding it. While he probably benefited from many aspects of his hospitalization, such as the discovery that most of the patients were far more seriously handicapped than he, it did appear that the MMPI profile helped him to face up to the exact nature of his character disorder and that the simplicity of the clean-cut peak communicated much more to him than the very many words that had been said to him from time to time by numerous employers regarding his hostile behavior.

The subject in Figure 2 was also hospitalized, and alcoholism and unemployment were the main entering complaints. He was assigned to group therapy and did not take the MMPI and other tests until a few weeks later. In group therapy his only participation consisted of attentive listening to the others, and when challenged about this he would firmly explain that he was just sizing up the situation, finding out what was going on, and that he had not yet determined whether he cared to share his personal affairs with the group. He would smile pleasantly in saying this, making an effort to hide his hostility and his fear of exposing himself.

He asked while taking the tests whether he might be allowed to learn the results and he subsequently took care of arranging for the appointment to go over his tests, which indicated that he had been sincere in making the request. As with the first subject, his real interest seemed to be mainly in the MMPI profile, and he listened intently as the profile was explained to him. He relaxed noticeably after being told that the low scores on *L* and *K* indicated that he had tried to represent himself honestly and that there clearly had been no attempt on his part to make himself look any better than he was. He said that he was very glad that the test could show this, for he had indeed been completely honest.

In explaining the profile to him, it was pointed out that although

FIGURE 2 *MMPI profile for male subject, age 38.* (Reproduced by permission. Copyright 1948 by The Psychological Corporation, New York, N.Y. All rights reserved.)

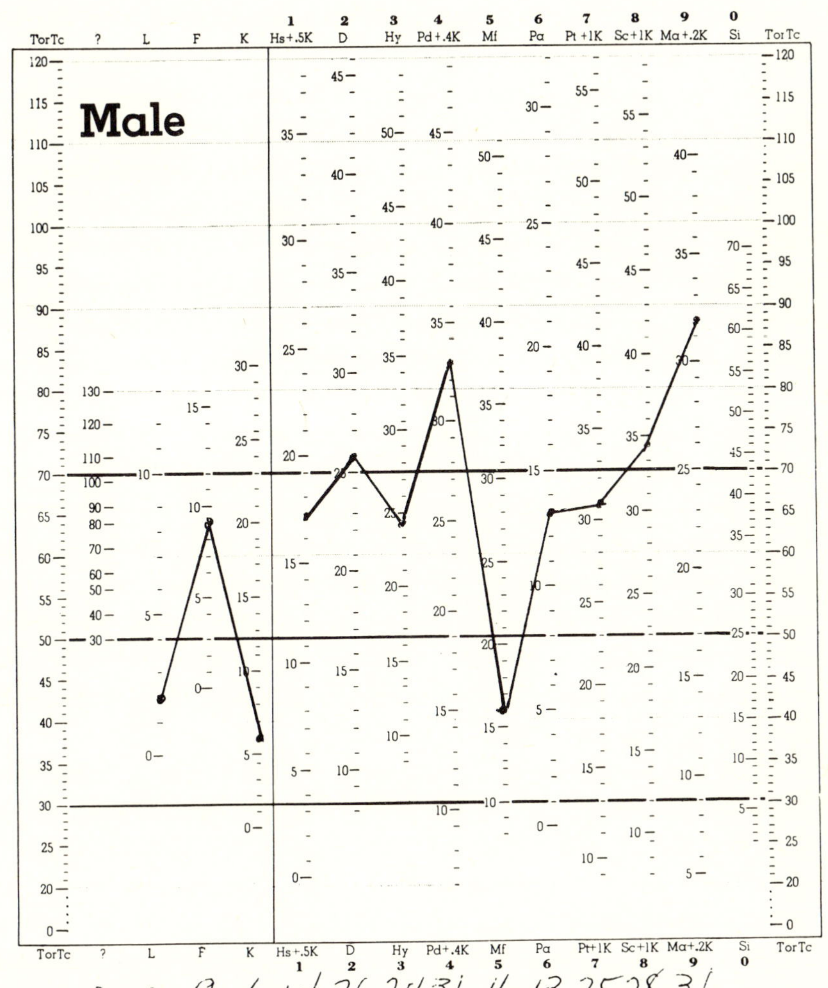

Raw Score 2 2 9 6 14 26 24 31 16 13 25 28 31 —

K to be added 3 2 6 6 1

Raw Score with K 17 33 31 34 32

he had some anxiety and probably at times resorted to the kinds of behavior that neurotic people use when they are anxious (*Hs, D, Hy,* and *Pt* all above one standard deviation), he was more likely to take some kind of action, such as his drinking, to reduce his anxiety and to simultaneously express his hostility, which was even more of a problem for him than his anxiety (*Ma* and *Pd*). The high *Sc* was interpreted as indicative of feelings of isolation and of being different from others, and the *Pa* as representing a certain amount of distrust. His behavior in group therapy was used as an example. He kept nodding while these explanations were going on, as if he were in agreement. Then he was asked, "Now if you were going to do something about this, what would you do?" His reply came promptly. He pointed to the very elevated *Ma,* saying, "Well, the first thing is to get this down. I think I can—in fact, I *know* I can." He then implied that his misbehavior involved more than his drinking, but he did not confess what. Then he went on, pointing to the *Pd:* "That ought to help to bring this down; in fact, I'm pretty sure it will." Again there were some vague allusions to matters he did not want to reveal fully, containing the suggestion that his misbehavior was the main cause of his hostile relations with other people, particularly his wife. He ended by pointing to the other elevated scores, saying that he didn't quite know how it would come about but that he expected that the other scores would probably be lowered if he took care of the more significant matters so clearly indicated by *Ma* and *Pd.*

As he talked, he began to assume the confident air of a man who knew what he must do. The day before he had requested discharge from the hospital, which was granted, and he departed immediately after the interview. There is no followup in this case, but it is used as an illustration of an unusually thorough response to an MMPI interpretation. Like the first subject, this man seemed to get a sense of direction from the MMPI profile that words alone had not conveyed to him.

Psychiatric residents with whom the MMPI has been discussed show much less interest in their own profiles than in the results of their projective tests. Later, however, as they struggle with the problems of diagnosing their patients, most of them seem to develop more interest in the MMPI as a clinical instrument.

Sentence Completion Methods

Goldberg (1965) has reviewed the literature on sentence completion methods and discussed the theoretical status of such techniques. Questions concerning the value of these instruments in any test battery need not be considered here; the reality is that one or another of them appears in many test batteries, particularly of the admissions or screening kind. Often the sentence completion affords the group-tested subject his best opportunity to express ideas and feelings in his own words, and this includes his own grammar, spelling, and handwriting.

Experience in discussing sentence completions with subjects leads to the impression that their greatest utility lies in eliciting history. Perhaps because of the great amount of censorship and conscious awareness that often goes into the making of the completions, subjects are likely to become defensive about any efforts on the examiner's part to make interpretations that go beyond the conscious content. "Reading between the lines" of a subject's own written words can be unwelcome, although the same subject will readily accept the interpretation of his visual perceptions on the Rorschach test, the significance of which he could not guess at when giving the response.

If other projective tests are available for interpretation such as Rorschach, MAPS, and TAT, it is better to concentrate on them first, after which the sentence completions may be viewed by the subject with increased insight and a more constructive attitude. Or selected completions may be referred to profitably from time to time as all the test findings are integrated. For example, a discussion of relationships to mother figures on the TAT and MAPS and of the attitudes toward females that can be inferred from the Rorschach can include the items on the sentence completion that refer to mother or other females. If there is a discrepancy between the inferences that come from the techniques that draw the least easily censored responses and the more conscious sentence completions, rich material for discussion ensues.

Sometimes the sentence completion contains material in the form of slips and misspellings that is invaluable for simple confrontation of the subject when the main purpose is to get him to acknowledge the presence of a problem area. For instance, one subject had been in trouble repeatedly for writing bad checks. He was found to have an I.Q. of 124, and he claimed two years of college. Although he spelled most of his words correctly, he misspelled the following key words: "Finachel oblacation." "Onorable discharge." *More than anything else he needed*—"gidence." *He felt inferior when*—"he was in the presents of rich people." *If only my mother*—"made my father help in the rasing of me." The tests were not interpreted to this subject, but it was a missed opportunity for what might have been a fruitful discussion.

The Thematic Apperception Test (TAT) [3]

Some of the shortcomings of sentence completion methods are present in TAT productions, but to a lesser degree. Many subjects feel that they can interpret their own TAT stories or that they can guess at the conclusions the examiner is going to make. Also, a good deal of conscious censorship often goes on in the making of the story. Many subjects assume that the examiner is going to believe that the stories are autobiographical, and when resistance is operating there may be a deliberate attempt to mislead the examiner.

Consequently, the first bit of information that the subject should have at the start of the TAT discussion is that it is invalid to treat the stories as autobiographical unless the subject himself says that they are. He can be instructed that the pictures tend to draw certain popular stories and that when these are given not much can be said about him that could not be said about anyone else. And he should

---

[3] Murray, H. A. (1943).

be reminded of the instructions (to tell what led up to the scene, what the subjects are thinking and feeling, and the outcome of the story). Any failure to follow the instructions or sudden deviation from the instructions makes good material for discussion, regardless of whether a story is in general constructed along popular lines. Themes which deviate markedly from those most commonly occurring are the ones on which to concentrate in the discussion, just as they are in all test interpretations.

Subjects may be asked to try to interpret their own stories, but usually this is not very fruitful, since self-interpretations usually consist of rationalizations that the subject then feels obliged to defend. Any trends that occur throughout the themes, such as mostly happy outcomes or vice versa, frequent death themes, and denial of violence in scenes which often draw such themes, are quite useful in giving a subject an idea of how his defenses operate in the area of interpersonal relations. This is particularly helpful if the same trends show up on other tests, so that a definite pattern of behavior can be demonstrated. For instance, a subject scolded the examiner for offering him so many unpleasant pictures, saying she would probably conclude that he was depressed and unpleasant, when actually it was her fault because of the pictures she selected. But on the MAPS test which came next he set up scenes that were far more disagreeable than his TAT themes had been, apparently quite unconscious of the fact that he was revealing his own problem rather than being a victim of the examiner's choices. When time came for the discussion and he was confronted with what had occurred, he at first tried to defend himself by explaining that all of the MAPS figures had disagreeable expressions on their faces. He gave up this defense and became thoughtful about his reaction after it was pointed out that he had failed to use any of the MAPS figures that looked calm or happy.

Any sudden changes in story-telling style, long delays, behavior such as sighing, laughing—or even belching—can be called to the subject's attention, with an invitation to some free association to the story involved. These behaviors can be tied up with similar signs on other tests, particularly MAPS and Rorschach. In general, the TAT serves best as a more surface level kind of support for inferences coming from other materials, such as the Rorschach and MAPS, the interpretation of which is less obvious to the subject.

Make a Picture Story Method (MAPS) [4]

This technique should perhaps be regarded as the best projective instrument for the discussion phase of testing. It is not easy to exercise very good censorship of what one is doing while at the same time selecting figures to set up dramatic scenes. Yet, the finished scene contains representations of the real world and of real people (aside from the mythological characters included among the figures), thus furnishing illustrative materials that are more readily meaningful than ink-blot responses.

It is, of course, possible to take the MAPS test defensively, which often consists of hamming up the scenes, making them improbable or ridiculous, on the assumption that if they are silly enough it will not be possible to interpret them. One of the great values of this technique is that it invites this sort of "acting out," and the ridiculous scenes are usually magnificent examples of how the subject operates when he is acting out—or acting up, as the case may be.

Some individuals set up comic or exaggerated scenes simply because it is fun, but the scenes are nevertheless revealing. The paper-doll quality of the figures stimulates a playful response, usually in the better-adjusted subject, and this need not necessarily be a sign of defensiveness. Usually the affect of the subject as he sets up the scene is the clue. Healthy subjects and many others enjoy using scenes and figures symbolically, and it is important to watch closely for attitudes and any signs of feeling in regard to the test materials and the task. Behavior while taking the test is as useful to discuss as the finished scenes themselves. For this reason one should record all of the subject's remarks after the test is offered to him and any other behavior, such as delays, rejection of figures, sorting patterns, etc.

The best transition to the MAPS comes immediately after the

[4] Shneidman, E. S. (1952).

TAT. The first scene (usually the living room) is shown to the subject and he is instructed, "You have been telling stories about pictures that have people in them. Now I am going to give you some scenes in which there are no people. Here are the people and this time you may choose anyone you like to put in the scenes." The figures are then laid in front of the subject in a neat pile, feet of figures facing the subject to ease the sorting, and he is instructed to "spread the figures out so you can see who is there." The table should be sufficiently cleared to allow for ease in spreading out the figures, and the first scene is placed in front of the subject to one side of the heap of figures. He is further instructed, "Put anyone you like in the scene and then tell me what is happening." This instruction is repeated if the subject hesitates after sorting the figures.

The subject should not be helped in sorting the figures. If he does not start to sort or if he only partly spreads them apart, he should be encouraged once or twice more to "spread them out so you can see who is there." If he does not comply and starts setting up the scene while the figures are still in a heap, he should be allowed to go ahead in his own way. A record should be kept of how he continues to handle the figures and how he copes with the problem of receiving new scenes if he has not spread the figures out and thus does not know what all the possibilities are for populating them. Some subjects who delay spreading out the figures give in after a few scenes and finish the spreading task, while others end up with many figures still covered, stirring around in them with one finger somewhat aimlessly as each new scene is offered, the figures ending up turned in all directions. Other subjects go to the opposite extreme, sorting the figures with compulsive thoroughness, in neat rows exactly the same distance apart, segregated according to sex, age, race, fantasy character, etc.

Many subjects engage in a running comment as they inspect the figures, and more often than not they pay no attention to the fact that their comments are being recorded. They may say later that they noticed, but that they supposed it was part of the test and they did not mind. Subjects who do comment on the recording of their remarks are usually either unduly defensive or paranoid.

Similar behaviors do not necessarily have the same meaning in each case, and for this reason at discussion time it is important to elicit, if possible, an account of the subject's feelings as he was offered the test and went about complying with the instructions. Some subjects are insulted by the playful character of the test, probably because they are very defensive and fearful of revealing themselves, while others are quite overwhelmed by the large number of characters to choose from, the factor of making a choice in itself, and probably other factors as well. It is extremely rare for subjects to become so resistant to the task that they refuse to try it altogether, but this did occur in the case of one applicant for psychiatric residency. His excuse was that the examiner had not allowed enough room to spread out "all those figures" (one half of a large desk had been cleared for him), and the assurance that many others had found the same amount of space to be ample did not persuade him.

Some subjects continue on with the TAT instructions in giving stories to the MAPS test, and there is no objection to this. However, the simple instruction "Just tell me what is going on" yields ample data for interpretation and discussion and adds an atmosphere of informality that seems to enhance the acting-out behavior that becomes so revealing in many cases. Questions may be asked about the stories, but a minimum of interference or intrusion on the part of the examiner is desirable. Titles to the scenes can be very revealing of attitudes and can be sought but not demanded. Some subjects populate scenes with characters that seem to them to belong in the scene without having verbalized to themselves any particular story or action. In these cases, a title may reveal more than the story which is made up as an afterthought.

The reader who is familiar with Shneidman's manual (1952) will note that the above suggestions about administration of the MAPS deviate in some respects from the manual. These deviations are by no means essential for a satisfactory use of the MAPS test for discussion purposes, but they add useful data.

Recognition of the importance of the subject's behavior on being confronted with and dealing with the materials of this technique came as an outgrowth of years of using the method in the assessment of psychiatric residents. In appraising this group, clues to their defensive structure are of paramount interest, and their approach to the MAPS test materials constitutes a good work-sample, yielding some information about degree and nature of defensiveness.

Selection of scenes deserves a few words. The use of a great many scenes leads to fatigue and justifiable resistance. At least a few everyday scenes like the Living Room, Street, and Bath Room should be used in the beginning. In the case of doctors and patients, the Medical scene often yields useful data. Following these, a transition to a few situations calling for more imagination helps the uncovering process. The Dream, Blank (blank card like all others, is offered with no special comment), Cave (the old, primitive home—what is back there?), Forest (the closing in of the neurosis; how does it feel and what is it about?), and Doorway (what lies ahead?) have frequently furnished valuable interpretive and discussion material. Usually, for the last scene, the subject is handed the remaining backgrounds with the suggestion that he select at least one more. It is desirable to use not over ten scenes at any one time, since many subjects seem to get tired of the task after 45 minutes to an hour.

The Rorschach Test [5]

Communicating how this technique is used in the discussion is a difficult task. There is so much variability to Rorschach responses, and Rorschach protocols vary greatly in their usefulness for this purpose. Other factors, such as the doubts that many clinicians have about the validity of ink-blot techniques, may render the examiner less secure in using the test in the discussion. If he has too many doubts, the Rorschach will not be included in the battery of tests, anyhow. For those who are skeptical but who still use the instrument because they feel they get something from it that other techniques do not offer, it may be some comfort to remember that the subject probably has not read the literature and may thus be willing to regard his performance with an open mind. He should be informed,

[5] Klopfer, B., et al. (1954); Beck, S. J. (1944).

of course, that the technique has its limitations and that there is controversy in regard to it, and be encouraged to take a hypothetical approach to its use.

Most subjects have more curiosity about their Rorschach performance than about any other test, and if the Rorschach is used, then it should be discussed. To fail to do so is to suggest that something has been held back that is too traumatic to bring out in the open.

Examiners who are accustomed to working with dreams in psychotherapy are likely to feel more comfortable with Rorschach responses than those who shun all kinds of unconscious materials. Getting the subject's associations to his Rorschach responses is as easy as getting associations to dream content, and this method can always be resorted to if there is any doubt about what to do. If such an approach is used alone, some of the value of the Rorschach is lost, but most subjects probably would be satisfied if their associations were discussed and related to the other materials, such as thematic test responses.

As with other techniques, the subject's behavior while taking the Rorschach is very important discussion material. Delays, changes in approach, manner of holding the cards, manner of responding to questioning in the Inquiry phase (willingness to account for what he has done or says he has seen, evasiveness, ability or inability to locate concepts clearly, and many other clues to attitudes and work habits) all indicate styles of behavior that are worthy of examination.

An example of the kind of behavior that can be discussed profitably comes from a test report:

> He made an obvious effort to appear assured, but sat shaking his feet constantly and squirming in his chair. Several times he announced that he was completely at ease and free from anxiety about testing, his foot—legs were crossed—swaying all the time. Instructions for all tests had to be repeated. Although instructions on the Rorschach were given in detail and rather explicitly, he asked questions to further clarify the situation. All questions were answered, and it appeared that there could be no misunderstanding. However, after Card IV, during which he changed his approach, he revealed that he had misinterpreted an answer to one of his questions.

> The question had referred to how many responses he should give, and the instructions had been that 3 or 4 responses on the average were sufficient and that fewer or no responses to a card occasionally occurred without reducing the value of a record. He remembered this instruction as being that it was necessary to spend three or four *minutes* looking at each card. (He had been told specifically that time was of little importance and to pay no attention to it.) He asked at the beginning whether his first impression should be given and was told that this was fine, whereupon he interpreted this to mean that he should give all impressions immediately and as fast as possible. This made recording difficult, so he was asked to give E. time to catch up. He was unable to go slower, although asked repeatedly to allow E. time to record. After giving 10 responses to Card III, he said, "That's probably enough . . . I could look on and find more and more things in there" and asked E. how her arm was holding out. Remarks of this kind throughout the record showed that he was aware of E.'s role, but he did nothing to make it easier.

Some subjects show marked variations in the quality of their responses, in the amount of time spent on the different cards, the number of responses per card, and their cooperativeness in giving specifications during the Inquiry. For instance, do cards which customarily yield sex responses arouse the greatest amount of defensiveness or perhaps elicit responses with the lowest form level? Or does the subject become defensive only when an effort is made to determine whether shading or color contributed to a concept? Or does the loose, smearing type of response occur only on the colored cards? The best use of such responses entails a certain amount of teaching the subject how the test is used, so it may not always be desirable to interpret these findings. However, in the discussion of the Rorschachs of psychology interns and psychiatric residents, who will soon be learning the method anyhow, nothing can be more important psychologically than for them to learn what arouses their defensiveness or what produces their acting out.

Variations in approach to the blots usually can be pointed out as possible indications of problem areas. Although sometimes such confrontations arouse an initial defensiveness, most subjects find their own behavior fairly convincing after it is called to their attention and do attempt to look beneath and beyond the behavioral signs of defensiveness.

Responses which seem to repeat the same theme over and over from one card to the next make especially useful discussion material, since they usually indicate a problem area with which the subject is struggling at the time. All aspects of the conflict may not be conscious, and the area may be very painful and touchy, such as a male–female identity conflict. But the projection of the struggle onto each ink blot in turn is indicative of so much pressure to cope with the problem that further attempts at repression are likely to be unsuccessful. The safest context in which to discuss such an area is that of the subject's own test perceptions, using his descriptive words and phrases to depict the feeling-tone that accompanies the conflict.

Repetitive themes, of course, are suggestive of obsessionalism and may be a bad prognostic sign, since the subject may get some gratification from his preoccupations. In these cases, the Rorschach is of great service as graphic material to illustrate to the subject how he has narrowed his world by his obsessional behavior.

More than with any other technique, and because an ink-blot response is strictly a subject's own doing, even if it is a popular response, it is important to watch for the use of pronouns. Any change to the pronoun "you" (for instance, subject says, "Now here you had two animals that were fighting and scratching each other.") is likely to be a sign of blaming the examiner for the response. A change to the pronoun "we" may represent a shared experience. A response such as "We had a mixture of different flavors of ice cream here" can lead to a discussion of how the subject tends to induce others to support his immaturity and self-indulgences. Some subjects habitually use the pronoun "you," and these are often very defensive individuals who resent having the implications of the use of the pronoun called to their attention. Others change the pronoun only at times. It is not uncommon for "you" to be responsible for responses containing sexual content, while sometimes "we" engage in this bit of voyeurism together. Before going over their protocols with the residents, every "you" and "we" is circled in red so that they stand out clearly. It is very important for this group of subjects to become aware of any "buck-passing" behavior.

Popular and very commonly seen responses do not furnish very useful content for discussion except insofar as any specifications deviate from the usual ones. Any deviation should be noted and perhaps discussed. It is well to tell subjects that popular responses given without any unusual elaborations do not yield any information regarding how the subject may differ from anyone else, for this saves considerable time. The future usefulness of the instrument probably is not impaired by telling a subject that a response is a common one after he has given it. In the case of a very limited Rorschach containing only popular and common responses, possibilities for discussion of the test are also limited. Such subjects can be encouraged at that time to look for more responses and to discuss their feelings about the blots. Subjects who give such records are usually satisfied with test discussions that stick to surface materials, showing little interest in probing into unconscious motivations and needs. Or they may prefer working with other methods, such as TAT or sentence completion.

Sometimes subjects get defensive about their perceptions because they assume that what they see must be what everyone else sees and that therefore their projections have no special significance for them as individuals. Usually such subjects are not the best candidates for test discussion because they are too naive or rigid or are lacking in psychological mindedness. With them it is necessary to explain that although there are indeed certain commonly seen percepts, the blots inspire extremely varied interpretations, and thus what a subject sees constitutes his choice from the large mass of possibilities and therefore has significance in showing something about him.

Other subjects attempt to explain their perceptions in terms of something they have seen or experienced very recently (such as seeing bears in Card II because of having recently been to Yellowstone Park). In general, this is a rigidity sign. It occurs frequently in brain-damaged individuals who are concerned with holding onto reality and also in individuals who place great emphasis on being "logical." Persuading them that there might be only an incidental relationship between seeing bears on Card II and a trip to Yellowstone Park may be difficult, if not impossible. When the response which is presumably inspired by the recent experience is an unusual one, it may help to remind the subject that he still is making a choice from his store of experiences and that this may have significance.

Subjects who show the most capacity for making use of the kinds of interpretations or confrontations that come from an ink-blot performance usually furnish protocols that have rich content for discussion. Original responses are the most useful and should be explored fully, getting the subject's associations and making an effort to relate them to historical material and other test responses.

Responses made up entirely of inside shading usually refer to an area of anxiety that the subject needs to work with consciously. For example, a subject who saw the emaciated figure of a man in the center shading of Card IV related the response to his current anxiety about his changing relationship to his still very robust father who had always been cast in the role of the villain and for whom he was developing some compassion because of his father's impending divorce. He was at the time threatened by the development of some belated affection for his father, and seemed to gain some useful insight from speculating about his need to depict such a weakened image in order to feel safe in the changing relationship. In another case, the seeing of a face of a beautiful girl in the shading on the right-hand side of Card II and the face of a very homely man in the shading on the opposite side furnished the clue to an unconscious sibling rivalry situation.

The Rorschach frequently surpasses other instruments in giving clues to attitudes, either conscious or unconscious. This is because Rorschach interpretation is less readily obvious to the subject than interpretation of the other most commonly used projective techniques. Also, the playful approach that some subjects adopt with the MAPS test can prove misleading, and a Pollyanna approach to the TAT can mask hostility or ambivalence. An example that led to remarkably valid hypotheses regarding what the father was like and the subject's attitudes toward his father and other authority figures illustrates the rich possibilities afforded by ink-blot materials. It comes from a test report which reflects accurately the use of interpretations made to the subject in the discussion:

His counter-phobic methods of dealing with Father and other authority figures are a little rough, but one has to admit they are sometimes funny.
To Card IV:
"Well, it looks like a giant with huge feet, and you're looking from below up at him and the next thing looks like a huge penis. And looks like you're looking up at the back rather than the front, and it looks like he's frizzy all over, like a rag doll that's gone through the washing machine too many times."

Note here use of "you're" instead of "I'm"—an employment of "buck-passing technique" to diminish his fears; also, the incongruity between the giant and a rag doll that gets put through the washing machine is an excellent example of a true counter-phobic effort. This is reinforced by the introduction of shading at this point. Then, as usual, he returns to elaborate:

"So many other things I was thinking of; it looks kind of threatening because it's *black* and so on—and on the other hand it looks kind of funny. Looks like a balloon in the sky, like at a circus you see a balloon man up in the air from directly below, and it looks like these arms out here might be wings."

The response suggests that in addition to being a washout, father can also be seen as a "wind-bag."
But:

"Looks like he's got heavy boots on—might be spurs."

The response suggests Father is also a bully. Or is he?

"Of course they're on the wrong part of the heel." (Subject pauses.)

"And then that head up there, looks like an embryonic head, like the neural canal—or a monster type of head."

Maybe Father is also infantile—or stupid—or idiotic. After another pause, the subject goes on:

"Looks like a shiny coat, like black ermine. Kind of glistens, kind of has a texture like that." (This refers to giant's coat.)

Did Father have something rich to offer after all? After this response apparently some guilt began to catch up with the subject, for he changed the "penis" into a dog's head "kind of looking up at you with sad eyes," which then changed to a response with more depressive significance:

"And then again it looks like it might be a skull with some of the teeth out of it down here." (Depression did not dispel his hostility, however, for this is elaborated in the Inquiry): ". . . the rest of the teeth knocked out somehow."

In this case, death of the father had interrupted the process of working through the conflict with the father, who had been an inconsistent authority figure. Discussion of the Rorschach perceptions seemed to be of value to the subject in clarifying and identifying his mixed feelings. At a conscious level, his feelings had consisted mostly of diffuse hostility, slightly tempered by guilt surrounding his own hostile acting out.

Problems in Paranoia

Because of the extreme amount of defensiveness that often accompanies paranoid conditions, this area deserves special treatment in this chapter. Paranoid test signs are not confined to the protocols of paranoid schizophrenics, and when they occur they do not necessarily indicate that thinking is delusional to the extent of being easily recognized as psychotic. The word *paranoid* has, in the minds of most people, become associated with schizophrenia (or craziness), with delusional thinking, with danger that might ensue from the paranoid's hostility, and with still other phenomena, all of which are generally regarded as undesirable or "bad." On the other hand, although still not altogether innocuous, it is much more socially acceptable to be "oversensitive," "lacking in confidence in others," "afraid to trust," "afraid that others don't mean well," etc. Even the word "suspicious" is not a good choice unless the subject himself introduces it, since people have rather negative associations to suspiciousness.

A subject who began psychotherapy after his tests were discussed with him and his lack of trust in women was pointed out, said during his third psychotherapy interview that he was not just "suspicious of women," but that he was discovering he was "paranoid" in general. In this case, of course, we were then free to use the word *paranoid,* but the usefulness of this word came from the fact that it was the patient's own. Whether he would have taken this term for himself if it had been introduced in the discussion by the examiner is a question that cannot be answered, but this is one of many examples that could be cited to demonstrate that a subject may do a good deal of processing of materials that come up in the discussion, often with deepening insight and reduced defensiveness concerning his pathology. This particular subject brought into therapy considerable conscious material demonstrating his paranoia, and his own frank labeling of it as something undesirable seemed to be helpful to him in the attempt to rid himself of this element of his personality.

His Rorschach contained so many paranoid signs (disembodied pairs of eyes, numerous unusual white space responses, etc.) that it might have been tempting to interpret these responses directly as signs of paranoia. However, since labels of this kind do not offer people much to work with, it is more helpful to point out sources of fear, if possible, so that there is something concrete to attach the paranoid ideation to. The naive subject usually finds the classic psychoanalytic explanation of the dynamics of the paranoid syndrome confusing and unacceptable, and the truly paranoid individual often greets such an explanation with extreme defensiveness. Thus, it is more helpful to him to start by selecting from his test responses those which offer the best chance for a conscious acceptance of sources of distrust.

In the case of the subject in question, the watching eyes were interpreted as indicative of feelings of being under surveillance or of being influenced, while the white space responses were said usually to indicate feelings of resentment and negativism. It was pointed out that many of the space responses occurred next to blot details usually interpreted as feminine. And, although he had mentioned himself that it was not realistic, he had felt obliged to put "stingers" on a butterfly perceived in the usual butterfly area of Card II, an area often seen as having female sexual characteristics. Then, to complete the interpretation, the signs of feelings about females which came through at a more conscious level on the thematic tests were used to illustrate the kind of interpersonal relationships he had projected between men and women.

Two examples from the thematic tests follow.

> *To TAT 18GF:* "This man right here is lily-livered and a physical weakling. Otherwise, he wouldn't let this woman strangle her or manhandle him. . . ."
>
> *To MAPS Living Room Scene* (Characters are young woman in short skirt, N-9, and Superman, L-5): ". . . Well this is a boy friend and a girl friend here, going to a costume party. She had previously told him to dress as a little boy so they could go as a little boy and a little girl—her skirt is too short for her age—or I'll make it appear such—but, as he told her, he is going dressed as Superman. And *she's* mad. So she's going to the party anyway, but she's going to be mad."

Not only the content but the slip in the first story and the effort of the female to infantilize the male in the second story are ideal discussion materials which most subjects would be willing to reflect on and would be able to retain for future consideration. The extension of his distrust to male figures was present but somewhat more benign and equally useful in illustrating to this young man the nature of his difficulties in interpersonal relations.

An excellent and easily used example of distrust comes from the same subject:

> *To MAPS Closet Scene* (The only figure is Santa Claus, L-3, who is placed in the closet): "Santa says, 'I'll bet those kids thought I was coming down the chimney.' And he says, 'They forgot all about the trap door in the closet.' And we'll call that, *Santa's Getting Sneakier Every Year.*"

In this case, discussion of the tests was immediately followed with psychotherapy with the examiner as the therapist. The patient being compulsive and paranoid, but not yet psychotic, the course of therapy would not be expected to be smooth under any circumstances. However, it did seem that use of the tests helped focus early on the significant problems and that the transference distrust which inevitably developed was worked through with unusual ease. Being able to point out to him that his feelings could have been predicted from the tests long before they occurred assisted him in maintaining his objectivity toward the therapist. His efforts to provoke the therapist to infantilize or defeat him so that he would not have to work to give up his neurosis were also predictable and could be referred back to his test projections in the same way.

This example of lack of trust in authority figures is taken from a test report written in 1961. The example concerns this 31-year-old man's response to the Blank scene of the MAPS test:

> It [the MAPS scene] was set up in that sort of unconscious way often employed by people who select figures to fill a scene and then determine the story after the figures are placed on the background. Santa [L-3] went in first, followed by the bloody man [M-7], the snake [A-2], the man with back turned and seated [I-2] (all strange associates for Santa). . . . Story: "Santa Claus, in reality Nikita Khrushchev, has just shot Jack Kennedy—in reality Jack Armstrong, the All-American Boy. While Mao Tse-tung, disguised as a boa constrictor, is about to bite Nehru—in reality Mahatma Gandhi, with padding and clothing. Mao, having disguised himself in the form of a snake, is soon seized and destroyed as the evil thing. While Nikita, although he has stamped on the All-American Boy, is so successfully disguised that people's notions sway themselves to recognize him as Santa Claus only, who, therefore, has committed no evil. The moral to this story is that if you project an image big enough it had better be a good image or it will not work. And the title is *The Triumph of Good Over Evil.*"

Before getting to the use of this story in the discussion, another example related to the same problem enriches the picture. This one concerns his response to the MAPS Forest scene:

> The journey into the neurosis, the Forest, is again a struggle with trust, but this time the figure around whom trust centers is the old woman [F-10]. Three children [C-2, -3, -11] are lost and they come upon the old woman, who offers milk and cookies, after which she says she will take them home. The older girl thinks she is a witch, but the little boy laughs at his sister and persuades the girls to go

> with the old woman, who takes them safely back home. (His very great need to feel that he can trust mother-figures and the overriding of the initial distrust were just as clearly displayed in his behavior toward the examiner in the testing and discussion interviews.)

In discussion, materials of this kind are most successfully handled together, along with all other examples in the protocols related in any clear way to the problem of trust in others. All such examples are read back to the subject before beginning the interpretation, and he is asked whether he can perceive for himself a trend. He may be asked to try to ignore his own interpretations made at the time, if there are any, such as the "moral" to the scene dealing with dictators on the MAPS Blank card. Whether or not the subject recognizes the continuity of the theme of trust from one response to the other, his associations usually help to increase the validity of any interpretations that will be offered to him. He can be helped by suggestions, such as that Santa is a "good" father figure, whereas Nikita and Mao are, according to his story, "bad" and deceitful fathers. He can be asked, "Which one of the characters represents you?" After helping him recognize that to him even the most benign authority-figures (Santa) are feared by him as having "evil" intentions, it can be pointed out to him that although mother-figures are not wholly trusted either, he is much less likely to misperceive their intentions. This subject selected the bloody man for himself and related his problem with authority figures not only to poor rapport with his father when he was a child (Father was seen as punitive, selfish, and competitive for Mother's attention) but also to recent changes in his relationship to his father. In the report this speculation followed the discussion.

> All the to-do about Santa in Nikita's clothing (or vice versa) seems to relate to the changing state of affairs between him and his father. Having aged, Father now would like to be regarded by the successful son as having been a good father; he is ready for the grandfather role which hardly fits with his more youthful paternal behavior. There may be some wish that Father would remain like Mao, un-

> disguisedly bad, so that he can be rejected without further conflict. The subject is both intrigued and apprehensive over becoming better friends with Father; he is not sure how far to trust him or how much of the change in Father comes from genuine regret and how much from fear of aging and pure selfishness. Father actually seems to be encouraging him to share Mother, and to the subject this comes a little late.

In the discussion, this insight into Father, which obviously was already available to the subject, was used to expand the consideration of how his perception of other authority figures might become distorted. This sort of application of the testing insights to relationships in "the here and now" is, of course, one of the chief benefits to be gained from test discussion. An example of the kind of data that could have been used in the above case for this purpose comes from the same report:

> In writing this, I am recalling his reaction to his interview with Dr. X and his very keyed-up state afterwards as he tried to figure out what was underneath some of the questions Dr. X asked. He kept saying it must have been a good interview, as if he badly needed to believe that the interview had gone well but was unable to allay his own anxiety because of his uncertainty about what was behind some of Dr. X's questions.

Not all paranoid subjects are able to tolerate even the most sensitive and diplomatic of test discussions. An individual with very well systematized delusions spontaneously asked at the start of testing whether he might be told the results of his tests. He was told that this would be possible and a few days later when he inquired again was given an appointment. The discussion began with a sentence completion test at the end of which he had written, "I would like to know the results of my tests." The test was used in an exploratory way to try to draw out his feelings, but he did not seem interested in exploring further any of the responses he had made and was vigorously defensive about those that referred directly to his delusional system. He soon turned away from the test in order to reiterate his beliefs, which included his idea that a male friend was bringing numerous women to his room at night, forcing him to furnish sexual gratification to these women, so that he was in a state of constant physical exhaustion from so much sexual activity. Since some subjects respond better to graphic symbols than to words, his response to Card IV of the Rorschach was read back to him:

> This looks like a—a cow—a bull that's been flattened on the ground . . . feet spread out . . . the head gave me the impression it was a bull . . . sprawled on the ground you know? (He was asked what the bull was doing there.) It's hard to say—you know how cows or calves, when they're out of water . . . could be anything—tongue hanging out . . . out of water or dead of starvation . . . I guess you could call 'em tongue-tied or something . . . I didn't exactly think of him as dead—sprawled out—near dead—not dead.

He was asked whether what had happened to the bull here could be a reflection of how he felt about what was happening to his own masculinity, and his immediate reply was that the image of the flattened bull could not possibly have any bearing on his feelings about himself, for how could he doubt his masculinity when night after night he had all those women? In this case, the need for the paranoid defense appeared to be so strong that no further effort was made at that time to make use of the tests, and the patient did not ask to pursue the test discussion.

Not all subjects who take over the discussion session in order to talk about whatever else interests them have paranoid ideation, but it does seem in looking back that more of the individuals who are strongly paranoid than those in other diagnostic categories have shown little tolerance for the kind of discussion session appreciated by most subjects. One young paranoid subject who had expressed an interest in knowing the results of his tests opened his discussion appointment by rebuking the examiner for paying attention to the tests, saying that what he wanted and needed was to talk and be listened to. Since his tests contained some very distressing responses, it seemed understandable that he might like to avoid looking at them, and he was allowed to use his appointment time as he liked—which proved to be for telling about traumatic events of his past. In individual psychotherapy, for a long time he was very resistant and expressed fear of being "brainwashed" into behaving and thinking like well people who hold jobs and conform to the conventional social order.

Another very paranoid subject seemed to be digesting the interpretations with no trouble, and left the discussion period with an appearance of having gained some useful insight and of being quite satisfied about it. But by the next day, he had completely distorted some of the discussion content. He was in psychotherapy with a resident who had been eager for the patient to undergo the test discussion. As soon as the unfavorable reaction was reported, the patient was returned for further discussion. He worked very constructively, drawing on historical material to help explain why he had developed the misunderstanding. The outcome here was good, but if there had been no opportunity for the second session, discussing his tests with him would have appeared to be a serious error. This is the only example from many years of experience with this procedure in which this kind of emergency has arisen. This is probably partly due to the fact that the patient was not the kind of subject who would ordinarily be chosen for the sort of confrontation that takes place in test discussion. But, in spite of the rarity of the occurrence, the case points up the necessity of followup and of being available to the subject for further appointments if necessary. (This patient had exhibited a very condescending, patronizing manner during the test administration. An honest discussion of his tests necessitated confronting him with his manner of alienating others. He required more help in working this through than a single session afforded, and consequently his paranoid defenses were temporarily exacerbated. With the help of psychotherapy, he was able, eventually, to abandon much of his unpleasant persona.)

Homosexuality

Homosexuality is in itself a sensitive subject for most individuals, and this difficulty is often enhanced by the fact that paranoia is a frequent accompaniment to the problem. Many times there are other personality characteristics which render these subjects more vulnerable than the majority.

The first example is a young adult male whose tests contain signs of homosexual conflict, paranoid ideation, and schizoid or borderline schizophrenic indications. The thematic tests contain fine examples that illustrate difficulties in achieving interpersonal closeness and deep feelings. The following quotations from the report written after the discussion demonstrate the kind of response which is easily discussed with most subjects, regardless of signs of weakness in ego strength:

> Ambivalence interferes constantly with TAT story construction. This is particularly dramatic on the mother–son card, 6BM, where an unusual element is introduced: ". . . Looks like she's talking to someone that's not in the picture." This is followed and preceded by much comment about the "homely" and "homespun" atmosphere of the picture, and he goes on: "It seems like it is some large problem. . . . There's a tone of something important to them, and yet the tone is of simple home-life, as if they were making arrangements for a burial—maybe her husband and his father just died—like mother and son. I guess I almost said husband and wife—I don't know—seems like somebody just died—like somebody came to the door, maybe the postman, and she'll open the door—simple, homespun—let's see, the—let's see. [pause] It doesn't seem like the situation is as grave as I might sound—seems like the mourning is for some friend. [pause] I feel like the situation here is very shallow—somewhat like the old comic strips."

In most cases, all that is necessary is to read back such a story to the subject, asking him to listen to it from the standpoint of what sort of feelings go into the relationships between the persons referred to in the plot. As this exercise is followed by other examples of similar response, the subject begins to listen for the manifestations of his problem. For instance:

> *To TAT Card 12M:* "It's two ideas . . . the man is probably a psychoanalyst. [But he] could be a raged, insane relative that's really out to kill this boy that's sleeping on the couch."

If the subject were contemplating going into psychotherapy or analysis, this response could be used to help him anticipate frightening and disruptive negative transference reactions if use of the response in this way were to meet with the approval of the therapist or analyst. However, with the present case for whom immediate therapy was not in the planning, the response was used simply to illustrate the ambivalence toward anyone close to him.

Two examples from the MAPS test broaden the perspective on this theme still further:

> *To MAPS Living Room Scene:* The hero is the amputee [M-18] who "has some type of affliction and how he's getting over it," and he is visited by both his minister and doctor. After a pause, the subject also includes the pup [A-1] saying, "Of course you could throw in the dog—make it a little less traumatic and—a—more—humane."

> *To MAPS Stage Scene:* This scene was his own choice from the remaining backgrounds. On the stage he placed four of the blank-faced figures [S-2, -3, -4, -5]. "I guess you could make it—just say that all of life is but a stage. [He is asked for the story.] Well, just a more or less generalized betrayal—think of Shakespearean things—that all of life is but a stage. [pause] There's no faces because this is just a generalized [pause] generalized situation—no faces—people there just symbolic of the different members of the family, each having a definite part to play." (The slip "betrayal," went unnoticed by him.)

A straightforward discussion of the implications of these themes, including the slip, led to historical data which was offered with a show of genuine feeling by the subject. In brief, Father was an overworked, emotionally distant, and very cranky man, perhaps accounting for the fact that, although in the Living Room two professional substitute parent-figures were introduced to help the crippled son, it was still necessary to "throw in" a dog in order to include the human sentiments of compassion and sympathy. Mother, he said, came from a long line of emotionally impoverished individuals. She never achieved any closeness to her children; she went through the motions (as if on a stage playing the role) of being a mother, but without ever showing any genuine warmth in the process. In describing his early life, the subject indicated in many ways that he felt crippled emotionally and, like the man in the Living Room, he was struggling to get over it. There seemed to be little doubt that a very thorough discussion in this case led to both broadened insight and ego-reinforcing reduction in guilt, for there were plenty of data to demonstrate that he had acquired his personality defects through good and sufficient cause. Some remarks about the discussion reflect the general climate of that phase:

> The discussion phase went quite well here. It was approached very supportively by pointing out the assets and then indicating the test signs for maladaptive defenses that interfere with the best use of the assets. His poor WAIS verbalizations . . . were interpreted as signs of insecurity, and his "paranoid" reactions to being tied up with the insecurity he feels with his father, who is cranky and distant and too busy to bother with him, leading to chronic feelings of being criticized, rather than being a true paranoia. Since he had some Rorschach responses with minus form level that seemed to be related directly to the father relationship, the illustrations of this could be made rather dramatically. Perhaps the most constructive insight that he obtained was that he showed more severe signs of disturbance in his relationship to his father than in that with his mother.

Because this subject included in his historical account of himself the information that he had recently embarked on a phallic-aggressive spree which he said he was enjoying, the test signs of passivity suggestive of homosexual inclinations were not interpreted. It seemed best that he have some more time to prove himself as a sexual athlete before exposing the underlying passivity, some of which would probably disappear with improvement in his self-concept and distance from his father. The new insight that women seemed to be the lesser of two evils could be anticipated to help the heterosexual process along.

In cases where there seems to be little doubt about the overtness of the homosexual behavior but in which the subject may have reasons for desiring to conceal the fact of his homosexuality, the problem in the discussion is quite different. It is no longer a matter of protecting the subject from insight which he might have trouble tolerating and which might lead to panic. Rather, it is a matter of how to approach the tests honestly and yet without forcing a confession the subject does not wish to make or without making the subject feel that he is in the position of being phony. Such a young adult male is referred to in these excerpts from the test report:

> Handling the discussion here called for tact but also for honesty. To gloss over any of it [the signs of homosexual dynamics] with this very exposed and accessible young man would, it seemed to me, be inviting increase in paranoia. He did not ever say to me in so many words that he is homosexual, and I did not invite any confessions of that sort. We confined ourselves to discussing the interfamilial relationships, how these were reflected in the tests and his dynamics. I used the word "homosexual" freely, but always in the context of historical and dynamic origins, attitudes, defensive adjustment, etc. I pointed out every response that he made that would have led me, in a blind analysis of his tests, to conclude that homosexuality had been the defensive way out of the conflict over the relationship with the seductive mother. When we finished we seemed to have arrived at a mutual conclusion that as a gentleman no other choice really had been open to him. Of course, we did not overlook the rebellious aspects of his choice, but we decided that various [other] females . . . had contributed realistically. . . . The aspect of seduction in the maternal relationship was probably the most useful single new element for him, but probably the complete frankness and acceptance expressed in the discussion did much to reduce his tensions, since he looked increasingly relaxed and happy as it proceeded.

The protocols in this case are long and rich, and it would be an enormous task to quote even those responses which led to the most significant insights. But most of the responses are delightfully transparent, showing that any unconscious material was very close to the surface. The Rorschach contains many overt sex responses and responses indicating an interest in his mother's body, her pregnancies, etc. When these were pointed out, he denied awareness of any boyhood sexual interest in his mother, but he soon recalled many examples of incidents in which his mother's overly affectionate attitude toward him had been noted by others, sometimes with jealousy. One response which hilariously lampooned the sexual goings-on between mature, parent-type figures helped to demonstrate to him his unaccepting attitudes re heterosexuality and rejection of sex with a mother figure, which apparently had generalized to all females. And a completely absurd Rorschach concept of a "madam" with a huge vagina made up of white space served further to express his attitudes toward sex with females and his negativism toward advice to experiment heterosexually.

Responses of this kind, given with pleasure and feeling, cannot be ignored in any test discussion. If the subject could not tolerate discussing them, he probably would not be able to give them in the first place. However, for those examiners who are squeamish about responses revealing the more sensitive kinds of pathology, the kind of affect expressed by the subject at the time of response can be a guide. If the affect is flat or very sober when the concept itself is improbable or ridiculous, then a more cautious approach is called for. In such cases, the unreasonable or distorted aspects of the concept can be pointed out and the subject can be instructed that this kind of thing generally is indicative of unresolved conflict and asked what his own associations are to the response. He is very unlikely to be able to offer any associations that cannot be pursued further with benefit. If he has no associations, the response can be dismissed as being unexplainable, at least for the moment. As mentioned elsewhere in this chapter, it should be made clear to the subject that all aspects of the test data cannot be expected to be found immediately interpretable.

Integration of an Interpretation

The following illustrates how data from several tests—in this case the WAIS, Rorschach, TAT, and MAPS—can be tied together in order to construct a working hypothesis for the consideration of the subject. Simply for instructional purposes, the hypothesis will be offered first, followed by some of the best of the supporting test data.

Hypothesis

The subject, a 46-year-old male, had a rigid, moralistic, but generous mother. Her generosity made it difficult for him to attain full autonomy, which he really would have liked to achieve. He got even with her for the infantilizing that had taken place (it really was not very great) by a certain amount of acting out (again not very great) and by taking veiled, hostile pot shots at her on occasions, particularly when her moralizing tendencies were showing. He did enough of this to prevent any serious buildup of hostility and tension within himself. Now a father, he was acting out some of the rebellion of his own youth by subtly encouraging his children to carry out some of the more immature of the acting-out behavior he had given up, thus getting some vicarious satisfaction out of their performing aggressive acts that were no longer appropriate for himself.

Data from WAIS

On the Comprehension subtest, which is heavily loaded with items pertaining to values and social behavior, he gave overlong replies (this never occurred on other subtests). He showed indications of denial; for instance, if he said something that upon reconsideration he disapproved of, he would order the examiner to "cancel out that last sentence." He did not behave as though he were dictating, but the role of the examiner as his recorder—and a laborious role it was indeed—became clear. When the *lost in the forest* item was reached he first asked, "Do you write down everything I say?" and then gave a half-page reply using the pronoun "you' 'six times, ending with, "You don't wish I should go into some of the things you would run into in Canada?" (E. indicated she could skip finding out how she would get out of the Canada woods!) At the end of the last item he asked, "Had you rather I use one-syllable words?"

The above responses suggest that this otherwise rather charming male got into a sort of transference reaction as a result of the nature of the Comprehension test, becoming aggressive against the examiner —and showing some versatility about it, we must admit.

Data from Rorschach

Card III: First seen are "two men, who seem to be lifting something jointly." Then: "Maybe they're two girls, on further consideration; have skirts on and seem to have boosoms and it's rather windy . . . the wind seems to be blowing from two directions at once, but that's how it is." (*Interpretation:* Cooperative males are displaced by the females, who take over—lifting a picnic basket in both cases—and the wind, blowing from two directions, implies tension and conflict. Mention of the "boosoms" gives additional orality to the perception, although dependency is present in both instances.

Card IV: The only response is the usual bear rug with the specifications, "A rather inexpert job of skinning . . . hanging down, forepaws, skin of forelegs seems to be in a dependent position. . . . The texture of the blot seems to have highlights and darker areas; looks like fur." (*Interpretation:* If this response is taken as symbolic of his masculine identity, he feels he plays the masculine role inexpertly, and he is troubled by his unresolved dependency needs; but at the same time the readiness to acknowledge the texture, although it came at the very last, indicates he is not in any really serious trouble in expressing and satisfying his own needs or in empathizing with the needs of others.)

Card VIII: Two badgers "have been wounded and are in a rather exhausted condition. Apparently bleeding from a chest wound . . . here's his left forepaw which seems to have a small pool of blood—at this point he seems to be dripping a drop of blood. . . . His right hindpaw is on solid ground, but he's dragging his left hindpaw from which a pool of blood seems to have formed and he's getting a drink from a pond—maybe the blood has stained the water." This is the only main response, but he followed the inquiry to this response with: "Here's another fantastic picture—

here's a blue corset with stays . . . but what the corset is doing there I don't know. I can't relate the animals to that concept." (*Interpretation:* In light of our hypothesis, one interpretation could be that the concept of the exceedingly badgered badgers calls up the association of the old-fashioned corset belonging to the rigid, moralistic mother. We might also suspect a touch of masochistic enjoyment in belaboring the extent of the injury, lending a feeling of justification to holding onto the acting-out behavior in order to get even with Mother, who is responsible for making the Id–Superego battle such a bloody one.)

Card VII: "A small bay with a boat landing and pier—with woody shore line and a couple of harbor lights on either side—protected by promontories—a pier—seems to be set in a swampy area, which would be the lowest place on the bay and more natural place to put a pier for easy accessibility." In Testing the Limits, when asked directly for "areas which resemble human genitals," he said of the pier: "This is a vagina—maybe I was beating around the bush when I called it a pier or boat or receding platform." (*Interpretation:* In spite of the bloody combat of Card VIII, a card with strong female connotations is a safe harbor and he makes an easy transition from safety to sex. The *FK* quality of the harbor scene suggests some well-tolerated anxiety, perhaps in respect to the dependency suggested by the idea of the harbor and perhaps the restrictions imposed by it and the lights which guarantee one does not go astray.)

Testing Limits on Card Least Liked: He chose Card I: "Gives me a rather upsetting feeling when I look at it—I feel an impulse of center struggle when I look at it. Maybe I put myself in the position of a man being harassed by a couple of witches." (Initial responses had been a man in the center leading a choir or orchestra and two witches on the side riding brooms.) (*Interpretation:* The ease with which he could get into transference reactions with females and then see through his own reaction is perhaps suggested by this response. Or we might wonder about the similarities between wife and mother. Also, as with Card III, there are other possibilities, such as competition with females, or an identity struggle, since the center detail of Card I is usually seen as a female.)

Card X: He gave eight responses to this card, two of which are particularly supporting to the main hypothesis: "Then in red, we have some strawberry jam that seems to have gotten smeared around.—The reason for that is that having raised several children I've seen many, many smears." (*Interpretation:* Note the pronoun "we," implying some sharing in the indulging in a little smearing; but note also how "we" don't ever quite take responsibility for having done it—it just "seems to have gotten smeared around" and in the Inquiry is blamed entirely on his children.)

The eighth and final response is to the popular crabs "with numerous arms that seems to be—have caught hold of a green jelly fish.—I just called it a jelly fish because it looked like something the crab was eating and that was as shapeless a mass as you could imagine and this green thing doesn't present any particular outline—don't know whether crabs eat jelly fish or not—guess they do." (*Interpretation:* If one borrows from Jungian symbolism and thinks of the crab "with numerous arms" as a mother symbol, then what Mother is doing becomes rather important. One easy possibility is that she is possessive and devouring. Also, what about the length that he went to to deny that the green objects have any shape, even to the point of assuring the examiner that they are "as shapeless a mass as *you* could imagine." [Italics are mine.] Not only the examiner, but many other subjects, imagine that the green objects are shaped like buck sheep jumping, and this subject had shown in some of his other responses to Card X a very good capacity to use the fine details of the blots in order to form some excellent shapes. Thus, the buck sheep was not beyond him, so one might ask whether seeing such a fine masculine symbol in the grasp of the devouring mother was too threatening. Or, alternately, whether he felt so much like a jelly fish in the grasp of the enveloping and devouring mother that this response won out over any other competing responses. The fact that he did not even get around to the popular crab response until the very last also deserves some passing mention.)

TAT, Card 6BM:

The son is a bank cashier who plays the horses. The story begins: "Well, let's call this *Contrition.* Here is a Lord-fearing—or God-fearing—uprighteous woman—widow—who has worked and saved to put her son through college—and she's looking out the window watching her picture of success crumble to nothing, knowing she cannot sell enough to cover his losses." (*Interpretation:* While not autobiographical, the picture of the uprighteous woman who furnishes the safe harbor by paying off the losses of the acting-out son is clear enough.)

MAPS Living Room:

Scene contains a father [M-19], policeman [M-5] and child [C-12]. "Policeman appears at the front door, announces that little Johnnie has broken a window and the father is saying, 'Why look at little Johnnie; he wouldn't break anybody's window.' Enough. [He is asked to go on.] Well, the child is in a very innocent position, and the father is in a similar position. I think they probably both know that the child broke the window but will only admit it as a last resort. And I think the policeman with the sort of smile on his face knows that he knows they broke the window." (*Interpretation:* Of course the slip "they" is quite supporting to the main hypothesis, and this story in general is fundamental to the part of the main hypothesis which states that he vicariously enjoyed and probably encouraged aggressive or rebellious behavior on the part of his children. It is noteworthy that no mother appears in the scene; this is strictly a matter between father and son.)

Discussion

In discussing with the subject the large amount of data that went into the leading hypothesis stated above—and there were still other supporting data that could also be used—several approaches could be followed. The approach employed here, in which the main hypothesis was stated before furnishing the supporting data, is not the best one to be used when discussing the test responses with the subject. As stated in the beginning, it was used to clarify the application of the technique only. Presenting hypotheses in advance to the subject who gives the test responses deprives him of the opportunity to participate in constructive self-discovery and also is likely to increase defensiveness. It has always worked well to read back with the subject all of his test responses, indicating to him that the task is to look for continuities and for any signs of how he handles certain key relationships, such as with females, males, mother-figures, father-figures, authority-figures, etc. The hypotheses that would gradually evolve in this way could be neatly and comprehensively stated only at the end, and whatever the subject was able to add to the data in the discussion would go into the hypothesis formation. If he made no comment at all, the hypotheses would be supported only by the test responses.

The majority of subjects respond best to participation in the making of the hypotheses to be derived from their tests. Most subjects who are approached in this manner seem to derive satisfaction from the control they have over the hypothesis formation through the giving of history and from discovering some new relationships themselves. Probably this is a big factor in a subject's willingness to work with the hypotheses. Furthermore, observation of how they work with the data and with the examiner adds valuable information in the assessment of ego strength, nature of defenses, flexibilities, rigidities, etc. In the assessment of psychiatric residents this is perhaps the most valuable of the data obtained.

In the case of the data cited above, the main hypothesis (which proved to have much historical data to support it) was developed by starting with the WAIS, going then to the Rorschach and last to the thematic tests. But it would have been possible to start with the TAT, then account for the reaction to the Comprehension by pointing to the "uprighteous" mother, proceeding then to the deeper level and more primitive representations on the Rorschach.

Conclusion

The Role of Assets

In this chapter the emphasis has been largely on communicating to the subject the unconscious, neurotic, or irrational aspects of his behavior. This should not lead to the impression that the more constructive and positive aspects of the personality that show up on the tests are neglected. Communication of such factors is not difficult and usually does not present as much of a problem in language choice or in persuading the subject to consider the observation.

The best use of the positive findings is to help the subject see how the more adaptive aspects of his personality can be utilized in helping him modify those behaviors that appear to lead to conflicts with his environment. Often this is equivalent to offering tools designed to perform a task which seemed insurmountable because no tools or only inadequate tools were available before. Hopefully, the subject will obtain an overview of his personality that will result in better recognition of emotional needs that affect behavior and better control of behavior.

Research Possibilities

Systematic investigation of the effects of the test discussion process should pose many of the same problems and possibilities as investigation of the effects of different styles of psychotherapy. A number of experimental designs can be suggested.

For example, it would be useful to know whether the method is more effective with one type of patient than another. Patients matched on important variables but belonging to different diagnostic categories can be used as comparison groups. It would, of course, be highly desirable for the same clinician to conduct the discussions for all groups. Probably no two clinicians will function the same way in carrying on a discussion, and variability at least can be reduced by having only one clinician for this purpose. It would be further desirable for the same clinician who conducts the discussion to do all the test administration as well, again reducing variability from group to group and from discussion to discussion.

While a comparison between schizophrenic and neurotic groups could be useful, experience so far suggests that other breakdowns within the diagnostic categories could give more precise information. For instance, comparisons of hysterics versus obsessive-compulsives or character disorders or paranoid schizophrenics, and so on, might be more helpful in identifying those populations which respond more favorably or more unfavorably to the discussion process.

Varying degrees of ego strength within the diagnostic categories might prove to be better criteria for suitability or unsuitability. Scores from tests like the MMPI could be used to separate the groups.

Criteria for evaluating the varying degrees of success of the discussion can be set up by the investigator and data sources can range from descriptive statements regarding how the subject makes use of the discussion period itself to long-term observations and followup. Interviews or questionnaires designed to explore the subject's recall of the discussion and how he believes he has made use of it or observations made by others could yield quantifiable data. Due to change of attitudes toward self and others, subjects sometimes improve in their feelings and behavior and yet are unable to verbalize any insights. Consequently, some sort of performance measure should be available in addition to the subject's verbal report.

Another research design could employ discussion combined with psychotherapy. Experience suggests that subjects who have entered psychotherapy immediately following test discussion focus unusually well on their central problems, getting quickly to conflict areas. Subjects matched for as many characteristics as possible (sex, age, intelligence, diagnosis, type of conflict, socio-economic status, education, etc.) could be assigned to one of four groups: a group receiving discussion alone, a group receiving discussion followed by psychotherapy, a group receiving psychotherapy but no discussion of tests, and a group receiving nothing beyond the initial workup required to select and match the subjects.

Again, it would be desirable to use the same discussant and therapist for all groups, but it might not be practical for one therapist to have so many patients in psychotherapy. Hence, the subjects in the two groups undergoing psychotherapy could be assigned on a random basis to a number of therapists of relatively equal experience using similar approaches. The therapists would serve as judges of whether differences existed between the two groups and whether these differences, if any, showed some degree of uniformity.

In order not to bias the therapists in advance, the design of the experiment should be concealed from them. Because the subjects would be likely to reveal details of the test discussion during the course of psychotherapy, it probably would not be possible to conceal the fact of the test discussion. Consequently, differences between the groups might be at least somewhat masked by scheduling a "discussion" period for all subjects following their testing. One group would then undergo a thorough discussion as described in this chapter, whereas the other group would be given a fairly routine interview in which the subject would take the lead, with the interviewer, interacting nondirectively and making no interpretations.

The followup evaluation of all the groups would need to be made by someone unfamiliar with the design and possessing as little as possible of the kind of information that would lead to bias.

These designs call for large expenditures of time. However, at a period in clinical psychology when one of the principal areas of that field is under attack—namely, testing, and particularly projective techniques and their efficacy—this could prove to be time well spent. For countless hours and much energy have gone into the development of all kinds of assessment techniques. If the body of information concerning these instruments is to be retained and used, broader applications for them should be developed. The questions discussed here are not yet fully answered. Does discussion of his own tests with a subject have a constructive or therapeutic effect? Do some kinds of subjects benefit from this experience while others do not? Does such an experience prior to psychotherapy or during psychotherapy expedite the therapy process?

Appendix. A Therapeutic Application of Psychodiagnostic Test Results[6]

The preceding paper[7] describes a teaching program employing administration of a number of psychological tests to psychiatric residents, followed by interpretation of his own test findings to each resident as a teaching device. Since the writer has taken responsibility for recommending this method and there are no manuals to guide those who may wish to attempt the final phase of the testing process—the discussion of the test results with the subject—some remarks about it seem in place here.

The therapeutic aspect of the test discussion phase has not been stressed in the foregoing paper, but a large number of the residents have commented that it has proved to be therapeutic and many of these have stated this with enthusiasm. In addition to residents, the author has employed test discussion in the psychotherapy of a wide variety of patients, including schizophrenics.[8] In no case has any resident or patient appeared to be harmed by the information given him, and the majority of patients have indicated that they liked knowing their own test results and have shown ability to use the data constructively and profit from the experience.

A discussion of the differences between psychological test interpretations which can properly be offered to subjects taking the tests and the kind of interpretations that are made in psychotherapy would be relevant here. However, it would be a difficult topic to treat fully in

---

[6] From Gertrude Baker, *Journal of Projective Techniques & Personality Assessment,* Vol. 28, No. 1, 1964, reprinted by permission of the copyright owner.

[7] Baker, Gertrude, and Ferguson, J. T. 1964. "Teaching Psychodiagnostic Testing to Psychiatric Residents." *J. Proj. Tech.* 28: 9–12.

[8] The writer of course never discusses the patient's test findings with him unless this procedure is requested by the referring doctor.

a short paper even if the differences were well understood. There are probably many more individuals doing psychotherapy, employing a variety of methods, than there are psychologists who undertake to share test results with their subjects.

The question has been raised whether interpretation of test results may not be as unsafe or emotionally upsetting as interpretations made in psychotherapy sometimes prove to be. This is at the present time a question that cannot be answered, since we do not have a great deal of data regarding the test interpretation process. The fact that subjects do not seem to be unduly disturbed by a discussion of their own test responses may be due largely to the method employed, which the writer has adhered to closely for many years (see particularly the outline in the last part of this paper).

Another question which can be raised appropriately is whether the test discussion may spark a need for psychotherapy, ending with the subject needing to go into psychotherapy. In the case of residents, approximately 180 of whom have undergone the test discussion process by this method, there have been no instances in which the discussion itself appeared to lead to a demand for therapy. In some instances it seemed to serve to diminish the immediacy of a previously expressed desire for therapy by furnishing tangible data upon which the subject could work by himself for some time. Frequently psychiatric residents are very eager for more self-insight before they enter the training program and such residents particularly welcome the opportunity to discuss their test results.

Before the discussion begins, the limits in terms of time are relatively well defined. As a rule, three or four hours are set aside for the first appointment, with the understanding that the discussion will last to the point of closure, with a good summary of the test findings being possible at the end. With a small number of very verbal subjects who give extremely long protocols or with the type of individual who interrupts frequently to insert history, resistance maneuvers, etc., a second session may be necessary. Interruptions are to be encouraged, of course, since this is the best way to learn about the effects of what the interpreter is doing and since they give the subject some opportunity to work through the information he is receiving.

It is a good idea to be flexible about time in order to suit individual needs, but always with the understanding that the discussion focuses mainly on the test findings and does not become conventional psychotherapy. With the majority of residents, one long interview suffices.

In rare cases, a third or fourth somewhat shorter session has been granted within a week or so of the testing in order to clear up additional questions. Also, in a few instances subjects return weeks or months or even years later with some specific question or questions that lead to reviewing the tests. By this time the residents have become so impressed with the necessity to keep the tests as a focus that they ask specifically whether the tests contain any information regarding their questions. The residents do not at any of these times make an attempt to persuade the tester to engage in conventional psychotherapy, although they often remark that "this is therapeutic." They seem to use the insights from the tests to enhance their own efforts at self-understanding, and apparently there is something about the kinds of insights that tests offer when properly used that is particularly applicable to gaining self-understanding at a level that is immediately utilizable.

With patients, the usage of time and length of appointments has to be more variable for a variety of reasons, including the patient's tolerance and the time available to others who may be involved in the discussion. Also, the prohibition that the test discussion is not intended to lead to conventional psychotherapy is usually less applicable, although of course the tester may frequently not be the therapist. Often the patient is about to begin therapy or is already in therapy, and the therapist, who in most cases in the writer's experience is someone who at one time has gone through the discussion process himself, usually has some clear ideas as to what he hopes to accomplish in having the test results discussed directly with the patient. Within the hospital setting usually the therapist sits in on the discussion, participating to varying degrees in it. This of course prepares the therapist to make further use of the test insights in the course of his psychotherapy with the patient. If the therapist does not sit in, it is important that he receive a report on what transpired. (One therapist who could not be present sent along his recorder by the patient, and a three-hour session was fully recorded for later use in therapy.)

One great advantage in beginning psychotherapy with a discussion of test results seems to be that it reduces defensiveness, perhaps because test data are more observable and tangible than interpretations or inferences offered by the therapist as the result of listening to the data the patient brings to the conventional therapy session. Or perhaps the patient attributes to tests some magical potency he is not willing to allow another individual to have. Certainly, it is true that tests furnish convincing examples of the patient's behavior that can be pointed out to him for illustrative purposes.

It would not be possible to offer a "cook book" for a process that necessarily must be characterized by a good deal of variation, depending on the subject's test protocols and personality and the skill and personality of the psychologist who undertakes the interpretation. This is truly an interaction process, a factor which adds to the complications that are likely to arise. It is probably appropriate to offer the warning that only the experienced and relatively secure psychologist should undertake such a discussion of test results.

In spite of skill in test interpretation and understanding of psychodynamics, probably few psychologists are able at first to discuss a subject's own projective—or even objective—test results with him without experiencing some anxiety. In writing test reports, as we point out a subject's pathology most of us are reassured by the fact that we do not need to share our remarks with the subject, who is usually one of those excluded from any detailed knowledge of his records by reason of confidentiality. Presumably, precautions regarding confidentiality are for the subject's protection, but they also offer tremendous shelter to us, the keepers of the records. If we knew in advance that we would have to share our reports with the subject, they would probably often read rather differently. It might be that they would contain a great deal more about assets as an ameliorating factor and perhaps overlook important aspects of pathology if we are timid. An overemphasis of the assets might prove to be just as pernicious as mentioning only the liabilities.

If we do not stand alongside the subject and face up to his liabilities with him as supportively as we face his assets, we are letting him down in a serious way. Of course, every psychotherapist knows this, and the purpose of this paper is simply the discussion of techniques for doing it while discussing a subject's test performance with him. The skilled psychologist is very likely to include in his report some remarks about the subject's strengths, so he does have some experience in verbalizing data that the subject would enjoy hearing were he to read his own test report. Most psychologists lack experience in using the kind of language or in employing methods that would present the liabilities of a subject to him in a fashion that would be constructive or even palatable for him to listen to.

Many of the less positive things psychologists say in test reports are couched in pseudoscientific jargon which satisfies them that they have nonjudgmentally dealt with a subject's shortcomings but which communicates little that is concrete or tangible to the subject. Or, if a subject does know the meaning of some of the jargon he is likely to take it as indicative of pathology that is frightening and that he does not have the skill or special training to deal with. For instance, to say, "You suspect people's motives," would be vastly more useful to the majority of individuals than saying, "You are paranoid."

Choice of language, then, is a very important element in making looking at himself via his test responses acceptable to the subject. A second and perhaps even more important factor in making this sort of test interpretation successful is the matter of the source of the interpretation—the subject's own tests, or his own actions in response to the test stimuli. The data are there before him and are not to be denied; it is not the psychologist who is accusing him of something—what he did is there to see. Probably it is these factors, along with choice of level and language usage, that help to prevent the making of the so-called "premature" interpretation from test data. Of course, any fear that an interpretation may be premature or unwise should lead to careful exploration at a safe level before attempting the interpretation.

It is true that the psychologist is "guilty" of making the interpretation, and therefore of course he will do well not to make interpretations without sufficient supporting data, which he can then use for illustrative purposes in order to encourage the subject to consider the test findings. For example, if a subject objects to something that is pointed out to him, such as that he seems hostile to women because he nearly always sees them on the Rorschach with heads or arms or other parts of the body "cut off," it will usually help motivate him to deal with the possibility of his hostility by turning to TAT or MAPS and pointing out, if they occur, the unusual number of instances in which unpleasant things happen to women. He may protest that in the TAT scenes it is already obvious that unpleasant things are happening, whereupon it can be impressive to him to turn to the MAPS and show him that in this medium where he had opportunity to put women in happier situations he still continued to plague them with misfortune. Of course, if other supporting data are not available, it is better not to press a suggested interpretation, for then it becomes a matter of the psychologist imposing his will, taking the responsibility for what happened on the tests away from the subject.

Differences in ego strength naturally make for differences in interpretation, and the approach in reviewing the tests of a psychiatric resident will not be the same as that in discussing a schizophrenic's test responses. However, it is an error to regard it as necessary to be so protective of the schizophrenic as to avoid all confrontations of him with his pathology. Fear of a patient's pathology sometimes leads to overprotective attitudes and measures which lack the qualities of accepting the patient along with his pathology and constructively dealing with the various manifestations of his illness. The supportiveness of the atmosphere in which the data are discussed is one of the most important features in working with patients of varying ego strength.

It may be useful to the psychiatric resident, for example, to permit some real guilt about immature modes of behavior to arise, whereas with the schizophrenic more effort to help him see realistic reasons for the origins of his immaturity could relieve him of some of the guilt. It is very common for schizophrenics and some neurotics to change the subject if an area becomes too painful, and usually this should be permitted, particularly in a first session. If a resident does this, usually it should be called to his attention, and consideration of the painful area should be pressed—unless something in the tests suggests that to do so would be contraindicated. To get away with cutting off a topic can result in the strong-egoed, highly aware individual suffering an anxiety attack following the discussion session. This may also be true for schizophrenics, but experience with them has led to few reports of this kind, perhaps because schizophrenia is a disease that exploits escape mechanisms.

A paper that would attempt to deal with all the varieties of problems so far experienced by the author in many years of using this technique would be much too long for journal publication. Furthermore, it is not possible to anticipate all the new problems that may arise in the experience of others. As a result of conducting a staff seminar on this subject in the fall of 1960, an effort was made to reduce the suggestions for undertaking the discussion to an outline of statements defining the procedure in a general way that is applicable for all types of subjects. This outline follows.

Interpretation of Psychological Test Data to Patients and Other Subjects

I. Communication—the first consideration.
   A. Avoid labels, scientific terminology; if subject uses them have him define his terms (so what is on his mind is clear to you and him) and discourage continued use of such terms.
   B. Teach him to think operationally and dynamically about himself in language that makes it possible for him to communicate to others besides yourself so he can make himself understood to his layman associates.

II. Making interpretations acceptable.
   A. *Always* lead from test data in making any interpretation or inference.
   B. Show subject the difference between fact and inference; stress the hypothetical nature of the procedure.
   C. But don't sell the tests short; don't be afraid to press an

interpretation if there are several examples of the same sort of behavior or implied feeling to back it up.

D. If an issue is tackled at all, the treatment should be full and frank at whatever level is chosen. There should be no side-stepping or maneuvers to tone down the impact once the issue is raised. At least two factors should determine whether to get involved in any area: (1) the subject's real need for defenses against insight into the area, and (2) the level of interpretation chosen. (For example, if tests of a male subject show castration anxiety and homosexual conflict, a more surface level of presentation can be chosen in which data indicating fear of, or hostility for, women are pointed out, or it might be noted that the subject always trims off projections or sees such areas as representing weak, fragile or gentle creatures, etc., suggesting he has qualms about being sexually very aggressive. The possibility of turning away from women to a homosexual solution would not be mentioned unless the subject himself introduced it, since it would be a further and still deeper *inference* and not really part of the test data. If the data include references to homosexuality, then by all means it should be included in the discussion and integrated with the other signs of sexual and interpersonal maladjustment. This can be extremely therapeutic, since it may give the subject his first dynamic insight into his homosexuality.)

E. Take time to be sure the subject gets the point. This is particularly important in interpreting the resistances, where he may be unusually dense.

F. If possible, amuse him; in working with resistances this is particularly helpful.

G. Size up his needs and respond to them. (There is usually a good dynamic relationship between socially acceptable needs and socially unacceptable ones, and most subjects mind less having the latter referred to if the former are also included and the interaction is pointed out. This improves objectivity more than almost anything else.)

III. Social climate of the interview.

A. It is partially a *sharing* experience, in which examiner and subject now sit back and look at the individual who took the tests (but don't carry this too far so that it becomes phony or artificial—we look at the individual but don't lose track of the fact that he is one of us).

B. The *didactic* aspect is also very important. The examiner should teach his subject psychodynamics, explain how symptoms and behavior patterns develop, if he thinks it will help to increase the subject's objectivity. He should forget precautions about "intellectualization," since the discussion is around the subject's own data and this is not intellectualizing.

C. The hypothetical approach adds to the objectivity and prevents negative transference, as does the process of arriving at decisions from multiple data. Resistance is reduced because of the legitimacy of making inferences as long as they remain inferences and are not transformed into "facts."

D. Sharing the tests reduces paranoia; test findings are shared with the subject rather than used to influence him or to shape his treatment without his awareness of our purpose.

E. Examiner influence: the examiner as he administered the tests is out there too, alongside the subject who took them, and should be looked at wherever possible. Subject should be informed that a good deal of research has been done on this and told of some of the results. This adds to the sharing experience and the reduction of transference and paranoia.

IV. Tolerance limits.

A. Examiner should not get carried away with his own magnificent insights and fail to note signs that the subject has had enough. These are usually manifested by the subject turning interpretations into opportunities for longer and longer periods of history giving, and it may be wise to abandon the tests for the time being and listen. Failure of the subject to return to the tests or to apologize for directing attention away from them is a sure sign he has had enough (but does not mean that what has been done so far is a failure).

B. If a subject, including a very fragile-egoed patient, stays with the tests, in most cases the interpretation should continue. It is untherapeutic to be overcautious.

Summary

This paper attempts to make more explicit the processes (referred to in the preceding paper) of interpreting a subject's own test results to him. Both learning about the use of tests and learning about one's own personality result from being the subject of such a procedure, giving the device a combined teaching and therapeutic value.

The wide variations in personality and test results, as well as among psychologists who may wish to undertake this task, make the formation of rules to follow difficult. Also, any attempt to unduly narrow the scope of this procedure at this stage seems inadvisable. However, some precautions and suggestions that have come out of years of experience with both patient and nonpatient subjects have been offered.

References

Baker, Gertrude. 1964. "A Therapeutic Application of Psychodiagnostic Test Results." *J. Proj. Tech.* 28: 3–8.

———, and Ferguson, J. T. 1964. "Teaching Psychodiagnostic Testing to Psychiatric Residents." *J. Proj. Tech.* 28: 9–12.

Beck, S. J. 1944. *Rorschach's Test. I. Basic Processes.* New York: Grune & Stratton.

Drake, L. E., and Oetting, E. R. 1959. *An MMPI Codebook for Counselors.* Minneapolis: The Univ. of Minnesota Press.

Goldberg, P. A. 1965. "A Review of Sentence Completion Methods in Personality Assessment." *J. Proj. Tech.* 29: 12–45.

Hathaway, S. R., and Meehl, P. E. 1951. *Atlas for the Clinical Use of the MMPI.* Minneapolis: Univ. of Minnesota Press.

Klopfer, B., et al. (Eds.). 1954. *Developments in the Rorschach Technique,* Vol. I. New York: World Book Co. *Ibid.,* 1956, Vol. II.

Murray, H. A. 1943. *Thematic Apperception Test Manual.* Cambridge: Harvard Univ. Press.

Shneidman, E. S. 1952. "A Manual for the MAPS Test." *Proj. Tech. Monograph* 1, No. 2.

Wechsler, D. 1944. *The Measurement of Adult Intelligence,* 3rd ed. Baltimore: The Williams & Wilkins Co.

———. 1955. *Manual for the Wechsler Adult Intelligence Scale.* New York: The Psychological Corp.

9

Florence B. Brawer

The Rorschach in Academic and Vocational Research: A Review

Although the Rorschach is most often considered to be a clinical tool, its use has not been limited to clinical practice. There are numerous situations where Rorschach interpretations are related to nonclinical populations and where individual evaluations extend to group situations and to specialized occupational fields. These varied applications are consistent with Rorschach's (1921) own statement that response content may provide information about a subject's interest in his work and thus widen the perceptions of his personality structure.

Generally, nonclinical investigations employing the Rorschach attempt to establish relationships between individual personality characteristics and effectiveness in specific educational and occupational areas. They try to predict academic success, to select the types of men and women who will be successful in certain occupational roles, and to describe the special environmental conditions most conducive to vocational satisfactions. Results of these many studies are both confusing and disquieting. In spite of some efforts to replicate the research, there have been few designs sufficiently clear that they add information without raising further questions or isolating other variables. Other studies have not lent themselves to extend investigations. As a whole, the research lacks both clarity and consensus.

Presented in three parts, this chapter deals with certain nonclinical aspects of the Rorschach technique—its roles in predicting academic and vocational success and in describing the outstanding characteristics of people involved in particular occupations. Although references to earlier publications will be cited occasionally, this text is primarily concerned with reports issued from 1956 to 1968 which deal with the Rorschach and occupational research. The first section summarizes the background of vocational and educational counseling and emphasizes the involvement of psychological determinants and psychological measures. It includes a cursory report of previous reviews concerned with the Rorschach in educational and occupational situations. The second section considers significant studies with the Rorschach in academic/occupational situations; it also refers to reviews by Patterson (1957), Spiegelman (1956), and Williams and Kellman (1956) which summarized Rorschach-related activities prior to 1956. Although only those journals and texts originally published in English have been examined, a lack of consistency in emphasis will soon become apparent. This is partially due to the fact that some literature simply appears more relevant to our subject than others, and partially to personal biases regarding what is considered of most interest. The final section focuses briefly on theoretical concerns. A general overall critique of the literature is offered, together with suggestions and recommendations for future directions.

From these reports of the literature, certain inferences may be drawn regarding the Rorschach's employment in vocational and academic situations. The kinds of clinical insights that may develop from its use are also relevant to many nonclinical situations. This chapter attempts to bring some of these interpretations into focus as, directly or through implication, it is concerned with the following questions: Why should the Rorschach be used for studies of vocational success? If predictions of future performance *can* be made, why should this be so? Or if not, why not? What links exist between psychological data and work/environmental data? What ones are still missing? Is it the process or approach to work that is simulated in the organization of the unstructured ink blots? Or is it, rather, the approach of new situations—work or otherwise—that these stimuli approximate? Can the Rorschach isolate individuals who will become successfully acclimated to their new occupational environments? Which specific signs might relate to what kinds of occupational and academic satisfactions?

Behind these questions lies the basic premise that the Rorschach, a clinically valid tool, also may be applied to nonclinical situations. It is therefore in a unique position to provide an in-depth awareness of the individual as he functions in his world of school and work.

History

Attempts to form a bridge between personality characteristics, individual differences, and occupational choices constitute a relatively old story in psychology. As early as 1820, Bessel noted that an astronomer's assistant had been dismissed for errors in observation and subsequently conducted

> the first experiments upon individual differences in a psychological function . . . He experimented upon himself and colleagues and found a wide variation in speed of response. This was the beginning . . . of a vast literature of the measurable differences among human beings. [Brayfield, 1965, p. 890]

Interest in these variables was further stimulated by Galton's (1883) emphasis on the psychological variabilities in different individuals as a field for scientific investigation, by Cattell's (1890) work with tests and measurements, and by Whipple's (1910) two-volume publication on physical and mental tests. Galton, Wundt (1880), Kraepelin (1892), and Bleuler (1912) were all concerned with techniques involving associations, but it was Jung (1918) who initially developed a systematic approach for applying associations to the study of unconscious processes. His experiments with word associations in conjunction with physiological measures of emotion then became the first of a type which Frank (1939) was to later identify as a "projective technique."

By 1910, sufficient material was reported that Munsterberg could summarize the applications of psychological testing in business and industrial situations. Shortly after, as part of the general wide-scale testing and selection programs of World War I, personality testing received increased attention as a field of study. Augmented by the birth of vocational, educational, and personal counseling, interest in the guidance movement was further nurtured by the national needs for training and reemployment that became important in the post-war years. Then, joining the already swelling armamentarium of techniques to assess individual personality patterns, interests, abilities, and aptitudes, Rorschach's experiments with ink blots were published in 1921. Here was the nucleus of a new, dynamic approach to human evaluation that stimulated the interest of psychiatrists; clinical, social, and industrial psychologists; anthropologists and educators. The depression of the Thirties, the intensified testing programs of World War II, and the vast and extensive activities of the Veterans Administration, working in collaboration with schools and colleges, swelled the demands for trained specialists and gave impetus to the instruction and preparation of qualified people in the techniques of guidance, individual assessment, and vocational counseling.

This period also inaugurated a shift from previous emphases upon cognitive and motor skills to global concerns with personality dynamics and interpersonal behaviors. There thus developed attempts to predict behavior in exceedingly varied situations. The Office of Strategic Services (OSS) Assessment Staff's appraisal of men and women recruited for special services during World War II represented "the first attempt in America to design and carry out selection procedures in conformity with so-called *organismic* (Gestalt) principles" (1948, p. 3). The OSS staff was charged with the development of procedural systems by which individual personality patterns could be revealed in order to facilitate reliable predictions concerning their usefulness. Because of the nature of the war activities, however, it was not possible to obtain adequate job descriptions for the thousands of candidates who were studied in the United States and abroad. Accordingly, predictions were made for individuals on the bases of instruments but without accurate knowledge of the situations in which they would perform and without definite criteria upon which the predictions could be evaluated. These deficiencies became major stumbling blocks in the OSS program. Today the problems are still evident, in spite of the extended efforts to understand people in particular situations.

Individual assessment, environmental or situational appraisal, and defined criteria are now seen as basic requirements for any personal guidance or organizational evaluation program. Determining the effectiveness of individuals functioning in various kinds of positions, discovering which students will succeed in what schools, and predicting what types of teachers will be most effective under what conditions are problems related to individual appraisal, both in and out of the armed forces. Stern, Stein, and Bloom emphasized the importance of increasing "the probability that individuals being selected for participation in these various kinds of institutional programs would do so with maximum efficiency and economy both for themselves and the institution in question" (1956, p. 23).

If they are to be valid and reliable measures of effectiveness, predictions of individuals functioning in prescribed situations must be incumbent upon the specification of criteria and defined objectives. This contention, initiated by Murray (1938) in his development of the individual need/environmental press concept, has been further elaborated by MacKinnon, Crutchfield, Barron, and Block (1958); Pace (1962; 1964); Pace and Stern (1958); and Stern, Stein, and Bloom (1956). Hahn and MacLean bridged the early and somewhat narrow beginnings in vocational assessment and personality appraisal to more direct relationships of a global nature when they reported:

> During the decade from 1930 to 1940, much attention was directed to methods of helping youth make appropriate educational and vocational choices, but developments in this area of interest were obscured during the following ten years by a shift in attention to the problems of clinical psychology. There was a tendency to consider the major problems of educational-vocational choice settled . . . [but] World War II caused attention to be directed toward personality dynamics and the role of learning in counseling and psychotherapy. [1955, p. 40]

Previous Reviews of the Rorschach in Academic-Vocational Appraisal

The specialized areas of clinical and counseling psychology combined forces in the common effort to fit individuals into specific academic and vocational situations. Instruments previously developed to appraise behavior were joined by the Rorschach, which moved from its exclusively clinical domain to a larger area of service. However, while the Rorschach's role has been reported in thousands of publications, Spiegelman had to qualify its use by pointing out that "the investigation, by means of the Rorschach, of the relations among vocational choice, success, adjustment, and personality is associated almost entirely with the name of Anne Roe" (1956, p. 439).

Also in *Developments in the Rorschach Technique,* Volume II (Klopfer et al., 1956), Snowden discussed the instrument in terms of assessing people who direct and administer organizational activities. Describing the clinical-industrial psychological approach, he suggested special applications of the Rorschach to appraise principal executives, study interpersonal relationships among top executives, and evaluate applicants for executive posts. No specific research in the industrial field was reported, but it was noted that the psychologist involved in group relationships with top management personnel

> has before him the richest sort of firsthand, continuously generating, raw data on the social behavior of the individuals in the group. If he also has available to him the Rorschach records of these individuals, he has the makings of a complex and arduous task, any progress in the accomplishment of which should contribute to his effectiveness in serving the individuals and the group. [Snowden, 1956, p. 587]

And further

> clinical psychologists working in industry have found new and fruitful uses for the Rorschach stemming out of the special demands of the field . . . the possibility for intensive, longitudinal, multilevel studies of normal productive individuals functioning together

> in a goal-directed hierarchical structure presents a challenging opportunity for much further research. [*Ibid.*, p. 592]

In 1956, Williams and Kellman introduced their chapter, "The Rorschach Technique in Industrial Psychology," with the statement:

> The youthfulness of the American movement in the utilization of projective techniques in vocational settings is marked by vigorous activity, as is evidenced by our lengthy (although selected) Rorschach bibliography covering its first ten productive years. [*Ibid.*, p. 545]

Publications dealing with various kinds and levels of occupational groups were cited, and training programs for several diverse areas were described. Selected Rorschach studies were also grouped according to the technique's administration as a group or individual tool. This survey of the literature to 1956 continues to be a valuable contribution, but its focus on method appears to be a displacement of emphasis. The important feature of the Rorschach—or, for that matter, the importance of any instrument employed to fulfill a specific task—is less the way in which it is administered or used than in how well it answers the problems in question. Instruments, audio-visual materials, lectures, and trips to the zoo may all merge together as media for solving particular assignments, teaching certain subjects, or evaluating individuals in delineated situations. They must be seen for what they are—instruments, processes, approaches to objectives. The danger of becoming "media-bound" would appear to express itself in a narrowing of focus and a lack of evaluation of the results attained.

More valid approaches in Williams and Kellman's chapter, however, are the suggestions that the Rorschach be used as one of a battery of instruments—projective and nonprojective—suggested by the needs of the vocational process under examination and that additional "objective data" be utilized to obtain an accurate clinical picture of the employee operating in his particular "work climate." Such information would include the personal and health histories, socio-economic-cultural adaptations, and general intellectual and educational data, as well as the job specifications, appraisals by both superiors and peers regarding the subject's adjustment, and an objective evaluation of the job performance. Certain goal-seeking principles for research in the industrial-psychological field are also specified:

1. Research design should be based on a holistic evaluation of the "vocational personality" within his life and work setting . . .
2. The use of batteries of projective instruments, as a part fulfillment of the first goal and as an interim technique until more inclusive designs are produced, will also minimize some of the trends toward "sign" and other mechanistic methods . . .
3. Development of clinical criteria in the validation of the Rorschach in vocational applications must be stimulated . . .
4. The development of fully descriptive "job specifications" for the vocations and professions under study will offer the best guarantee that employer and other "work climate" biases will be taken into account . . .
5. A corollary to the expanded use of the clinical method in vocational processes is the simultaneous expansion of training and retraining of clinicians for the industrial setting, and of industrial psychologists in the clinical method . . .
6. Specific configurational determinations for individual vocational entities . . . hold promise for the isolation of Rorschach factors . . . that could be of great practical and theoretical importance. Replication and validation studies, as well as extension of this approach to other positions and vocational categories, should be actively encouraged . . .
7. For a philosophical and methodological orientation in research in applied as well as experimental areas, we can do no better than to quote Hertz who suggested that the Rorschach . . . "is an instrument which works under the critical eye of the clinician. The task of the Rorschach worker, for the statistician, indeed for all who are are interested in personality theory and projective methods, is to find out why" (Hertz, 1951, p. 332).

[Williams and Kellman, 1956, pp. 573–575]

The concept of fields, classified in terms of interest areas and levels of educational and professional experience and training, was discussed by Hahn and MacLean (1955). Subsequently, Super noted that success has been defined generally as the level which is

> attained on the occupational ladder . . . [and] it is only in recent years that there is any indication from research that personality is related to success. Few studies had attempted to ascertain personality differences associated with occupational levels, and when the attempt was made (Paterson and Darley, 1936) the results were negative. As better methods have been tried, relationships between personality and occupational level have been found, in line with the substantial evidence that there are interest and value differences between occupational levels . . . The room for personality variations at each occupational level may be great enough to obscure the relationship between personality and success, but they have begun to merge. [Super, 1957, p. 236]

Pointing to the absence of comprehensive work with personality techniques in the field of occupational psychology, Roe suggested that in spite of limited evidence, there seemed to be no doubt that

> some specialized occupations, at least, do attract persons who resemble each other in some personality characteristics . . . Although those who follow a particular occupation may tend to show certain personality patterns more often than other patterns there will be many in the occupation who do not have a modal pattern. My own studies suggest that the deviates may have a particular contribution to make, in part because they may look at problems in slightly different ways than the others. It is probable that some basic correspondences, interests at least, are essential, and that the extent and number of deviations from the mode vary enormously from one occupational group to another. [1956, p. 80]

Reviewing the literature concerned with occupational fields and personality characteristics, Roe abstracted seventeen Rorschach studies of specialized occupational groups: social workers, insurance salesmen, metallurgists, engineers, physicists, biologists, paleontologists, psychologists, clergymen, anthropologists, organists, commercial artists, artists, and copywriters. Perhaps of greatest potential value in this context was the emphasis upon Maslow's (1950) hierarchical arrangement of basic needs for occupational selection. This concept —holistic, functional, and dynamic—would appear to have meaning for the understanding of motives which underlie the determination of particular behaviors and the choices of certain occupations by different types of individuals.

Snowden, Spiegelman, and Williams and Kellman, then, leaned positively toward projective devices for industrial assessment; and Roe also used the Rorschach, but with less enthusiasm. Patterson, however, was much less in favor of the technique for vocational counseling. He pronounced a lack of agreement with

> the general assumption that projective tests are, or would be, of great value in vocational counseling. The assumption does not appear to be supported by adequate evidence. This is not to imply that personality factors are not important in vocational success; they certainly are. But it has not been shown, in the opinion of the writer, that the aspects of personality tapped by projective tests bear any significant, useful relationships to vocational success. [1957, p. 535]

Supporting Kelly's disenchantment with the Rorschach (Kelly and Fiske, 1951) and Cronbach's (1955) suggestion to abandon its use except in research studies, Patterson continued:

> The widespread use of projective techniques, and their enthusiastic acceptance and extension in all areas of applied psychology, with so little critical analysis of their value, is amazing. Such techniques are not infrequently regarded as the criterion against which other evidence, including actual behavior, is judged. [*Ibid.,* pp. 550–551]

Still another review, limited in the number of cited publications but large in the extent of bias against the Rorschach, was that of Super and Crites. In reference to previous reviews, they summarized by stating that

> the evaluations of these reviewers have varied from optimistic enthusiasm for the Rorschach in the vocational setting to hypercritical rejection of it. The favorable comments have generally acknowledged the lack of empirical support for the vocational use of the Rorschach but have rationalized the negative research evidence by pointing to deficiencies in it or inadequacies in the experiments which have produced it; the unfavorable opinions have often been based upon exacting criteria of research excellence. [1962, p. 563]

Discussing two very early studies that attempted to predict success on the job with Rorschach performance (Pietrowski, 1944; Anderson, 1949) it was suggested that although personality patterns do not seem to differentiate occupations,

> it is quite possible that personality can act as a suppressor variable in the prediction of vocational success and vocational satisfaction. This is, given a particular pattern of aptitudes and interests, a worker may be more or less successful and satisfied in his job depending upon the extent to which his personality affects the fulfillment of his vocational capabilities. [*Ibid.,* p. 570]

They concluded that the Rorschach "may yet" be a valuable tool in vocational counseling but that much more is needed to be known.

Thus we see that both the history and the "review of reviews" present sometimes ambiguous and frequently contradictory findings. What, then, is the research picture for the literature not previously presented? How is the Rorschach seen today as it relates to occupational and academic predictions and patterns? The following portion of this chapter deals with material published from 1956 to 1968.

The Literature Since 1956

Today there is very little that remains unquestioned. Both individuals and organizations are subject to examination and, frequently, to attack. Developments in the areas of personality and environmental assessment suggest relationships between existing phenomena, but there is considerable confusion about relevant dimensions and the instruments used to appraise them. Among the techniques that have been under scrutiny is the Rorschach, and, in recent years especially, there have been published numerous pro and con discussions concerning its use. Some of these are founded upon definite research; others are clearly tinged with unrelated and subjective conclusions.

The purpose of this section on the Rorschach is to present current considerations about its function in occupational and academic settings, to discuss the relevant literature since 1956 and to support a major contention—that, basic to the many questions revolving about man and his world, there exists a certain foundation upon which to build new insights. The Rorschach is hardly the whole answer but, like other instruments, it can help point to some of the answers. Until better tools are developed and more definite criteria of behavior are designated, there is a need to refine the instruments currently available and to better understand their use. This section deals with the Rorschach as a means of learning more about people in prescribed vocational and educational situations.

Surveys

Both a review and a representative bibliography of studies concerning Rorschach content presented by Draguns, Haley, and Phillips (1969) may be of interest to those dealing with personality and occupational forces. On the other hand, Roe, who has done perhaps the most work in this area, reported with Mierzwa (1960) that only a handful of the investigations reported from 1957 to 1960 were concerned with Rorschach evaluations in occupational fields. In spite of some new books dealing with projective techniques, there have been fewer accounts of research with this instrument. Examinations of a number of journals, as well as a thorough search of *Psychological Abstracts,* indicates that the number of articles dealing with the Rorschach—as either focal point or medium employed—has declined substantially in the past four years, 1965–1968. This declination is even more marked when articles are considered which report the instrument's effectiveness in determining personality patterns of individuals engaged in specific vocations, delineating features of certain occupational "types," or making predictions of academic success and adjustment.

The literature reports a number of studies that employ the Rorschach for purposes of predicting occupational and/or academic success as well as investigations that use the Rorschach to describe particular characteristics of people functioning in specialized fields. In order to review a representative number of these reports, the material will be classified according to special fields of concentration. There are various other approaches that might be employed to further the purposes of this chapter—for example, examining the preponderance of certain determinants among special groups of people, describing degrees of constriction, utilizing form-level approaches in terms of the ego-strength construct. However, the emphasis here is on the Rorschach as a tool, technique, and medium, rather than as the major focus. Accordingly, its use is seen in terms of its contributions to understanding people engaged in various occupational and academic activities. The Rorschach, then, will be examined as it functions in reported studies of specialized activities: in medical and medically affiliated fields; the military; academic prediction studies; artistic-creative populations; management and industry; scientific fields; and teacher effectiveness.

Medical and Medically Affiliated Group Studies

Investigators in various fields have found that predictions of performance from academic to occupational situations pose intractable problems. In a large-scale effort to relate school activities and postgraduate success, the medical school performances of 507 physicians were correlated with their occupational effectiveness after graduation. Of 847 intercorrelations stemming from the earlier isolation of 200 variables, 97 percent were found to be of zero-order magnitude. These results suggested that "psychologically, performances in school-like situations do not closely resemble the performances in the world-of-work situations" (Taylor, Price, Richards, and Jacobsen, 1966, p. 3).

Other investigators have also attempted to discover particular characteristics that might isolate one subgroup of the population from others and that might define dimensions unique to special groups. This type of definition appears particularly important in situations where limited numbers of individuals are selected for highly professional activities. Society cannot afford to educate people who are not likely to function effectively in the areas for which they have been prepared. Similarly, potential candidates for specialized vocations need not expose themselves to excessive frustrations if the possibilities of failure or extreme dissatisfaction outweigh those of success. It is most important that selection of procedures be better developed—structured upon the available knowledge of people, specific occupations, typical environmental settings, and the way in which work areas fit into society's requirements.

Assuming that medical students differed sufficiently from other college students to invalidate the use of previously established "college student" norms, Rossi and Neuman (1961) examined 199 subjects. All four classes of medical students enrolled in the University of Utah College of Medicine were administered batteries of tests, including the Rorschach given in group form according to Harrower-Erickson and Steiner (1945). All protocols were scored according to Klopfer (1954), with the addition of the Beck (1933) Z score. In general, the results were consistent with the earlier medical students' norms published by Harrower-Erickson and Steiner (1945) and with theoretical expectations. There was not, however, the greater production of *At* percepts attributed earlier to medically affiliated groups by Molish, Molish, and Thomas (1950) and by Dorken (1954). And Rossi and Neuman's conclusion that the Rorschach can be profitably used to distinguish special subgroups was inconsistent with Eron's (1954) comparison of medical and divinity students, wherein the Rorschach was seen as an "unjustifiable" selective device for medical students. The facts that Eron's population consisted of only 35 medical and 35 divinity students and that these subjects were from Yale University, a school employing extremely careful initial selection procedures and conceivably choosing students who tend to demonstrate similar personality traits, may well account for the Rorschach's inability to distinguish subject matter subgroups.

Mindess' (1957) investigation of student nurses utilized four instruments: the Rorschach, the Wechsler-Bellevue Intelligence Scale (1944), a short case history form, and personal interviews. Before beginning nurses' training, 80 women ranging in age from 17 to 29 were interviewed, tested, and given a case history form to complete.

Each Rorschach protocol was scored according to the Klopfer method and, since ego strength was considered significant in the ability to cope with the stresses involved in nurses' training, each was also rated according to the Rorschach Prognostic Rating Scale (RPRS) (Klopfer, Ainsworth, Klopfer, and Holt, 1954). Twelve of the original 80 candidates dropped the program. The progress of the remaining 68 was followed for one year, during which time a series of academic grades and efficiency-on-ward ratings were obtained. These independent supervisor ratings were based upon four criteria: (1) dependability (Does the student attend to her duties?); (2) care of patient (Is her attitude pleasant?); (3) relationship with superiors (Does she resent authority?); and (4) relationship with peers (Does she work well in a team?). Product–moment correlations were computed for the pretraining test scores and actual training achievement indicated by a combination of grades and ratings.

The case histories appeared to be barren of any prognostic value, since every girl had sketched a rosy picture of her life and denied any serious problems; subsequently they were not utilized in the prediction of training success. Full-scale IQ scores obtained from the Wechsler, the total RPRS score, and a combination of these two scores were correlated with academic grades, ward ratings, and combined nurses' grades. Results showed that the academic grades and ward ratings correlated at .439; the IQ and academic grades at .434, and the IQ and combined nursing grades at .457 (all significant at the .01 level). When correlated separately, the ward ratings did not significantly relate to either IQ or RPRS but the RPRS academic grade correlation of .281 was significant at the .05 level. The multiple correlation of the IQ and the RPRS and the total nurses' ratings (academic grades and ward evaluations) was .50, again significant at the .01 level. Intelligence, as measured by the Wechsler, and ego strength, as assessed by the RPRS, were thus found to be significantly related to achievement in nurses' training.

In appraising this study, it was suggested that Mindess' report pointed to a

> quite serious problem in reasoning from success in training and success on the job. . . . It is particularly important in studies of

> physicians, nurses, therapists, etc. That is that actual performance in the occupation may not be (and probably is not) sufficiently closely related to grades and other training measures to make studies of students of any marked utility in this field. Here note that ward grades, which one can reasonably assume most closely represent professional performance, are not related to either of the test measures used. [Roe and Mierzwa, 1960, p. 285]

Even if the ward grades had been highly related to the other measures, however, this would still have been an indication based upon prediction of success during the training period, not success in actual job performance. While one may well argue that ward ratings would be highly related to future on-the-job ratings, we do not yet know what the important underlying factors might be in the students' performances in training. This is consistent with findings from the large study of physicians (Taylor, Price, Richards, and Jacobsen, 1966), reported earlier, which strongly indicated the negative relationships between academic prediction and postgraduate success. What would be extremely helpful in this regard would be a longitudinal study of pretraining prediction, training and/or academic success evaluation, and posttraining appraisal. The latter measures should be based upon success on the job as defined by predetermined criteria, success with both "superiors" and colleagues or fellow-workers, and intra-individual successes as determined by the assessees' own evaluations of their occupational satisfactions.

Holt and Luborsky (1958) used the Rorschach as a major instrument in their study of psychiatrists at the Menninger Foundation. The results of this large-scale investigation suggested that when the Rorschach, Strong, and Wechsler-Bellevue scores were examined statistically, the multiple correlations were less valid than clinical evaluations utilizing the Rorschach and Wechsler as principal instruments. The special Thematic Apperception Test manual that was developed on this same project proved to be more successful than the Rorschach manual, although the authors suggested that further study might be fruitful in yielding more efficient clues. They also reported that no brief battery of procedures was better than that used by the

Admissions Committee and that a "single projective technique was *not* adequate for this kind of prediction. Even though the Rorschach or TAT cannot be used alone, they probably do contribute usefully in the context of a rounded body of data" (Holt and Luborsky, 1958, p. 215).

An important point stemming from this study was that the investigator who studies "normals" should be aware of the enormous range of all types of responses and should realize that many techniques do not provide sufficient information about such issues as adequate coping behavior. It was suggested that

> a special word of caution may be in order regarding the Rorschach test for anyone who has not had considerable experience in giving it to intelligent persons who are not seeking treatment. An applicant often perceives the Rorschach situation as one in which he ought to let himself go as much as possible, give free-associative material, or demonstrate the liveliness of his imagination by what are essentially primary process operations in his perceptual-associative functioning. The result often bears a superficial resemblance to schizophrenic productions: There may be extensive autistic elaborations, arbitrary combinations or fusions of images, or a massing of sexual content. If the tester has any doubt, he can quickly establish the true nature of these productions by re-administering the test with the instructions to leave out that kind of material; when it is truly pathological in origin, the subject cannot long exclude it from consciousness. Internal checks on the significance of such material, whether it represents pathological break-throughs or regression in the service of the ego, can be seen in the preservation of formal properties such as the accuracy of form perception, the balance of locations and determinants, or the like. [*Ibid.,* p. 326]

Roe and Mierzwa pointed out that the major result of this study was "the demonstration of just how complex the selection problem is, and how inadequate our techniques still are. Inadequate still, but not without promise" (1960, p. 284).

Still viewing the Rorschach in terms of special population subgroups, Thomas, Ross, and Freed (1965) examined 586 medical students at Johns Hopkins. In a two-volume publication, the authors suggested that the Rorschach responses of their subjects permitted an objective approach to Rorschach evaluation and that, since the responses resembled in many ways responses of college students and college graduates, they provided normative data for young adults of superior intelligence in general and for medical students in particular. Regarding the frequency of key words included in the Area Index, it was suggested that

> with this analysis as a guide . . . , the actual 'popularity' of popular responses in a given group of subjects may be judged and potential new popular percepts detected. In this way, the *P* score for the Rorschach test may be brought into relationship with considerations of time, place, and person. In addition popular descriptive and verbal terms may be identified. On the other hand, the significance of the unusual or 'sick' response may be greatly enhanced if it can be expressed in precise terms as to its degree of uniqueness for the particular group under study. [Vol. II, p. xxxiv]

In his foreword to Volume I, Lenkau wrote that the large-scale systematic indexing of Rorschach responses through the use of a computer program resulted from the continued attempts to find ways in which collected data could be more "scientifically productive." He pointed out that the particular method of computerizing and tabulating data

> represents a new and modern method for communicating the content and location of responses of a large group of protocols for comparison with other groups and also furnishes a normative standard against which other highly intelligent groups may be measured. It offers a new approach, not yet fully explored . . . for judging deviations from the norm by particular individuals. [1964, p. vi]

The efficient processing of valuable data is only one answer to one problem, although certainly a significant problem. Any attempt to program material about medical students should be considered in terms of the demands of the medical profession "in field."—What, indeed, is the role of the physician in the urban society? Among rural populations? In a society where systems like organized medical programs may offer potential solutions to caring for vast numbers of people? In areas where the physician still functions as a free practitioner? What are the features that make for success in practice after the student has graduated from medical school? Are these related to the type of school he attended, the type of person he is or the setting in which he has chosen to work?—These are just a few of the many questions that demand answers if we are to understand the medical man of today and tomorrow.

Military Applications

Since 1965, little has been written about the Rorschach's application in military selection and appraisal, in spite of the fact that our current war efforts have focused the attention of many Americans on the military. In the literature searched, only two investigations appeared relevant to this subject.

The study by Rohrer, Hoffman, Bagby, Herrmann, and Wilkins was not discussed in reviews previously cited, although it was published in 1955. One thousand Marine candidates for officer's commissions and 374 Navy officers were administered the Rorschach in group form. The results suggested that the group Rorschach did not differ from the individually administered Rorschach in information obtained and that, when used for research purposes, the group method was superior to the individual approach. This finding is inconsistent with Molish's (1956) review of the Rorschach in military psychology and psychiatry, where it was pointed out that the use of large-scale Rorschach techniques previously applied to problems of selection and screening large military populations had not provided encouraging results. However, the limitations of the instrument for prognostic purposes were not necessarily considered a function of the technique itself but of the inadequate norms, statistics, and criteria for comparing groups and, especially, the current lack of knowledge about the possible compatibility between the various neurotic mechanisms and successful military adjustment. The Rorschach was found to be most valuable in decisions regarding the fitness of particular subjects where there is a question of adjustment to a special military environment. Especially in "stress situations induced by combat conditions, the use of the test has great value in determining how pathological the reaction to stress may be and whether removal from the forward combat area is advisable" (Molish, 1956, p. 816). Again, as with the OSS findings, the importance of relating test findings to social and environmental structures becomes apparent.

Like industry and other occupational areas, the military might be considered in terms of Roe's field/level hypothesis (1954), where field points to the activity focus and level suggests the amount of responsibility involved. One might, for example, function in military systems at several different levels. By separating these levels and appraising the individual according to the particular level at which he will be expected to operate, the predictability of tools like the Rorschach might well be increased. This same concern for levels might apply also when people are considered for promotions. The excellent chief petty officer may possess the apparent prerequisites for advancement, but certain other factors, such as a lack of organizational ability, may be operating to prevent him from becoming an effective Naval warrant officer. Conversely, if he has worked in a particular capacity for a number of years, he may not possess the necessary abilities to adapt to new positions; thus, a promotion would not be desirable. This concept of levels, of course, must not be regarded as only applicable to the military. It operates in all occupational fields.

Academic Areas

The literature dealing with the prediction of academic performance is probably as voluminous as any of the material concerned with the educational world. In spite of this tremendous interest and, occasionally, the deep insight into the people and the problems, and in spite of new and refined techniques to measure human effectiveness, we still know little about what ingredients make for success in different academic enterprises. The most general and, simultaneously, the most accurate statement is that success or failure in education continues to be judged on previous successes or failures. Questions of learning ability, motivation, and teaching techniques remain subordinate to that point. Attempting to predict success in life on the basis of academic grades attained is, however, a precarious exercise. Hoyt's review of 46 studies relating grade point averages and adult achievement corroborates the ineffectiveness of college performances as the predictor of future success. From these investigations it was concluded that "college grades have no more than a very modest correlation with adult success no matter how defined" (1965, p. 45), although suggestions were offered for the more effective control of differences among colleges and work settings and for more adequate definitions of criteria and measuring devices to assess adult achievements.

Before going into the very few studies in which the Rorschach has been used recently for purposes of academic prediction, brief reference will be made to some studies conducted prior to 1956 which have not been previously reviewed in the literature examined. None of these investigations change the presently rather discouraging picture of judging academic "success"—and one might well ask, just what does academic success really mean in and to the life pattern of an individual? However, the research needs to be mentioned, if only because it may suggest future directions for examination, just as the work with physicians and medically related personnel described earlier also has implications for extended studies with different populations.

Much has been written about the relationship of Rorschach *W*:*M* responses, intellectual aspiration and organizational interest (Beck, 1933; Klopfer, Kirkner, et al., 1954; Hertz, 1960). However, Ryan (1951) reported that the Rorschach failed to differentiate between academic underachievers and overachievers. In another study of academic achievement (Prest and Ryan, 1953), Davidson's (1950) 19 signs of adjustment did not discriminate among overachievers, normal achievers, and underachievers, although there were nonlinear relationships between certain Rorschach variables and achievement. These led to a portrayal of the overachiever as overconventional and conforming (high *P*); practical minded: tending to "see what is there" and exhibiting stereotyped thinking (high *A*); manifesting "little introversion or self-preoccupation" (as indicated by low *M*) and "probably immature" (*FM*). This type of analysis, based upon the examination of Rorschach configurations in well-defined groups at different levels of achievement, appears to be a potentially productive line of procedure which necessitates further research.

Again using Rorschach configurations in association with college achievement, McArthur and King (1954) found that protocols dominated by inanimate movement and color responses differentiated two groups of subjects: 137 referrals to Harvard's Department of Hygiene for academic and/or personality difficulties and 74 controls, Harvard upper classmen selected at random from the student list. In a study by Cooper (1955), 77 male and female freshmen students were given the Ohio State Psychological Test (Toops, 1940) and a modified version of the group Rorschach, scored by Munroe's (1941) Inspection Method. The test data were correlated with grade point averages for three semesters' school work. The Ohio State predicted grades with a correlation of approximately .50; the Rorschach and grades were not significantly related for the women, but for male students the correlation was significant at the .05 level. These findings did not concur with Munroe's earlier studies with college women at Sarah Lawrence, wherein the Rorschach proved a better predictor of independent faculty ratings of students' academic standings than did the ACPE (1951) test of general scholastic aptitude. That Munroe's results have not been replicated in other investigations may be due to the fact that schools in which traditional marking systems are employed differ from experimental colleges such as Sarah Lawrence. In this context, Cronbach suggested that we need inquiry which will point out "the elements or patterns in the Rorschach (that may be associated with particular behaviors and criteria) rather than to attempt blind prediction of marks or over-all ratings" (1950, p. 81).

The literature just cited was published prior to 1956. Since that time, the material searched yielded only three investigations dealing with either Rorschach prediction of school performance or with Rorschach responses of children in different grades. At the elementary level, Ledwith (1959) studied 291 children between the ages of 6 and

11 who were divided into a longitudinal group of 138 subjects and a control group of 153. The children in the longitudinal group were tested annually for six consecutive years; thus, a total of 981 Rorschach protocols were analyzed and normative data were provided for twenty Rorschach indices: *R, W, D, d, Dd, S, F, M, FM, m, CF, K, FK, c, C′, FC, C, A, H,* and *P*.

Three hundred fifty-six entering freshmen at Adelphi College were also tested upon college entrance, and at the end of the first year each was assigned quality points (Sopchak, 1958). Tetrachoric correlations between these points and the test scores showed that (1) the relationship of high school grades and the Rorschach was low; (2) the California reading and language test scores were related to the ACPE scores, but the combination of the two did not relate to the Rorschach except at a low level; (3) high school averages correlated better with quality points than any psychological test—the usual result for such investigations. Munroe's findings were not supported.

Schmeidler, Nelson, and Bristol (1959) used the Rorschach as both a decision-making and a predictive tool. Six hundred thirty-three freshmen at Barnard College were given the Rorschach in groups or, in a few cases, responded to a self-administered form. Protocols were scored according to Munroe's technique and then divided into three groups in the ratio of 1:2:1 good, fair, and poor adjustment. After the students' expected four-year period at school had expired, their college records were scored for such features as academic honors, withdrawal before graduation, extracurricular honors, probation time, engagement in few extracurricular activities, and evidence of severe psychological difficulties. The Rorschach ratings of adjustment, examined also after the four-year period, showed "significant or suggestive" relationships in the anticipated direction to each of the above criteria of college performance. It was found that the 58 women who had been rated as potentially creative achieved more honors and showed different college records from the other students. Thus, even when the Rorschach was

> given and interpreted under less than ideal conditions, and even when the qualitatively different diagnoses . . . are disregarded,

> Rorschach findings are relevant to college behavior. Since, further, many of the criteria for college performance applied to actions in the junior and senior years, and the Rorschachs were administered at the beginning of the freshman year, our data indicate that the Rorschach can make successful group predictions over a fairly long time span, during a period of life when considerable personality change ordinarily occurs. [*Ibid.,* p. 33]

The authors, all members of the college staff, felt that both they and the class advisors

> could reach their decisions about students more readily and with more confidence when they could consult the Rorschach interpretations. Since they wisely do not make decisions on the basis of these interpretations alone, they probably use them chiefly to suggest new directions to consider in a difficult case, or to confirm their ideas in doubtful cases. The pattern of use over the four years of college indicates that the test was helpful both when they were forming first impressions of the students, and also, later, when they had grown to know the students more intimately . . . In making more specific recommendations, we suggest that there are at least four areas in which Rorschach interpretations can profitably be used in a college setting: psychotherapy, social encouragement, academic advice, and vocational guidance . . . In every case where psychotherapy had been recommended on the basis of the Rorschach it had been needed . . . A girl who tries too hard to be noticed, but whose Rorschach indicates that she respects and accepts adult authority, might in the course of conferences with a staff member be given hints or outright advice.

Regarding academic performance,

> the general relevance of Rorschach ratings to college performance suggests that interpretations in this area can tentatively be accepted as valid . . . and potential academic difficulties can . . . be spotted in the Rorschach . . . As for suggested limitations of college use of freshman Rorschach, the flexibility of human behavior accounts for some of the changes in . . . actual behavior. The test may be valid at one time and yet change later. [*Ibid.,* p. 36]

In an effort to clarify the concept of the "normal" personality, 64 outstanding men and women—all elected student council members of three small liberal arts colleges—were studied over a two-year period of time, with normality defined as

> the ability to maintain an harmonious and productive relationship with the environment and with the self. The normal person was assumed to be a "going concern", able to maintain a reasonably positive balance between outer pressures and inner needs without intolerable expenditures by the environment or by the self. [Cox, 1956, p. 70]

The Rorschach and TAT were administered individually; each student also took a scholastic aptitude test and engaged in six hours of interviews with a staff psychiatrist. In addition, the parents were interviewed by a case worker in the student's home. On the basis of a psychiatrist's appraisal, each student was classified into one of three groups: Group A (approximately 43 percent of the total population) maintained a high level of functioning with apparent ease; Group B (36 percent) bought adjustment at an appreciable cost, showing some neurotic traits; Group C (approximately 19 percent) "struggled with great insecurity or hostility, or both, and seemed to be less successful than the others in maintaining the outward aspect of smooth adjustment" (Cox, 1956, p. 71) .

After analysis of the material, results were compared with a set of data that had been derived from another group (D) of 22 students who were known to be neither comfortably nor successfully adjusted in their college communities. It was found that the mean numbers of Rorschach responses for the four groups were not statistically significant (Group A offered 39.4 responses; Group B, 46.8; Group C, 39.9; and Group D, 30.9) and that there was no single refusal of a plate with the student council groups and but one with group D. There was, however, wide variability in *M* production (ranging from 0 to 30 responses), the results showing essentially that emotional disturbance (in Group A) tended to deplete *M* production in both quantity and quality. Student council members were predominantly introversive, with differences between the groups here being statistically significant. Several indices of favorable adjustment were consistent with the categories into which the students were placed. Other significant signs were determined by employing two new quantitative measures: a Morbidity Score, stemming from content, and a Discomfort Score, derived by summing *m, k,* and *K* responses. It was suggested that further comparisons be made by studying students in psychiatric treatment since the results of this investigation seemed to be "getting at genuine differences between the comfortable and effective personality and one that is somewhat less so" (*ibid.,* p. 77).

An incidental finding with a group of undergraduate students is relevant to issues regarding the Rorschach as predictor of academic success. Kleinman and Higgins (1966) found that the 49 females in their investigation produced more human movement responses than did the 49 males. This was similar to but statistically more significant than Felzer's results and was interpreted as stemming from "differential sex-role expectations concerning the use of fantasy" (1955, p. 440).

Although decidedly limited in populations, studies such as these may eventually lead to better understanding of the college student and to better means of helping him with his occupational choices. This is consistent with the position expressed by the College Entrance Board (1963) when it suggested that research with "existing personality" or "non-intellective" tests should be encouraged because no available instrument is yet sufficiently studied to warrant acceptance for admission decisions. One of the problems in using the Rorschach in large-scale studies of college students, of course, is related to difficulties in time. Such publications as the Johns Hopkins' volumes (Thomas, Ross, and Freed, 1965) and further developments in computer retrieval systems for specialized information dissemination (Gorham, 1965; 1967) may allow further extension of the technique.

Throughout this section on the Rorschach and academic performance/prediction, there has been an underlying emphasis which views individual evaluation, no matter how accurate, as dependent upon accurate evaluation of the environment. In 1962, Pace pointed out that

> there is a long and distinguished history of research on the characteristics of college students . . . but there is no comparable history of research aimed at describing the characteristics of colleges . . . the experiences and conditions for student learning and living which the college provides . . . define the environment, the college culture, the campus atmosphere. [Pace, 1962, pp. 44, 45]

Suggesting that the model for studying behavior is the interaction between personality needs and environmental press, as prescribed by Murray (1938), Pace further described the press of the college environment "as a kind of operational definition of objectives or major emphases" (Pace, 1962, p. 61). In order that our understanding of college students be valid and meaningful, it must be met by an appropriate degree of knowledge about the types of schools in which they function, the predetermined criteria of success in those situations and, finally, the relationships of the students' personality characteristics to the many facets of the collegiate atmosphere. Only under such a structure can the many attempts to predict academic performance have value for both the special populations in question and similar groups that will follow.

Studies of Artistic Groups

Creativity, of course, knows no set boundaries. It is a concept that cuts across all efforts to separate vocational and academic situations from solely psychodiagnostic ones. In this respect, many studies conducted on the so-called creative person and many investigations seeking to establish ways of isolating certain types of "creativity" are essentially involved with particular groups of individuals, although their primary purpose may not have been the description of group characteristics. Although creativity is not limited to artistic groups, for the purposes of this chapter the concept will be discussed only in terms of specialized artistic subgroups.

Patterns of cognitive functioning characterizing creative individuals rather than questions of motivation, ego processes, or related activities occurring during the actual creative process [1] were examined by Hersch (1962). His study was based on the conceptual framework of Werner (1957), who described development in terms of degrees of differentiation and integration and postulated the ability to utilize processes at varying developmental levels. This progression–regression phenomena may be depicted in terms of value judgments of good–bad or developmental functioning of maturity–primitivity; self-actualization and dedifferentiation of ego boundaries (Maslow, 1950); and "regression in the service of the ego" (Kris, 1952) wherein normally preconscious or unconscious material becomes accessible to consciousness. The hypothesis tested was that "in situations in which responses can be developmentally ordered, creators will show a more ready availability of both relatively mature and relatively primitive responses than non-creators" (Hersch, 1962, p. 193).

Sixty subjects were divided into three groups, relatively homogeneous in terms of age and intelligence:

1. Twenty eminent artists, chosen from Roe's (1946b) data, all of whom had made cultural contributions that have been generally acknowledged.
2. Twenty individuals who were in no way distinguished for creativity in any culturally ascribed form and from whom there were no indications of psychosis.
3. A schizophrenic group of 14 hospitalized patients described as "of the paranoid type" and six patients whose diagnoses of schizophrenia were distributed among other sub-classifications.

Rorschachs were administered individually to each of the 60 subjects. The responses were classified developmentally according to the Genetic Scoring System (Phillips, Kaden, and Weldman, 1959), which rates categorized responses as relatively primitive or mature, following Werner's rationale. Of the six response categories studied, Movement, Integrative, and Form Dominant Responses were considered to be mature; Form Subordinate, Physiognomic, and Primitive Thought Responses were seen as primitive. Artists gave more Move-

---

[1] For an encompassing study of the creative process, see Koestler's *The Act of Creation* (New York: Macmillan Co., 1964).

ment and Form Dominant Responses than did the schizophrenics and also more Physiognomic Responses. Neither the Form Subordinate nor the Primitive Thought Responses discriminated significantly between the two groups. Physiognomic Responses, including those in which the blots are considered to have affective and symbolic qualities ("gay," "troubled," "unhappy") were offered in only six cases in the combined normal and schizophrenic groups; 49 such responses were offered by the artists. Hersch concluded his report by noting that

> the creator is able to subordinate and utilize his primitive operations in a manner that is rare in schizophrenia . . . the primitive functioning of the creator is more circumscribed, with mature operations readily available while the schizophrenic is relatively limited to genetically early functioning . . . [Therefore] we might say that for the creator primitive operations may be exploited toward the production of the highest cultural achievements, while for the schizophrenic primitive operations serve the pathological purposes of symptom formation. [1962, p. 198]

The statement is similar to Barron's remarks about the creative process:

> there are times when it is a mark of greater health to be unruly, and a sign of greater inner resources to be able to upset one's own balance and to seek a new order of selfhood.
>
> The ability to permit oneself to become disorganized is . . . quite crucial to the development of a very high level of integration. Because we are capable of reflecting upon ourselves, we are committed, willy-nilly, to an artistic enterprise in the creation of our own personality . . .
>
> Certain facts concerning temporary upset and agitation in especially healthy or potentially healthy persons can thus be explained in terms of the creative act necessary in order to achieve integration at the most complex level. [1963, p. 4]

In Eiduson's (1958) comparison of artist and non-artist, the TAT and the Rorschach were administered to a group of "normal" artists, a group of neurotic artists, and a control group of non-artist businessmen. The artists showed the most marked differences in their ways of thinking and perceiving and were more original, unusual, and novel than the business-oriented subjects. They also appeared to be more sensitive to their own needs as well as to the needs of others. The characteristics found typical of the artists are not those that later typically harden into neurotic patterns.

A more recent investigation of the relationship between artistic creativity and Rorschach responses was an outgrowth of previous findings suggesting that production of whole responses held up more consistently than other Rorschach variables in designating artistic creativity (Anderson and Munroe, 1948; Harrower and Cox, 1943). Rawls and Boone (1967) attempted to statistically verify the power of whole response production as discriminating between artists and non-artists and to evaluate the effectiveness of this power by increasing whole response production through a specific instructional set. Under a set of regular instructions and a whole response set, the number, quality, and percentage of whole responses produced by a group of 16 male and 8 female artists were compared with similar responses of 16 male and 8 female non-artists. Both groups of subjects offered a greater number of wholes under the *W* response set, but the artists produced a significantly greater number of *W*'s, regardless of set. Under the instructional set to produce only whole responses, the artists scarcely increased their own production while the non-artists almost doubled their percentages of acceptable wholes. The questions might thus be asked: Is there a relationship between Rorschach whole response production and artistic creativity? And if whole response ability can be increased through a specific response set for non-artists, can non-artists be taught to develop a whole perceptibility that also encourages artistic expression in them? Upon further examination of the Rorschach protocols, it was suggested that artists are not nearly as inhibited as non-artists in their impressions and responses, that artists more frequently offer percepts of an abstract nature, and that they are less stimulus bound and less concrete than non-artists.

> Precision alternatives occurred far more frequently among non-artists. This type of response appeared most often under the whole

> response set when a subject's supply of whole responses for a particular stimulus was already limited. In an effort to increase the number of responses, the non-artist, in essence, began repeating himself. Thus, artistic creativity appears to be reflected by facility in change of set which manifests itself in greater production of different whole responses. [Rawls and Boone, 1967, pp. 21–22]

Management and Industrial Positions

In 1955 it was suggested that while clinical psychology has contributed greatly to personnel appraisal with its techniques for exploring motivations and dynamics, data from projective techniques must be matched with specific requirements of a job situation and used to explore human functioning rather than human deviation and disintegration (Brower, 1955). In view of this position and Snowden's (1956) more enthusiastic regard for the Rorschach's value in industrial and organizational assessment, it is interesting to note that only a limited number of studies have been devoted to these special problems. A plausible reason for this disregard may be the barrage of criticism flung at psychological testing by the 1966 Congressional Inquiry into Testing. The unique green-covered *American Psychologist's* (1965) special issue on testing and public policy presented a series of diverse positions by Inquiry participants. Since testing for governmental positions and testing for other administrative organizations share certain common semblances, much that was written in this journal is pertinent to our concern here. Several speakers, for example, denounced psychological tests because they "were not based on scientific evidence" or were "of little value" in personnel work. Smith stated that

> the validity of tests for predicting training or educational achievement is quite different from their validity for predicting performance in actual work. Generally speaking, we have no tests or test batteries which validly predict performance in areas of special talent or skill such as art, music, creative writing, medicine, engineering, executive ability, or scientific research. [*Ibid.*, p. 909]

Conversely, Brayfield suggested that he knew of "no other professional tool which has matched the effectiveness of psychological tests in assisting individuals to realize their civil and human rights," (1965, p. 889) and Ives (1965) pointed out that

> personality testing, interpreted by a competent professional psychologist, will in my opinion give a better evaluation of what the person is really like than other methods short of prolonged personality study. The tests which might be compared to x-ray of the personality, when combined with other evidence . . . , should provide our best present means of deciding whether a given person will be suitable, for example, to represent us abroad, as in the Peace Corps, or undertake highly secret or specialized work as in the intelligence service . . . I prefer . . . the more subtle so-called projective tests such as the Rorschach or Thematic Apperception Test, administered as part of a complete battery. [*Ibid.,* p. 899]

Supporting test use in the Peace Corps, Shriver said that

> in our selection process, we will continue to employ qualified professionals who can apply their skills, tact, sensitivity, and validity. Our psychologists have said, and our experience has borne them out, that a selection process must depend on a conglomeration of considerations. No one test, nor any one procedure, can be counted upon. [*Ibid.,* pp. 876–877]

Still other statements raised questions for further investigation:

> There are many other problems, not only in selection, but in all areas of personnel management, that cry out for new insights and better measurement tools . . . I see a compelling need for research concentration on questions like these:
>
> How can we understand the real nature of work and the meaning of work in relation to changes in occupational demands and opportunities?
>
> How can we place people in those positions where they can contribute most to their organizations as they satisfy their own career needs?
>
> How can we improve the appraisal of those qualities of personality and experience which are not amenable to objective written testing?

> How can we understand better and apply more effectively the processes of human observation and judgment essential to all of the facets of personnel management—in selection, in performance appraisal, and so on? [Macy, 1965, p. 884]

Pertinent to the general problem of industrial testing, Michael suggested that Bloom's taxonomic system for describing curriculum objectives in behavioral terms could be extended to the assessment of various job requirements, including top management.

> Almost any suggestion that could be made as to possible ways in which psychological tests might be designed to yield higher predictive validities has probably occurred to each of the testing experts . . . The pressing need is to obtain more nearly adequate criterion measures. At the risk of restating the obvious, one could say that two broad avenues exist for the realization of higher validities in differential tests . . . improving communication . . . (and) continuous research and development. [1957, p. 486]

Of the few recent publications concerned with the Rorschach's use in industrial management, Piotrowski and Rock's *Perceptanalytic Executive Scale* (1963) is the largest single work. Included in this material, of interest to both the trained psychologist and the personnel manager, is a survey of the literature which identifies characteristics of successful business executives. The scale is based upon the process of Rorschach interpretation described earlier by Piotrowski (1957) and contains

> no fixed traits but perceptanalytic personality elements that are hardly ever manifested in overt behavior in their pure form . . . [It also] contains no fixed traits that a visual inspection of the executive would reveal. We can validate our scale only by checking the . . . conclusions drawn from scores computed from the entire scale with its six parts, or inferred from one or several parts . . . The exceptional person with great strength and potentialities is not penalized . . . The scale, and especially the entire ink blot test record, are equally sensitive to desirable and undesirable action-tendencies and attitudes. The scale measures attitudes and drives determining achievement on the job; it provides an inventory of particular assets or weaknesses. [1963, p. 11]

Stemming from the more traditional approaches to Rorschach interpretation, this development was described in terms of thirty-two test component signs. Fifteen of the signs were considered to be positive indices and seventeen negative. A protocol's final score is derived by finding the algebraic sum of the weights (varying from +4 to −3 points assigned to each sign) of the positive signs minus the weights of the negative signs. Part One of the scale is concerned with human movement responses, Part Two with animal movement responses, and Part Three "contains a variety of miscellaneous test components other than movement responses" (*ibid.,* p. 34). Similar scales might be developed upon this type of rationale and designed for different populations.

Another departure from the traditional Rorschach technique is the Structured-Objective Rorschach Test (SORT), designed by Stone (1958) so that people who have had no special training in administration, scoring, and interpretation of the traditional Rorschach could use the standard blots. The SORT was developed to measure temperament patterns in vocational and personnel counseling, with the manual providing norms for an adult sample of over 8000 subjects: professional and semi-professional groups, students, mechanical workers, office workers, and salesmen. SORT ratings have been validated against supervisory ratings with a high degree of correlation, but much further research is needed because many studies employing it have concentrated on clinical problems rather than on vocational situations (Langer, 1962; Langer, Hayes, and Sharp, 1963; Langer and Hicks, 1966; Weinlander, 1967).

Hicks and Stone (1962) evaluated the SORT's effectiveness in discriminating between successful and unsuccessful managers by administering a comprehensive battery of tests to 76 supervisors of a medium-sized operation. Ratings by both peers and superiors of overall performance, promotability, and versatility were related to test results, with the SORT correlating highest with supervisors' evaluations of versatility. In a study using Beck's (1933) Z score, the Z failed to differentiate among non-executive groups, skilled, semi-skilled, and unskilled, although it reflected some characteristics of top-level managers (Otis, 1959). Phelan investigated "the relationship between performance of a battery of predictors as to promotion to administrative positions and the ultimate promotion and success in promotion of the men in question" (1962, p. 102). A fairly heterogeneous group of 94 nonadministrative men from 18 industrial organizations, ranging in age from 18 to 43 and in education from high school to specialized college majors, were examined for first-line supervisory positions. Each man was rated in terms of promotability. Eventually, one man from each industrial group was promoted to a management position and in 12 of the 18 groups the person subsequently promoted was also independently selected by the personnel man. In spite of the acknowledged variance among management positions in different companies and the difficulties in specifying job descriptions, predictions regarding fitness for administrative positions were found to be feasible. The holistic approach to test interpretation yield higher correlations with the criterion (prediction of promotability to administrative positions) than did individual objective test scores. Projective tests, taken singly, did not predict promotability of a highly significant level, but the Rorschach and TAT responses combined were the best predictors (median rho $= .56$; $p = .10$).

Perhaps a fruitful way of looking at top management is in terms of general traits, special attributes, and awareness of the job requirements. For example, people in industry functioning at top administrative levels are expected to be intelligent—but intelligent in what ways? Are the best qualified people the ones who can interact with others on social levels? Are they able to integrate material at highly developed conceptual levels? Are they adaptable in the sense of being willing to adjust to new ideas and new processes or do they build on past experiences? What part do innovation tendencies play in the role of top managers? These are questions that might be asked; perhaps their answers may be found in Rorschach protocols that are interpreted in terms of both content and certain qualitative ratios: *M: W; M: (FC, CF+C)*; form-level ratings of specific cards; etc. It is very possible that top management in various occupations offers similar Rorschach records, but this, as well as other hypotheses, demands verification.

Scientific Fields

The literature prior to 1955 reports a fair number of studies in which the Rorschach was used to delineate special characteristics of people operating in specific scientific areas. Many of these investigations were conducted by Roe—scientists and technicians (1946a), biologists (1950), physical scientists (1950), anthropologists (1952), and psychologists (1952). Since 1955, however, only one report in the literature searched deals with the Rorschach as a medium for studying scientists. Eiduson's study of scientists in their psychological worlds suggests the prevailing tendency to stereotype the scientist.

> The "inspirational" and mystical hypotheses had supported the idea that the origin and nature of the scientist's creative mental processes were unknown, that separation and uniqueness were somehow essential ingredients of his creative productivity, and that all attempts to study creativity intimately would run the risk of destroying the very things that they set out to investigate. [1962, p. 7]

Scientists—Their Psychological World is an account of 40 male physical scientists engaged in research pursuits. Exploiting the myths and the mysteries, this book may be viewed as an interaction of clinical, social, and occupational dimensions of its subjects. The sample itself was smaller than but similar to Roe's populations; it consisted of 16 biologists, 12 chemists, 6 geologists, and 6 physicians who ranged in age from 28 to 65 years, with a mean of 41.7 years. All held the doctoral degree, had been in science for an average of fifteen years beyond their graduate work, and were affiliated with a university or other academic installation on the West Coast. Their work activities varied from positions in which they did all the experimental or theoretical work themselves to directing research by others, from teaching to administrative duties. Their academic ranks ranged from full to assistant professors and their publications varied in number from the most prolific's output of over 200 scientific books and articles to a minimum of three. All, however, considered themselves to be research scientists.

These men were examined from five different points of view: (1) developmental histories and personal backgrounds; (2) adult personality structures; (3) cognitive styles; (4) self-images; and (5) relationships to their nonscientific worlds—family, community, work and play patterns. Through both actuarial and clinical procedures, the comparative study of the 40 subjects elicited common denominators of personality and behavior. The Rorschach and the TAT, augmented by open-ended depth interviews, provided psychological data which were, subsequently, independently submitted to three clinical psychologists and rated according to assigned variables. These ratings described the subjects' "characteristics of thinking and perceiving, their personality structures and emotional pictures, the kinds of motivation to which they respond—variables culled from the literature on the creative person in general, and the scientist in particular" (*ibid.*, p. 4). This special way of translating clinical data into a selected rating scale seems to be a particularly valuable way to treat psychological test results.

The personality appraisals showed that the subjects had "emotional and motivational characteristics . . . [which were] more different than alike" (*ibid.*, p. 113). They were similar, however, in some respects—in their intense involvements with things intellectual, in their wide-ranged emotional responses to the work structure, in their emotional independence and in the tremendous role of self invested in their work. Their greatest similarities—in fact, the only ways in which they were all alike—existed in their cognitive approaches. All had developed certain ways of thinking and perceiving, of combining and reorganizing percepts. Interestingly, in describing their own creative processes, these men—who had been trained in the objective, the rational and logical—showed "a high degree of respect for the irrational, the unconscious" (*ibid.*, p. 145).

Teachers and Teachers-in-Training

The many attempts to predict teacher performance have failed to isolate consistent and significant dimensions of effectiveness, despite the vast amount of literature surrounding the problem and the multifarious measures and criteria employed (Barr, 1955; Dixon and Morse, 1961; Heil, 1960). The quests for single qualities to characterize effective teachers have resulted in disparate conclusions, while the individual dimensions historically used to predict success have failed in their generalizability (Dana, 1962). Research dealing with this problem and employing the Rorschach to assess teachers or teachers-in-training, however, suggests some interesting findings.

Measures of flexibility-rigidity were used with 28 intern teachers in the Harvard-Newton program of 1964 (Sprinthall, Whiteley, and Mosher, 1966). Their Rorschach protocols were evaluated according to dimensions evolving from Rokeach's (1954) focus on the openness or closedness of belief systems. Ratings based on the Rorschach were consistent with the ratings given to the teachers by classroom observers. The research supported the basic hypothesis that there is a positive relationship between Rorschach measures of cognitive flexibility and effective teaching.

Student teachers again were examined in an attempt to factor analyze Rorschach variables most prominent among "normal" adult students. Sultan (1965) administered individual Rorschachs to 98 women students, scoring the protocols according to the Klopfer system and certain designated content variables. The factors were then compared with Cattell's (1949) personality factors. Although the Rorschach was found to be important in establishing certain results, it was suggested that it not be used as the "all-round technique" for assessing personality.

With a similar population, another attempt was made to identify clusters of personality attributes which may contribute to student teaching success (Lewis, 1966). Prior to their entrance to North Texas State University, the Structured-Objective Rorschach Test (SORT) (Stone, 1958) was administered to 283 students. The scores obtained were correlated with grade point averages earned in student teaching courses and with ratings by college coordinators who had been asked to designate the greatest strengths and weaknesses of the subjects. Significant correlations among Practical, Deduction, and Moodiness attributes of the SORT and success in student teaching led to suggestions that the technique be used in counseling programs for teacher admissions, that followup studies be made of the activities of first-year teachers, and that useful criteria be developed for evaluating student teaching.

The SORT was again used with a group of 133 students enrolled in educational psychology courses as secondary education majors (Weinlander, 1967). The 44 male subjects tended to demonstrate more anxiety than the 89 females, but they showed better control of emotional energy in terms of abstract thinking, as indicated by higher theoretical (*W*) scores. These findings were contradictory to those of Cox and Leaper (1959), who reported, on the basis of the SORT, higher anxiety levels for women than for men.

The problem of predicting teaching success was again pointed out by Symonds and Dudek:

> There is a voluminous quantity of ongoing research to find ways of diagnosing teacher effectiveness for the purpose of discovering a method or methods which can be used in teacher selection. But to date the results have been on the whole disappointing. Tests of knowledge and ability yield low correlation with any criterion of teaching effectiveness. Attitude inventories appear promising, but the results are inconsistent. Some exploration in the use of projective techniques has gone forward but the results, although suggestive, have not yet demonstrated their practical usefulness. [1956, p. 227]

A correlation of .60 was established between the investigators' Rorschach-based estimates of teaching effectiveness and independent estimates of the top- and bottom-rated teachers, based on acquaintance with each individual's teaching performance. Four factors were found to discriminate between the two groups of teachers: personality organization, judgment and reasoning, capacity to relate to others, and aggression. More meaningful, perhaps, than the actual factors was a discussion about the ways in which the individual teachers were assessed, the word comparisons of different responses, and the various Rorschach reports.

Two other studies have been reported in which teaching interns were evaluated on the bases of three measures: independent supervisor ratings, the Rorschach, and the Adaptive-Flexibility Inventory (Brawer, 1967)—a word association technique designed to evaluate dimensions of ego strength. Subjects for these investigations were junior college teaching interns engaged in a preparation program at UCLA (Brawer and Cohen, 1966; Cohen and Brawer, 1967).

The Rorschach was administered in group form; an individual inquiry ranging from 10 to 25 minutes was also conducted for the purpose of clarifying questions regarding determinants, locations, and popular responses. Each Rorschach protocol was scored according to the Klopfer system and assessed on the bases of two quantitative and two global or holistic approaches: a quantitative or sign rating, the Rorschach Prognostic Rating Scale (RPRS) (Klopfer et al., 1954), a global assessment of general adjustment, and a global assessment of cognitive-integrative level.

1. The quantitative assessment consisted of the sum of thirteen signs especially selected for these subjects. A numerical rating was assigned to each sign, representing the extent to which the individual's Rorschach protocol fit the criteria suggested by Rorschach interpretative hypotheses. The specific signs included three measures of form-level ratings; *M; F%*; *M; FM* and color relationships; movement (*M, FM, m*) relationships; *FK, Fc,* and *F* relationships; chromatic–achromatic ratios; ratio of *FC:* (*CF* + *C*); and *A%*.
2. The RPRS, developed as a measure of ego strength and a means for predicting an individual's response to psychotherapy, was designed to quantify in an objective way the "intuitions" or "hunches" of experienced clinicians. The total RPRS weighted scores were used in the prescribed manner; the sums of the three movement scores were also used alone, as suggested by Sheehan, Frederick, Rosevear, and Speigelman (1954).
3. The measure described as the "global assessment of general adjustment" was a purely subjective evaluation. Each protocol was rated according to the respondent's potential adaptability to a first-time teaching situation and according to his expected

ability to cope with the sometimes great modifications dictated by a transition in role.

4. A second global approach was used to assess the Rorschach responses on a cognitive-integrative level. This, too, was a general rather than a strictly numerical system. Form-level highs and lows, number and quality of *M* responses, proportion of pure form determinants, number of responses, the types and percent of location categories, and the amount of differentiation in *W* responses were considered. On the bases of these criteria, each Rorschach protocol was rated on a five-point scale, following the first five classifications suggested by Bloom in *The Taxonomy of Educational Objectives* (1956): Knowledge = 1; Comprehension = 2; Application = 3; Analysis = 4; and Synthesis = 5.

Results of these ratings showed that in the sign assessment procedures, seven specific signs were significantly correlated with independent supervisors' ratings of the junior college teachers who served as subjects. The total of the global evaluation and the assessment of integrative ability were also highly significant. The RPRS and the global assessment of general adjustability were significant but at a lower level. Accordingly, global approaches to Rorschach interpretation were found to be as effective as sign approaches in predicting independent ratings of the teaching intern populations.

Of more meaning, however, than the mere focus on a sign or global approach was the suggestion that a basic concern must be the selection of signs or a "global set" relevant to the subjects tested, to the demands of the employment situation, and to the environmental conditions into which the subjects will move. Following this rationale, decisions concerning specific modes of interpretation of data become subordinate to the fundamental issue of choosing specific determinants which appear to be directly related to a unique group in its special setting.

Using this same population of junior college teaching interns, it was found that teachers possessing qualities of adaptability and flexibility (as noted by the Adaptive-Flexibility Inventory) were rated higher by their supervisors (college presidents or deans of instruction) than those teachers who did not show high measures of these dimensions. These features were seen as essential to the ability to change role or to make a successful transition from student to teaching positions.

In order to make a successful transition, the first-time teacher must make intense personal adjustments to the demands of the new situation where he finds a different status, a different role, and completely different patterns of reward and reinforcement. Indeed, a fundamental rationale in teacher preparation programs is that the transition from college student into professional teacher—or professional other—is a personal commitment requiring many adjustments; thus, the difficulties apparent in the many attempts to predict occupational success by earlier test measures.

The same suggestion that was offered in the section on the military might well apply here. Promotions demand certain personal adjustments just as do role changes in general. It would seem important that school administrators look to the person *as person* as well as to his tenure status before assigning advancements. An effective teacher might be a poor supervisor and a good supervisor could well be inadequate in the role of dean of instruction. Dimensions such as flexibility–rigidity may provide better ways of looking at academic personnel than those currently employed.

Single Studies of Miscellaneous Groups

The final discussion of the Rorschach as a medium to further knowledge about people in specialized occupational groups will be concerned with four very different investigations. The first deals with college students and their subsequent vocational choices; the others range from Rorschach responses of missionaries, through inquiry into the human movement responses of strippers, to the differentiating Rorschach reactions of nuns and college women students. Brief mention will also be made of differences in subsets of specialized anthropological groups.

French's (1959) report of various recorded measures on a selected sample of undergraduate students was one of a series of Studies in Career Development undertaken at Harvard. Although previous researchers had found various measures that distinguished occupational groups (French, 1956; Harrower and Cox, 1943; Heath, 1945; Roe, 1956), few studies report time lags between the test administration and the designation of occupation. Accordingly, French asked whether occupational choices could be predicted on the basis of the Rorschach and other measures. Using the criterion "successful living within the college community" for the selection of a group of 232 Harvard sophomores, Rorschach protocols and other data were compared with subsequent occupational choices. Job descriptions were recorded and examined in relation to the material obtained from the group Rorschach, socio-economic information, and recorded physical characteristics. Analysis of variance and multivariate group analysis showed that aeronautical engineers, writers, and architects all provided high numbers of *M*. "Neutral variables" seen as indicating "neurotic repression, impulsive explosiveness, obsessive notions, and inner anxieties" were found in those subjects who indicated high family influence in their occupational choices.

In another study, Rorschachs were administered to 206 American missionaries who belonged to eleven major missionary boards and subsequently worked in the foreign field (Shah, 1957). After seven years, the data were analyzed in terms of Munroe's (1945) Inspection Technique. No significant differences were found between those missionaries who had been rated as "successful" and those rated "unsuccessful," although there was a trend which suggested that "unsuccessful" missionaries tended to be less well adjusted than those described as "successful."

Wagner's (1965) investigation of Piotrowski's (1957) hypothesis—that *M* responses represent prototypal tendencies expressed motorically—implies that the Rorschach has, indeed, hit almost all fields of endeavor. In order to locate and isolate this kind of *M*, it was felt desirable "to select as criteria certain occupations which, by their very nature, demand a narrow and specific set of attitudinal and behavioral correlates" (Wagner, 1965, p. 522). Decidedly "exhibitionistic," the occupation selected was that of stripper. Subjects consisted of 7 women, all moderately successful in their field, whose average age was 27.7 and whose mean number of years as stripper was 8.2. Control subjects were matched to the experimental group by age. In this group of 21 women, 7 had been previously diagnosed psychiatrically as psychoneurotic, 7 as schizophrenic, and 7 as "normal." The strippers showed significantly more exhibitionistic *M*, operationally defined as a human movement response involving an activity performed for the benefit of an audience—for example, skating, dancing—and/or exhibitionistic enhancement of the individual through costumes and adornment.

Zax, Cowen, and Peter (1963) compared the Rorschach responses of 40 novice nuns and 40 college women who rated each of the ten Rorschach blots on 21 semantic differential scales (Osgood, 1957). The nuns generally rated the ink blots toward the more positive extremes of the evaluation scales and, occasionally, toward the more potent extreme of the potency scales. The social desirability ratings of 28 nuns were then compared with those of 28 students, again with the result that the nuns tended toward the extreme ratings—more positively extreme ratings on those adjectives rated as positive and more negative ratings on those generally rated as negative. In their ratings of neutral adjectives, the nuns were found to vary more than the college women.

Other studies conducted with members of different occupational subgroups in specialized anthropological populations have shown certain differences in Rorschach responses. Edgerton's (1969) intensive investigation of Africans in Uganda and Kenya differentiated herders from farmers of the Pokot tribes when the Rorschachs were evaluated globally. However, factor analyses of certain Klopfer scoring categories and various quantitative relationships did not distinguish the farming and herding groups of the four tribes examined. Such an approach bears further investigation with other subgroups in various cultures.

Overview

This chapter has sketched history, cited reviews, and abstracted literature. Still, the questions remain unresolved as to whether the Rorschach does or does not facilitate understanding of people in different occupational fields, or whether it does, indeed, aid in predicting academic and vocational success. These are confusing issues—issues whose answers are dependent upon definition of criteria, definition of objectives, knowledge of individual behavior patterns, accuracy of report, and awareness of environmental factors. The questions originally posed in the introduction to this chapter are similarly unresolved. They have not been answered in terms of "black and white" or "yes or no," but certain findings do suggest avenues of progress.

Some investigations support the use of the Rorschach, indicating that it is predictably and concurrently valid. Others suggest that it adds nothing to our armamentarium of information. And still others vehemently declare that not only does the Rorschach add nothing, it also confuses the issue! It would still appear, unfortunately, that one may approach the problem with an avowedly biased attitude and, after surveying the literature, only have his own biases reinforced. On the other hand, the researcher who chooses to view the Rorschach as a technique—a medium—for achieving a designated purpose or goal may find his efforts reaping results to support his choice of the instrument. While it is apparent, then, that the questions regarding the relationships among the Rorschach, academic prediction, occupational choice, and vocational knowledge are still unanswered, certain trends among investigations do appear and certain points do need emphasis:

1. First, the number of Rorschach studies has diminished over the years. The reasons behind this reduction, of course, are multiple. Succinctly, however, they may be seen as due to difficulties in handling the technique; the trend away from using tests per se toward more general attempts to investigate interactions of people within groups; the ambiguity surrounding the problems of validity; the

increased attention to the psychology of occupations as theory in terms of role constructs and typologies rather than in terms of the individual dynamically involved with a special field of work.

All of these factors enter the picture to a greater or lesser extent. To single out two special predicaments—time and training pressures—a series of investigations in which responses to the Holtzman inkblots are data processed may provide a structure for machine scoring the traditional Rorschach technique. Here again, the publications resulting from the extensive Johns Hopkins program may make scoring and interpretation of the Rorschach a more feasible operation, since handling the data is one of the greatest obstacles to Rorschach use. The pendulum might thus swing back to a period of greater employment of this tool.

2. The second conclusion formed from this investigation of the literature is that, despite some early and important baseline thinking, many studies employing the Rorschach still lack definitive criteria. Once again the relations of personality, interests, and aptitudes to occupational choices and success must be seen in terms of individual environmental interactions. It may never be possible nor desirable to study the "whole personality" as an independent entity, but it is possible to follow the individual in different phases of his life and in his relationships with people in various situations.

3. Selection of medium is dependent upon definition of goal—and justification for using the Rorschach, or any other tool, should be with the expectations that it will lead to the attainment of specified objectives. It is important to ascertain whether a specific measure—in this case, the Rorschach technique—is the most expedient, the most sensitive, and potentially the most rewarding instrument for use in a particular investigation with a special group of subjects functioning in a prescribed setting. This approach does not eliminate the serendipitous possibility of discovery, nor does it negate the potential for creative insights and bisociative discoveries. It does, however, define a beginning and an end. It poses hypotheses that can be tested by means of selected media. Beyond that, definition can reduce the ambiguous and, simultaneously, encourage the introduction of unknowns which in themselves may become potential avenues for the

future study and future understanding of man as he functions in our confusing, stimulating, tenuous world of today.

References

American Council Psychological Examination (ACPE). 1951. Princeton, N.J.: Educational Testing Service.

American Psychologist. 1965, Vol. 20, No. 11, Washington, D.C.: American Psychological Association.

Anderson, R. G. 1949. Rorschach test results and efficiency ratings of machinists. *Pers. Psychol.* 2: 513–524.

Anderson, Irmgard, and Munroe, Ruth. 1948. Personality factors involved in student concentration on creative painting and commercial art. *Rorschach Res. Exchange,* 12: 141–154.

Barr, A. S. 1948. The measurement and prediction of teaching efficiency: A summary of investigations. *J. Exper. Ed.* 16: 203–283.

Barron, Frank. 1963. *Creativity and Psychological Health.* Princeton, N.J.: Van Nostrand Co.

Beck, S. J. 1933. Configurational tendencies in Rorschach responses. *Am. J. Psychol.* 45: 433–443.

Bleuler, E. 1912. Affektivität, suggestibität, paranoia. *New York State Hospital Bull.* 4: 481–601.

Bloom, B. S. (Ed.). 1956. *Taxonomy of Educational Objectives,* I: *Cognitive Domain.* New York: McKay Co.

Brawer, Florence B. 1967. The concept of ego strength and its measurement through a word association technique. Doctoral dissertation. University of California, Los Angeles.

———, and Cohen, Arthur M. 1966. Global and sign approaches to Rorschach assessment of beginning teachers. *J. Proj. Tech. Pers. Assess.* 30: 536–542; December.

———, and Spiegelman, J. Marvin. 1964. Rorschach and Jung: A study of introversion-extraversion. *J. Anal. Psychol.* 9: 137–149; January.

Brayfield, A. H. 1965. Testimony before the Senate Subcommittee on Constitutional Rights of the Committee on the Judiciary. *Am. Psychol.* 20: 888–898.

Brower, Daniel. 1955. The applicability of projective techniques to personal appraisal. *Pers. Psychol.* 8: 235–243.

Cattell, James McKeen. 1890. *Physical and Mental Measurements.* London: Macmillan.

Cattell, R., Saunders, D., and Stice, G. 1949. *The Sixteen Personality Factor Questionnaire.* Champaign, Ill.: Institute of Personality and Ability Testing.

Cohen, Arthur M., and Brawer, Florence B. 1967. Adaptive potential and first year teaching success. *J. Teach. Ed.* 18: 174–185.

College Entrance Examination Board. 1963. A statement on personality testing. *Coll. Bd. Rev.* 51: 11–13.

Cooper, J. G. 1955. The inspection Rorschach in the prediction of college success. *J. Ed. Res.* 49: 275–282.

Cox, F. N., and Leaper, P. M. 1959. General and test anxiety scale for children. *Australian J. Psychol.* 11: 70–80.

Cox, R. D. 1956. The normal personality: An analysis of Rorschach and thematic apperception test responses of a group of college students. *J. Proj. Tech.* 20: 70–77.

Cronbach, L. J. 1950. Studies of the group Rorschach in relation to success in the college of the University of Chicago. *J. Ed. Psychol.* 41: 65–82.

———. 1949. Statistical methods applied to Rorschach scores: A review. *Psychol. Bull.* 46: 393–429.

Dana, R. H. 1962. The validation of projective tests. *J. Proj. Tech.* 26: 182–186.

Davidson, Helen H. 1950. A measure of adjustment obtained from the Rorschach protocol. *J. Proj. Tech.* 14: 31–38.

Dixon, W. R., and Morse, W. C. 1961. The prediction of teaching performance: Empathic potential. *J. Teach. Ed.* 12: 322–329.

Dorken, H., Jr. 1954. A psychometric evaluation of sixty-eight medical interns. *J. Can. Med. Assoc.* 70: 41–45.

Draguns, J. G.; Haley, E. M.; and Phillips, L. 1969. Studies of Rorschach content. A review of the research literature, part I: Traditional content categories. *J. Proj. Tech. Pers. Assess.* 1: 3–32.

Edgerton, Robert B. (in press). *Adaptation and Continuity: A Comparison of Pastoralists and Farmers in Four East Africa Societies.* Berkeley: University of California Press.

Eiduson, Bernice T. 1958. Artist and nonartist: A comparative study. *J. Pers.* 26: 113–128.

———. 1962. *Scientists: Their Psychological World.* New York: Basic Books.

Eron, L. D. 1954. Use of the Rorschach method in medical student selection. *J. Med. Ed.* 29: 35–39.

Felzer, S. B. 1955. A statistical study of sex differences on the Rorschach. *J. Proj. Tech.* 19: 382–386.

Frank, L. K. 1939. Projective methods for the study of personality. *J. Psych.* 8: 389–413.

French, W. L. 1956. The relationship between various measures recorded on a selected group of Harvard undergraduates and occupation twelve years later. Doctoral dissertation. Harvard Graduate School of Education.

———. 1959. Can a man's occupation be predicted? *J. Couns. Psychol.* 6: 95–101.

Galton, F. 1883. *Inquiries into Human Faculty.* New York: Macmillan.

Gorham, D. R. 1965. The development of a computer scoring system for inkblot responses. *Proceedings of the Ninth Congress of the Interamerican Society of Psychology,* pp. 258–270. Miami Beach: Interamerican Society of Psychology.

———. 1967. Validity and reliability studies of a computer-based scoring system for inkblot response. *J. Cons. Psychol.* 31: 65–70.

Hahn, M. E., and MacLean, M. S. 1955. *Counseling Psychology*. New York: McGraw-Hill.

Harrower, G. J., and Cox, K. J. 1943. The results obtained from a number of occupational groupings on the professional level with the Rorschach group method. *Bull. Can. Psychol. Assoc.* 2: 31–33.

Harrower-Erickson, M. R., and Steiner, M. E. 1945. *Large Scale Rorschach Techniques*. Springfield, Ill.: Charles C Thomas.

Heath, C. W. 1945. *What People Are*. Cambridge, Mass.: Harvard University Press.

Heil, L. M. 1960. *Characteristics of Teacher Behavior and Competency Related to Achievement of Different Kinds of Children in Several Grades*. New York: Brooklyn College.

Hersch, Charles. 1962. The cognitive functioning of the creative person: A developmental analysis. *J. Proj. Tech.* 26: 193–200.

Hertz, M. R. 1951. Current problems in Rorschach theory and technique. *J. Proj. Tech.* 15: 307–338.

———. 1960. The organization activity. In *Rorschach Psychology* (Edited by M. A. Rickers-Ovsiankina.) New York: John Wiley.

Hicks, J. A., and Stone, J. B. 1962. The identification of traits related to managerial success. *J. App. Psychol.* 46: 428–432.

Holt, R. R., and Luborsky, L. 1958. *Personality Patterns of Psychiatrists, Vol. I: A Study of Methods for Selecting Residents*. New York: Basic Books.

Hoyt, D. P. 1965. *The Relationship Between College Grades and Adult Achievement: A Review of the Literature*. Iowa City, Iowa: American College Testing Program.

Ives, Margaret. 1965. Testimony. *Am. Psychol.* 20: 898–901.

Jung, C. G. 1918. *Studies in Word Association*. London: William Heinemann.

Kelly, E. L., and Fiske, D. W. 1951. *The Prediction of Performance in Clinical Psychology*. Ann Arbor: University of Michigan Press.

Kleinman, Roger A., and Higgins, Jerry. 1966. Sex of respondent and Rorschach *M* production. *J. Proj. Tech. Pers. Assess.* 30: 439–440.

Klopfer, B.; Ainsworth, M.; Klopfer, W.; and Holt, R. 1954. *Developments in the Rorschach Technique,* Vol. I. New York: World Book Co.

———; Kirkner, F. J.; Wisham, W.; and Baker, G. 1954. Rorschach prognostic rating scale. In *Developments in the Rorschach Technique,* Vol. I. (Edited by B. Klopfer and others.) New York: World Book Co.

Koestler, Arthur. 1964. *The Act of Creation*. New York: Macmillan.

Kraepelin, E. 1892. *Ueber die beinflussung einfacher psychischer vorgange durch arzneimittel; experimentelle untersuchungen*. Jena: Gustav Fisher Verlag.

Kris, E. 1952. *Psychoanalytic Explorations in Art*. New York: International Universities Press.

Langer, Philip. 1962. Social desirability and acquiescence on the SORT. *Psychol. Report.* 11: 531–534.

Langer, Philip; Hayes, W. G.; and Sharp, H. C. 1963. Effect of anxiety and induced stress on the structured-objective Rorschach test. *Percept. Mot. Skills.* 16: 573–580

———, and Hicks, T. C. 1966. The structured-objective Rorschach test: A question of choice intensity. *Percep. Mot. Skills.* 22: 439–442.

Ledwith, Nettie H. 1959. *Rorschach Responses of Elementary School Children.* Pittsburgh, Pa.: University of Pittsburgh Press.

Lenkau, P. V. 1965. Foreword in *An Index of Responses to the Group Rorschach Test: Studies on the Psychological Characteristics of Medical Students.* (Edited by C. B. Thomas and D. E. Ross.) Baltimore: The Johns Hopkins Press.

Lewis, James N. 1966. The relationship of attributes measured by the structural-objective Rorschach and success in student teaching. Doctoral dissertation. Denton, Texas: North Texas State University.

MacKinnon, D.; Crutchfield, R. S.; Barron, F.; and Block, J. 1958. An assessment study of Air Force officers, I: Design of the study and description of the variables. *USAF WADC Tech. Rep.* No. 58–91, Pt. 1, X153.

Macy, J. W. 1965. Psychological testing and the public service. *Am. Psychol.* 20: 883–887.

Maslow, A. H. 1950. Self-actualizing people: A study of psychological health. *Personality.* 11–34.

McArthur, C. C., and King, S. 1954. Rorschach configuration associated with college achievement. *J. Ed. Psychol.* 45: 492–498.

Mindess, H. 1957. Psychological indices in the selection of student nurses. *J. Proj. Tech.* 21: 37–39.

Molish, H. B. 1956. The Rorschach test in military psychology and psychiatry. *Am. J. Orthopsychiat.* 26: 807–817.

———; Molish, E. E.; and Thomas, C. B. 1950. A Rorschach study of a group of medical students. *Psychiat. Quart.* 24: 744–774.

Munroe, Ruth. 1941. Inspection technique. *Rorschach Res. Exch.* 5: 166–191.

———. 1945. Prediction of the adjustment and academic performance of college students by a modification of the Rorschach method. *App. Psychol. Monogr.* No. 7. Stanford University Press.

———. 1945. The Rorschach test: A report of its use at Sarah Lawrence College. *J. High. Ed.* 16: 17–23.

Munsterberg, H. 1907. The third degree. *McClures Magazine.* 29: 614–622.

Murray, H. A., and others, 1938. *Exploration in Personality.* New York: Oxford University Press.

Osgood, C. E.; Suci, G. J.; and Tannenbaum, D. H. 1957. *The Measurement of Meaning.* Chicago: University of Illinois Press.

Office of Strategic Services. 1948. *Assessment of Men.* New York: Rinehart.

Otis, Leon S. 1959. What does the Rorschach Z score reflect? *J. Cons. Psychol.* 23: 373–374.

Pace, C. R. 1962. Implications of differences in campus atmospheres for evaluation and planning of college programs. In *Personality Factors on the College Campus.* (Edited by R. L. Sutherland and others.) Austin, Texas: The Hogg Foundation, University of Texas.

———, and Stern, George G. 1958. An approach to the measurement of psychological characteristics of college environments. *J. Ed. Psychol.* 49: 269–277.

Paterson, D. G., and Darley, J. G. 1936. *Men, Women, and Jobs.* Minneapolis: University of Minnesota Press.

Patterson, C. H. 1957. The use of projective tests in vocational counseling. *Educational Psychology Measurement.* 17: 533–555.

Phelan, J. G. 1962. Projective techniques in the selection of management personnel. *J. Proj. Tech.* 26: 102–104.

Phillips, L.; Kaden, S.; and Waldman, M. 1959. Rorschach indices of developmental level. *J. Gen. Psychol.* 94: 267–285.

Piotrowski, Z. A., et al. 1944. Rorschach signs in the selection of outstanding young male mechanical workers. *J. Psychol.* 18: 131–150.

———, 1957. *Perceptanalysis.* New York: Macmillan.

———, and Rock, Milton R. 1963. *The Perceptanalytic Executive Scale: A Tool for the Selection of Top Managers.* New York: Grune & Stratton.

Psychological Abstracts. Washington, D. C.: The American Psychological Association.

Rawls, James R., and Boone, Jerry N. 1967. Artistic creativity and Rorschach whole responses. *J. Proj. Tech. Pers. Assess.* 31: 18–22.

Roe, Anne, 1946a. A Rorschach study of a group of scientists and technicians. *J. Cons. Psychol.* 10: 317–327.

———. 1946b. Artists and their work. *J. Pers.* 15: 1–40.

———. 1949. Analysis of group Rorschachs of biologists. *J. Proj. Tech.* 13: 25–43.

———. 1950. Analysis of group Rorschachs of physical scientists. *J. Proj. Tech.* 14: 385–398.

———. 1951. A psychological study of eminent biologists. *Psychol. Monogr.* No. 14, 65.

———. 1952. Analysis of group Rorschachs of psychologists and anthropologists. *J. Proj. Tech.* 16: 212–224.

———. 1953. A psychological study of eminent psychologists and anthropologists and a comparison with biological and physical scientists. *Psychol. Monogr.* 67: 2.

———. 1954. A new classification of occupations. *J. Couns. Psychol.* 1: 215–220.

———. 1956. *The Psychology of Occupations.* New York: Wiley.

———, and Mierzwa, John. 1960. The use of the Rorschach in the study of personality and occupations. *J. Proj. Tech.* 24: 282–289.

Rohrer, J. H., Hoffman, E. L., Bagby, J. W., Herrmann, R. S., and Wilkins, W. L., 1955. The group administered Rorschach as a research instrument: Reliability norms. *Psychol. Monogr.* 59: No. 393.

Rokeach, Milton. 1954. The nature and meaning of dogmatism. *Psychol. Rev.* 61: 194–204.

Rorschach, H. 1921. *Psychodiagnostics,* 5th ed. (pub. 1951). New York: Grune & Stratton.

Rossi, A. M., and Neuman, G. G. 1961. A comparative study of Rorschach norms: Medical students. *J. Proj. Tech.* 25: No. 3.

Ryan, F. J. 1951. Personality differences between under and over-achievers in college. Doctoral Dissertation. New York: Columbia University.

Schmeidler, G. R.; Nelson, M. J.; and Bristol, M. 1959. Freshman Rorschachs and college performance. *Gen. Psychol. Monogr.* 59: 3–43.

Shah, S. A. 1957. Use of the Inspection Rorschach Technique in analyzing missionary success and failure. *J. Proj. Tech.* 21: 69–72.

Sheehan, J. G.; Frederick, C. J.; Rosevear, W. H.; and Spiegelman, M. 1954. A validity study of the Rorschach Prognostic Rating Scale. *J. Proj. Tech.* 18: 233–239.

Shriver, S. 1965. Suggestions to the American Psychological Association. *Am. Psychol.* 11: 876–877.

Smith, K. V. 1965. Testimony. *Am. Psychol.* 20: 907–915.

Snowden, R. F. 1956. Top management and the Rorschach technique. In *Developments in the Rorschach Technique,* Vol. II. (Edited by B. Klopfer and others.) New York: World Book Co.

Sopchak, A. L. 1958. Prediction of college performance by commonly used tests. *J. Clin. Psychol.* 14: 194–197.

Spiegelman, M. 1956. The Rorschach technique in social psychology. In *Developments in the Rorschach Technique,* Vol. II. (Edited by B. Klopfer and others.) New York: World Book Co.

Sprinthall, N. A.; Whitely, J. M.; and Masters, R. L. 1966. A study of teacher effectiveness. *J. Teach. Ed.* 17: 93–106.

Stern, G. G.; Stein, M. I.; and Bloom, B. S. 1956. *Methods in Personality Assessment.* New York: The Free Press.

Stone, J. B. 1958. *S–O Rorschach Test.* Los Angeles: California Test Bureau.

Sultan, E. E. 1965. A quantitative investigation of the Rorschach Inkblot Test as applied to student teachers. *Brit. J. Soc. Clin. Psychol.* 4: 197–206.

Super, D. E., and others. 1957. *Vocational development: A framework for research.* New York: Bureau of Publications, Teachers College, Columbia University.

———, and Crites, J. O. 1962. *Appraising Vocational Fitness.* New York: Harper & Row.

Symonds, P. M., and Dudek, S. Z. 1956. Use of the Rorschach in the diagnosis of teacher effectiveness. *J. Proj. Tech.* 20: 227–235.

Taylor, C. W.; Price, P. B.; Richards, T. M.; and Jacobsen, T. L. 1966. Grades as substitute criteria or as predictors of physician performance. *Psychiat. Spec.* 3: 1–3.

Thomas, C. B.; Ross, D. C.; and Freed, E. S. 1965. *An Index of Responses to the Group Rorschach Test: Studies on the Psychological Characteristics of Medical Students.* Baltimore: The Johns Hopkins Press.

Toops, H. A. 1940. *Ohio State University Psychological Examination.* Chicago: Science Research Associates.

Wagner, Edwin E. 1965. Exhibitionistic human movement responses of strippers: An attempt to validate the Rorschach. *J. Proj. Tech. Pers. Assess.* 29: 522–524.

Wechsler, D. 1944. *The Nature and Classification of Intelligence.* Baltimore: The Williams & Wilkins Co.

Weinlander, Mary L. 1967. Validity of the variables on the Structural-Objective Rorschach Test (SORT) among alcoholics, neurotics, and psychotics. *J. Gen. Psychol.* 110: 91–94.

Werner, H. 1957. *Comparative Psychology of Mental Development,* revised ed. New York: International University Press.

Whipple, G. M. 1910. *Manual of Mental and Physical Tests.* Baltimore: Warwick & York.

Williams, Gertha, and Kellman, S. 1956. The Rorschach technique in industrial psychology. In *Developments in the Rorschach Technique,* Vol. II. New York: World Book Co.

Wundt, W. 1880. *Grundzuge der Physiologischen Psychologie.* Leipzig: Engelman.

Zax, Melvin; Cowen, Emory L.; and Peter, Mary. 1963. A comparative study of novice nuns and college females using the response set approach. *J. Abn. Soc. Psychol.* 66: 369–375.

Index of Names

Abbey, D. S., *46*
Abt, L. E., 143, *204*
Adelson, J., 306, *317*
Ainsworth, M. D., 272, *319,* 399, *433*
Allison, J., 300, 303, 309, *317*
American Council Psychological Examination, 431
American Psychologist, 431
Ames, L. B., 100, 101, 112, 114, *140*
Anderson, I., 414, *431*
Anderson, R. G., 395, *431*
Arlow, J., 265, 271, *317*

Bachrach, H., 43, *45,* 309, *317*
Bagby, J. W., 403, *436*
Baker, G., 321, 328, 374, *383, 433*
Barr, A. S., 422, *431*
Barron, F., 284, 294, *317,* 389, 413, *431, 434*
Bateson, G., 256, *260*
Bauman, G., 210, 213, 246, *260, 261*
Beck, S., 83, *97*
Beck, S. J., 11, 13, *45,* 345, *383,* 398, 405, 418, *431*
Bell, N. W., 143, *204,* 256, *261*
Bergan, J. R., 43, *45,* 310, *317*
Blanchard, W., 210, 211, *260*
Blatt, S. J., 278, 300, 303, *317*
Bleuler, E., 387, *431*
Block, J., 389, *434*
Bloom, B. S., 389, 425, *431, 436*
Bohm, E., 12, *45*
Bolgar, H., 109, *140*
Boone, J. N., 414, 415, *435*
Bower, T. G. R., *140*
Brawer, F. B., 424, *431, 432*
Brayfield, A. H., 387, 416, *431*
Brenner, C., 265, 271, *317*
Bristol, M., 407, *436*
Brower, D., 415, *431*
Brown, F., 83, 96, *98*

Cattell, J. McK., 387, *431*
Cattell, R., 422, *431*
Child, I. L., 306, *317*
Christensen, P. R., *320*
Claparède, E., 119, 130, *141*
Cohen, A. M., 424, *431, 432*
Cohen, I. H., 32, *45,* 279, *317*
College Entrance Examination Board, *432*
Cooper, J. G., 406, *432*
Cornelison, A. R., *205*
Cowen, E. L., 428, *437*
Cox, F. N., 423, *432*
Cox, K. J., 414, 427, *433*
Cox, R. D., 409, *432*
Crites, J. O., 394, *436*
Cronbach, L. J., 394, 406, *432*
Crutchfield, R. S., 389, *434*
Cutter, F., 210–212, 216, 249, 255, 257, *260, 261*

* Numbers in italics refer to pages on which full reference listings appear.

Dana, R. H., 422, *432*
Darley, J. G., 393, *435*
Davidson, H. H., *45,* 182, 183, *205,* 405, *432*
Décarie, T. G., 129, *141*
Derman, B. I., 310, *317*
Dixon, W. R., 422, *432*
Dorken, H., Jr., 398, *432*
Draguns, J. G., 396, *432*
Drake, L. E., 333, *383*
Draper, W. A., *320*
Dudek, S. Z., 281, 305, *317,* 423, *436*
Dworetzki, G. (*see also* Meili-Dworetzki), 102, 119, *141*

Edgerton, R. B., 428, *432*
Eiduson, B. T., 413, 420, *432*
Ekstein, R., 48, 60, 77, *80*
Epstein, N. B., 210, 215, *261*
Erikson, E. H., 302, *317*
Eron, L. D., 398, *432*

Farberow, N. L., 209, 210, 212, 216, 249, *260, 261*
Feirstein, A., 300, 303, 310, *317, 318*
Felzer, S. B., 410, *432*
Fenichel, O., 51, *80*
Ferenczi, S., 14, *45*
Ferguson, J. T., 328, 374, *383*
Fiske, D. W., 394, *433*
Flavell, J. H., 106, *141*
Fleck, S., *205*
Fox, J., 104, *141*
Frank, L. K., 387, *432*
Frederick, C. J., 424, *436*
Freed, E. S., 401, 410, *437*
French, W. L., 427, *432*
Freud, S., 14, *45,* 264, 265, 267, 268, 272, *318*
Friedman, H., 13, *45*
Fromm, E., 43, *45,* 297

Galton, F., 387, *432*
Gardner, R. W., 37, 42, *45,* 274, 302, 309, *318, 319*
Getzels, J. W., 284, *318*
Gill, M. M., *46,* 265, 267, 271, *318, 320*
Ginsparg, S., 36, *45*
Goldberg, P. A., 339, *383*
Goldberger, L., 278, *318*
Gorham, D. R., 410, *432, 433*
Gray, J. J., 286, 301, *318*
Grygier, T., 293, 301, *318*
Guilford, J. P., 284–288, *318, 320*

Hahn, M. E., 389, 392, *433*
Haley, E. M., 396, *432*
Haley, J., *260*
Harrower, G. J., 414, 427, *433*
Harrower-Erickson, M. R., 398, *433*
Hartmann, H., 48, *80,* 272, *318*
Hathaway, S. R., 333, *383*
Havel, J., 32, *45,* 58, *80,* 273, 278, 282, 290, *319*
Hayes, W. G., 418, *434*
Heath, C. W., 427, *433*
Heath, D. H., 33, 35, *45,* 310, *318*
Heil, L. M., 422, *433*
Hemmendinger, L., 13, *45,* 101, 102, *141*
Herrmann, R. S., 403, *436*
Herron, W. E., *80*
Hersch, C., 306, *318,* 412, 413, *433*
Hertz, M. R., 103, *141,* 392, 405, *433*
Hicks, J. A., 418, *433*
Hicks, T. C., 418, *434*
Higgins, J., 410, *433*
Hoffman, E. L., 403, *436*
Holt, H. W. v., Jr., 300, *320*
Holt, R. R., 32, 35, *45,* 58, *80,* 266, 267, 271–273, 276, 278, 282, 288, 290, 298-301, 311, *318–320,* 399–401, *433*
Holtzman, W. H., 58, *80*
Holzberg, J. D., *205*
Holzman, P. S., *318*
Hoyt, D. P., 405, *433*
Hunt, J. McV., 106, *141*

Inhelder, B., 120, 126, 127, 137, 138, *141*
Ittelson, W. H., 60, *81*
Ives, M., 416, *433*

Jackson, P. P., *260*
Jackson, P. W., 284, *318*

Jacobsen, T. L., 397, 400, *436*
Jenkins, T. N., 299, *319*
John, E. R., 303, *319*
Jung, C. G., 387, *433*

Kaden, S., 412, *435*
Kafka, H., 295, *319*
Kahn, M. W., 36, *45*
Kay, E., *205*
Kelley, D. M., *45*
Kellman, S., 386, 391, 392, *437*
Kelly, E. L., 394, *433*
King, S., 406, *434*
Kirkner, F. J., 405, *433*
Klein, G. S., 309, *318, 319*
Kleinman, R. A., 410, *433*
Klopfer, B., 12, *45,* 103, *141,* 272, *319,* 345, *383,* 390, 398, 399, 424, *433*
Klopfer, W. G., 3, *8,* 83, 97, *98,* 211, *319, 433*
Koestler, A., 412, *433*
Kraepelin, E., 387, *433*
Kris, E., 264, 265, 272, 305, *319,* 412, *433*
Kutash, S. B., 60, *81*

Langer, P., 418, *434*
Leaper, P. M., 423, *432*
Leadwith, N. H., 406, *434*
Lenkau, P. V., 402, *434*
Levine, M., 101, *141*
Levy, J., 210, 215, *261*
Lewis, D. J., *320*
Lewis, J. N., 422, *434*
Lidz, T., *205*
Lindner, R. M., 3, *8,* 83, *98*
Linton, H. B., *318*
Lohrenz, L. J., 37, 42, *45,* 274, *319*
Loveland, N., 210, 213, 214, *261*
Luborsky, L., 38, *45,* 400, 401, *433*
Lunt, P. S., 145, *205*
Lyons, J., 311, *319*

McArthur, C. C., 406, *434*
MacGregor, R., 256, *261*
MacKinnon, D., 389, *434*
MacLean, M. S., 389, 392, *433*
Macy, J. W., 417, *434*

Martin, R. M., 311, *319*
Maslow, A. H., 393, 412, *434*
Masters, R. L., *436*
Mayman, M., 16, *46,* 274, 311, *319*
Meehl, P. E., 333, *383*
Meili-Dworetzki, G. (*see also* Dworetzki), 103, *141*
Mierzwa, J., 396, 400, 401, *435*
Mindess, H., 398, *434*
Molish, E. E., 398, *434*
Molish, H. B., 398, 402, 403, *434*
Morse, W. C., 422, *432*
Mosher, 422
Munroe, R., 406, 414, 427, *431, 434*
Munsterberg, H., 387, *434*
Murphy, L. B., *81*
Murray, H. A., 340, *384,* 389, 411, *434*
Myden, W., 268, 269, 282, 305, *319*

Nelson, M. J., 407, *436*
Neuman, G. G., 398, *436*

Oberlander, M. I., 310, *319*
Oetting, E. R., 333, *383*
Office of Strategic Services, 388, *434*
Oppenheimer, J. R., 110, *141*
Orgel, J., 306, *319*
Osgood, C. E., 253, *261,* 428, *434*
Otis, L. S., 418, *435*

Pace, C. R., 389, 410, 411, *435*
Paterson, D. G., 393, *435*
Patterson, C. H., 386, 394, *435*
Peter, M., 428, *437*
Phelan, J. G., 418, *435*
Phillips, L., 3, *8,* 83, 96, 97, *98,* 396, 412, *432, 435*
Piaget, J., '112, 115, 117, 120–124, 26–28, 130–132, 137–139, *141, 142*
Pine, F., 288–291, 295, *320*
Piotrowski, Z. A., 7, *8,* 395, 417, 427, *435*
Prest, 405
Price, P. B., 397, 400, *436*
Pryor, D. B., 33, *46*
Psychological Abstracts, 435

Rabkin, J. G., 36, 43, *46*

Ramsay, M., 43, *46*
Rapaport, D., 12, 34, *46*, 58, 60, *81*, 272, 273, 295, 297, *320*
Rawls, J. R., 414, 415, *435*
Richards, T. M., 397, 400, *436*
Robbins, L. L., 37, *46*
Rock, M. R., 417, *435*
Roe, A., 306, *320*, 390, 393, 396, 400, 401, 404, 412, 420, 427, *435*
Rogolsky, M. M., 281, 300, *320*
Rohrer, J. H., 403, *436*
Rokeach, M., 422, *436*
Roman, M., 210, 213, 246, *260*, *261*
Rorschach, H., 385, *436*
Rosevear, W. H., 424, *436*
Ross, D. C., 401, 410, *437*
Rossi, A. M., 398, *436*
Ryan, F. J., 405, *436*

Sapin, D., 212, 216, *261*
Saretsky, T., 36, *46*
Saunders, D., *431*
Schachtel, E. G., 83, *98*, 311, *319*
Schafer, R., 3, *8*, 12, 22, 24, 26, 28, 29, 31, *46*, 58, 64, *81*, 83, 97, *98*, 269, 297, 310, *320*
Schlesinger, H. J., 309, *319*
Schmeidler, G. R., 407, *436*
Sechehaye, M. A., 60, *81*
Sengstake, C. B., *320*
Shah, S. A., 427, *436*
Sharp, H. C., 418, *434*
Sheehan, J. G., 424, *436*
Shneidman, E. S., 342, 344, *384*
Shriver, S., 416, *436*
Silverman, D. K., 306, *320*
Silverman, L. H., 290, 296, *320*
Singer, M. T., 210, 213, 216, 254, *261*
Smith, J. G., 3, *8*, 83, 96, 97, *98*
Smith, K. V., 415, *436*
Snowden, R. F., 390, 415, *436*
Sobler, D. T., *205*
Sonoda, B. C., *320*
Sopchak, A. L., 407, *436*
Spence, D. P., *318*
Spiegelman, J. M., *141*, 386, 424, *431*, *436*
Sprinthall, N. A., 422, *436*
Stein, M. I., 389, *436*
Steiner, M. E., 398, *433*
Stern, G. G., 389, *435*, *436*
Stice, G., 431
Stone, J. B., 418, 422, *433*, *436*
Suci, G. J., 253, *261*, *434*
Sullivan, J. J., 301, *320*
Sultan, E. E., 422, *436*
Super, D. E., 393, 394, *436*
Swartz, J. D., *80*
Symonds, P. M., 423, *436*

Tannenbaum, D. H., *434*
Taylor, C. W., 397, 400, *436*
Thomas, C. B., 398, 401, 410, *434*, *437*
Thorpe, J. S., *80*
Toops, H. A., 406, *437*

Vogel, E. F., 143, *204*, 256, *261*

Wagner, E. E., 427, 428, *437*
Waldman, M., 412, *435*
Walker, R. G., *46*
Wallerstein, J., 48, 61, *80*
Wallerstein, R. S., 37, *46*
Warner, W. L., 145, *205*
Weakland, J., *260*
Wechsler, D., 330, *384*, *437*
Weinlander, M. L., 418, 423, *437*
Weissman, S. L., 143, *204*
Werner, H., 412, *437*
Whipple, G. M., 387, *437*
Whitely, J. M., 422, *436*
Wild, C., 306, *320*
Wilkins, W. L., 403, *436*
Williams, G., 386, 391, 392, *437*
Wilson, R. C., 284, *320*
Wisham, W., *433*
Wolff, P. H., 106, 109, *142*
Wright, N., *46*
Würsten, H., 121, *142*
Wundt, W., 387, *437*
Wynne, L. C., 210, 213, 216, 254, *261*

Zax, M., 428, *437*
Zukowsky, E., 36, *46*

Index of Subject Matter

Academic performance, prediction of by Rorschach, 404–411
Academic research, use of Rorschach in, 385–431
Accommodation, 111–112
"Acting out," 146, 153, 162, 170, 176, 200, 342
Actors, 290–292
Adaptive assets, 113, 371
Adelphi College, 407
Adolescence, 117–118
Alcohol addiction, 24–25, 170, 333–335
Alcoholism and consensus Rorschach, 249–254
American Negro, 212
Anatomy responses, 398
Anxiety and reaction time, 50–51
Anxiety state, 32, 152
Architects, 427
Artists, creative, 264–265, 279–280, 282–290, 307–308, 411–415
Associative processes, 424
Authority, attitude to, 355, 356, 357, 370
Autism, 29
Average form-level rating, unweighted, 36

Barnard College, 407
Barron-Welsh Art Scale, 292–293, 294, 295
Behavior problems in children, 195–197
Bernreuter Personality Inventory, 34
Biologists, 420–421
Block Design, 331–332
Brick Uses Test, 284, 289, 290, 291, 294, 302
"Burnt-out" schizophrenic record, 56

C responses in children, 103, 113–114, 116; interpretation, 152, 157, 170, 182, 191, 201
C′ responses, interpretation, 202
Case histories, in sample case studies, 143–260
Case studies, adults, 90–95, 364–370
Castration, 162
"Cathexis," 85
CF responses, scoring, 176, 182, 201
Character disorders, 24
Chemists, 420–421
Child development, general, 4, 100–140
Children: development of perception in, 102–103, 105–113, 119–121, 124–127, 136–138; emotional and social development, 128–132, 139–140; and memory, 127–128, 138–139
Children, use of Rorschach with: age patterns, psychological significance of, ages 0–2, 110; ages 2–7, 111, 116–117; ages 7–12, 117; school age children, 100–101, 103–105, 107, 406–407; clinical application, 133–134

Color responses, and ego functioning, 68, 70
Compulsive, 31
Confabulation, 20, 72, 75
Confabulatory combination, 104–105
Consensus reactions vs. individual responses, 254–257
Consensus Rorschach, administration of, 209–211, 249, 253–254; examples of protocols, 216–242, 244–248; scoring of, 259–260; with a reference group, 249–254; and theory of content polarities, 216–248
Constriction, 25, 28, 29, 195
Contamination, 39
Content, interpretation of: miscellaneous categories, 58–59; polarities, 216–217, 225–226, 243, 246–247, 249, 255–256
Content analysis, of polarities in consensus Rorschach, 216–248; and reaction time, 59
Creativity, general, 6, 14, 32, 86, 264–265, 268, 275–276, 305–309, 384, 411–415; and adaptive regression, 279–295 and libidinal content, 296–297; and orality, 298–304; and primary process, 295–298, 309–310
Criticalness, 63–64, 66, 73

D responses, interpretation, 156
Davidson Rorschach Adjustment Signs, 182–186
DD responses, interpretation, 274, 276–277, 280, 289
DE responses, interpretation, 274, 276–277, 280, 289
Defense mechanisms, 79, 138
Dependency needs, 170, 175, 331, 366
Development, concepts of, 101–102, 106–113
Diagnosis, discussion with patient, 326–330; from symbolic responses, 95–96
Diagnostic use of the Rorschach, 321–383
Doctors, 90
dr responses, 156
Draw-a-Person Test, 33
Dreams, 266–267, 346
Drug addiction, 196
DW responses, 156
Dysphoria, 152

Ego, boundaries, 60–63; functioning, Rorschach indicators of, 2–3, 47–80; strength and weakness, 13, 34, 37, 39, 325–326, 399
Ego defensiveness, 34, 67–68, 176, 273–274, 276–277, 333
Ego processes, 47–49, 56–58, 60–63, 69, 70–72
Engineers, 427
Equilibrium, Piaget's theory of, 115–119, 135–136
Examiner, relations with subject, 87

F responses, interpretation of, 15–21
F responses, scoring, 24, 36–37, 42, 116, 156, 161, 176, 185, 191, 196, 201
F+ responses, 12, 15–17, 18, 22
F− responses, 15, 19
F%, 23, 25, 26, 27, 28–30, 151, 182, 191, 282
F+%, 28
(*F*+ or *F*−), 1
Fabulation, 58
"The Family Rorschach," 213–214
Fantasy, 27, 86, 94, 152
FC responses, interpretation, 182, 201, 202
Fc responses, interpretation, 185, 201
Feedback, 6
FK responses, interpretation, 367
Flexibility, 294–295, 296, 304, 309–310, 423–424
FM responses, interpretation, 125, 137, 152, 156, 161, 162, 170, 176, 182, 185, 196, 201, 202, 203
Form level, and stimulus acceptance, 52–56; and reaction time, 50–52; and scoring system, 15–20

Form-level rating, comparisons, 22–32, 34, 39; in clinical practice, 21–22; interpretation, 20–22, 37–38; the rating scale, 11–13, 15–20, 424–425; validity of 32, 41–43
Form perception, 15–18
Freudian theory, 6
Fs responses, 19, 21
Fv responses, 12–13, 18–19
Fw responses, 17–18
Fw+ responses, 22

Genetic structuralization, 124
Geologists, 420–421
Gestalt function in projective tests, 88
Gestalt psychology, 4, 104, 113–114, 119, 121, 124, 389
Group dynamics, 243–248, 254–255
Group methods, 209–211, 213–215, 216, 243–248, 249–254
Group Rorschach Test, 211–212

H responses, 338
Hanfmann-Kasanin Test, 299, 303, 304
Harvard University, 406, 427
Health-Sickness Rating Scale, 38–39
Holtzman Inkblot Test, 286
Homosexuality, 212, 305, 327, 359, 364
Hostility, 156, 175

Identification, 162–164
Images, mental in children, 124–127, 137–138
Imaginal resources, 85, 94–95
Impulses, ego-alien, 87; neurotic, 170, 176; primitive, 162, 185, 203
Industrial psychology, use of Rorschach in, 385–431
Industrial testing, 414–416
Inquiry, 20, 21, 75, 275–276, 346–347
Intellectual manner of approach, 49
Intelligence, 12, 115, 122–124, 284, 286, 290, 291, 308, 399
"Interaction testing," 213, 246
Interpersonal relationships, 252–253
Interpretation, technique of, 364–370
Interpretative hypotheses, 3, 88–89, 106, 364–370, 374

Johns Hopkins University, 40, 430

K responses, interpretation, 202

LSD, 196

M responses, interpretation, 116, 138, 152, 156, 176, 182, 203, 409–410, 418, 427–428
m responses, interpretation, 202
Ma responses, interpretation, 338
Make-a-Picture-Story Test (MAPS), 341, 342–345, 354, 356, 361, 369
Marijuana, 196
Masochism, neurotic, 147
Medical students, 397–398, 401–403
Memory, structure of, 127–128
Menninger Foundation, 400
Military applications of the Rorschach, 403–404
Minnesota Multiphasic Personality Inventory (MMPI), 34, 316, 327, 333–339, 354, 372, 379
Minus form level, interpretation, 116
Missionaries, 427
M:W ratio, 419

Obsessive-compulsive, 30
Oedipus complex, 187, 191
Ohio State Psychological Examination, 290, 406
Oral phase, 302
Oral responses, in creativity tests, 298–301
Organic brain damage, adult, use of Rorschach in, 326–327
Organized responses in children, 103
Originality, 116

P responses. *See* Popular responses.
Paranoid, 352–359
Pathognomic signs, 20
Peace Corps, 415, 416
Perception, effects of the needs on, 65–66
Perception vs. intelligence, 122–124
Permeability, 86–87

Perseveration, general, 75; magic wand, 104
Personality assessment, individual, 99–100, 420
Personality tests, objective, 330–359, 414–416
Physicians, 397, 399, 420–421
Popular responses, interpretation, 70–71, 74, 156, 281, 349, 402
Prediction of academic and vocational success, 385–431
Primary and secondary processes, 32–33, 36, 57–60, 71–72, 264–266, 267–268, 282
Primary process scoring, 268–275, 309–310, 311–317
Primitive responses, analysis, 412
"Pripro," 279, 280, 281, 292
Projective techniques: general, 401; theory of, 387, 390–392
Psychiatrists, 400
Psychoanalytic theory, 4, 139, 264–268, 301, 305–306
Psychodiagnostic tests (testing): therapeutic application of, 374–383; related to Rorschach, 324–325, 328–329, 330–359
Psychogram, 151, 163
Psychopathology, in family of three generations, 140–204
Psychosomatic illness, 32, 327
Psychotheraphy. conventional, 323–324

R (total number of responses), 32, 116, 153, 201, 282
"Reaction schemata," 109
Reaction time, 50–51, 56–57, 59–60
Reality, inner vs. outer, 60–63
Reality orientation, 153
Reality testing, 13–15, 18, 20, 21, 24, 27, 49, 67, 68, 73, 78–79, 151
Regression, 6, 34, 109, 282–283; adaptive vs. mal?daptive, 264–266, 271–272, 277–279; creative, 279–295, 305–309
Reiss-Davis Child Study Clinic, 47
Remarks, 74
Repression, 29
Response, adequacy of, 62–64; content of, 57–58; general, 12–13, 347–352
Role dimensions, 216–248
Role playing, 252, 256–257
Rorschach, consensus. *See* Consensus Rorschach.
Rorschach, the: definition of, 48; other forms and techniques, 5–7, 133–134, 345–352, 385–431; use and qualities of, 4, 6–7
Rorschach examination, administration of, 392; computerizing results, 402
Rorschach Prognostic Rating Scale (RPRS), 3, 399, 424
Rorschach protocol, examples of, 64–80, 90–96, 136–137, 147–203, 366–368

S responses, interpretation, 195, 353
Sadism, 170
Saxe Sentence Completion Test, 333
"Schemata," 110–111, 128–129, 138
Schizophrenia, general, 25, 28, 36, 61, 146, 152, 210, 310, 412–413
Schizophrenic adolescents, 79–80
Scholastic Aptitude Test, 286
Science, use of Rorschach in, 420–421
Self-concept, 96
Sentence completion methods, 339–340
Sex areas, of cards, 163–164, 175–176
Sex responses, 161–162, 175–176, 182, 186, 201
Sexual disturbances, 211, 212
Sexual roles, 162–164, 175–176, 177, 185, 253
Sexual symbolism, 195
Shading responses, interpretation, quantitative, 161, 186, 349–350
Sibling rivalry, 203
Social behavior of individual, 252–254, 255–258; family and consensus Rorschach, 211, 215–217, 243–248; family relationships, 143–260; groups, behavior of, 211–216, 243–248

Stimulus acceptance, 56–57
Strippers, 428
Stroop Color-Word Test, 293, 299, 302, 303
Structured-Objective Rorschach Test (SORT), 7, 418–419, 422–423
Students, college, 34, 37, 404–411, 427
Suicidal trends, 27, 28, 223, 224, 245
Sydenham's chorea, 147, 157
Symbolic responses: general, 83–96; criteria of, 84–85; diagnosis of, 95–96; interpretation, 88–89
Symbolism, 126

TAT. *See* Thematic Apperception Test.
Teachers, prediction of performance by Rorschach, 421–426
Testing the limits, in sample cases, 367; with color, 191
Tests, psychological, discussion with patient, 321–383
Thematic Apperception Test, 248, 288, 289, 290, 291, 292, 340–342, 343, 354, 369, 379, 400, 419
Theory, 4, 216–248
Therapy, from symbolic response studies, 96; from test discussions with patient, 322–326, 374–383
Thought processes in children, 136–137
Top management, 415–421
Twins, identical, 37

Unconscious, the, 87

Validation (validity), discussion of, 2
Validation, problems of: pertaining to intelligence tests, 329–330
Vocation and personality, 393–396
Vocational guidance, 7, 330
Vocational use of the Rorschach. *See* Industrial psychology, use of Rorschach in.

W responses, in artists, 414–415; development of, 102; interpretation, 120, 156, 175
Wechsler Adult Intelligence Scale (WAIS), 330–332, 365–366
Wechsler-Bellevue Scale, 213, 291, 292, 293, 398, 400
Witkin Embedded Figures, 301–303, 304
W:*M* ratio, 201
Writers, 283–290

Z score, 103, 418

Card Index

I: 64–66, 91, 147–148, 153, 157–158, 164–165, 171, 178–179, 187, 192, 197, 367. **II:** 66–68, 91, 148, 153–154, 158, 165, 171, 179, 188, 192, 197. **III:** 68–69, 91, 148, 154, 158–159, 165–166, 171–172, 179, 188, 192–193, 197–198, 366. **IV:** 69–70, 92, 149, 154, 158–159, 166, 172, 179–180, 188, 193, 198, 366. **V:** 70–71, 92, 149, 154, 159–160, 166, 172, 180, 189, 193, 198. **VI:** 71, 73, 92, 149–150, 155, 160, 166–167, 172–173, 180, 189, 193–194, 199. **VII:** 73, 92, 150, 155, 160, 166–167, 173, 180, 189, 194, 199, 367. **VIII:** 73–74, 93, 150, 155, 160–161, 167–168, 173–174, 180–181, 190, 194, 199–200, 366–367. **IX:** 74–75, 93, 150–151, 155, 161, 168, 174, 181, 190, 194–195. **X:** 75–76, 93–94, 151, 155–156, 161, 168–169, 174–175, 181, 190–191, 195, 200, 367–368.

A B C D E F G H I J

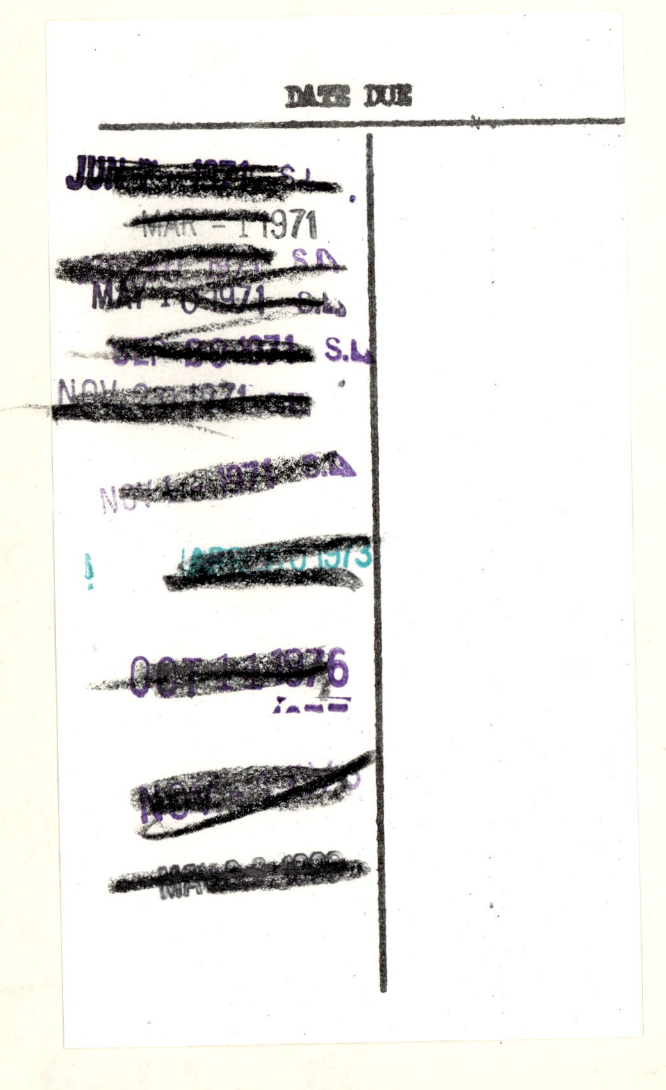
DATE DUE
MAR - 1 1971